Anatomies of Revolution

Recent years have seen renewed interest in the study of revolution. Spurred by events like the 2011 uprisings in North Africa and the Middle East, the rise of Islamic State, and the emergence of populism, a new age of revolution has generated considerable interest. Yet, even as empirical studies of revolutions are thriving, there has been a stall in theories of revolution. *Anatomies of Revolution* offers a novel account of how revolutions begin, unfold, and end. By combining insights from International Relations, Sociology, and Global History, it outlines the benefits of a 'global historical sociology' of revolutionary change, one in which international processes take centre stage. Featuring a wide range of cases from across modern world history, this is a comprehensive account of one of the world's most important processes. It will interest students and scholars studying revolutions, political conflict, and contentious politics in Sociology, Politics, and International Relations.

GEORGE LAWSON is Associate Professor in International Relations at the London School of Economics and Political Science. His books include: *Global Historical Sociology*, co-edited with Julian Go (Cambridge, 2017); *The Global Transformation: History, Modernity and the Making of International Relations*, co-authored with Barry Buzan (Cambridge, 2015); and *Negotiated Revolutions: The Czech Republic, South Africa and Chile* (2005).

Anatomies of Revolution

George Lawson
London School of Economics and Political Science

CAMBRIDGE
UNIVERSITY PRESS

CAMBRIDGE
UNIVERSITY PRESS

University Printing House, Cambridge CB2 8BS, United Kingdom

One Liberty Plaza, 20th Floor, New York, NY 10006, USA

477 Williamstown Road, Port Melbourne, VIC 3207, Australia

314–321, 3rd Floor, Plot 3, Splendor Forum, Jasola District Centre, New Delhi – 110025, India

79 Anson Road, #06-04/06, Singapore 079906

Cambridge University Press is part of the University of Cambridge.

It furthers the University's mission by disseminating knowledge in the pursuit of education, learning, and research at the highest international levels of excellence.

www.cambridge.org
Information on this title: www.cambridge.org/9781108482684
DOI: 10.1017/9781108697385

First published 2019

Printed in the United Kingdom by TJ International Ltd. Padstow, Cornwall

A catalogue record for this publication is available from the British Library.

ISBN 978-1-108-48268-4 Hardback
ISBN 978-1-108-71085-5 Paperback

For Kirsten, Jake, Xavi, and Kasper

Contents

Contents

Acknowledgements

I wrote most of this book in Highbury, North London. In the late fourteenth century, rural workers marched on Highbury and burned down its manor house as part of what became known as the Peasants' Revolt. In nearby Stoke Newington can be found the Newington Green Unitarian Church, also known as the Meeting House, which was frequented during the eighteenth century by a number of prominent dissenters, most notably Mary Wollstonecraft and Richard Price. Amongst those who came to hear Price speak were Thomas Paine and Thomas Jefferson. Heading towards where I work, at LSE, can be found Clerkenwell Green, perhaps the epicentre of revolutionary London. Over the centuries, Clerkenwell Green and its surrounds have been home to Chartists, Suffragettes, and a myriad of groups supporting independence movements around the world. During Lenin's exile in London, the communist newspaper *Iskra* was published here in a building that is now the Marx Memorial Library. Down the road in De Beauvoir Town, over 300 communists, including Lenin, Stalin, Trotsky, Kollontai, and Luxemburg met (in a church no less) over two weeks in May 1907 in order to develop a common revolutionary programme that could overthrow Tsarist Russia and build a communist state.

These are just some of the many revolutionaries who have made London their home or headquarters. The list ranges from the well-known figures above, to which could be added Karl Marx, Simón Bolívar, and Ho Chi Minh, to lesser-known characters such as Madan Lal Dhingra and Francisco Caamaño. Marx is buried in Highgate cemetery, the area where I grew up. At school, I met the children of Chilean activists who had fled Pinochet's Chile and, more frequently, the sons and daughters of those exiled from apartheid South Africa. Occasionally, children whose parents worked at the nearby Soviet Trade Delegation would come and play football in the park; they were usually accompanied by minders to ensure that Cold War enmities did not transfer onto the pitch.

Revolution, therefore, has always been around me. But not just me. Revolution is around all of us, without us always noticing it. Experiences of revolution are central to the making of the modern world – their legacies live on in systems of government, constitutions, legal codes, military strategies, holidays, monuments, music, and more. Yet, in the contemporary world, revolution often appears as an attenuated force, a once radical project that has now been domesticated, made safe for a world of communicative capitalism and low-intensity democracy. This book argues against this view. In part, it does so by showing that revolutions remain a live force in a world of injustice, oppression, exploitation, and debasement. In part, it does so by exploring how revolution changes over time and place – the secret of its longevity is its adaptability. This book unravels the multiple pathways – or anatomies – that revolutionary processes take.

Anatomies of Revolution has taken a long time to write. I began sketching it out during the 2011 Arab uprisings, which crystallized a number of issues I wanted to explore in more depth: the relationship between non-violent movements and coercive power, revolution and counter-revolution, international and domestic politics, revolutionary success and failure, and more. I initially set out to write a short book for Polity Press, then something more developed for the Configurations series at the University of Michigan. Many thanks to Louise Knight at Polity and Melody Herr at Michigan for their interest in the project.

Since 2011, I have given talks on and around the book at more events than I can remember. I have also taught the subject for several years, something that students tend to associate with one-way diffusion, but which is actually an acutely interactive process. And I have taken whatever opportunities have arisen to avail friends and colleagues of the argument, more often than not learning enormously from these engagements. All this means that I won't – or can't – thank everyone. Sorry. I will, however, highlight two people who provided extraordinarily helpful comments on the book's penultimate draft: Tarak Barkawi and Ayşe Zarakol. I am very fortunate to count on Tarak and Ayşe as both friends and intellectual comrades. Cambridge University Press solicited three detailed reports on the book, which were extremely useful in clarifying its contribution and avoiding some dead ends. Those concerned have now outed themselves as Jack Goldstone, John Foran, and Daniel Ritter – I am very grateful to all three, as I am to John Haslam at the Press for his interest in the project and for shepherding it through the review process. My thanks also too to those who read – and improved – key parts of the book: Kelly-Jo Bluen, Matt Dixon, Tanya Harmer, Kevan Harris, Adrian Rogstad, Eric Selbin, and Will Rooke. I have also benefited from discussions over the years with Jamie Allinson, Colin Beck, Mlada Bukovansky, Erica Chenoweth, Julian Go, Patrick Jackson, Neil Ketchley, Jeppe Mulich, Sharon Nepstad, and Justin Rosenberg. Early on in the process, Paul Kirby and Nawal Mustafa provided useful insights into how to frame the book. The University of Sydney, and in particular Colin Wight, provided a hospitable space in which to finish it.

Then there is my family: Kirsten, Jake, Xavi, and Kasper. Here I am somewhat stumped about what to say. In most acknowledgements, authors thank their families for their help in writing their books. I don't understand this. Almost without exception (Kirsten take a bow), my family has done whatever it can to stop me writing *Anatomies*. I don't blame them. Books take parents away from children and, even when I was physically there, I wasn't always mentally present. Yet still the kids persisted in wanting me to do anything but work. This, it seems to me, is exactly what families are for. So if mine is unusual in this respect, I wouldn't have it any other way. I am very glad to have been pushed and prodded and poked away from the book by all three children and, sometimes, by my wife. Books come and go, even ones that have taken this long to write. Families are forever. And the latter is much more important than the former.

This is why I am dedicating this book to Kirsten, Jake, Xavi, and Kasper, not for helping me, which they haven't, but for insisting that I give them attention when I didn't want to, and for telling me to stop working when I felt that I couldn't. It turns out that they were right and I was wrong. And I love them very much for showing me that.

Introduction
The Rights and Wrongs of Revolution

What Are Revolutions?

There are two main ways of approaching the study of revolution in the contemporary world – and they are both wrong. On the one hand, revolutions appear to be everywhere: on the streets of Kobane, Caracas, and Tehran; in the rhetoric of groups like Podemos and Black Lives Matter; and in the potential of technologies to reshape people's lives. Rarely do weeks go by without a revolution of one kind or another being proclaimed. In recent years, figures as varied as Abu Bakr al-Baghdadi, Emmanuel Macron, Tarana Burke, Xi Jinping, Tawakkol Karman, and Elon Musk have been labelled as revolutionaries, while the hugely popular musical Hamilton, and the even more popular Star War series, have eulogized revolutionary struggle. This broadening of the concept of revolution goes beyond its take-up by the mass media and in popular culture – www.revolution.com is a venture capitalist firm, www.revolution.co.uk is a software company, and www.revolution.com.au is a flea and heartworm treatment for dogs and cats. But is revolution really just a marketing trope, investment strategy, or pet service? And can it be street mobilization, social movement, and technological breakthrough at the same time?[1] If revolution is everywhere, perhaps it is nowhere.

This issue is complicated by an equally common, but apparently contradictory, belief – that revolutions are irrelevant to a world in which the big issues of governance and economic development have been settled. In the contemporary world, revolutions 'offer little promise and pose little threat' (Mayer 2001: 3). With the passing of state socialism in the Soviet Union, it is supposed, revolutions appear more as minor disturbances than as projects of deep confrontation and systemic transformation.

---

[1] The fracturing of the practice of revolution is matched by a decentring of the academic study of revolution. Although it is possible to find lots of work on revolutions around the academy, this often takes place outside the province of 'revolutionary studies'. Rather, revolution is studied in multiple disciplines under diverse sub-headings: contentious politics, social movements, civil resistance, terrorism, civil war, etc.

What is left, for good or for bad, are pale imitations: anaemic (small 'r') revolutions rather than 'real', 'proper', 'authentic' (big 'R') Revolution.

Both of these positions are untenable. While the former makes revolution so all-encompassing that it becomes an empty term without substantive content, the latter fails to see the enduring appeal of attempts to overturn existing conditions and generate alternative social orders. The primary aim of this book is to generate a more judicious appreciation of the place of revolution in the contemporary world, examining how revolutions emerge, how they unfold, and how they end. Its central task, therefore, is to unravel the *anatomies of revolution*.[2]

This is a major undertaking. It is made harder by the fact that revolutions are not static objects of analysis, but processes that change in form across time and place – there is no supra-sensible revolutionary form from which empirical references can be drawn. Revolutions have been conducted by nationalists in Algeria and Angola, slaves in Haiti, constitutionalists in America and France, communists in Russia, China, Nicaragua, and Afghanistan, radical military groups in Libya and Ethiopia, peasants in Mexico, Cuba, and Vietnam, a curious coalition of leftists, students, merchants, and clergy in Iran, and an even curiouser mix of Islamists, youth, labour organizations, and 'ultra' football fans in Egypt. At the same time, the concept of revolution exists in every major language group in the world. A study of its etymology would need to take in the Greek concepts of *epanastasis* (revolution), the Arabic terms *thawra* (revolution), *inqilab* (*coup d'état*), and tamarrud (rebellion), the notions of *mered* (rebellion), *hitkomemut* (uprising), *meri* (revolt), and *kesher* (plot) in classical Hebrew, the Chinese word *geming* (change of life, fate, or destiny) and the Latin verb *revolvere* (to return).

Probing deeper into the European meaning of the term reveals further diversity. In Ancient Greece, the idea of revolution was linked to the movement contained within Aristotle's trinity of democracy, oligarchy, and tyranny. In the Middle Ages, the concept was used to denote something circular, the turning of wheels rather than fundamental rupture, as in the elliptical movement of planets surveyed by Copernicus in his *De revolutionibus orbium coelestium* ('On the Revolution of Celestial Spheres'). During the Early Modern period, the term began to be associated with sudden, dramatic political changes (Harris 2015: 27, 34; see Rachum

---

[2] The term 'anatomies of revolution' bears a deliberate resemblance to Crane Brinton's *The Anatomy of Revolution*, first published in 1938. Whereas Brinton found a single 'anatomy of revolution' in the 'great revolutions' of England, America, France, and Russia, the goal of this book is to highlight the multiple pathways that revolutionary processes follow, emphasizing the overlap between revolutions and other forms of social change, and drawing on a greater range of cases than Brinton considered.

1999 for an account that stresses earlier origins). By the early part of the nineteenth century, the constitutional revolutions of America and France had become seen as archetypal – the latter in particular crystallized the notion of revolution as a deliberate act, signified by the emergence of a distinct category of *révolutionnaire* (revolutionary) (Baker 2015: 95, 102). From this point on, revolution was a future-oriented act – an ongoing project of potentially unlimited duration. During the twentieth century, revolutions became primarily associated with violent ruptures from one type of social order (capitalist and/or colonial) to another (socialist and/or post-colonial). After the collapse of the Soviet Union, many commentators argued that revolution had taken another turn, becoming variously 'unarmed' (Ritter 2015), 'negotiated' (Lawson 2004), conjoined with reform programmes to generate a new category of 'refolution' (Garton Ash 1989), or reconnected with older notions of return, as captured in Jürgen Habermas's (1990) notion of 'rectifying revolutions'. In the present day, as noted above, revolution is increasingly caught between two extremes: denigration on the one hand, catch-all term on the other.

All this presents a considerable, but not insurmountable, challenge. The first task is to establish some boundary conditions around revolution as a field of enquiry. This book does so in two ways. First, rather than examine revolution either in the sense of epochal change (e.g. 'the Neolithic revolution') or as breakthroughs in specific spheres of social life (e.g. 'the information revolution'), this book is concerned with revolutions geared at the takeover of political power, whether the main site of political power is a state, city-state, empire, kingdom, or principality. In other words, my focus is on specific revolutionary projects rather than macro-structural transformations or domain-specific shifts, except when these impact (as they often do) on state-centred movements.[3] As discussed below, this still produces a wide canvass, requiring that points of differentiation are drawn both within revolutions, such as the distinction between social and political revolutions,[4] and between revolutions and other forms of social change, such as civil wars, *coup d'états*, rebellions, transitions, and reform programmes. Second, for reasons of analytical coherence, this

---

[3] This is not to say that transformations that take place in particular domains of social life, such as the industrial revolution or the Revolution in Military Affairs (RMA), do not impact significantly on state-centred movements, just that this is not their central locus.

[4] Political revolutions feature a turnover in state leadership and institutions; social revolutions embrace political, economic, and symbolic fields of action. Examples of the former include the uprising against Ferdinand Marcos in the Philippines in 1986; the archetypal illustrations of the latter are France, Russia, China, and Cuba. For more on this distinction, see: Goldstone (2001: 143); Foran (2005: 8).

book restricts its canvass to modern revolutions.[5] It is worth briefly elaborating on these two points.

The relationship between processes of social change is a close one, both analytically and empirically. Indeed, this book argues that revolution is part of a broader family of processes associated with social transformation. First, a number of revolutions in the modern era were preceded or succeeded by civil wars, including those in France, Russia, China, Cuba, Nicaragua, Afghanistan, and Angola. Thomas Paine and Edmund Burke, hardly natural bedfellows, shared the view that England's Glorious Revolution in 1688 was both a revolution and a civil war (Armitage 2015: 67). Second, the effects of *coup d'états* can, on occasion, be revolutionary. The coup by Augusto Pinochet in Chile in 1973, the putsch against the monarchy led by Muammar Qaddafi in Libya, and the Francoist *golpe militar* in Spain set in motion radical economic and political programmes that significantly recast their societies. At the same time, coups have often preceded revolutions: the regime of Fulgencio Batista in Cuba was caught up in several coup attempts during the late 1950s, something that allowed the revolutionary forces led by Fidel Castro to build up support in the eastern highlands before advancing on Cuba's cities. Third, rebellions (here used synonymously with revolts) are also closely associated with revolutions. Often, disenfranchised groups from slaves to peasants have been in a state of virtually continuous rebellion, taking part in processes that have induced revolutions from Haiti to Nicaragua, and from Algeria to Mexico. Fourth, transitions from authoritarian to democratic orders often overlap with revolutionary dynamics, most obviously in the negotiated settlement that ended apartheid in South Africa in 1994. Finally, although reform movements are usually seen as distinct from, or as barriers to, revolutions, there are several occasions when reforms by governments have hastened rather than prevented revolution. In eighteenth-century France, for example, the programme of limited reform instigated by Louis XVI emboldened the provincial *parlements* (appeal courts), the newly empowered bourgeoisie, and peasants taking part in rural uprisings. As Alexis de Tocqueville (1999/1852) notes, the weakness of the monarchy was revealed by its reforms, allowing the middling classes of burghers and merchants to press for more radical changes. Defeat in the Seven Years War with England, the example of

---

[5] Modern is less a temporal designation – and still less a normative one – than it is an analytical one. In other words, modern is taken to mean a specific configuration of industrial capitalism, rational-bureaucratic statehood, and 'ideologies of progress', such as socialism, nationalism, and liberalism. For more on this understanding of modernity, see Buzan and Lawson (2013, 2015). For an analysis of revolutions in the pre-modern world, see: Shaban (1979); Finley (1986); Ober (1998); Syme (2002); Arjomand (2019).

a successful revolution in America, and the growth of new ideas like nationalism coupled with elite fracture in turning reform into revolution.

Revolution, therefore, appears in relation to, rather than opposition from, other forms of social change. Civil wars, *coup d'états*, rebellions, transitions, reform programmes, and revolutions are intimately connected, overlapping and running into each other at a number of junctures (Lawson 2006b). However, although revolutions bleed – sometimes literally – into other processes of social change, they also retain a relative autonomy from them. In their most basic sense, revolutions can be understood as the reorganization of everyday life – they seek permanent shifts rather than temporary changes to the texture of social relations. In this way, revolutions consist of several dimensions simultaneously: a symbolic revolution that seeks to destroy pre-revolutionary tropes and reforge new forms of symbolic order; a political revolution that aims to overthrow the old regime and reconstruct systems of governance; and an economic revolution that intends to recast relations of production, value, and exchange. In short, a revolution is a *collective mobilization that attempts to quickly and forcibly overthrow an existing regime in order to transform political, economic, and symbolic relations.*

Each aspect of this definition is important: 'collective mobilization' contrasts with processes of elite-driven change, many of which can be radical – China since its 1978 'opening up' and some contemporary Gulf monarchies serve as cases in point; 'quickly' distinguishes revolutions from longer-running processes of evolutionary change, such as the several centuries of British parliamentary reform; 'forcibly' illustrates the importance of conflict, compulsion, and transgression to revolutions – contained forms of contention ranging from civil rights legislation, extending the suffrage, or introducing shock-therapy programmes may have dramatic consequences, but this does not equate to the forceful opening of previously restricted orders conjured by revolutions; 'overthrow' exemplifies the extra-constitutional component of revolutions, while also distinguishing them from more partial processes such as democratic transitions; both 'transform' and the inclusion of political, economic, *and* symbolic orders illustrate the systemic quality of revolutionary change; 'attempt' signifies that there are many more unsuccessful than successful revolutions and a large number of revolutionary situations that do not lead to revolutionary outcomes. If this book included only successful cases, its discussion would be limited to a handful of well-trodden cases.[6]

---

[6] Colin Beck (2018) finds that research on revolution is, in general, skewed towards a few landmark cases: Nicaragua, France, Russia, Cuba, Iran, Vietnam, and China. Overall, Beck finds three main biases in the social science of revolutions: first, towards major social

The point is not to see this definition as a template to which revolutions must comply. Such a move would not only elide the variety of forms that revolution takes, it would also struggle to make sense of unsuccessful revolutions and the many revolutionary situations that do not lead to revolutionary outcomes. The definition offered above is, therefore, best seen as a flexible abstraction rather than as an empirical straight-jacket, an analytical first cut by which to examine diverse revolutionary pathways. As subsequent chapters make clear, revolutions are dynamic processes that change over time and place. The measure of the success of this definition is not how well it represents each episode of revolution, but how useful it proves to be for two tasks: first, clarifying the various pathways that revolutions take; and second, highlighting both differences and overlaps between revolutions and other forms of social change.

Although revolutions have existed, at least in some form, throughout human history, their greatest impact has been felt under global modernity – the configuration of political, economic, and symbolic processes that have served to recast domestic and international orders over the past two to three centuries (Buzan and Lawson 2015). The resulting constellations – the modern states-system, industrial capitalism, and major political ideologies – are structural formations that contain a global reach. In many ways, therefore, global history over the last two centuries or so is a shared story. Struggles for and against imperialism, the extension of capitalism around the world (and resistance to its spread), the emergence of universalist doctrines, and technological developments have, with varying degrees of coercion, brought the world within some kind of commons. In this sense, modernity is, as Ernest Gellner (1988) puts it, a 'tidal wave' of homogenizing pressures. But the tsunami has not been evenly felt. Although processes such as industrialization, imperialism, and rationalization have affected most parts of the world, they have not done so in a uniform manner. Indeed, the dislocation wrought by modernity has provoked a multiplicity of responses: market openness and protectionism, democracy and authoritarianism, religious renewal alongside secularism. At its heart, therefore, modernity is a contradictory

revolutions; second, towards twentieth-century uprisings; and third, towards revolutions seen to be progressive. According to Beck, 75 per cent of historical-comparative books on revolution focus on 'leftist' or 'democratic' revolutions, while only 15 per cent survey religious or 'reactionary' cases, almost all of which examine the 1979 Iranian Revolution. This is a big problem. It means that conservative revolutionary movements are omitted, from fascism to militant Islamism. It also means that, if revolutions are successful by definition, then most studies are selecting on the dependent variable. This, in turn, means that there is not enough study of *why* so many revolutionary movements are unsuccessful, not least because of successful counter-revolutionary projects. These issues are picked up in the following chapter.

process, one marked by greater affluence but also rising inequality, and global forms of governance alongside drives for local autonomy. It is a profoundly ambivalent set of processes (Adorno and Horkheimer 1997/ 1944). And it is within this ambivalence that revolutions have assumed their most virulent form.

This introduces the final reason why *modern* revolutions are the focus of this book – revolutions have had a major impact on the development of modern social orders. Martin Wight (1978/1946: 92) wrote in the late 1970s that over half of the preceding 500 years had featured some kind of conflict between revolutionary and counter-revolutionary states. The period since the publication of Wight's book may well be the most revolutionary in history – we are living in a 'new age of revolution' (Goldstone 2016: ii). Although, as this book will chronicle, no revolution has delivered in full on its promises, revolutions have bought dramatic changes in their wake. The French Revolution introduced the notions of nationalism and popular sovereignty, concepts of political 'left' and 'right', the metric system, and a conflict between absolutism and republicanism that dominated European politics during the nineteenth century. The Russian Revolution pioneered a model of state-led industrialization that was a powerful draw for many states around the world during the twentieth century. The Chinese, Vietnamese, and Cuban revolutions exemplified variants of southern revolution that resonated around the insurgent 'Third World' during the Cold War. The Egyptian Revolution of 1952 established a form of military-led social transformation that inspired revolutionary movements in the region during the 1950s and 1960s, just as comparable uprisings in Tunisia and Egypt inspired unrest in North Africa and the Middle East in 2011. The 'people power' uprisings in Eastern and Central Europe in 1989 have served as the lodestone for a range of unarmed revolutions in the contemporary world. Whichever form revolutions have taken, they stand as a challenge to status quo authority, both at home and abroad, by virtue of the example they set in overcoming seemingly overwhelming forces and in their capacity to generate substantial changes both to the texture of their home societies and to international orders. Revolutions and the *avoidance* of revolutions, whether through autocratic modernization, reform programmes, or counter-revolution, are not occasional punctuation marks, but the very grammar of modern world history.

Why Revolutions Matter

Revolutions matter, therefore, in three ways: as *substantive* processes that have played a central role in shaping the modern world; as *analytical* categories that overlap with, but do not fully merge into, other processes of social transformation; and as *normative* projects for and against which people have fought and died. This book examines these issues in reverse order. The next section of this chapter concentrates on the normative aspect of revolutions, looking at how revolutionary utopias have both inspired and appalled. The following chapter takes a first cut at the analytical issues most closely associated with the study of revolutions, exploring themes of continuity and change, whether revolutions 'come' or are 'made', to what extent revolutions should be seen as international or domestic processes, and the difficulties of theory building given the diversity of revolutionary experiences. Chapters 2 and 3 take a more fine-grained approach to these issues, establishing a historicist, relational, inter-social understanding of revolutionary situations, trajectories, and outcomes. This, in turn, provides the parameters for Chapters 4, 5, and 6, which demonstrate the pay-off of this approach to six revolutionary episodes: England, Chile, Cuba, South Africa, Iran, and Ukraine. Chapter 7 examines one of the main forms that revolution has taken in the contemporary world – 'negotiated revolution'. Chapter 8 examines the prospects for the theory and practice of revolution in the contemporary world.

As a whole, the book aims to make three main contributions to the study of revolutions. First, it develops an *inter-social* account of revolutionary change.[7] Despite attempts to incorporate international factors into the study of revolution, for the most part, international processes tend to be seen either as the facilitating context *for* revolutions or as the dependent outcome *of* revolutions (Lawson 2015a). The result is an analytical bifurcation between international and domestic in which the former serves as the backdrop to the latter's causal agency. An inter-social account overcomes this binary by showing how transboundary relations form an interactive crucible for each and every case of revolution, from the desire to 'catch-up' with more 'advanced' states to the role of ideas in fermenting unrest across borders. Chapter 2 outlines the parameters of a *descriptive* inter-social account that recognizes the centrality of transboundary entanglements to revolutions, and an *analytical* inter-social account that theorizes the ways in which interactions between social sites play a constitutive role in how revolutions begin,

---

[7] The term 'inter-social' is preferred to alternatives such as intersocietal, international, and inter-state in that it does not presume that the objects of analysis are societies, nations, or states, respectively. Throughout the book, 'inter-social' is used interchangeably with 'transboundary'. For more on this, see Chapters 1 and 2.

develop, and end. The key contention here is that revolutions are inter-social all the way down.

Second, this book historicizes revolutionary dynamics. This goes beyond any claim that 'history matters'. Most social scientific studies of revolution use history to test and refine their accounts, while some of the most important scholarship on revolutions has been conducted by historians (e.g. Palmer 1959, 1964; Rudé 1964; Brinton 1965/1938; Moore 1966; Bailyn 1967; Hill 1975; Furet 1981, 1999; James 2001/1938; Dubois 2004; Sewell 2005; Adelman 2006; Pincus 2009; Ferrer 2014). Rather, what this claim entails is a need to *historicize* revolutions by being attentive to the constitutive impact of time and place on revolutionary practice and theory. This is different from seeing history primarily as a means of testing theory or as a foundation for coding and experimentation. It is a position that starts from the premise that all revolutions are singular in the sense that the events that produce a particular revolution are not replicable because contexts are never completely alike. This insight, one that many revolutionaries themselves have often been resistant to, is joined with a second claim: that singular events produce sequences – or plots – that can be abstracted and used to explain other revolutionary episodes. Part I uses multiple episodes of revolutionary change to construct ideal-typical anatomies of revolutionary situations, trajectories, and outcomes. Part II refines these revolutionary anatomies through a series of historical illustrations. Part III develops, and explores the edges of, a group of revolutions in the contemporary world: 'negotiated revolutions'. In each case, the goal is to combine narrative and abstraction in a way that provides an explanation of a particular revolutionary episode, while simultaneously generating portable insights into the wider genus of revolutions. Throughout the book, history and theory are treated not as binaries, but as co-constitutive (Barkawi and Lawson 2017).

The book's final contribution stems from taking seriously the idea that revolutions are not a single thing (McAdam et al. 2001: 226). This may seem like an obvious claim. Yet much of the social science of revolution proceeds by identifying revolutions as a particular class of phenomenon, breaking them down into their constituent parts (a range of core attributes, necessary and sufficient conditions, independent and dependent variables, etc.), and measuring the fit between these components and cases that conform to – or challenge – these attributes. This book proceeds differently. It starts from particular revolutionary episodes, ordering these episodes into clusters of social action that, in turn, yield causal configurations that reoccur across time and place. Such analysis does not require any kind of historical homology – there is a basic acceptance of variation in terms of initial conditions, sequences of events, combinations of causal mechanisms, and outcomes (Tilly 2005: 28). The goal is to demonstrate that alongside the singularity of historical experience can be found recurrent causal patterns – interactive dynamics that shed light on diverse revolutionary episodes. The difference between this approach and much existing scholarship is akin to taking a photograph or shooting a film. Most approaches do the former, holding certain conditions constant by taking a snapshot of a particular moment in time, then testing the generalizability of this snapshot to other instances of the phenomena. This book does the latter, seeing social reality as a moving spectacle that requires analytics to be adjusted to changing conditions. The aim is to move away from a view of revolutions as bundles of properties towards a relational concept of revolutions as 'entities-in-motion' (Lawson 2017: 77).

Anatomies of Revolution, therefore, seeks to develop a global historical sociology of revolution in which the inter-social provides the 'global', the concern with historicizing revolutions provides the 'historical', and the relational constitutes the 'sociology'. If global historical sociology examines the inter-social dynamics that enable the emergence, reproduction, and breakdown of social orders, then revolutions must play a central role in its agenda (Lawson 2017). After all, revolutions are the archetypal instance of social breakdown and reemergence. Beyond this contribution, the book introduces a number of concepts to the study of revolution: *revolutionary sovereignty* (Chapter 1), *causal configurations* (Chapter 2), *the protest spiral* (Chapter 6), and *the moderation curse* (Chapter 7). The bulk of this book, therefore, is concerned with why, when, and how revolutions take place. But behind these dynamics lie more basic impulses. Lurking behind scholarly analysis of revolutionary change are fundamental questions about the rights and wrongs of revolutionary struggles.

Revolutionary Rights and Wrongs

Revolutionaries can never be innocent.[8]

Why have people been willing to lay down their lives in support of, or in opposition to, projects that promise a radical transformation of existing conditions? Many of those who take part in revolutions, whether in the revolutionary vanguard or amongst its rank-and-file, may do so for

---

[8] This acute observation is made by the narrator in Viet Thanh Nguyen's 2015 novel about the Vietnamese revolution: *The Sympathizer*.

instrumental reasons, something recognized by a substantial literature on the rationality of revolutionary actors (e.g. Popkin 1979; Taylor 1988; Goldstone 1994; Aya 2001; Wood 2003). But in many ways, revolutions appear to be irrational processes, motivated less by logics of expected utility than by a sense of collective outrage, hope, and solidarity. As James Scott (2012a: 22) argues, revolutions are utopias that offer the possibility of both material plenty and ideological fulfilment. In their most basic sense, revolutions are normative projects closely bound up with notions of rightful rule and rightful resistance – their promise is earthly salvation.

Revolutionary utopias are at once a means of critiquing existing conditions, explaining their inequities, and offering a path to an alternative future. Using the term utopia in this way means returning to the sense employed by the progenitor of modern utopian visions, Thomas More (2003/1516). For More, utopia had two foundational elements: first, the possibility of a better world; and second, the belief that it could be made. More built on two Greek words – *eutopia* (good society) and *outopia* (nowhere) – to signify an image of an alternative order: something superior to current conditions, but also man-made and achievable. Early Modern utopian thinkers such as More, Francis Bacon, and Henry Neville produced works of considerable imagination, coupling this imagination with careful attention to detail, providing maps and alphabets, and specifying the form that everyday rituals should take – mealtimes, the size of households, forms of acceptable sexual conduct, and the like (Bruce 1996). Early Modern utopias were imbued with claims to truth that were as much about fostering ideal forms of organization as they were about the idealization of people or nature. Utopias, therefore, can be understood as hybrids of fiction-practice that offer a mirror to existing conditions, critique the status quo, and promote a novel institutional order (Gordin et al. 2010: 13). Utopias are both imaginaries *and* exercises in institution building rooted in a particular reading of past, present, and future conditions. Before anything else, revolutions are utopian in this double sense: movements intended to perfect both thought and deed, bringing these two dimensions together in a harmonious relationship mediated by idealized political, economic, and symbolic orders (Lawson 2008).

In this broad sense, contemporary revolutionary projects share a family resemblance to medieval Millennial movements that outlined a series of stages along which human affairs travelled, promising to hasten the path towards an end-time in which everlasting freedom would be delivered, whether this point of freedom was to stem from religious salvation, a communist state, or a liberal kingdom of ends. As John Gray (2007), Martin Malia (2006), and others have argued, modern understandings of revolutions stem, at least in part, from redefinitions of spirituality during the European Reformations in which personal, direct contacts between believer and deity came to replace those governed through inter-mediaries, whether this was clergy or other representatives of organized religion. The movements across Europe by Anabaptists, Hussites, and Lutherans challenged social orders based on forms of authority that claimed to serve as direct representatives of God's will. These movements acted as forerunners both directly to uprisings such as the Dutch Revolt of 1566 and more indirectly to later movements that sought to overturn existing social orders via a legitimating ideology based on a sharp dis-tinction between virtuous rulership and righteous resistance. The dreams of deliverance of Early Modern radicals contained the belief that 'good' would inevitably triumph over 'evil'. In the process, revolutions came to be seen less as accidents of history than as forces of nature in which right and reason could work hand-in-hand (Rachum 1999). It is possible to discern a line, therefore, which navigates between medieval eschatology, Jacobinism, Bolshevism, and, finally, to the contemporary day, imper-fectly drawn and uneven though it might be.

On the one hand, revolutionary utopias are bound up with notions of emancipation, captured in projects that both critique existing conditions (usually understood as a combination of economic exploitation, political subjugation, and cultural debasement) and provide the contours of an alternative institutional order. On the other hand, some critics associate revolutionary utopias with dystopian nightmares. For critics like Gray and Malia, the submerging of revolutionary methods, tactics, and strat-egies behind ideals of salvation is the proximate cause of the campaigns of terror conducted by revolutionaries from Robespierre to Mao. These campaigns, it is argued, are rooted in the notion that the powerless must release themselves from conditions of servitude through 'divine violence' (Benjamin 1999/1921; also see Sorel 1999/1908).

This latter view – of revolutionary utopias as necessarily bound up with the legitimation and use of violence – is one that many advocates of revolution have embraced. Georges Sorel (1999/1908) saw revolutionary violence as fundamental to ridding societies from bourgeois decadence and advancing the emancipation of the working class. Frantz Fanon (2001/1961: 74) contended that 'violence is a cleansing force. It frees the native from his inferiority complex and from his deeper inaction; it makes him fearless and restores his self-respect'.[9] Leon Trotsky (2007/

---

[9] The first English language edition of Fanon's *Wretched of the Earth* included a preface by Jean-Paul Sartre that was just as dedicated as Fanon to the necessity of violence in post-colonial struggles. Hence, Sartre (1965: 21) wrote, 'to shoot down a European is to kill

1920: 82) expressed his disdain for the 'Kantian-clerical, vegetarian-Quaker prattle' of those who condemned Bolshevik methods during the Russian Civil War. Mao (1927: 27) shared Trotsky's understanding of the necessity of revolutionary violence:

A revolution is not the same as inviting people to dinner, or writing an essay, or painting a picture, or doing fancy needlework; it cannot be anything so refined, so calm and gentle, or so mild, kind, courteous, restrained and magnanimous. A revolution is an uprising, an act of violence whereby one class overthrows another ... to right a wrong it is necessary to exceed proper limits, and the wrong cannot be righted without the proper limits being exceeded.

Frequently, it seems, revolutionaries have justified repression within an ideal of violence-as-necessity. For Sorel, Fanon, Trotsky, Mao, and others, overcoming the inequities of bourgeois society, colonial rule, Tsarist autocracy, or imperial domination was impossible without violence. In this understanding, revolutionary regimes used the guillotine, mass purges, and other forms of violence in order to demonstrate the cleansing virtue of revolutionary struggles. French revolutionaries railed against the corruption of the nobles, priests, and *canailles* (commoners) who had been bought off by foreign toxins. In contrast, the revolution preached a simple form of truth, one rooted in the moral perfection that arose through revolutionary virtue. It was not without reason that Robespierre was known as 'the incorruptible', nor that he sought to establish a 'Republic of Virtue' through the 'Cult of Reason'. The guillotine was employed by French revolutionaries as an 'educational device for creating a new and pure revolutionary humanity' (Moore 2000: 132). From the use of the guillotine and the slaughter of counter-revolutionaries in the Vendée region of western France at the end of the eighteenth century to the massacres perpetrated by self-proclaimed revolutionaries in China, Cambodia, and elsewhere, so violence has appeared not just a means to an enlightened end but as an emancipatory force in its own right.

Beyond the condemnation – and endorsement – of revolutionary violence lies a deeper debate about the repressive character of revolutionary regimes. Michel Foucault, for example, saw the desire of revolutionaries in France to classify, discipline, and foreclose social practices as acutely repressive.[10] For his part, Friedrich Nietzsche (2003/1886) claimed that

two birds with one stone, to destroy an oppressor and the man he oppresses at the same time: there remains a dead man and a free man'.

[10] Foucault was less condemnatory of other revolutions, most notably the 1979 Iranian Revolution, which he saw as embodying a new form of political subjectivity. Foucault wrote a number of essays and articles on the revolution. On 13 February 1979, his column in the Italian newspaper *Corriere della Sera* – 'A Powder Keg Called Islam' – claimed

the revolution in France represented the triumph of a 'slave morality' aimed at levelling difference and plurality, seeing in modern revolutions a new form of violent tyranny. And François Furet (1981) argued that the French Revolution merely replaced one form of absolutism (dynasticism) with another (popular sovereignty). The result, for Furet, was a totalitarian belief in *le peuple* (the people) that squashed individual liberty in the service of *la volonté générale* (the general will). Some revolutionaries have been similarly concerned with the ways in which revolution could be subverted to dictatorial ends, hence Trotsky's (1972/1937: 64) withering attack on Lenin: 'Lenin's methods lead to this: the party organization at first substitutes itself for the party as a whole; then the central committee substitutes itself for the party organization; and finally, a single "dictator" substitutes himself for the central committee.' Reminiscent, perhaps, of Xi Jinping's appropriation of power in China in recent years.[11]

For some, therefore, the dictatorial features of modern revolutionary utopias arise from the attempt to *create* the correct conditions for liberty to arise – in other words, in flattening, by force if necessary, differences of class, race, gender, religion, and nation. From Robespierre to Castro, revolutionaries have sought to generate the conditions – via a vanguard party, programmes of education and re-education, control of the media, and a powerful coercive apparatus – through which notions of freedom, whether liberal, communist, or post-colonial, are to be realized. Again, many revolutionaries have not only recognized, but embraced, this tendency. Che Guevara (1968: 9) argued that the aim of the revolutionary regime in Cuba was to ensure that 'there is no life outside the revolution'; to that end, 'society as a whole must become a huge school'. Fidel Castro famously told intellectuals in Cuba that 'within the Revolution, everything goes; against the Revolution, nothing'.[12] Generating a revolutionary society in Cuba meant more than effecting changes in state personnel, reforming governance structures, or altering conditions of

---

that, 'the historical significance of the Iranian Revolution will be found not in its conformity to a recognised revolutionary model, but instead in its potential to overturn the existing political situation in the Middle East ... an "Islamic" movement can set the entire region ablaze, overturn the most unstable regimes, and disturb the most solid ones. Islam – which is not simply a religion but an entire way of life, an adherence to a history and a civilization – has a good chance to become a gigantic powder keg at the level of hundreds of millions of men'. On this last point, Foucault proved to be prescient. For a critical view of Foucault's engagement with Iran, see Afary and Anderson (2005); for a more sympathetic account, see Ghamari-Tabrizi (2016).

[11] Thanks to Jack Goldstone for alerting me to this comparison.

[12] This is a line from Castro's 'Words to Intellectuals' speech at the National Cultural Council in Havana in June 1961, available from the Castro speech database: http://lanic.utexas.edu/project/castro/db/1961/19610630.html, accessed 19 September 2018.

economic production and distribution. Rather, the revolution required the control of every sphere of social life, from formal sites of authority to informal rituals ranging from wedding ceremonies to public holidays. Modern revolutionaries sought nothing less than the construction of a new, more perfect, revolutionary being.

For critics, the attempts by revolutionary regimes to homogenize both individuals and social order, and to generate an organic unity between the two, meant that modern revolutions were necessarily totalitarian. This made them dangerous 'vogues' that validated heinous acts (Colburn 1994: 89), 'high-modernist faiths' that tried, but failed, to perfect the human condition (Scott 1998: 199, 204, 273), or 'secular religions' seeking 'sacralization after the death of God' (Shorten 2007: 164). Such narratives are, at best, partial. As Alberto Toscano (2010: 202) points out, critics often associate revolutions with 'fanatical' utopianism as an 'ideological force-field' by which to validate their own positions.[13] Critics of revolution, Toscano argues, favour a contained form of political subjectivity in which revolutions should be limited in form and ambition – their model is America rather than France. Such a view runs into two objections. First, liberalism, whether embedded in particular states or projected internationally by powerful states, has often been the target of revolutionary critiques. The democratic illusion, it is argued, has served to suppress the radical transformation of existing orders. This issue is discussed further in Chapters 7 and 8. Second, for those struggling against colonialism, autocracy, and other forms of bondage, revolution has often appeared as the 'only way out' (Trotsky 1997/1932: 167; also see Goodwin 2001). In this view, revolutions are processes through which the downtrodden, the excluded, and the dispossessed have risen up against conditions of servitude in order to demand justice, freedom, and an end to indignity. Revolutions are the 'perennial shout of "enough"!' (Gerassi 1971: 4).

Two forms of revolutionary utopianism, therefore, sit side by side. In contrast to the notion of revolution-as-tyranny sits an alternative reading of revolutionary utopianism, one deeply engrained with the overcoming of tyranny. In this latter understanding, revolutionary repression is not the product of an internally driven totalitarian hard-drive, but the result

---

[13] It should be noted that revolutionaries have frequently used 'utopian' and 'utopianism' as terms of abuse. Lenin, for example, railed against Bukharin's 'utopian' schemas in discussions over whether the Bolsheviks should recognize national self-determination and carry out economic reforms. Marx too regularly denounced the 'utopianism' of those who opposed the 'scientific reason' of historical materialism. But as E. H. Carr (1969: 14) points out, Marx's combination of 'prophet moralist' and 'cool scientist' made him the embodiment of modern utopianism.

of struggles rooted in old-regime brutality and counter-revolutionary hostility – frequently revolutions have become radicalized in the midst of struggles against their adversaries. The Jacobins seized control of the French revolutionary state during the war with Austria, just as Ayatollah Khomeini used the conflict between Iran and Iraq to crush secular opposition in Iran (Goldstone 2011: 16). In similar vein, the war communism of the Bolsheviks during the Russian Civil War did not derive from arbitrary power, but from the precarious nature of the regime as a blockaded fortress on the brink of collapse (Trotsky 2007/1920: 23; also see Losurdo 2015).[14] Throughout modern history, the attempt by counter-revolutionary regimes to restore the old order has often unleashed a 'white terror' to match the repressive policies carried out by revolutionary regimes (Mayer 1971: 97). As the next chapter discusses, Edmund Burke and Henry Kissinger belong to the study of revolution just as much as Thomas Paine and Fidel Castro.

Revolutionary states have rarely, if ever, delivered on their promises. No states do. But revolutionary movements have provided a means for those living in despair and indignity to reject their conditions and force the opening of exclusionary social orders. Surveying the history of the last few centuries, it is difficult to see how core features of the modern world – the overturning of colonial rule, the break-up of empires, the end of slavery, female suffrage, the establishment of formal racial equality, and the emergence of mass education and welfare systems – could have taken place, at least on a comparable scale, without revolutions. English Levellers, American constitutionalists, Haitian slaves, French *sans-culottes* (commoners), Russian workers, Chinese communists, Cuban guerrillas, Nicaraguan peasants, Iranian *bazaari* (merchants), Czech students, and Tunisian Islamists have conducted revolutions precisely because alternative means of inclusion were closed to them. It is a rare elite that gives away its power voluntarily. The results of revolutionary uprisings have been radically imperfect. But their impact has been profound and, to a great extent, beneficial for many people around the world.

The Two Faces of Revolution

Revolutions, therefore, are at once both liberating and totalizing processes, movements that offer freedom but which ensnare their participants

---

[14] War communism involved a range of measures, including compulsory labour, rationing, collectivization, and the expropriation of grain. It was instituted during the civil war at a time when the Bolsheviks faced the seizure of almost all of their coal and metalworking production, and the blockade of most of their oil, cotton, and food producing regions.

behind new forms of political, economic, and symbolic authority. In normative terms, revolutions are essentially contested. On the one hand, they represent the most intense means through which publics around the world have attempted to overcome conditions of injustice. In this sense, revolutions represent the outer limits of the politics of the possible, expressions of an apparently universal proclivity to challenge forms of gross inequity. On the other hand, this expression – and the struggle it generates – is always excessive, incorporating methods that are necessarily transgressive. This transgressive excess leads revolutions away from emancipation and towards tyranny. As John Dunn (1972: 4) argues, there are two, apparently diametrically opposed projects contained within revolutions:

Revolutions, like the temple of Janus, have two faces. One is elegant, abstract and humanitarian, an idyllic face, the dream of revolution and its meaning under the calm distancing of eternity. The other is crude, violent and very concrete, rather nightmarish, with all the hypnotic power, loss of perspective and breadth of understanding you might expect to go with nightmares.

Perhaps, therefore, revolutions are best seen as both tragic necessities and as necessarily tragic.

Having set out the main contours of the normative field within which the concept and practice of revolution is debated, the following chapters seek to move the debate beyond revolutionary rights and wrongs towards an understanding of the sociological anatomies of revolution. Although I return to normative issues in Chapter 8, the principal aim of this book is not to conduct a full assessment of these issues.[15] Rather, it is to offer a novel account of revolutionary situations, trajectories, and outcomes. This task begins, in the next chapter, with a survey of the main themes within which the study and practice of revolution have taken place.

---

[15] As Fred Halliday (1999) points out, revolution lacks the tradition of normative thinking afforded to related processes, such as the debate around 'just war' – there is precious little debate around issues of *ius ad revolutionem* and *ius in revolutione*. The best survey of the issue remains Geras (1989). For attempts to assess the ethics of resistance and revolution within the parameters established by just war theory, see: Buchanan (2013); Finlay (2015); Gross (2015). For a wider discussion of the relationship between law, ethics, and revolution, see: Kelsen (2007/1945); Brunkhorst (2014).

Part I

Theories

Part I takes three successively deeper cuts at theorizing revolutions. The first chapter introduces the main debates in the study of revolution: processes of continuity and change; the relationship between international and domestic dynamics; the question of whether revolutions contain general tendencies, or whether they must be studied on a case-by-case basis; and the degree to which revolutions are made by people on the ground or are the result of macro-social forces. Moving beyond the binaries suggested by these debates, the chapter outlines the contours of a historicist, relational, inter-social approach to revolution. This approach is deepened in Chapter 2, which seeks to fulfil the promise – if not yet the reality – of 'fourth generation' approaches to revolutionary theory. It outlines a four-stage research process: first, examining the sequences that particular revolutions take; second, assembling these sequences into analytical narratives that are logically coherent and supported by the available evidence; third, abstracting the causal configurations through which revolutions take place; and fourth, assessing the ways in which these causal configurations explain revolutions in multiple settings. The goal is to demonstrate that, alongside the singularity of historical experience can be found recurrent revolutionary pathways. Chapter 3 demonstrates the pay-off of this approach through analysis of the causal configurations that underpin revolutionary situations, trajectories, and outcomes. This provides the basis for the historical work that follows in Part II ('Histories') and the analysis of contemporary revolutions that serves as the basis for Part III ('Prospects').

1   Revolutionary Dynamics

A Long Time Ago in a Country Far, Far Away

In 1791, a rebellion broke out in the French colony of Saint-Domingue, the smaller, western part of the island of Hispaniola, situated not far from Cuba. Although Saint-Domingue was small, it enjoyed a lucrative role in the world economy, producing half of the world's coffee and 40 per cent of its sugar (Klooster 2009: 84). Saint-Domingue's colonial potentate, France, was heavily dependent on the island, which supplied two-thirds of the metropole's overseas trade (James 2001/1938: xviii). So substantial was this trade that the value of crops produced in Saint-Domingue during the 1780s was worth more to the French treasury than the combined merchandise returned to Spain from all of its colonies (Klooster 2009: 84; Stephanson 2010: 199). No wonder that Saint-Domingue was known as the 'Pearl of the Antilles' and its capital, Cap Français (Le Cap), as 'the Paris of the Antilles' (Landers 2010: 55). French Saint-Domingue was 'the envy of Europe … the Eden of the New World' (Ferrer 2014: 1).

Beyond its leading role in the production of coffee and sugar, Saint-Domingue was a central node in one of the most important tradable commodities of the time – slaves. During the 1780s, 30,000 slaves per year were imported from Africa to Saint-Domingue (Stephanson 2010: 204); between 1770 and 1790, the slave population of the island nearly doubled (Polasky 2015: 139). As a result, the island was home to the largest population of slaves in the region: slaves represented 89 per cent of the island's population (Hunt 2010: 26). These slaves were highly valuable, worth three times as much as the value of the land and buildings in the colony combined (Klooster 2009: 91). But despite their value, slaves were subject to abject conditions both on the passage to Saint-Domingue and during their time in the colony itself. Whipping was an everyday part of life on the estates and plantations, while strict punishments were meted out to those who tried to escape: branding and severed ears for a first offence; further branding and severed hamstrings for a second offence; execution for a third offence. Large numbers of slaves died from mistreatment, malnourishment, and disease. For those who survived, their lives were ones of immiseration and indignity.

Large numbers of slaves allied to wretched conditions produced a fertile environment for insurrection – Saint-Domingue was home to a number of slave revolts in the latter part of the eighteenth century. The 1791 rebellion had a more pronounced edge to those that had gone before. Partly this was due to the broader context of upheaval that followed the French Revolution of 1789, which was an event of consequence not just for France, but also for its overseas possessions. Indeed, the victory of the revolutionaries in France allowed Saint-Domingue's *gens de couleur* – an elite minority of freed slaves and mulattos (mixed race European-Africans) – to lobby the new government in Paris for the recognition of full political and civil rights. At the same time, the colonial elite (*grands blancs*) saw the 1789 revolution as an opportunity to lobby for commercial autonomy from the metropole, something made pressing by heightened inter-imperial competition which, amongst other things, fostered metropolitan demands for exclusionary trade regimes (Adelman 2008: 327–8). In this, they were aided by ideas of self-rule and nativism, which acted to reconfigure notions of sovereignty within imperial territories. They were also aided by an uprising amongst black slaves in the northern part of the country. Initially, the demands of the slaves were limited to the abolition of reviled practices, most notably the use of the whip. Over time, however, slave demands became more radical, cultivating a movement that sought the overthrow of slavery, mulatto domination, and French colonialism. This uprising was to have major repercussions not just for Saint-Domingue, but also for the wider world.

In the period following the August 1791 uprising, Saint-Domingue became embroiled in a multifaceted conflict: slaves fought against French colonial forces; mulattos fought alongside the French against slaves; and various factions joined the French in order to fight foreign forces, mainly from Spain and Britain, who exploited the conflict as part of both the broader machinations of European geopolitics and as part of the war against post-revolutionary, and later, Napoleonic France. All of this was overlaid by deep social divisions, most notably race. After a long campaign, black insurgents under the leadership of Toussaint Louverture, Jean-Jacques Dessalines, and Henri Christophe defeated the French in 1800. Two years later, Napoleon ordered the re-invasion of the island under the command of his brother-in-law, Charles Leclerc. Leclerc arrested Louverture, who was sent to France and imprisoned at Fort de Joux in the Jura Mountains. He died the following year. Despite Louverture's death, remaining black forces won crucial battles at Crête-à-Pierrot and Vertières, culminating in French surrender in November 1803. On 1 January 1804, Dessalines became Governor-General of the independent republic of Haiti.

The revolutionaries in Haiti, evocatively labelled by C. L. R. James (2001/1938) as the 'black Jacobins' in order to stress the many connections between the slave forces and their counterparts in France, established a rule premised on constitutional egalitarianism. The 1805 constitution not only formally abolished slavery, it also guaranteed equal rights before the law, property rights, and freedom of belief, while insisting that 'no person is worthy of being a Haitian who is not a good father, good son, a good husband, and especially a good soldier'.[1] The last clause is worth particular attention. Dessalines, known after 1805 as Emperor Jacques I, led a society that placed military power at its apex. He fortified the country and forced Haitians either into armed service or to work on the land. Dessalines also instituted a programme of terror against both former colonialists and local rivals. His view of revolution was stark: 'To make a revolution, to succeed at it, one needs to do only two things: cut heads and burn houses' (in Ferrer 2014: 256). Not for the last time, revolutionary ideals of freedom, equality, and justice were tempered by oppression. Once again not for the last time, the apparent victors of the revolution became its victims. Haiti's former slaves were subjugated behind new structures of repression, while Dessalines himself fell captive to the revolution's bloody aftermath. In 1806, on his way to fight rebel forces, Dessalines was murdered by his own advisers. Thereafter, Haiti fragmented into a 15-year civil conflict between the State of Haiti, run on autocratic lines by Henri Christophe (after 1811, known as King Henri I of the Kingdom of Haiti) in the north of the territory, and a somewhat less autocratic Republic of Haiti in the south, with Alexandre Pétion as president (President for Life from 1816).

The revolution in Haiti had cascading effects. In France, it became increasingly difficult to square the principles of the 1789 revolution – liberty, equality, fraternity – with the slave trade, particularly after the Haitian uprising demonstrated the capacity of slaves to resist, fight, and govern for themselves. Even before the revolution in Saint-Domingue had been concluded, the universality of discourse around rights was challenged by racial discrimination, leading to debates over whether the revolutionary constitution should be extended to the colonies. The Society of the Friends of the Blacks (Société des Amis des Noirs), including major revolutionary figures such as Brissot, Condorcet, and Mirabeau, argued

---

[1] Available at: http://faculty.webster.edu/corbetre/haiti/history/earlyhaiti/1805-const.htm, accessed 19 September 2018.

that slavery could not stand alongside revolutionary claims of universal rights and equality. In April 1792, male *gens de couleur* in Saint-Domingue were granted full civil rights. The following year, the French colonial commissioners abolished slavery in the territory. In 1793, Jean-Baptiste Belley, a *gens de couleur* representing northern Saint-Domingue, became the first non-white to take up a seat in the National Assembly. And in February 1794, the revolutionary regime in Paris extended emancipation throughout the French colonies. In Britain, too, the experience of Haiti and other slave rebellions acted as a spur to the abolitionist movement. Although both colonialism and slavery proved to be resilient features of nineteenth-century international order (the emancipation decree was revoked by Napoleon in 1802), the Haitian Revolution served as a catalyst for debates that, over time, deinstitutionalized slavery and formal racial discrimination around the world.

Further afield, the revolution ended Saint-Domingue's role as a major exporter of sugar and coffee, presaging the relative decline of the Caribbean as a central node within global economic circuits (Geggus 2010: 85; also see Geggus 2002). It also presaged a shift in relative power within the Americas – after the defeat in Haiti, Napoleon effectively abandoned the French imperial project in the region, selling the 'Louisiana territory' to the United States and, as a result, greatly adding to the capabilities of the United States. The effects of this reorientation in French policy also had a number of unintended consequences. Napoleon's occupation of Spain and Portugal in 1807–8 provided a window of opportunity for independence movements throughout the Iberian Atlantic. These movements were, in turn, encouraged by the revolutionary government in Haiti, particularly the administration in the southern part of the country led by Pétion, which first sheltered Simón Bolívar and many of his supporters, and then supported their struggle through the provision of arms and personnel in exchange for a commitment to abolish slavery.[2] Pétion argued that the Americas should be made free of 'Spanish monsters', and called for Africans, Amerindians, and black Americans to settle in Haiti (in Geggus 2010: 99). Pétion's administration also formulated an 'anti-slavery foreign policy' that sought to liberate slave ships sailing near Haiti and initiated a 'free soil' policy that welcomed enslaved fugitives (Ferrer 2012: 58). If the example of Haiti acted as a spur to a number

---

[2] Christophe's regime was more cautious than Pétion's on this front. Christophe was content to run migration campaigns that encouraged people of colour, particularly African Americans, to move to Haiti. But he was anti-interventionist when it came to exporting the revolution. In this sense, his regime had a dual identity: revolutionary at home, 'normal' abroad. Thanks to Christian Cantir for exchanges on this point.

of uprisings in the region, it also acted as a spur to counter-revolution. In Cuba, Haiti's revolution was taken as a warning – in response, there was a hardening of both enslavement and the plantation system. The expertise of Haitian refugees helped Cuba to double both its number of sugar mills and its productive capacity in the two decades after the revolution (Ferrer 2014: 36). By 1820, Cuba was the largest sugar producer in the world.

The Haitian Revolution therefore formed part of a transnational field of contention that brought into question multiple strands of late eighteenth-century international order: the superiority of European coercive power; the legitimacy of colonial rule; an economic system premised on the trafficking of African slaves; and the ways in which racism and slavery challenged emergent notions of liberty and emancipation. For the study of revolutions, the example of Haiti – after the United States, the Western Hemisphere's oldest republic – is important for several reasons. First, there are the many features that led up to the revolutionary crisis itself, not least the ways in which a domestic crisis conjoined with international turbulence in turning local protests into a general uprising. Second, there are the intricacies of revolutionary events themselves – the competing factions, rival sites of authority, and shifting alliances – that served to radicalize the movement and make its outcomes unpredictable. Third are the nuances that lie within revolutionary struggles, such as the exemption granted to members of the Polish Legion, some of whom had fought on the side of the French, from the programme of terror waged by Dessalines on the grounds that they too were a subjugated people.[3] Fourth, there are the contradictory outcomes of the revolution itself. Despite its defeat, France continued to claim de jure sovereignty over Haiti, only granting Haiti partial recognition in 1825, and full recognition in 1838. Even then, Haiti was forced to pay an indemnity to its former colonial power, a debt that took 100 years to redeem. The complex status of the island, involving 'multiple layers of recognition and non-recognition' (Gaffield 2015: 184), was a barrier to both growth and de facto sovereignty. Fifth are the dynamics of revolution and counter-revolution that help to explain why Haiti's outcomes were so contradictory. During the conflict, up to 60,000 Haitian refugees resettled in the United States, Canada, Cuba, and the Caribbean (Jasanoff 2010: 38). These refugees served as a counter-revolutionary lobby, the forerunners to later diasporas from Russia, Cuba, and Iran. Finally, Haiti demonstrates the ways in which a 'peripheral' polity can be generative

---

[3] Dessalines also spared many priests, health workers, and skilled workmen, as well as some Englishmen and Americans – his terror had a pragmatic edge.

of discourse and policy in the 'metropole'. News about the revolution was widely reported in Europe. William Wordsworth wrote a glowing ode 'To Toussaint Louverture', while the revolution played a significant role in Hegel's formulations of master–slave and lordship–bondage (Buck-Morss 2000: 844; Fischer 2004: 24–33). But despite the interest shown towards Haiti by Europeans at the time, later analysts of revolutions downplayed its influence.[4] Although Eric Hobsbawm (1962: 4) wrote that 'the world revolution spread outward from the double crater of England and France', the experience of the Haitian Revolution suggests a more polycentric character to the age of revolution.

The Haitian Revolution therefore provides a range of insights into dynamics that lie behind both the study and practice of revolutionary change: processes of continuity and change – that revolutions promise radical transformation, yet are constrained by domestic and international pressures; the centrality of multiple international dynamics to revolutionary anatomies; the question of whether revolutions contain general tendencies, or whether they must be studied on a case-by-case basis; and the degree to which revolutions are made by people on the ground and how much they are the product of broader symbolic, economic, and political fields. The rest of this chapter explores these four themes in more detail.

Continuity and Change

Perhaps the greatest cliché in revolutionary folklore is that revolutions change everything. Indeed, the notion of revolution-as-rupture has been much fuelled by revolutionaries themselves. From Robespierre to Guevara, revolutionaries have claimed to be starting history from a 'year zero' in which symbolic, political, and economic relations would be cast afresh. 'We have it in our power', wrote Thomas Paine (2004/1776: ix), 'to begin the world over again ... The birthday of a new world is at hand'. Paine (1999/1791: 92) went on to write stirringly of the association between modern revolutions and social transformation:

What were formerly called revolutions were little more than a change of persons or an alteration of local circumstances. They rose and fell like things of course, and had nothing in their existence or their fate that could influence beyond the spot that produced them. But what we now see in the world, from the revolutions of America and France, are a renovation of the natural order of things, a system

---

[4] One notable exception within revolutionary scholarship is Eric Selbin (2010: 143), who argues that Haiti is 'the world's most important revolutionary process', albeit one that 'virtually everyone ignores'.

of principles as universal as truth and the existence of man, and combining moral with political happiness.

Paine saw this new concept of revolution as extendable well beyond America and France. Hence (Paine 1999/1791: 191),

The iron is becoming hot all over Europe. The insulted German and the enslaved Spaniard, the Russ and the Pole, are beginning to think. The present age will hereafter merit to be called the Age of Reason, and the present generation will appear to the future as the Adam of a new world.

The concept of revolution-as-rupture as formulated in the Atlantic revolutions that began in the final quarter of the eighteenth century spread around the world over the next two centuries (Miller 2011: ch. 1). Hence, Leon Trotsky (1997/1932) spoke of the need for 'permanent revolution' in order to stoke the fires of global insurrection,[5] while Ayatollah Khomeini, Iran's Supreme Leader following the 1979 revolution, invoked the potential of revolutions to change the world: 'State boundaries are the product of a deficient human mind ... The revolution does not recognize borders and frontiers, it will go through them ... Until the cry "There is no God but God" resounds over the whole world, there will be struggle' (in Abrahamian 1993: 49).

To some extent, Paine, Trotsky, and Khomeini kept their promises. The revolutions in America, France, Russia, and Iran had major effects both on their home societies and the wider world. Indeed, for much of modern world history, the conflict between revolutionary movements and their opponents has constituted one of the central dramas in world politics. Just as the French Revolution ushered in the long nineteenth century with its conflict between absolutist monarchies and constitutionalist movements, so the Russian Revolution introduced to the twentieth century its central motif: the clash – both ideological and geopolitical – between state socialism and democratic capitalism. Other revolutions can claim almost as great an impact: the Cuban Revolution as the exemplar of the possibilities of guerrilla warfare; the Chinese Revolution of the radical potential of the peasantry; the Iranian Revolution as the event that unleashed a militant form of Shi'ism onto the world stage. The impact of revolutions, therefore, is substantial. Revolutions, by virtue of the example they provide in overcoming apparently insurmountable forces, in generating substantial changes both to the texture of their home societies and international order, and in the power of example they provide for oppressed people, do change the world.

---

[5] Although the term 'permanent revolution' is usually attributed to Trotsky, it is a term that was first used by Marx. On this, see Edelstein (2015).

But this is only part of the story. Revolutions are usually major disappointments, often ending in defeat, re-subjugating those who bought them about, and leading to the establishment of domestic tyranny – the story of Haiti is not a one-off. Indeed, as the previous chapter showed, critics of revolution see them as little more than malevolent disturbances to the stability of international order. Edmund Burke, to take one example, saw the French Revolution as a fundamental challenge to the underlying fabric of the European states-system. Burke (1993/1790: 58) described the revolution as a 'tragi-comic scene' set in motion by 'philosophical fanatics' intent on spreading a 'monstrous fiction' that would lead to 'unsocial, uncivil, unconnected chaos'. For Burke, the French Revolution rejected ancient liberties and trampled on the traditions that sustained the 'European Commonwealth'. The revolution's opposition to property, hierarchy, rank, and rightful privilege served to break the social bonds required to maintain order (Bourke 2015: 741). The 'moral degeneration' of France provided little more than 'a new school of murder and barbarism' (Burke 2005/1792: 269).[6] Crucially, Burke linked domestic and international revolution. The zealotry of the revolution, he argued, meant that it was compelled to spread outwards; there could be no strategy of containment and no negotiation with 'the mother of monsters' (Burke 1999/1796). Burke (1999/1796) called for armed counter-revolution legitimized by what he called the 'law of neighbourhood': that radical change in one state affected others in their 'vicinity' to the extent that, if necessary, revolutions could be suppressed by force.[7]

Over the two centuries since Burke's writing on the French Revolution, counter-revolution has continued to exist as an international project. Many US administrations, particularly during the Cold War, chose to actively support counter-revolutionary movements, even when this led to collaboration with insalubrious characters such as Suharto in Indonesia, Ferdinand Marcos in the Philippines, and Mobutu Sese Seko in Congo (known as Zaire for much of his rule). In the Americas, considered by most US administrations as their sphere of influence, US backing for these regimes included the provision of funds, training, and arms

---

[6] Burke had a quite different take on the American Revolution, which he saw as a legitimate defence of liberty, property, and Anglosphere community. On this, see: Mosher (1991); Spinner (1991); Bourke (2015).

[7] Burke's views of the revolution hardened during the 1790s. *Reflections on the Revolution in France* sought to 'quarantine' the 'revolutionary plague' and 'keep it at a distance'. However, his 1796 *Letters on a Regicide Peace*, from which the second half of this paragraph draws, favoured an armed doctrine of counter-revolution that would directly confront French attempts to create a 'universal empire'. On the changing tenor of Burke's ideas of counter-revolution, see: Welsh (1995); Hampsher-Monk (2005); Simms (2011); Bourke (2015).

to figures like François (Papa Doc) Duvalier and Jean-Claude (Baby Doc) Duvalier, the father-and-son despots of Haiti during much of the Cold War period, as well as autocrats such as Manuel Noriega, Augusto Pinochet, and Anastasio Somoza. The Western Hemisphere Institute for Security Cooperation, formerly known as The School of the Americas, has educated tens of thousands of students, including Noriega, in techniques often used in counter-revolutionary campaigns. Justification for US support for authoritarianism during the Cold War was often legitimized by the threat of revolution which, it was argued, would lead to the imposition of communism and the strengthening of the influence of the Soviet Union. Hence, Cordell Hull, Secretary-of-State under Franklin Roosevelt, is claimed to have said of one Latin American ruler (most likely Rafael Trujillo, the dictator-president of the Dominican Republic) that, 'he may be a son-of-a-bitch, but at least he's our son-of-a-bitch'. And Henry Kissinger, perhaps the archetypal figure of US Cold War counter-revolutionary realpolitik, sustained a consistent doctrine of counter-revolution in order to justify US interventions around the world, including Vietnam, in the interests of what he saw as higher order needs of US power, international stability, and security from revolution.[8]

It is not only international projects of counter-revolution that prompt the failure of revolutions to fulfil their promise of total change. There are also domestic constraints on incoming revolutionary regimes: alternative political coalitions, recalcitrant members of the armed forces, old regime loyalists, and others. France's counter-revolution, for example, began at home, most notoriously in the ruthless pacification of opponents of the revolutionary regime in the Atlantic region of the Vendée, which led to the death of around 20% of the region's population (Malešević 2017: 121; also see Tilly 1964). If domestic counter-revolution is, in part, a direct confrontation between revolutionaries and status quo forces, counter-revolution also takes place in more indirect fashion, though the sinews of bureaucratic power. Any takeover of the state requires accommodations with the technocrats of power: civil servants, members of the coercive apparatus, local officials, and more (Mulholland 2017: 370). The incoming regime relies, at least in the short term, on tax inspectors, teachers, health professionals, police officers, and comparable figures to continue doing their jobs. Without this administrative continuity, the state would collapse. Yet the loyalty of these groups is to the state rather than

---

[8] Kissinger took many of his cues from the arch counter-revolutionary of the modern era, Prince Klemens von Metternich, one of the architects of European dynastic order during the early-to-mid nineteenth century. Kissinger wrote his PhD thesis on Metternich, later publishing it in book form: Kissinger (1999).

the revolution. This is also the case with members of the coercive apparatus. The deep embedding of the coercive apparatus within the state, as well as the frequent use of force by revolutionary regimes against their adversaries, means that no revolution has sought to destroy it. Beyond conducting a purge of those considered to be too close to the old regime, revolutionaries not only inherit the existing coercive apparatus, they also tend to extend its prerogatives.[9]

There is more continuity therefore between old and new regimes than either advocates desire or opponents fear. This includes informal sites of continuity that restrict the possibilities of radical change, not least the norms, habits, and mores that inhabit what Jeffery Paige (2003: 28) calls the 'hidden abodes of everyday life'. The capacity of revolutionary regimes to recast these deep-rooted associations and beliefs is limited. Even the French Revolution, the paradigmatic revolution of the modern era, had less of an impact than is commonly thought. Much of the initial revolutionary project was overturned by the restoration of the Bourbons in 1815 and many of the families who enjoyed positions of influence under the *ancien régime* retained their privileges during the first half of the nineteenth century. According to Alexis de Tocqueville (1999/1852), one of the revolution's most astute – if partisan – chroniclers,[10] the centralization of French administrative institutions, usually heralded as products of the revolution and the Napoleonic era, were, in large measure, inherited from the old regime. Tocqueville recognized the stickiness of both bureaucracies and habits in the face of revolutionary innovation. As he wrote in 1852, 'nothing, or almost nothing, has changed since 1789 ... the revolution stirred up society rather than changed it' (Tocqueville 1999/ 1852: 8; also see Furet 1981: 25).

At the same time, revolutionary regimes are often weak when they seize power: the new government in France faced opposition both from sections of the old regime and the revolt in the Vendée; Russian Bolsheviks fought a major war with old guard 'whites' and foreign armies; in China, Mao Zedong and the Chinese Communist Party took three decades to complete their seizure of power. The institutions and customs of the old order became reinvested in the revolutionary regimes of France, Russia,

---

[9] Prominent exceptions include the 'negotiated revolutions' in Central and Eastern Europe in 1989. I return to this point in later chapters.

[10] Tocqueville's analysis of 1789 was drawn, in part, from his experience of the events of 1848. In early 1848, Tocqueville served as a member of the Chamber of Deputies, using this platform to warn his fellow delegates about the impending crisis. After the revolution, Tocqueville was elected to the Constituent Assembly, serving as Vice President of the Assembly and, later, as Minister of Foreign Affairs. He was dismissed from office following the coup by Louis-Napoleon in 1851.

and China, just as they did in Haiti, Mexico, Cuba, Iran, Nicaragua, Vietnam, and elsewhere. Given the domestic weaknesses of revolutionary regimes, the stickiness of symbolic tropes, and the counter-revolutionary tendencies of leading states in the international system, it is hardly surprising that revolutions have often ended in disappointment. It is also little surprise that revolutionary regimes have frequently responded to domestic and international opposition by becoming despotic. Dessalines' campaign of terror against his opponents two centuries ago is not a novel feature of revolutionary states; rather, it is the norm.

Overall, therefore, revolutions neither fulfil the expectations of the romantics who advocate them, nor become the dystopias feared by those who promote their overthrow. In order to understand the significance of revolutions, it is important to cut a swathe through both of these myths: the exaggerated fantasies of revolutionaries themselves and the claims of those, often conservative, analysts who deny the importance of revolutions to domestic societies and international relations. Revolutions do not start history afresh, but nor can they be reduced to mere footnotes in history. Rather, revolutions involve the forceful breakdown of the old order and the attempt to reconstruct forms of political, economic, and symbolic authority. Revolutions have a formative effect on the societies where they occur, on the regions in which they take place, and on the wider international order with which they interact. Yet the stickiness of old-regime institutions and symbolic fields curtail the transformative capacities of revolutionary regimes, while many elements of the revolutionary programme are never initiated. The first theme in studying revolutions, therefore, is to unravel the dynamic between established ties and the capacity of revolution to institute programmes of radical change. It was not just in Haiti that the ambivalent, even contradictory, features of revolutionary transformations have been made apparent.

International or Domestic?

Most revolutionaries have emphasized the international elements of their uprising. Toussaint Louverture, for example, insisted that Haiti could not go it alone. Louverture invested substantial political capital in securing French support for the revolution, a project that backfired when Napoleon ordered the retaking of Haiti by General Leclerc. As noted in the previous section, this invasion led to Louverture's death in French custody before Haitian forces had completed their victory.

Beyond the insistence by revolutionaries of the international dimensions of their struggle lie more general connections between revolutions and international processes. Three stand out. First is the notion held by revolutionaries that the international system – whether understood as imperialist, capitalist, racist, or a combination of all three – operates as a structure of oppression. Second, there is the sense that revolutionary states pose a challenge to this system, one that is overtly emancipatory. And third, there is the internationalism of revolutionary states: that their struggle is not contained by the limits of state borders or power politics, but one that transcends existing boundaries (Halliday 2008). Marx and Engels (1967/1848: 46–7), for example, thought that communism could not exist 'as a local event. The proletariat can only exist on the world-historical plane, just as communism, its activity, can only have a world historical existence'. Lenin made this point starkly: 'global class, global party, global revolution' (in Halliday 2008: 70). In 1968, protestors in European capitals chanted: 'Paris, London, Rome, Berlin, we shall fight and we shall win.' Some of the principal intellectual currents of the 68-ers were drawn from the work of 'Third World' figures such as Mao and Ho Chi Minh. Che Guevara (1968: 62) globalized these sentiments into a 'battle cry' of anti-imperialism in his 'Message to the People of the World':

How close and bright would the future appear if two, three, many Vietnams flowered on the face of the globe ... what difference do the dangers to a human being or people matter when what is at stake is the destiny of humanity. Our every action is a battle cry against imperialism and a call for the unity of the peoples.

Revolutionary movements, therefore, run counter to many of the ground-rules of international order (sovereignty, the sanctity of international law, and diplomacy), proclaiming ideals of universal society and global insurrection. Revolutions challenge international order in a number of ways ranging from disrupting existing patterns of trade and inter-state alliances to questioning whole systems of rule. To take one example, the challenges of the Bolshevik Revolution were short-term, prompting the withdrawal of Russian forces from the First World War; medium-term, in the provision of support for like-minded movements – the Soviet Union invaded Poland in 1920, provided aid for German revolutionaries in 1923, supported the republicans during the Spanish Civil War from 1936 to 1939, and helped to install socialist regimes in Europe and Asia during the late 1940s; and long-term, in the establishment of a systemic alternative to democratic capitalism. As with other revolutions, the outcomes of the Bolshevik Revolution included new alliances that, in turn, induced a conflict between the revolutionary state and a counter-revolutionary coalition that sought to contain it.

The Bolshevik Revolution, like those in Haiti, France, China, Cuba, Iran, and elsewhere challenged the credibility of the existing international system and, with it, the credibility of the system's great powers. This, naturally, prompted a response: in order to justify their position at the apex of the international system, great powers must act decisively in the face of a revolutionary challenge (Bisley 2004: 56). Occasionally, this action takes place in support of the revolutionary movement, as with the 1989 revolutions in Central and Eastern Europe. More frequently, great powers act to suppress such revolutions, seeing them as threats to international order, as was the case in Haiti, France, Russia, Algeria, Vietnam, and elsewhere. Burke's notion that the French Revolution was likely to 'infect' its neighbours stands as an illustration of this tendency. As he told the House of Commons in 1791, when it came to containing the Jacobin virus: 'Holland might justly be considered as necessary a part of this country as Kent' (in Simms 2011: 109). In terms of its vision and character, counter-revolution is just as internationalist as revolution.

Counter-revolution is aimed at containing the triple challenge – normative, ideological, and strategic – that revolutionary states represent (Bisley 2004: 55; also see Scott 1982). Intervention by counter-revolutionary states is both informal, covering covert practices and cultural ties, and formal, taking in propaganda, training, aid, and the provision of arms. Nick Bisley (2004: 52–3) distils these two forms of aid into five sets of activities: first, direct military intervention, as in US intervention alongside white armies during the Russian Civil War; second, financial aid and clandestine support for counter-revolutionary forces, as with US support for Nicaraguan Contras or Mujahedeen groups in Afghanistan and Pakistan during the 1980s; third, low scale harassment, such as propaganda campaigns, public diplomacy, and the jamming of radio signals common to Western strategies in Eastern and Central Europe during the Cold War; fourth, deprivation, such as sanctions, of the kind that the United States has sustained against the Iranian and Cuban revolutionary regimes; and fifth, disruption, through the non-recognition of revolutionary states and associated practices, such as the expulsion of Cuba from the Organization of American States (OAS) in 1962. Counter-revolutionary policies frequently combine two or more of these activities. US involvement in the Russian Civil War included a financial package ($450 million for the post-Tsarist government and almost $200 million for use against the Bolsheviks after the October Revolution), armed intervention (9,000 American troops were sent to Siberia and nearly 5,000 to North Russia), plus assistance in the form of food relief, medical aid, and the like (Tardelli 2013).

On occasion, counter-revolutionary forces succeed in rolling back revolutions – examples include much of continental Europe in 1848–9, the Dominican Republic in 1965, Grenada in 1983, and Syria in 2011. More frequently, these campaigns lead to protracted struggles between the revolutionary regime and counter-revolutionary forces. Although counter-revolutionary forces often enjoy a military superiority over revolutionary movements, the latter contain a political advantage, particularly in terms of legitimacy. For example, although the 1968 Tet Offensive by the North Vietnamese was a military success for the United States and its allies, it marked a political defeat for counter-revolutionary forces, so much so that military requests for funding were thereafter refused by Congress and President Johnson decided not to stand for re-election (Mack 1975; Willbanks 2007: chs. 6–7). A similar assessment can be made of the French military victory over the Front de Libération Nationale (FLN) in Algeria, which was eroded by both the illegitimacy of its methods, particularly the widespread use of torture, and the FLN's concerted, and highly successful, public information campaign (Connelly 2003; Byrne 2016). Regardless of outcome, the crucial point is that revolution and counter-revolution are less two entities than one, joined in a shared, if mutually destructive, relationship.

Revolution and war are also tightly meshed. On the one hand, revolutionary states are far more likely than other states to enter into violent civil war: over one million people died in the Mexican Revolution and the country's subsequent civil unrest between 1910 and 1917, around three million Russians died in the civil war between 1917 and 1921, and close to five million Chinese were killed in the first five years of Mao's post-1949 revolutionary regime (Westad 2012: 322; Beissinger 2014: 6). On the other hand, revolutionary states are both twice as likely as non-revolutionary states to induce inter-state war and much more likely to win these wars (Maoz 1989: 204; also see Carter et al. 2012; Colgan 2013). This is, in part, because revolutionary states devote far greater resources to their militaries than non-revolutionary states – major social revolutions have been followed by an average 264 per cent increase in defence budgets (Carter et al. 2012: 452).

As Stephen Walt (1996) notes, revolutions intensify the prospects of war in three ways. First, revolutions provide a window of opportunity for states to improve their position vis-à-vis other states – because revolutionary regimes are beset by civil strife and elite fracture, other states may seize the chance to attack the revolutionary regime. Second, this window of opportunity generates 'spirals of suspicion' as the uncertainty produced by the revolution heightens levels of insecurity that, in turn, raise threat perceptions (Walt 1996: 33). Finally, revolutionary states seek to export their revolution both as a way of shoring up their fragile position at home and because of their ideological commitment to an alternative international order. Concomitantly, counter-revolutionary states assume that the revolution will spread unless it is 'strangled in its crib' and that revolution will be relatively easy to reverse (Walt 1996: 43). This 'perverse combination' of insecurity and overconfidence heightens the prospects of inter-state conflict (Walt 1996: 40). By increasing uncertainty and fear, by altering capabilities, and by raising threat perceptions, revolutionary states begin a process that, quite often, engenders inter-state conflict. A mutual lack of understanding on both sides of the revolutionary confrontation, augmented by ideological polarization, produces an unstable international environment. War between revolutionary and counter-revolutionary forces emerge from an 'over-reaction to over-perceived revolutionary dangers' (Mayer 1977: 202).

Revolutions, therefore, are always international events. At times, the international effects of revolution are symbolic – for example, Haiti was the first independent state to recognize the legitimacy of the Greek Revolution in 1820. At other times, it is material – the Cuban revolutionary regime has provided armed support to a range of liberation movements, as well as humanitarian assistance to states throughout the global south. Yet there is a paradox at the heart of the relationship between revolutionary states and the international system – revolutionary states must establish relations with other states and co-exist with the system's rules, laws, and institutions, even while professing to reject these practices. Although the Declaration of the Rights of Man claimed that 'the sovereignty of peoples is not bound by the treaties of tyrants', the French revolutionary regime signed a resolution on non-intervention in 1793, stating that 'the invasion of one state by another state tends to threaten the liberty and security of all' (Armstrong 1993: 217–18, 227). Even when they did annex territory, revolutionaries appealed more to old regime treaty law than to revolutionary principles (Kolla 2017: 119). For their part, the Soviet revolutionary regime enjoyed a selective approach to international law, arguing through the principle of 'socialist legality' that promises must be kept (*pacta sunt servanda*) and that new circumstances invalidated previous treaties (*rebus sic standibus*). In this way, foreign loans were annulled, but rules on the treatment of prisoners of war upheld. Following détente in the early 1970s, Chinese–US relations were normalized. This saw China end its support for black radical groups and switch its allegiance in Angola from the Soviet-backed MPLA (Movimento Popular de Libertação de Angola) to UNITA (União Nacional para a Independência Total de Angola), a group supported by both the United States and apartheid South Africa (Frazier 2015: 206–7).[11]

Pressures to conform therefore act as a counterweight to claims of self-reliance and global insurrection. Despite challenging existing forms of international order, revolutionary states play their part in reproducing regimes governing trade, alliances, and security. On the one hand, revolutionary states exhibit a particular form of *revolutionary sovereignty* – a claim that simultaneously legitimizes international intervention and domestic autarchy. On the other hand, in order to function as states, revolutionary states are forced to give up many of their revolutionary aims.

Given the closeness of the relationship between revolutions and international relations, it is curious that the international components of revolution have not received more attention, particularly from scholars of International Relations (IR) (Lawson 2011, 2015a; Rao 2016). IR scholarship has usually treated revolutions as problems to be solved rather than as constitutive of international order (for exceptions, see: Walt 1996; Halliday 1999; Bukovansky 2002; Panah 2002; Anievas 2015; Rao 2016; Allinson 2019). This residual disciplinary location may be the result of broader silences regarding the ways in which contentious politics have shaped the development of modern international order.[12] Whatever the reason, it is striking that IR's neglect is matched by the relatively sparse accounts of the international features of revolution within revolutionary theory more generally. As the next chapter shows, many third and fourth generation revolutionary theorists claim to have attended sufficiently to the international components of revolutions. Yet these accounts have not yet theorized the multifaceted role played by international processes in the causes, trajectories, and outcomes of revolutions.

[11] The relationship between communism and African American movements was long-standing. Marx wrote extensively about slavery in his writings on the civil war. And Lenin raised the 'Negro Question' at the Second Congress of the Communist International in 1920; shortly afterwards he wrote a letter to American communists urging them to engage more directly with African Americans. The issue of racialized capitalism – how capitalism and racism went hand in hand – was a central concern for figures like W. E. B. Dubois, who was hosted by Mao during a high-profile visit to China in 1959. On this, see: Robinson (1983); Zimmerman (2016).

[12] If the conservative agenda of mainstream IR provides some rationale for its neglect of revolutions, it is more surprising to see the way in which revolutions dropped off the radar of Comparative Politics during the 1990s and 2000s. In recent years, however, revolutions are making something of a comeback – see: Beissinger (2007, 2014); Bunce and Wolchik (2007, 2011); Weyland (2009, 2012); Levitsky and Way (2010, 2013); Slater (2010); Carter et al. (2012); Colgan (2012, 2013); Slater and Smith (2016).

Universal or Particular?

The third theme in the study of revolutions is the question of whether there are general characteristics that hold for all revolutions, or whether revolutions are so distinct that they must be studied on a case-by-case basis. The next chapter discusses this issue in depth. This section briefly surveys the two issues that are most often seen as essential to revolutions: violence and newness.

In the modern era, revolutions have usually been seen as fights to the finish in which one side vanquishes the other: the 1789 revolution in France ushered in a decade of domestic strife, opening the way to Napoleonic dictatorship and continental war; the Bolshevik Revolution was followed by a four-year civil war in which foreign armies and their proxies fought the Red Army; and the two stages of the Chinese Revolution, first to establish a republic and then to build a communist state, were separated by a battle for domestic authority that lasted for three decades. Even after these revolutions, the new regimes struggled to impose their authority on their wider societies. Robespierre's Terror, Stalin's forced collectivization and purges, and Mao's Cultural Revolution were all attempts to shore up revolutionary regimes from opposition at home and abroad, real or imagined. The storming of the Bastille, the raid on the Winter Palace, and the Long March undertaken by the remnants of Mao's army became part of revolutionary folklore, symbols of the might and right of the revolutionary struggle. If revolutions were to succeed, it seemed, they had to be violent.

Reflecting the violent struggles espoused by revolutionaries both in word and deed, revolutionary scholarship has tended to equate revolutions with fights to the finish in which nothing less than death or victory would suffice. As noted in the previous chapter, both theorists and practitioners of revolution have often seen the basic essence of revolution as violence. But such a focus disguises a more complex relationship between revolutions and violence than is commonly understood (Gurr and Goldstone 1991: 338–40). In the nineteenth century, there were regular discussions within revolutionary groups about the balance to be struck between 'physical force' and 'moral force'. At the beginning of the twentieth century, revolutionaries in Russia, Iran, Turkey, and elsewhere sought radical change not through violent overthrow, but through uprisings that aimed at shifting sovereignty away from imperial courts towards representative assemblies and written constitutions (Sohrabi 1995; Kurzman 2008; Chalcraft 2016: 168–72). This form of struggle remained somewhat latent until the 1970s, when non-violent movements became more commonplace. Of the 67 authoritarian regimes dismantled between 1972 and 2002, it is claimed that over 70 per cent were the result of non-violent uprisings (Nepstad 2011: 4–5). Since the end of the Cold War, unarmed protests have become the preeminent form of revolutionary mobilization.

Oftentimes, there is no clear either-or between violent and non-violent campaigns. Both have existed simultaneously within the same protest movement (as with South Africa's African National Congress and its militant wing Umkhonto we Sizwe) or developed from one to the other (as in the Philippines during the 1970s and 1980s). Very few movements operate in the total absence of violence if, by violence, we include the destruction of property, hand-to-hand fighting, or the throwing of objects like stones and bottles, all of which can harm and, on occasion, kill. Violence and non-violence are not binary opposites, but a continuum. They are also in the eye of the beholder – Palestinian protestors armed with stones or Venezuelan activists throwing 'poopootov cocktails' (an adaptation of Molotov cocktails containing human and animal faeces) are not non-violent to their opponents. Indeed, regimes use stone throwing, attacks on property, hand-to-hand fighting, or even violent rhetoric as a rationale for denouncing their opponents and deploying their coercive apparatus. Definitions of violence and non-violence are ambiguous, subject to interpretations that are, in turn, dependent on context and political position.[13]

At the same time, many revolutions are relatively peaceful seizures of power. Violence stems, for the most part, from battles *after* the initial takeover of state power, resulting from the need by revolutionary regimes to shore up their rule in the face of domestic and international counter-revolution, a cycle that can be observed, for example, in Iran by way of its war with Iraq and the ruthless measures employed against the regime's domestic opponents. At the same time, post-revolutionary violence has often not been committed *by*, or directed *at*, the state, but arisen from the absence *of* the state. For example, in the years after the 1789 revolution in France, alongside the well-known counter-revolutionary struggles, conscription riots, and anti-tax protests were 'ordinary', scattered forms of violence, many of which stemmed from the lack of a central authority – the settling of scores and personal feuds, brigandage, and so on (Tarrow 2015: 33–4). The relationship between violence and revolution is therefore complex. Violence may be seen as intrinsic to revolutionary

---

[13] Tilly (2003) distinguishes usefully between armed protest (i.e. guns and bombs) and violent protest (rock throwing, hand-to-hand fighting, etc.). If this distinction is followed, a large number of contemporary protest movements are unarmed, but violent (Kadivar and Ketchley 2018). I come back to this point in Chapter 7.

struggles, as it was by figures like Lenin or Fanon, or as an illegitimate tactic of revolutionaries, as it is by many contemporary activists. Either way, there is no universally applicable association between revolution and violence – the connection between them is contingent rather than fixed.

The second characteristic often assumed to be essential to revolutions is the idea of newness. Many analysts demand that, to be considered as 'proper' revolutions, uprisings must be legitimized by a utopian vision that promises nothing less than the remaking of domestic and international order. However, demanding that every revolution conjure a new world vision would disqualify almost every instance from being labelled as a revolution. 'Third World' revolutionaries from Mao to Castro have fused a basic grounding in Marxism with nationalism and populism. Ayatollah Khomeini often linked an understanding of revolutionary Islam with a quasi-Marxist concern for the dispossessed and downtrodden, arguing that: 'Islam represents the slum dwellers, not the palace dwellers'; 'In a truly Islamic society there will be no shantytowns'; and perhaps his most obviously hybrid rallying cry: 'Oppressed of the world, unite' (Abrahamian 1993). Other figures from the Islamic world also illustrate this fusion of 'Che Khomeinism' (Gellner 1981). Shi'ite figures such as Ali Shariati combined an engagement with Marxism (developed in Shariati's case as a graduate student at the Sorbonne) with Islam – hence his call for a 'red' or 'revolutionary' Shi'ism (Bayat 2017: 35–48).[14] Sunni radicals, too, have demonstrated a capacity for ideological eclecticism: Abul ala Maududi, the founder of the Jamaat-e-Islami party in Pakistan, was strongly influenced by Lenin, while other Sunni radicals, including Hassan al-Banna, founder of the Muslim Brotherhood, adopted a Gramscian view of strategy in forming his critique of *jahiliyyah* (secular, ignorant) states and societies (Bayat 2008: 104). In these instances, Islamic appeals, combined with nationalism, populism, and quasi-Marxian rhetoric, have served as repositories for long-standing grievances.

All revolutionaries, therefore, employ eclectic symbolic tropes, looking to the past as much as to the present or future in legitimizing their uprisings. Russian revolutionaries consciously modelled their experience on the French revolution. Both Mensheviks and Bolsheviks saw themselves as the Girondins and Jacobins of their day, even if the Bolsheviks

---

[14] Shariati's particular strength was 'injecting radical meanings into stock scriptural terms': jihad shifted from crusade to liberation struggle; *shahid* from martyr to revolutionary hero; the story of Cain and Abel became a metaphor for class struggle; and Imam Hossein was, in Shariati's reckoning, an early day Che Guevara (Abrahamian 2008: 144).

portrayed the October revolution as the antithesis of 1789, marking the triumph of the fourth estate (the proletariat) over the third estate (the bourgeoisie). As Marx (1968/1852: 96) himself recognized in his discussion of bourgeois revolutions, revolutionaries often look backwards for their unifying message:

And just when they seem engaged in revolutionizing themselves and things, in creating something that has never existed, precisely in such periods of revolutionary crisis they anxiously conjure up the spirits of the past to their service and borrow from them names, battle slogans and costumes in order to present the new scene of world history in this time-honoured disguise and this borrowed language. Thus Luther donned the mask of the Apostle Paul, the revolution of 1789 to 1814 draped itself alternately as the Roman Republic and the Roman Empire, and the revolution of 1848 knew nothing better than to parody, now 1789, now the tradition of 1793 to 1795.

The utopian vision of revolutionaries, therefore, does not necessarily emerge as a set of original precepts. Rather, revolutionary ideology coalesces around a blend of the time-honoured and the novel. Longstanding ideals of freedom, justice, dignity, and equality are as central to revolutionary rhetoric as claims of remaking the world anew. More generally, equating revolutions with inalienable, essential features such as violence and newness reduces them to static objects of analysis. But as the Introduction argued, the meaning and practice of revolutions has changed over time, depending on the contexts in which they emerge and how events unfold. This does not mean that revolutions share no similarities, just that these similarities are not timeless properties or fixed attributes. As such, the study of revolution requires a shift from an 'attribute ontology' to a 'process ontology' (Jackson 2010), premised on the particular sequences through which revolutionary events take place. From these sequences of events, it is possible to abstract causal pathways that serve as a baseline for examining diverse episodes of revolution. The next chapter lays out such an understanding of revolutionary anatomies.

Do Revolutions Need Revolutionaries?

The final theme in the study of revolution concerns the debate around structure and agency: the question of whether revolutions are the result of intentional action by purposeful agents, or of broader constellations – demographic changes, patterns of class conflict, processes of modernization, and so on – that take place seemingly out of the reach of revolutionary participants. At first glance, this may seem like an odd question. After all, revolutions are particular processes that take place at particular times and which involve particular people. Eric Selbin (2008: 130) makes this point well:

Whatever else they may be, revolutions are fundamentally about people: created by people, led by people, fought and died for by people, consciously and intentionally constructed by people ... if the question is why revolutions happen here and not there, now and not then, and among these people and not those, we must focus on people.

Despite the force of Selbin's point, the debate around structure and agency remains a live one, not least because the most influential traditions of revolutionary theory argue that, although in a basic sense revolutions are 'made' by people operating in a specific context, revolutions are principally the product of broader structural alignments. Revolutions succeed or fail depending on certain underlying conditions: responses to shifts from agricultural to industrial production (Moore 1966); state crises emanating from military defeat and elite fracture (Skocpol 1979); long-term changes in population densities (Goldstone 1991), and so on. Given the right conjuncture of structural forces, revolutions have to occur: 'revolutions are not made, they come' (Skocpol 1979: 17).[15]

Not only is this question – whether revolutions need revolutionaries – an important theoretical debate, it is also one that affects the practice of revolutions. For example, although the Soviet Union supported a number of revolutionary movements around the world, it tended to do so only when it considered the objective conditions for revolution to be ripe. Such an understanding goes back to Marx's view of revolutions as rooted in contradictions within the existing mode of production. For Marx, the structural engine of capitalist society resided in the antagonisms between classes arising from the domination of the proletariat by the bourgeoisie, a relationship in which the former were reduced to the wage-slaves of the latter. To be sure, Marx argued (1967/1848: 83), 'capitalism has accomplished wonders far surpassing Egyptian pyramids, Roman aqueducts and Gothic cathedrals'. But the secret behind capitalism's accomplishments was its dual subjugation: first, of nature by man; and second, of the proletariat by the bourgeoisie. The role of the communist was to reveal the true nature of these relations, steering workers away from the temptation of reformist movements. For Marx, conflict with capitalist society should be open and direct.

---

[15] Skocpol here echoes the words of the American reformist lawyer, Wendell Phillips. The full quote from Phillips reads: 'Revolutions are not made, they come. A revolution is as natural a growth as an oak. It comes out of the past. Its foundations are laid far back.' Eric Selbin (2008: 133) reverses the dictum: 'revolutions do not come, they are made'.

Over the past century or so, Marx's approach to revolution has been subject to considerable critique. For the purposes of this book, two stand out. First, Marx overemphasized the centrality of class conflict to revolutions. Despite rhetorical claims to the contrary, revolutions have rarely been struggles between the proletariat and the bourgeoisie over ownership of the means of production. Rather, revolutionary movements have been forged out of complex, shifting coalitions, often with disparate aims, motives, and intentions. Indeed, Robert Dix (1984: 433) labels revolutionary movements 'negative coalitions' because the only thing protestors share is a desire to be rid of a particular regime or ruler.[16] Second, although Marx studied revolutions, particularly bourgeois revolutions, in detail, his theoretical approach bore few resemblances to concrete episodes of revolution. In 1848 and 1871, revolutions around Europe were either hijacked by the bourgeoisie or successfully resisted by old regimes. Likewise, in countries such as Germany and England where conditions appeared most ripe for revolution, no such uprisings occurred. It was only after Marx was dead that communist revolution took place in Europe – in Russia, a country in which an absolutist Tsar presided over an economy dominated by subsistence agriculture. During the twentieth century as a whole, those countries Marx considered to be 'backward' proved more susceptible to revolution than the 'advanced' states of the capitalist core that Marx thought were most vulnerable to revolution, hence Antonio Gramsci's comment that the Bolshevik Revolution was a 'revolution against Karl Marx's *Capital*'.

The failure of revolutionary movements in 'advanced' states prompted a revision of Marx's work by his successors. In order to conduct revolutions on the ground, Lenin, Trotsky, Mao, and others relaxed the structural content of Marx's theory. For Lenin (1917, 1970/1923, 1987/1901–2, 1992/1918), a successful revolution required a committed revolutionary movement – a vanguard party that united groups behind a common cause. Lenin tied his analysis of the agentic role of the vanguard party to a structural analysis of revolutionary crisis. Russia, he argued, neither had the most organized revolutionary party in Europe, nor was it the most ripe for revolution; rather, Russia was the 'weakest link' in the capitalist chain. It was, therefore, most susceptible to the activities of a committed revolutionary party. This association between Russia's structural place in the world economy and the agentic role of a revolutionary

---

[16] Interestingly, Marx and Engels' (1968/1852) *Eighteenth Brumaire* recognizes intra-class factionalism and the centrality of cross-class alliances in its *description* of the events of 1848 and after in France, even as Marx sought to relate these to a mode of production *analysis*.

party was also captured by Trotsky's (1997/1932) notion of 'uneven and combined development' (see also Gerschenkron 1962; Rosenberg 2010; Anievas 2015). Trotsky claimed that relatively 'backward' countries were more likely to experience revolution than those states that experienced first-hand the long-term development of industrialization, urbanization, and agrarian reform ushered in by modern capitalism. As Trotsky put it (1997/1932: 29), 'backward' nations could make 'special leaps' to overtake 'advanced' countries within a relatively short timeframe. The 'whip of external necessity' generated by international pressures (in the case of Russia – British and German industrialization) led to unstable amalgams of the archaic and the advanced. In these circumstances, Trotsky (2007/1920) argued, a vanguard party could exploit the opportunities created by structural instabilities. Without the intermediate buffer presented by a domestic bourgeoisie following the failure of the 1905 revolution in Russia, the country experienced not a two-stage revolution as predicted by Marx, but the immediate overthrow of Tsarist rule. These understandings of the ways in which the agentic role of professional revolutionaries went hand-in-hand with the structural conditions for revolution was extended by Marxists in the 'Third World'. The cornerstone of Mao's strategy was simple: the revolutionary party did not have to win the war, it merely had to avoid losing it. This strategy allowed for a gradual ripening of revolutionary conditions, with military struggle only taking place when the revolution was deeply implanted within the population. At that time, the revolutionary party could seize a favourable moment in which to assume power, just as the Bolsheviks had done in October 1917.

As Marx's theory of revolution was extended by the practice of Marxist-inspired revolutionaries, the structural dimensions of his theory were grafted onto accounts of strategic action. Lenin, Trotsky, Mao, and others argued that, although Marx provided the basic impetus for understanding why revolutionary crises were chronic features of capitalist orders, revolutions could be made in seemingly unpromising conditions with sufficient strategic nous and strength of purpose. As Marx's precepts spawned later generations of Marxian inspired activists, it became clear to many that, even if revolutions were the locomotives of modern society, they required committed revolutionaries to guide, channel, and nurture them. The strategies employed by Marxist-inspired revolutionaries owed much to the circumstances they found themselves operating within.

The ways in which Marxists linked the structural dimensions of revolution to the strategic agency of revolutionary movements are mirrored by other structural accounts. For example, although Barrington Moore (1978: 322, 401) saw capitalist modernization as fundamental to the

development of revolutionary processes, he also argued that modernization was unlikely to lead to revolution without the appearance of 'sudden
and intolerable outrages' in which the popular classes were 'awakened
from anaesthesia' and their anger directed towards a revolutionary project. Indignity and injustice may be fostered by conditions of domination,
Moore argued, but they were only released as revolutionary sentiments
through the organization of a vanguard movement. In similar vein, Theda
Skocpol (1979) also struggled to maintain her 'resolutely non-voluntarist'
approach. 'Voluntarist' factors were central to the three cases – France,
Russia, and China – seen by Skocpol as paradigmatic: China was an
example of a two-stage revolution separated by thirty years of agitation
by the Chinese Communist Party (CCP); the Russian revolution was, to
some extent, made by the Bolsheviks who, as noted above, had a highly
developed strategy of revolution; and ideology was a central factor in
uniting revolutionaries in all three cases. For his part, Jack Goldstone
(1991: 27) supplemented his account of the ways in which demographic
bulges destabilized social orders with an understanding of how ideology
and political culture both mobilized opposition and provided a unifying
frame through which regimes were stabilized. As with Marxists, these
accounts augmented their *theoretical* account of the structural conditions
that lay behind revolutions with *historical* analysis that stressed the role
played by strategic action, organizational capacity, and political ideology.

Despite their common starting point in macro-analysis, therefore,
most structural approaches recognize the importance of agentic factors
to experiences and explanations of particular revolutions. This raises
two points. First, pressures for change are not just the result of macro-
patterns – they are also the result of bottom-up action by revolutionary
movements, action that helps to create the space in which revolutionary
transformation can occur. Second, social structures are emergent
rather than static. In other words, social structures are relatively fixed
configurations of social relations that are established through interactions
between events and wider social fields. The social world often appears to
be one of stasis and constraint, held together by naturalized norms and
habits, as well as apparently timeless institutions: families, bureaucracies, states, empires, and so on (Abbott 2016). But such a view occludes
the ways in which the social world is continuously being produced,
contested, disassembled, and recrafted. What is different about revolutionary periods is that the context in which social action takes place
is open and the goals of revolutionary contestation are far-reaching.
Revolutions differ from other forms of unruly politics by their transgressive character – in other words, by their scope, depth, intensity, and
effect.

If, as even the most ardent structural approaches to revolution appear to recognize, dynamics of revolutions cannot be discerned solely through macro-conditions, the opposite holds for those accounts that highlight the micro-foundations of revolutionary change. Most prominent here are rational choice approaches (Popkin 1979; Taylor 1988; Gould 1995; Lichbach 1995; Aya 2001; Wood 2003). For rationalists, revolutions take place if the expected utility or satisficing motivations of individuals direct them towards revolutionary activity. If new events or crisis stimulate mass protests, weakening the state and making protests more likely to succeed, revolutionary mobilization can gather pace quickly (Kuran 1995). It follows, therefore, that the study of revolution entails attention to the logics of those who make the action happen. To this extent, the joining of individual preferences into protest networks that, in turn, cohere into revolutionary movements provides insights into the emergence of revolutions within apparently stable social orders (Goldstone 2001: 163–5).

If rational choice approaches benefit from an acute understanding of the micro-foundations of strategic action, they contain two major weaknesses: first, insufficient attention to non-instrumental motivations, including emotions; and second, a failure to conjoin micro-action with analysis of the broader social fields within which revolutions take place. On the former, rational choice approaches omit the collective solidarity that lies at the heart of protest movements. Affective loyalties, such as compassion and trust, and moral emotions, such as indignation and pride, form emotional fields within which protestors are mobilized (Kane 1997; Jasper 1998, 2011; Gould 2009). Some emotions, particularly fear, tend to foster inactivity. Others, such as anger and hope, are more likely to fuel contestation. These emotions are heightened by moral shocks, which act as catalysts to underlying sentiments of outrage, injustice, and anger. Both moral shocks and emotional fields resonate via frames that connect individual grievances to wider struggles. These frames, understood as 'schemata of interpretations' through which people 'locate, perceive, identify, and label events' (Goffman 1974: 21), diagnose existing conditions, communicate a solution to these problems, and act as a call to arms (Snow and Benford 1988, 1992). Frames also help to denote which events and experiences become seen as significant (Snow and Benford 1992: 138; Johnston and Noakes 2005; Polletta 2006). If emotions are the 'fire in the belly' of revolutionary movements (Gamson 1992: 32), their omission by rationalist approaches is a major shortcoming – revolutionary movements are attempts to overcome fear, channel anger, foster hope, and restore dignity.

Relational approaches open up a second front against rational choice approaches. Despite a previous association with rationalist accounts of social action, the most developed relational accounts have been produced by Charles Tilly and his collaborators (e.g. McAdam et al. 2001). Tilly et al. argue that notions of interests are not fixed, but produced through contestation. For example, the term 'workers' was used to mobilize French protestors and sustain a sense of collective identity *during* the 1848 uprisings (Gould 1995: 63–4). The use of 'workers' as a frame helped to cohere disparate strands of protest into a single movement and identify who was inside and outside the revolution. Similarly, during the early 1790s, when the very existence of the French revolutionary regime was threatened by war, political factionalism became a treasonable offence – all opponents became labelled as counter-revolutionaries and subject to new legal measures, such as revolutionary tribunals, which befitted the state of emergency (Tarrow 2015: 41, 49). As these examples illustrate, revolutionary frames are produced in and through struggle: debates, demonstrations, songs, images, chants, occupations, strikes, street theatre, SMS messages, tweets, and more. Revolutionary action is produced by, and must be understood through, the thick contexts within which it takes place.

Revolutionary action is, therefore, forged contextually. That said, it is possible to identify mechanisms – 'a delimited class of events that alter relations among specified sets of elements in identical or closely similar ways over a variety of situations' (McAdam et al. 2001: 24) – that occur in different historical cases. The task of the analyst is to examine the ways in which distinct revolutionary settings yield recurrent patterns, highlighting the causal mechanisms that explain why certain sequences of events occur and reoccur (Tilly 2002: xi).[17] A parallel to such enquiry can be found in meso-level history – an attempt to recognize the specificity of particular historical conjunctures, while simultaneously noting the propensity of causal mechanisms to reoccur in diverse historical settings (Little 2000: 105). As Daniel Little (2000: 109) puts it: 'a central task of "meso-history" is to discover both the unifying dynamics and the differentiating expressions which these abstract [causal] processes take in

---

[17] Tilly and co did not always practice what they preached. For example, McAdam et al. (2001) used the concept of 'environmental mechanisms' (such as demographic pressures and economic slumps) to denote the context within which contentious episodes emerged. However, such mechanisms were often employed as static templates that established the parameters for contentious activity. In this way, revolutionary situations were conceived as primarily 'structural', while 'agency' was more associated with revolutionary events. The result was a reinforcement of the bifurcation between structure and agency.

different historical settings'. This book joins the attempt to link meso-level history with meso-level social scientific enquiry.

The balance between purposive action and contextual conditions – the question of whether revolutionaries make revolutions or revolutions make revolutionaries – is at the heart of debates about revolutionary theory and practice. Particularly crucial to the argument that follows is the way in which Tilly and others raise the possibility of meso-level configurations that take place in apparently discrete instances of revolution. Given this, the aim of revolutionary theory should be the articulation of *revolutionary anatomies*: flexible analytical constructs that simplify historical circumstances into ideal-typical sequences that, in turn, serve as a means of facilitating empirical enquiry. In this way, the complexity of revolutionary action is contained, but the richness of revolutionary diversity is maintained. The next chapter explores these meso-level dynamics in more detail.

2   Within and Beyond the Fourth Generation

Introduction

The previous chapter examined the main debates in the study and practice of revolutions. This chapter takes a deeper cut at these issues. Discussion takes place in two sections. First, four generations in the study of revolution are unpacked, illustrating the ways in which revolutionary theory has developed over the past century. Although this approach can foster an overly tidy picture of the development of revolutionary theory, and uproot contemporary approaches from their classical inheritance, there are two benefits to thinking in generational terms: first, it works as a heuristic device by which to parse theories of revolution; and second, it helps to illuminate the build-up of a self-conscious canon in the study of revolutions (Stone 1965; Goldstone 1980, 2001; Foran 1993a). In the second section, 'fourth generation' approaches to revolutionary theory are extended through the three – historicist, relational, inter-social – commitments highlighted in the Introduction. Such an understanding of revolution, it is argued, is immanent within many fourth generation accounts, yet remains an agenda still to be fully realized.

From Three Generations to Four

To date, there have been four main generations in the study of revolutions. The first is associated with figures like George Pettee (1938), Crane Brinton (1965/1938), and Pitirim Sorokin (1925). First generation figures, many of them historians, were often critical of revolution. Brinton, for example, considered revolutions to be analogous to a fever. For Brinton, the initial symptoms of a revolution, which could take generations to gestate, stemmed from a loss of confidence within the old regime as a result of rising expectations within the general population (itself the product of economic development), the emergence of new political ideologies (particularly within the intelligentsia), and the intensification of social tensions (which he associated with physical 'cramps').

Next, Brinton argued, a revolutionary force challenged the old regime. A revolutionary crisis emerged, with 'dual power' (from the Russian *dvoevlastie*) as its core feature. This crisis was resolved through the take-over of state power by the revolutionary regime that, although initially moderate, became radicalized both because of its ideological fanaticism and through its struggles with counter-revolutionary forces. The 'delirium' of radical extremists within the new regime embarked on a campaign of terror that, 'like Saturn, devoured its own children' (Brinton 1965/1938: 121).[1] Delirium was followed by convalescence, illustrated by the stage of Thermidor, a period of calm that Brinton associated with the fall of Robespierre in July 1794 and the end of revolutionary Terror. In the long-term, Brinton (1965/1938: 17) wrote, 'the fever is over and the patient is himself again, perhaps in some ways strengthened by the experience, immunized at least for a while from a similar attack. But certainly not made over into a new man'.[2]

There are two main weaknesses with Brinton's account and, by implication, first generation approaches. The first stems from a Parsonian reading of social order in which revolutions are considered to be deviations from standard settings of system equilibrium. Revolutions are less irregular fevers that disturb an otherwise consensual social order than processes deeply embedded in forms of contentious politics. As the last two chapters showed, revolutions overlap with civil wars, revolts, rebellions, and other forms of unruly politics analytically, conceptually, and empirically. The second weakness in Brinton's account is his suggestion that all revolutions, or at least all 'great revolutions', follow the same sequence: symptoms, cramping, fever, delirium, and convalescence. Although there are causal sequences within revolutions, these are multiple rather than singular in form – there is no essential pathway to which all instances of revolutions conform. On the contrary, revolutions are confluences of events that are historically specific, but which share certain causal configurations. These configurations – or revolutionary anatomies – are the subject of Chapter 3.

After the Second World War, a second generation of revolutionary theorists emerged, many of them seeking to explain the relationship between modernization and uprisings in the 'Third World'. Figures like James Davies (1962) and Ted Gurr (1970) argued that, during

---

[1] The comparison stems from a remark by Pierre Vergniaud who, on 13 March 1793, told the National Convention that: 'It must be feared that the Revolution, like Saturn, will devour its own children one after the other.' Vergniaud was guillotined later that year.

[2] For a comparable view of the 'infectious' character of revolutions from the standpoint of disciplinary IR, see Rosenau (1964).

periods of modernization, public expectations rose alongside an expansion in social, economic, and political opportunities. Davies (1962: 52) observed that an initial period of rapid growth associated with modernization was followed by an economic downturn, a process he labelled: the J-Curve. The J-Curve came about through increased levels of public frustration as anticipated notions of material development failed to take place. Ted Gurr (1970: 13) reconceptualized this process as 'relative deprivation' – the gap between what people expected to get and what they actually received.[3] For Gurr, unrealized *aspirations* were disappointing, yet tolerable; unrealized *expectations* – the false hopes bought about by exposure to new ways of life and ideas, and an awareness of the paucity of one's situation compared to others – were intolerable. In this way, the discrepancy between individual's sense of entitlement and their substantive capacity to achieve these goals established value discontent that, ultimately, became actualized in revolutionary uprisings. For both Davies and Gurr, the frustration and aggression that resulted from relative deprivation formed the basis for revolutions to take place.

Although second generation approaches offered some insights into why people revolt, they had much less to say about how, where, and under what circumstances they were likely to do so. Modernization on its own has no necessary link to revolution. Revolutions have taken place in industrialized states (e.g. the 1989 revolutions in Eastern and Central Europe), poor, predominantly rural countries (e.g. Angola, Afghanistan, China), and middle-income states (e.g. Cuba, Egypt). Sometimes, 'traditional' sources of authority have proved to be not just resilient, but vehicles for rapid autocratic modernization, as in contemporary Gulf monarchies. At the same time, as Theda Skocpol (1979: 34) queried: 'what society … lacks widespread relative deprivation of one sort or another'? As a concept, relative deprivation appears to be so general that it can apply to all cases of revolution, as well as large numbers of societies where revolutions do not take place. Without connecting the concept to other factors that make up revolutions – the role played by a state's coercive apparatus, the degree of fracture within a ruling elite, the role of a revolutionary party in mobilizing protest, and so on – accounts based on relative deprivation struggle to scale-up from micro foundations to meso and macro revolutionary processes. On its own, relative deprivation says something about the basic underpinnings of dissatisfaction, but little about how this is transformed into a revolutionary uprising. Rod Aya

---

[3] Although Gurr is widely associated with the term 'relative deprivation', it first appears in the work of W. G. Runciman (1966).

(1990: 23) summarizes this shortcoming effectively: 'grievances no more explain revolutions than oxygen explains fires'.

A third generation of revolutionary theory emerged in response to the shortcomings of second generation theorists. As discussed in the previous chapter, a range of predominantly structural theorists, including Barrington Moore (1966), Eric Wolf (1969), Theda Skocpol (1979), and Jack Goldstone (1991), saw revolutions as determined by the emergence of particular macro-level alignments. Revolutions took place, succeeded, or failed according to responses by the bourgeoisie and the peasantry to the commercialization of agriculture (Moore 1966), the role of 'middle peasants' in turning local forms of unrest into revolutionary uprisings (Wolf 1969), state crisis emanating from international conflict and elite fracture (Skocpol 1979), and demographic changes that destabilized social orders by placing pressures on state coffers, thereby weakening the legitimacy of governments and generating new forms of intra-elite competition (Goldstone 1991). Third generation theorists tended to incorporate international factors – uneven capitalist development, military conflict, and patterns of migration – into their accounts. Overall, the right combination of international and domestic factors served as the proximate causes of revolution.

As the last chapter discussed, the main difficulty with structural (and, therefore, third generation) theories was that their advocates found it difficult to explain how revolutions were made in unpromising circumstances and why revolutions did not occur when the right structural conditions were in place. As John Foran (2005: 12) noted, when explaining actual instances of revolution, agency, contingency, political culture, ideology, values, and beliefs 'slipped in through the back door' of structural theories.[4] As a result, analysis of revolution, partly rooted in the need to explain multi-class revolutions in Iran, Nicaragua, and Afghanistan mobilized, at least in part, by religious sentiment, awakened interest in how ideology and political culture shaped revolutionary mobilization. Theorists began to look beyond accounts of efficient causation towards causal sequences. John Foran (2005: 18–23; also see Foran 1993a: 13–14) argued that revolutions in the 'Third World' emerged from the intersection of five sequential conditions: dependent state development, which exacerbated social tensions; repressive, exclusionary, personalistic regimes, which polarized opposition; political cultures of resistance, which legitimized revolutionary opposition; an economic downturn, which acted as the 'final

---

[4] Occasionally they came in through the front door. Goldstone (1991: 27), for example, noted the ways in which ideology and political culture could both mobilize opposition and provide a unifying frame through which regimes could be stabilized.

straw' in radicalizing opposition; and a world-systemic opening, which acted as a 'let-up' of external constraints. For Foran (2005: 203), 'political fragmentation and polarization, economic difficulties, and outside intervention occur together in mutually reinforcing fashion'.

Foran's study, along with those of Parsa (2000), Goldstone (2001, 2003, 2009), Selbin (2010), and others (e.g. Sharman 2002; Sohrabi 2002; Lawson 2004, 2005; Kurzman 2008; Beck 2011, 2014, 2015; Ritter 2015), served as the advent of a fourth generation of revolutionary scholarship (for a historian's assessment of this literature, see David-Fox 2017). Fourth generation scholarship sees revolutions as conjunctural amalgams of systemic crisis, structural opening, and collective action, which arise from the intersection of international, economic, political, and symbolic factors. Jack Goldstone (2001: 172) argues that fourth generation approaches intend not to establish the causes of instability (because there are too many to capture), but to extricate the 'precariousness of stability'. In other words, fourth generation approaches focus on how international factors, such as dependent trade relations, combine with elite disunity, insecure standards of living, and unjust leadership to challenge state stability (Goldstone 2003: 77–81). For Goldstone (2001: 173), the range of factors that disturb state legitimacy makes stability 'fundamentally problematic'. State instability is the necessary precondition for the generation of revolutionary crisis – protests can be defeated by an entrenched elite and an infrastructurally embedded state that retains control of the means of coercion. If the state is able to carry out its core functions, if the coercive apparatus stays intact, and if an elite remains both unified and loyal to the regime, successful revolutions cannot take place. In this way, fourth generation revolutionary theory shifts the object of analysis from 'why revolutions take place' to 'under what conditions do states become unstable'?

Assessing Fourth Generation Approaches

Fourth generation scholarship provides several advances on previous generations of study. First, there is recognition that revolutions take place under a myriad of circumstances. As Jack Goldstone (2001: 172) notes:

Analysts of revolution have demonstrated that economic downturns, cultures of rebellion, dependent development, population pressures, colonial or personalistic regime structures, cross-class coalitions, the loss of nationalist credentials, military defection, the spread of revolutionary ideology and exemplars, and effective leadership are all plausibly linked within multiple cases of revolution, albeit in different ways in different cases.

For Goldstone (2003: 37), as for other fourth generation theorists, revolutionary diversity means that they are best seen as emergent processes that arise from a multiplicity of causes. This understanding of revolutions as emergent processes rather than static entities is an important amendment to previous generations of scholarship. As this book explores, revolutions are not reducible to a set of fundamental characteristics. On the contrary, their meaning and form shift according to dynamics rooted in both their local instantiation and broader inter-social relations. Second, as noted above, fourth generation scholarship recognizes the slippage within many third generation accounts, which tended to rely on ad hoc agentic factors, such as decisive leadership and effective coalition-formation, even as these factors are disavowed for the purposes of theory-building. A resurgence of interest in the symbolic features of revolutions, such as the mobilizing potential of revolutionary stories (Selbin 2010), has strengthened an agentic (re)turn in the study of revolutions. Finally, many fourth generation approaches have highlighted the necessarily international features of revolutionary change, from issues of dependent development to the impact of revolutions on inter-state conflict.

However, despite these advances, fourth generation scholarship remains an agenda to be fulfilled. None of the moves claimed by fourth generation accounts have, as yet, been fully realized. First, although contemporary accounts are more sophisticated than previous accounts of revolutionary change in the range of cases they observe, the number of factors they assess, and the methodological tools they employ, they remain attached to the same underlying sensibility that bedevilled previous generations of study, seeking to capture revolutions within 'general linear reality' (Abbott 1988). The result is that, rather than rethink the basis of their theoretical wagers, fourth generation approaches have tended to add more variables and include more cases, producing what Charles Kurzman (2003: 117) calls 'multivariate conjuncturalism'. Second, fourth generation approaches tend to reinforce rather than eliminate the binary between structure and agency, thereby reiterating some of the weaknesses of third generation accounts. And third, fourth generation approaches retain a limited sense of the international as providing either a facilitating context for revolution (e.g. through a focus on uneven development) or as the dependent outcome of revolution (e.g. through a heightening of inter-state competition). As such, they fail to realize the full potential of an inter-social approach. These three shortcomings, and some proposed remedies, are discussed in turn.

Historicism

Major concepts like revolution carry with them a sense of both coherence and permanence. Although definitions of revolution vary, almost everyone agrees that they are rapid transformations, usually involving mass, violent action from below. However, as the Introduction to this book showed, the concept of revolution has *historical* points of origin: 1688, 1776, 1789, 1917, 1989, 2011, etc. Yet, even when these 'eventful' points of origin are noted, there is a subsequent process of reification that serves to lend the concept of revolution an existence apparently outside of time, place, and history. This appearance – revolution as an abstract concept floating above world historical events – is often taken to be the source of its durability. However, the durability of revolution arises from precisely the opposite reason – from its capacity to adapt to many times and many places. The concept of revolution has not just been forged *in* history, it has been remade and contested *through* history. The threads of revolution run from England, America, France, and Haiti to Mexico, Russia, China, Cuba, Vietnam, Iran, Nicaragua, Eastern and Central Europe, the Middle East and North Africa, and up to the present day. Revolution as concept and practice has been remade in these events. Revolution is not an abstract concept that exists outside history, but one that is forged and reforged in history.

This insight is the starting point for a historicist approach to revolutions. A commitment to historicism means taking seriously the constitutive impact of time and place on revolutionary practice and theory. This involves more than simply being attentive to history. Revolutions have been one of the staples of both disciplinary History and historical sociology for many decades, so much so that it could be said that everyone who studies revolution is a historian in the sense that history is always there, in the theories that are developed and tested, and in the concepts that specialists of revolution deploy. It does not follow, however, that students of revolutions make for very good historians. To the contrary, work on revolutions has often been constructed via a division of labour between theory-building, explanatory social scientists and story-telling, descriptive historians, a binary that is premised on a number of overlapping distinctions: methods (a focus on secondary sources vs. primary sources); aims (the identification of regularities vs. the highlighting of contingencies); orientation (nomothetic vs. idiographic); sensibility (parsimony vs. complexity); scope conditions (analytic vs. temporal); levels of analysis (structure vs. agency), and more (Lawson 2012). Taken together, these distinctions promote a sense in which theory and history are distinct enterprises. But theory does not inhabit a realm that is exterior to history. Rather, theories arise historically, formed amid the encounters between theorists and the events they experience and, sometimes, take part in – note the example in the previous chapter of Marxian approaches to revolutions. All theories are living archives of events and experiences, living because theories are not only derived in and from history, but because they are also recrafted as they encounter new histories. In other words, theories are assessed and reassessed, made and remade through ongoing encounters with history (Barkawi and Lawson 2017).

A historicist approach to revolutions therefore starts with a double critique: first, of the view of revolution as an abstract concept that exists outside history; and second, of the sense in which revolutionary theory is separable from the history it both studies and emerges from. What lies behind both claims is the hold of general linear reality: the assumption that 'the social world consists of fixed entities (the units of analysis) that have attributes (the variables)' (Abbott 1988: 170). In this understanding, the interaction of attributes leads to stable patterns; patterns that persist regardless of context. Although they claim to be rejecting such a wager, fourth generation accounts are often wedded to this notion of revolutions as collections of properties. Indeed, debate within current scholarship tends to centre around which properties are essential or contingent to particular revolutions or clusters of revolutions. Jack Goldstone (2009), for example, highlights 12 components of colour revolutions, which he traces from the revolution of the United Provinces against Spanish rule in the sixteenth century to present-day instances in Ukraine and elsewhere. In other work, Goldstone (2014a: 16–19) lists the necessary and sufficient conditions that induce an 'unstable equilibrium' that, in turn, foster revolutionary situations: fiscal strain, elite alienation, popular anger, shared narratives of resistance, and favourable international relations, such as the withdrawal of support by a patron for a client. These conditions are generated by a range of causes, from demographic pressures to new forms of exclusion, which foster instability and, thereby, act as the 'fundamental causes of revolutions' (Goldstone 2014a: 21–5). Such analysis, like other fourth generation approaches, contains the assumption that revolutions consist of core attributes and necessary conditions, albeit with due regard, at least in principle, to the complexity of the social world and to variation within revolutionary experiences.

In contrast to this identification of core revolutionary attributes, this book sees revolutions as historically specific processes. In a strict sense, the diversity of revolutionary instances noted by Goldstone in the quote at the beginning of this section dictates that all explanations are case-specific – revolutions are particular event-complexes that combine in historically discrete ways. Because the specific processes within which revolutionary event-complexes cohere is singular and, therefore, unrepeatable, the timing of revolutionary events is crucial. If reforms by an incumbent elite take place sufficiently early, they may decompress revolutionary mobilization, as in many monarchies in North Africa and the Middle East in 2011; too late, and they are likely to fail, as in Tunisia and Egypt the same year. There is, therefore, no single attribute that can be associated, measured, or coded in relation to reform attempts by a state during a revolutionary situation. In similar vein, *when* a revolutionary movement appears is just as important as *how* it is organized. For example, there may be few differences between the organizational capacity of the Syrian opposition that fought Bashar al-Assad after the 2011 uprising and the movement that toppled Zine Ben Ali in Tunisia in January 2011. If anything, the former showed a greater capacity to mobilize and sustain its struggle. The latter was successful not because of a set of fixed attributes, but because it was the *first* such struggle in the region. Oftentimes, revolutionary waves become less successful the further away they travel from their original point of instigation: first, because revolutionaries in states outside the original onset of the crisis overstate the possibilities of revolutionary success, placing too much weight on dramatic news from elsewhere and drawing conclusions from relatively sparse information (Weyland 2012: 920–4); second, because revolutionaries enact their protests in increasingly inhospitable settings – regimes learn how to demobilize their challengers (Della Porta and Tarrow 2012: 122; also see Beissinger 2007; Weyland 2010); and third, because authoritarian state–society relations do not disappear overnight (Lawson 2005; Way 2008, 2011). Such studies indicate that revolutionary scholarship should be concerned less with the fact of emergence than with the time and place of emergence.

Fourth generation approaches to revolution often claim to recognize that revolutions are not composed of fixed attributes. But they do not always sustain this wager in their empirical analysis. The difficulty, as Alexander Motyl (1999: 23) points out, is that revolutions are not tangible objects that can be touched:

Revolutions do not exist as materially tangible 3-D objects, in the sense that we say that rocks and trees and airplanes exist as physical things. We can throw, touch or board the latter, we can use all or some of our senses to comprehend their physical reality, but we cannot do the same for revolutions. We cannot, like homicide investigators, draw a chalk line around a revolution, nor can we place it in an infinitely expandable bag. We cannot touch it, taste it, or for that matter even see it. Naturally many eyewitnesses to revolution claim to have seen it, but in reality what they saw were events and processes and people and things that, together, are called revolutions.

Such an understanding reconceptualizes revolutions as 'webs of interactions' with effects that change according to when and where they are instantiated (McAdam et al. 2001: 13; Tilly 2004: 9). To this extent, it makes little sense to ask: 'is "x" a revolution'? Such an exercise means comparing a dynamic process against an inert checklist. But revolutions do not have ascribed properties. Nor do they contain fixed attributes. Revolutions are sequences of events that attain their significance as they are threaded together in and through time. To put this in Abbott's terms (1988: 179), revolutions are 'closely related bundles' whose meaning arises from the order and sequence within which their events are knitted together.[5]

If revolutions are singular bundles of events, perhaps they are best examined on a case-by-case basis? Such research is certainly valuable in terms of its sensitivity to detail. However, this mode of analysis tends to generate what Daniel Little (1995: 52) calls 'combinatorial explosion', reducing history to a series of apparently random hiccups. At best, this runs the risk of producing a laundry list of causes that includes a large number of weak or insignificant factors. At worst, such an approach collapses into arbitrariness and ad-hocery. Because there are always events that go unobserved, there can be no total explanation of revolutionary processes, however forensic the analysis. It is no more possible to have a total history than it is to have a total theory. If all historical events are overdetermined in that 'there are more causes than outcomes' (Adams 2005: 10), then all analysis underdetermines the 'true causal story' by necessity (Little 1995: 53; also see Flyvbjerg 2001). All analyses are acts of suppression that simplify history in order to explain 'why this and not that' (Kirby 2012: 90). Theories denote what is significant and insignificant about a sequence of historical events. Attributional accounts carry out this task by testing the weight of causal factors that are taken to be necessary for particular outcomes. Yet, such a wager cannot eliminate the effects of the

---

[5] Some caution is needed here. Such an understanding resembles attempts by some previous scholarship (e.g. Goldstone 1991: 31–7) to see causation in revolutions as nonlinear, interactive, and multi-scalar. Goldstone (1991: 10–12) argues that different types of political crisis contain combinations of eight elements, ranging from degrees of popular revolt to changes in property ownership. For Goldstone, revolutionary episodes contain a *particular* rather than *essential* combination of these elements. In similar vein, the Boolean approach employed by Foran (2005) bears a family resemblance to the approach taken here by virtue of its stress on the *interdependence* of five causal factors. This reinforces the point that this book seeks to works within, as well as beyond, fourth generation revolutionary theory.

causal factors that lie outside the scope of a particular theory – it simply represses them. For their part, accounts that stress extreme particularity fail to see that events are part of broader concatenations that provide a shape – however difficult to discern – within historical development. If the former is historical without being historicist, the latter is historicist without being historical.

This book takes a different tack. The implication of seeing revolutions as contextually specific event-complexes leads to the production of analytical narratives that reconstruct how revolutions begin, endure, and end. This task is helped by the fact that, even during periods of radical uncertainty like revolutions, social action is not random. Rather, social action is embedded within fields of action that constrain behaviour and give meaning to these actions (Flyvbjerg 2001; Fligstein and McAdam 2012). In 'normal times', social orders are relatively stable – they are constituted by fields of action that are patterned in relatively sticky, predictable ways. At the same time, many fields of action, such as gender, class, and race relations, are so deeply entrenched as to be resilient against attempts at radical transformation. In 'abnormal times', such as revolutions, the possibilities open up of dramatically reshaping fields of action and categories of meaning (Goldstone and Useem 2012: 39, 45). Revolutions are attempts to break existing fields of action and embed new institutional orders. This twin process of displacement-replacement occurs in several fields of action – economic, political, symbolic – simultaneously.

Although, therefore, as the above quote from Alexander Motyl (1999: 23) makes clear, it is not possible to 'draw a chalk line around a revolution', it is possible to speak of revolutions as 'events and processes and people and things that, together, are called revolutions'. In this sense, revolutions are more like traffic jams than solar eclipses (Tilly 1993: 7). Whereas the latter are the result of regular celestial motion that follows a precise schedule under stable conditions, the former vary in form and severity, and develop for a number of reasons. This does not mean that there are no regularities to traffic jams. They are linked to rush hours, bad weather, roadworks, traffic light sequencing, breakdowns, accidents, and so on (Tilly 1993: 7). Although there can be no equivalent to predicting solar eclipses from these factors (for example, bad weather may or may not lead to a traffic jam), the combination in which these factors arise yields recurrent patterns. Like traffic jams, revolutions are, at least in part, stable accumulations of interactions. They contain situational logics, which emerge as events cohere in meaningful fields of action. These fields of action are exposed through the construction of analytical narratives that filter revolutionary events into idealized causal pathways. Analytical narratives are *structured stories about coherent sequences of events and actions* (Aminzade 1992: 457–8; also see Bates et al. 1998, 2000). They are interpretative to the extent that they identify connections that are taken to be meaningful (Reed 2011: 162). They are also tools of simplification in that they emphasize certain sequences of events and downplay others. But analytical narratives are also systematically constructed and logically coherent, providing a means of differentiating significant and accidental causal configurations, and seeking to produce enduring insights into concrete episodes of revolutionary change (Jackson 2010: 193; Little 2016: 257).

Such an approach cuts against the grain of orthodox approaches to causation. But it fits within a more pluralistic definition of causal analysis (Cartwright 2004; Mumford and Anjum 2014): how and/or why a particular outcome occurred where and when it did. Most revolutionary theory works from a regularity-deterministic view of causation, establishing associations between objects that are separated, or at least separable, in time and space (Kurki 2006: 192; Wendt 1998: 105). In these accounts, efficient causation acts as a push-and-pull between determinant and regularity: when A (determinant), then B (regularity) (Kurki 2006: 193; Kurki and Suganami 2012: 403). If a particular outcome (y) can be traced to a particular cause (x), then the inference is that a set of outcomes (y-type regularities) can be traced to a set of causes (x-type determinants). The interaction between attributes produces constant cause explanations that focus on stable relationships between variables, whether these variables are contextual or transhistorical. Lying behind this wager is the view that social entities are collections of properties that can be disaggregated and the co-variation between their properties assessed.

The problem is that, in processes as complex as revolutions, it is nigh on impossible to draw necessary links between causes and outcomes across time and place – there are endemic problems of 'interference' and 'prevention' (Mumford and Anjum 2014), plus confounding effects produced by the timing, order, and sequencing of events. As noted above, *when* an incumbent regime carries out reform tells us much about whether they will be successful. Protests that prove to be existential in one setting are either repressed or wither away in another. The centrality of context to assessments of revolutionary success and failure highlights the benefits of a shift to *configurational causation* – a concern for the ways in which events and sequences are ordered into causal complexes (also see Mahoney and Thelen 2015: 7). If events are the 'substrate of the social world' (Abbott 2016: 2), then causal configurations arise from the ways in which events are bound together sequentially. Four concepts underpin this view: *events* are singular historical happenings; *sequences* represent the ways in which events are linked with other events, forming event-complexes; *ordered* refers to the ways in which event-complexes are given meaning and, thereby, stability and coherence; *configurations* are causal explanations of revolutionary episodes generated by the logical ordering of a sequence of revolutionary events and their application to other cases. In this understanding, causation is not constant, but contextual.[6] And it is not the product of independent entities, but the result of interdependent, non-linear event-complexes. Configurational causation moves away from the claim to naturalism that underpins regularity-determinist accounts to one that stresses the construction of critical configurations: *robust, enduring interactions between sequences of event-complexes that reoccur across diverse revolutionary episodes.*

Such an understanding helps to more fully realize the promise of fourth generation approaches to revolution. Current scholarship tends to be caught in a bind: accepting the multiplicity of revolutionary episodes, while retaining an attributional approach that requires revolutions to fulfil certain elemental conditions. Identification of the context-laden interactions that constitute revolutionary processes generates a dual benefit: intimate knowledge of concrete revolutionary episodes alongside understanding of how revolutions are sedimented within wider fields of action. This produces a four-stage research process: first, examining the sequences that particular revolutions take; second, assembling these sequences into analytical narratives that are logically coherent and supported by the available evidence; third, abstracting the causal configurations through which revolutions displace-replace fields of action; and fourth, assessing the ways in which these causal configurations explain revolutions in multiple settings (also see: McAdam et al. 2001: 13; Tilly 2002: xi; Tilly 2004: 9; Pouliot 2015: 239–40).

This mode of research tacks between historical and theoretical registers, being sensitive both to the singular character of revolutionary events and the possibility of generating insights across a range of revolutionary episodes. In the first instance, causal configurations emerge locally (Pouliot 2015: 237). But although causal configurations are contextually located, they can also travel (Mahoney and Thelen 2015: 17; also see: Falleti and Lynch 2009; Pavone 2019). Causal configurations can therefore be used to construct ideal-typical anatomies of revolutionary causes, trajectories, and outcomes (as in Chapters 4, 5, and 6), or to develop typologies of revolutions (as in the family of 'negotiated

---

[6] Context is not synonymous with chance or coincidence, but refers to the sense in which, during revolutions, multiple futures co-exist in a context that is radically uncertain. For more on this, see Ermakoff (2015: 110).

revolutions' explored in Chapter 7). However they are used, the first step in fulfilling the promise of fourth generation revolutionary theory lies in the development of historicist enquiry that leads, in turn, to a commitment to configurational causation.

Relational Social Action

The second step in fulfilling the promise of fourth generation approaches is to move beyond the analytical bifurcation that is often drawn, explicitly or implicitly, between structural preconditions and strategic action. Although fourth generation approaches usually claim to be doing just this, there remains a sense in which culture, ideology, and leadership are grafted onto structural preconditions in order to generate a complete explanation (McAdam et al. 2001: 196; Sharman 2002: 1). For example, Misagh Parsa's (2000: 12, 25, 279) self-consciously 'synthetic' account of the Iranian Revolution focuses on the structural vulnerability of the Shah's regime and the ways in which a 'hyperactive state' politicized market interactions. At the same time, the dependency of the Iranian state on foreign backers, most notably the United States, along with elite fracture as the patronage system of the Shah weakened, 'set the stage' within which various groups, from clerics to *bazaaris*, acted (Parsa 2000: 7, 21). In Parsa's account, therefore, state vulnerability provided the structural precondition for the emergence of a revolutionary situation. Once this precondition was established, additional variables, ranging from the formation of opposition coalitions to the mobilization of collective sentiment, explained the timing of the revolution (Parsa 2000: 7, 25). Such a dichotomy – empirically present, if theoretically disavowed – is a regular feature of fourth generation accounts.

This tendency towards analytical bifurcation is problematic in that it reinforces two, equally unsatisfactory, myths: agent-centric theory builds on the myth of the person as a pre-existing entity, while structural accounts build on the myth of society as a pre-existing entity. To put this another way, whereas a focus on structure tends to reify relatively fixed patterns of social relations as things-with-essences, an emphasis on agency imagines a pre-existing, asocial individual whose motivations, interests, and preferences come pre-packaged. Both positions are unsatisfactory. Indeed, both rest on an assumption that their basic units of analysis are static, whether this assumes the form of a volitional subject or a macro-structure of some kind. However, as fourth generation accounts have shown, analysis of revolutions cannot assume the stability of a set of universal factors that are easily transplanted to diverse settings. Rather, analytical priority must be given to the ways in which relations between social sites *constitute* revolutionary dynamics. All social structures are relatively fixed configurations of social action, just as all social action takes place within relatively fixed configurations of social ties. There is no such thing as non-structured action (Emirbayer and Goodwin 1996: 364; Fligstein and McAdam 2012: 48–9; Pouliot 2015: 258). Social life takes place in fields of practice that are formed by patterns of events and experiences. Extending fourth generational accounts requires moving beyond binaries of structure and agency towards a relational approach that conceptualizes social action as taking place within these broader patterns.

This point is made clearer by differentiating between entities and entities-in-motion (Go and Lawson 2017). Entities are the subject matter of substantialist approaches, which see the basic units of enquiry as fixed substances, whether these substances are things (such as revolutions), people (as in expected utility models), or systems (as in world-systems analysis, which parses a single global structure into core, periphery, and semi-peripheral units, each of which is defined through a set of essential attributes).[7] In substantialist thought, entities contain a finite set of core attributes, as in Skocpol's (1979: 287) understanding of social revolutions as the 'rapid, basic transformations of a society's state and class structures, accompanied and in part carried through by class-based revolts from below'. The continuing hold of Skocpol's definition funnels the study of revolution towards a handful of 'great revolutions': England, Haiti, France, Mexico, Russia, China, Cuba, Vietnam, Nicaragua, and Iran. Not only does this limit enquiry to a small number of cases, it also struggles to make sense of those cases considered by Skocpol to be archetypal. If revolutions must be 'rapid', it is difficult to see how China's three-decade-long struggle conforms. If revolutions must transform 'state structures', then France does not qualify – republicanism was a short-lived experiment eclipsed first by Napoleonic empire and then by the restoration of the monarchy. If revolutions must both be 'class-based revolts from below' and transform 'class structures', then few if any revolutions meet this standard. As the last chapter showed, revolutions are cross-class coalitions that are bound up in complex dynamics of continuity and change. In this way, Skocpol uproots the study of revolutions from a wider universe of cases that do not conform to her definition,

---

[7] To be clear: the distinction between the two approaches does not revolve around the use of terms such as system, state, or revolution, but in how these terms are understood. For substantialist approaches, they are categories that denote a checklist of criteria. For relational approaches, they are a tool by which to simplify interactive patterns of social relations.

while simultaneously mischaracterizing those she considers seminal to her categorization.

The point is not that Skocpol's definition is *particularly* difficult to square with diverse revolutionary experiences. All theories are tools of simplification – their value arises not from their capacity to explain everything, but from their capacity to generate useful insights into particular domains of social life. The problem is that any definition rooted in the attempt to ascribe revolutions with a set of essential characteristics both occludes the empirical subject matter it claims to explain and fails to capture the sense in which revolutions are entities-in-motion. As Daniel Little (2016: 14) puts it: 'molecules of water preserve their physical characteristics no matter what … social things can change their properties indefinitely'. Theoretical work is not about providing a blueprint. And requiring that revolutions fulfil a set of inalienable characteristics distorts understanding of how revolutions change according to historically produced circumstances. As Chapter 6 illustrates, many post-Cold War revolutions have distinct trajectories in terms of their embracing of unarmed repertories and their fostering of despotically weak states (Lawson 2004, 2005, 2015b). Studies that stay within a substantialist framework cannot easily capture this shifting topography. Rather, a substantialist baseline is likely to see either conforming or non-conforming parts of a pre-existing script. More fruitful, this book argues, is the adopting of a relational stance that examines the contextually bound, historically situated configurations that emerge from diverse revolutionary episodes.

The contrast between substantialist and relational approaches is stark. Attributional approaches study the cross-case variation between a number of either independent or interdependent casual factors. Skocpol (1979), for example, worked with a Millian logic that linked prior social structures to a limited number of revolutionary outcomes. As noted above, some fourth generation work sought to move beyond this logic. Foran (2005) used Boolean analysis to identify interdependent factors that combined to generate either successful or unsuccessful revolutions. Goldstone (2014a) examined clusters of conditions that facilitated state breakdown, even as he allowed the resulting outcomes to be emergent, forged from the interaction of diverse actors and circumstances. Neither of these approaches, rich as they are, fully escape the attempt to work *from* necessary conditions *to* particular outcomes. However, a small difference in context may make a big difference in outcomes (Mumford and Anjum 2014: 225). Working from this assumption, this book seeks to move beyond Millian baselines towards an approach that is oriented around a view of revolutions as event-complexes, set in motion by a range of interactions among diverse actors operating in rapidly changing social fields. Millian approaches are not well suited to incorporating this thick notion of context (Falleti and Lynch 2009; Falleti and Mahoney 2015; Pavone 2019). The remedy is to trace the emergence of revolutionary event-complexes in distinct geographic and temporal contexts, and from this diversity of revolutionary experiences, discern comparable causal configurations: the centrality of shifting client–patron relations to how revolutions begin, the use of revolutionary stories to how they play out, and the symbiotic relationship between revolution and counter-revolution to their outcomes. Revolutions do not have uniform structures, but they do have shared forms.

An Inter-Social Approach

The third way in which the promise of fourth generation approaches remains unrealized is in its failure to generate a fully fleshed-out inter-social approach.[8] The term inter-social is preferred to alternatives such as intersocietal, international, and inter-state in that it does not presume that the objects of analysis are societies, nations, or states, respectively. Rather, it examines the relationship between 'external' and 'internal' dynamics wherever these are found: in ideas that cross borders, amongst networks of revolutionary actors, in asymmetrical market interactions, and more. An inter-social approach is concerned with the ways in which differentially located, but interactively engaged, social sites affect the development of revolutions without containing a prior presumption of what these social sites are.

Both third and fourth generation theorists often claimed to have sufficiently incorporated the international aspects of revolutions into their analyses. In response to the relative neglect of international factors by first and second generation work, third generation theorists included a range of international factors in their accounts. Goldfrank (1979: 143, 148–51) argued that the roots of revolutions lay in the 'world capitalist system' and its 'intensive international flows of commodities, investments, and laborers', 'great power configurations' (such as a shift in the balance of power), a 'favorable world situation' (such as changing client–patron relations), and a 'general world context' (such as a world war, which served to preoccupy great powers). Skocpol (1979: 14) famously argued that 'social revolutions cannot be explained without systematic reference to *inter*national structures and world historical development' (emphasis in

---

[8] Parts of this section draw on Lawson (2015a, 2016).

original). Skocpol (1973: 30–1; 1979: 19–24) highlighted the formative role played by two international factors in the onset of revolutions: the uneven spread of capitalism and inter-state (particularly military) competition. Both of these factors were embedded within 'world historical time', by which Skocpol (1979: 23) meant the overarching context within which inter-state competition and capitalist development took place. Tilly (1990: 186) also highlighted the importance of inter-state competition, arguing that: 'All of Europe's great revolutions, and many of its lesser ones, began with the strains imposed by war.'[9] Goldstone (1991: 24–5, 459–60) widened this focus by noting the ways in which rising populations across a range of territories served to foster state fiscal crises (by increasing prices and decreasing tax revenues), heighten elite fracture (as competition between patronage networks was sharpened), and prompt popular uprisings (as wages declined in real terms). Finally, Katz (1997: 13, 29) noted the ways in which 'central revolutions', such as France in 1789, fostered waves of 'affiliated revolutions' (also see Markoff 1996; Sohrabi 2002; Beck 2011).

The retrieval of the international by third generation revolutionary theorists has been extended by a number of fourth generation theorists. Jack Goldstone (2014a: 19, 21–2) highlights a variety of ways through which 'favorable international relations' serve as the conditions for societal instability, plus lists a range of factors, from demographic changes (such as rising populations) to shifting inter-state relations (such as the withdrawal of external support for a client), by which international processes help to cause revolutions.[10] Of John Foran's (2005) five 'indispensable conditions' that have enabled revolutions in the Third World to take place, two – dependent development and world-systemic opening – are overtly international. Charles Kurzman (2008) has noted the ways in which a wave of constitutional revolutions in the early part of the twentieth century spread over widely dispersed territories, from Mexico to China. Kurzman (2008: 8) argues that this wave acted as a 'dress rehearsal' for later events, most notably the 1989 revolutions in Central and Eastern Europe. Colin Beck (2011: 193) sees such waves as likely

---

[9] Despite this statement, Tilly's concern with the generative power of warfare was integrated more into his analysis of state-formation than it was his account of revolutions. Indeed, the role of war (or any international factor) in fostering revolutionary situations is absent from Tilly's (1978) major work on the subject – *From Mobilization to Revolution*.

[10] This scholarship sits in parallel to recent work on the transnational dimensions of contentious politics, which stresses the co-constitutive relationship between domestic and international mechanisms (e.g. Bob 2005, 2012; Tarrow 2005, 2012, 2013; Weyland 2014). The word 'parallel' is used advisedly. With some exceptions (e.g. Tarrow 2012: ch. 4; Tarrow 2013: ch. 2; Weyland 2014), the literature on contentious politics is not well integrated into the study of revolutions.

to increase 'as the level of world culture more rapidly expands', an argument that finds support in Mark Beissinger's (2014: 16–17) database of revolutionary episodes, which shows a marked increase in both the depth and breadth of revolutionary waves over the past century. Daniel Ritter (2015: 5) emphasizes the ways in which an international context characterized by the 'iron cage of liberalism' traps authoritarian states into accepting at least the rudiments of democratic practices. If authoritarian regimes are to maintain the benefits of ties with Western states, from arms to aid, then they must open up a space for non-violent opposition to emerge – the structural context of *international* liberalism provides an opening within which *domestic* non-violent opposition can mobilize.

Given this proliferation of interest in the international components of revolutions, it could be argued that contemporary revolutionary scholarship has solved the 'problem' of the international. It is certainly the case that these accounts have gone a considerable way to opening up a productive exchange between revolutionary theory and the international – this book aims to build on the insights of Goldfrank, Skocpol, Goldstone, Foran, Kurzman, Beck, Ritter, and other pioneers. However, the book also seeks to extend the insights of this scholarship by demonstrating how the international has not yet been theorized 'all the way down'. Three motivations lie behind this claim. First, despite increasing attention to the multiple connections between revolutions and the international, this relationship remains unevenly examined, being highly visible in some work (e.g. Foran 2005; Kurzman 2008; Beck 2014; Goldstone 2014a; Ritter 2015), yet all but invisible in others (e.g. Parsa 2000; Goodwin 2001; Thompson 2004; Slater 2010).[11] Clearly, there is much still to do in terms of mainstreaming international factors into the analysis of revolutions. Second, use of the international is often reduced to a handful of factors. In Skocpol's analysis, for example, inter-state competition is a surrogate for military interactions, particularly defeat in war. Hence: 'wars … are the midwives of revolutionary crises' (Skocpol

---

[11] Parsa's (2000) deployment of the international is restricted to the ad hoc activities of international organizations (such as the International Monetary Fund) and non-governmental organizations (such as the International Red Cross). Goodwin's (2001) use of the international is limited to the observation that states inhabit an international system of states. Thompson (2004) barely mentions international factors at all. Slater's (2010) account of Southeast Asian revolutionary movements explicitly excludes the international dimensions of these movements from his theoretical apparatus, even as the empirical sections of his book are saturated with such factors. Such a bifurcation parallels Barrington Moore's (1966: 214) account of revolutions, which reduced the theoretical impact of international forces to 'fortuitous circumstances' even as his empirical account relied heavily on them (on this point, see Skocpol 1973).

1979: 286). As the next chapter shows, such a view neglects the ways in which a cornucopia of international processes, from transnational cultural repertoires to inter-state alliance structures, affect the onset of revolutions. Third, much revolutionary scholarship has incorporated international factors via a strategy of 'add and stir', grafting international factors *onto* existing theoretical scaffolding rather than integrating such factors *within* a single framework. This point is worth examining in more depth.

As noted in the first section of this chapter, John Foran (2005: 18–23) sees revolutions in the 'Third World' as emerging from the interaction of five 'indispensable conditions': dependent development, which exacerbates social tensions; exclusionary, personalistic regimes, which polarize opposition; political cultures of opposition, which legitimize revolutionary movements; economic downturns, which radicalize these movements; and a world-systemic opening, which denotes a 'let-up' of external constraints. Two of Foran's five causal conditions are overtly international: dependent development and world-systemic opening. Yet these factors contain little by way of causal force. The first, dependent development, is a virtually universal condition of core–periphery relations – to paraphrase Skocpol's (1979: 34) comment on the ubiquity of 'relative deprivation': what 'peripheral' society lacks widespread dependence of one sort or another on a metropole? Even given Foran's (2005: 19) rendering of dependent development as a specific process of accumulation ('growth within limits'), the concept is wide enough to be applicable to every 'Third World' state. This is something borne out by Foran's (2005: 255) own analysis, in which dependent development appears as a near constant of both successful and unsuccessful revolutions.[12] In other words, the causal weight attributed to dependent development is nil; it serves as the background condition within which revolutions may or may not take place. In this sense, to posit relations between polities as dependent is less to assert a causal relationship than it is to describe the condition of every peripheral state around the world. Without further specificity as to the quality and quantity of dependent development, the term becomes little more than an inert backdrop.

At first glance, Foran's (2005: 23) second international category – world-systemic opening – by which he means a 'let-up' of existing

---

[12] Foran lists three exceptions (out of 39 cases) to the condition of dependent development – China (1911) (seen as a partial exception), Haiti (1986), and Zaire (1996). Yet it is difficult to see how these cases are free of dependent development in any meaningful sense. More convincing would be to see the three cases as ultra-reliant on wider metropolitan circuits, something Foran (2005: 254) seems to recognize in his depiction of Haiti and Zaire as cases of 'sheer underdevelopment'.

international conditions through inter-state wars, depressions, and other such crises appears to be more promising. Yet, here too, the causal agency of the international is significantly curtailed as world-systemic opening is seen merely as the final moment through which the 'revolutionary window opens and closes' (Foran 2005: 252). In other words, the structural preconditions that lie behind revolutions lie elsewhere – in *domestic* regime type, cultures of opposition, and socio-economic conditions. World-systemic opening is the final curtain call on a play that has largely taken place elsewhere.

In this way, both of the international components of Foran's analysis are limited to walk-on roles: dependent development is the background from which revolutions may or may not occur; world-systemic opening is the final spark of a crisis that has been kindled elsewhere. The sequence through which Foran's multi-causal analysis works is highly significant: international (dependent development), domestic (exclusionary, repressive regimes), domestic (cultures of opposition), domestic (economic downturns), international (world-systemic opening). The fact that Foran's sequence differentiates international and domestic in this way reproduces the analytic bifurcation that his analysis – and fourth generation theorists more generally – hoped to overcome. Such a bifurcation occludes the myriad ways in which Foran's ostensibly domestic factors are deeply permeated by the international: exclusionary regimes are part of broader clusters of ideologically affiliated states, alliance structures, and client–patron relations; cultures of opposition are local–transnational hybrids; socio-economic conditions are heavily dependent on market forces that transcend state borders. Rather than integrate the international throughout his casual sequence, Foran maintains an empirical and theoretical bifurcation between domestic and international. And he loads the causal dice in favour of the former.

Foran's deployment of the international is emblematic of fourth generation revolutionary scholarship. For instance, Jack Goldstone (2001: 146), although clear that international factors contribute in multifaceted ways to both the causes and outcomes of revolutions, is equally clear about the division of labour that exists between these two registers:

Although the international environment can affect the risks of revolution in manifold ways, the precise impact of these effects, as well as the overall likelihood of revolution, is determined *primarily* by the internal relationships among state authorities, various elites, and various popular groups. (Emphasis added)

In similar vein, Goldstone (2014a) makes much of the ways in which international factors serve as important conditions for, and causes of, revolutions. Yet, with the exception of noting the propensity of revolutions to stoke inter-state war, international factors largely drop out of Goldstone's account of revolutionary processes and outcomes. In this way, even fourth generation scholarship that claims to fully incorporate international factors into its analysis can be seen as containing two shortcomings: first, the maintenance of an analytical bifurcation between international and domestic; and second, retaining a residual role for the international. How might an approach that sought to more thoroughly integrate the international into the study of revolutions proceed?

An inter-social approach to revolutions starts from a simple premise: events that take place in one location are both affected by and affect events elsewhere. A number of transnational histories have pointed to the ways in which revolutionary events contain an international dimension that supersedes the national-state frame (e.g. Stone 2002; Adelman 2008; Hunt 2010). To take one example, the onset of the French Revolution cannot be understood without attention to the expansionist policies of the French state during the seventeenth and eighteenth centuries – between 1650 and 1780, France was at war in two out of every three years. This bellicosity, a product of pressures caused by developments in rival states as well as domestic factors, brought increased demands for taxation that, over time, both engendered factionalism in the *ancien régime* and led to chronic state debt (Stone 2002: 259–60; Hazan 2014). World trade too played its part in destabilizing the French state, fostering an underground economy, particularly in tobacco and calico, which heightened dynamics of rebellion and repression (Kwass 2013: 16–20; also see Bossenga 2010; Hunt 2013). The interactive dimensions of international relations also affected events during the revolutionary period. For example, in 1792, as the Jacobins were losing influence to the Girondins, leading Girondins pressed the state into international conflict.[13] As France's foreign campaigns went increasingly badly, the Committee of Public Safety, a leading site of Jacobin authority, blamed the Girondins for betraying the revolution and committed France to a process of domestic radicalization: the Terror (see Hazan 2014: 299–303 for a critique of the use of this term). In this way, domestic political friction induced international conflict that, in turn, opened up space for heightened domestic polarization. The Jacobins identified the Girondins as unrevolutionary traitors, while identifying themselves as the guardians

---

[13] At the heart of the generalized Girondin–Jacobin conflict was a personal clash between Brissot and Robespierre. As Brissot called (successfully) for war with Austria, arguing that French troops would be greeted as liberators, Robespierre responded with an apposite prognosis: 'personne n'aime les missionnaires armés' ('no-one likes armed missionaries'). This is a lesson that subsequent revolutionaries have been slow to learn.

of the revolution, a process that prompted a wave of popular militancy, most notably the *levée en masse* (Stone 2002: 194–208; Crépin 2013; Hazan 2014).

In addition to the dynamic role played by inter-social relations in both fostering the revolutionary situation and revolutionary trajectories in France, inter-social relations also played a fundamental role in the outcomes of the revolution. First, the revolutionary regime annexed Rhineland and Belgium, and helped to ferment republican revolution in several neighbouring countries, including Holland, Switzerland, and Italy. Second, the revolution prompted unrest throughout Europe, including Ireland, where a rebellion against English rule led to a violent conflict and, in 1800, the Acts of Union between the United Kingdom of Great Britain and Ireland. Third, the threat from France was met by extensive counter-revolution in neighbouring states. In England, for example, habeas corpus was suspended in 1794, while legislation ranging from the Seditious Meetings Act to the Combination Acts was introduced in order to contain the spread of republicanism. Although the French did not generate an international revolutionary party, many states acted as if they had done just this, instituting domestic crackdowns in order to guard against the claim made by Jacques-Pierre Brissot that: 'we [the French revolutionary regime] cannot be at peace until all Europe is in flames' (cited in Palmer 1954: 11).

An inter-social approach builds from this understanding of the generative role of transboundary entanglements. Empirically, an inter-social approach charts the ways in which relations between people, networks, and states drive revolutionary dynamics. Recall, for instance, the multifaceted inter-social dimensions of the Haitian Revolution discussed in the previous chapter: its embedding within circuits of capitalist accumulation, slavery, and colonialism; its embroilment in inter-state wars; and its impact on the development of uprisings in Latin America and beyond. Highlighting these empirical connections, whether direct or indirect, realizes the *descriptive* advantages of an inter-social approach. To date, the development of such a descriptive inter-social approach has been most evident in transnational, global, and economic history (e.g. Armitage and Subrahmanyan 2010). However, the richness of this scholarship has not been matched by work that adequately explores the *analytical* advantages of an inter-social approach. Analytically, an inter-social approach is concerned with the ways in which the logics of differentially located, but interactively engaged, social sites affect the causal pathways of revolutions. Such interrelations take many forms: the withdrawal of support from a patron, the pressures that emerge from the fusion of 'advanced' technologies in 'backward' sectors of the economy, the transmission of revolutionary ideas, the desire to emulate both revolution and counter-revolution, and so on. In both descriptive and analytical forms, inter-social interactions are less the product of revolutions than their drivers.

The promise of an inter-social approach rests on its capacity to theorize what otherwise appears as empirical surplus: the logics contained within the inter-social dynamics that constitute revolutionary processes. Inter-social relations form an interactive crucible for each and every case of revolution. The external whip of international pressures, added to the uneven histories within which social orders develop, produce an inter-social logic that has not, as yet, been effectively theorized in the study of revolutions.[14] It is the task of an inter-social approach to identify these dynamics and demonstrate their generative role in the formation of revolutionary processes. Although it can be difficult both analytically and descriptively to avoid using nation-state frames, there is no sociological rationale for maintaining the bifurcation between international and domestic. Revolutions are amalgams of transnational and local fields of action. This book outlines the ways in which transboundary entanglements, ranging from the symbolic transmissions that accelerate or redirect revolutions to dynamics of revolutionary/counter-revolutionary contestation, play constitutive roles in how revolutions begin, endure, and end. Revolutions are inter-social all the way down.

Within and Beyond the Fourth Generation

Seeing revolutions in a substantialist sense serves to reify them as static categories, precluding analysis of their causal configurations as these are instantiated in time and across space. Although fourth generation approaches claim to be moving away from a focus on inalienable characteristics, they often remain trapped in accounts that stress contextless attributes, abstract regularities, ahistorical variables, and timeless properties. Such accounts may be historical, but they are not historicist. For many social scientific studies of revolution, history appears as a monochrome flatland by which to confirm or, at best, tweak theoretical claims. A historicist mode of reasoning works differently: it recognizes the situated logics of revolutionary events, highlights their key features, orders these into intelligible analytical narratives, and examines their

---

[14] A partial exception is the Marxist debate on uneven and combined development. On this, see: Horowitz (1969); Deutscher (1984); Matin (2006); Rosenberg (2006, 2010, 2016); Anievas (2015).

utility in explaining other cases. A historicist approach outlines a space in which theory and history are driven together rather than pulled apart.

To a great extent, revolutionary theory is hampered by the debt it owes to powerful studies of the field, not least Skocpol's (1979) reinvigoration of the subject in her classic *States and Social Revolutions*. The research programme Skocpol helped to generate has been highly productive, but its agenda has run its course. It cannot, by virtue of its substantialist commitments, respond effectively to the diverse contexts within which revolutions emerge. Nor can its bifurcation between structure and agency capture the relational character of revolutionary action. And nor can such analysis fully accommodate the ways in which revolutions are inter-social all the way down. Many of these critiques were also made by the pioneers of the fourth generation of revolutionary theory, which promised a break with the attributional approach associated with Skocpol, a renewed emphasis on temporality, and greater attention to the international features of revolutions. Yet this chapter has explored the ways in which fourth generation approaches remain an agenda to be fulfilled. There has been a stall in theories of revolution even as empirical studies of revolutionary episodes are thriving. It is time for revolutionary theory to catch up. The rest of the book is an attempt to realize this task.

3   Anatomies of Revolution

Patterns in History

On 20 April 1894, two anarchists – Giuseppe Farnara and Francis Polti – were found guilty at the Old Bailey in London of a plot intended to destroy capitalism. The evidence that convicted Farnara and Polti came from the testimony of an engineer and a chemist who went to the police after becoming suspicious of two foreigners trying to buy lengths of iron piping and pints of sulphuric acid, plus the evidence of the two men's landlord, who discovered extremist literature in their bedroom. The defendants were sentenced to 30 years in jail. In many ways, this case bears the hallmarks of a contemporary terrorist trial – a small network of committed activists using the latest technologies in order to pursue their agenda. Substitute capitalism for *kafir* (unbelievers), extremist pamphlets for militant Salafi magazines, and the combination of iron piping and sulphuric acid for a mixture of iron shrapnel and explosives, and the comparison becomes even more acute.

This vignette highlights the ways in which it is possible to draw patterns in history. The previous chapter made the case for an approach that recognizes the situated logics of revolutionary events, but which also uses these logics to explain multiple cases. This chapter explores the pay-off of such an understanding of revolutions. Its goal is to map 'how particular configurations of ideal-typified factors come together to generate historically specific outcomes in particular cases' (Jackson 2011: 10, 114). Ideal-types serve as tools by which to clarify history – they organize social life into internally consistent, logical constructs (Weber 2004/1903–17). Such an 'analytical ordering of reality' probes the ways in which particular sequences of events interact during revolutionary processes so that typical causal pathways can be identified and compared, acting as portable insights for a range of diverse cases (Weber 2004/1903–17: 63, 67; Bellin 2012: 142; Kalberg 2012: ch. 5).

The main task of the chapter, therefore, is to develop ideal-typical accounts of revolutionary situations, trajectories, and outcomes. The insights drawn from this analysis are not attributional in that they identify a class of phenomenon and test their co-variation. Rather, they start from particular revolutionary episodes and order features of these episodes into clusters of event-complexes. This, in turn, yields causal configurations that reoccur across time and place. The goal is to demonstrate that, alongside the singularity of historical experience can be found recurrent patterns: modular organizational forms, such as a vanguard party or people power movement; common performances, such as demonstrations, strikes, occupations, slogans, and songs; and shared outcomes, such as the propensity of revolutionary states to construct powerful coercive apparatuses. As with the example of the nineteenth-century anarchists and twenty-first-century terrorists, these regularities emerge as patterns in history – critical configurations that contain enough flexibility to accommodate empirical variation, but which retain sufficient strength so that their logics are robust across time and place.

Revolutionary Situations

A revolutionary situation is defined by a regime and an opposition advancing competing, but exclusive, claims to the same polity (Tilly 1993: 10). Revolutionary situations often emerge in eras of international upheaval, in which state effectiveness is threatened by inter-state conflicts, economic crisis, and shifts in prevailing patterns of hierarchy, authority, and rule. In short, revolutions thrive in 'abnormal times', a point recognized vividly by Mao: 'there is great chaos under Heaven; the situation is excellent'. In this sense, both the breakdown of semi-colonial monarchies at the beginning of the twentieth century and the winding-down of the Cold War at its end acted as a spur for revolutionary change. In the case of the former, the collapse of the Persian, Ottoman, and Chinese monarchies induced a 'crisis period' that fostered the conditions for revolutionary situations to emerge (Hobsbawm 1986: 18). In the case of the latter, as long as revolutionaries framed their story as one of a 'return to normalcy', emancipation from the Soviet yoke, or as liberation from a system whose time had passed, so the great powers welcomed what had previously been outcast states into international society (Lawson 2004).

Shifts within the international system therefore provide the fuel for revolutionary change. Crises of international order, featuring breakdowns in existing international hierarchies, often prefigure revolutionary waves – groups of revolutions that arise from a similar context, have linked objectives, and share common features, whether in terms of their organizational form (e.g. a horizontalist people power movement), tactics (e.g. a commitment to non-violence), and/or symbolic repertoires (e.g. shared slogans or colours) (Markoff 1996; Katz 1997; Sohrabi 2002; Beck 2011). States most susceptible to these openings are those on the semi-periphery of the international system, dependent geopolitically and economically on other states, and facing challenges to 'modernize' from more 'advanced' states (Goldfrank 1975, 1979; Skocpol 1979). Often, the desire of these states to carry out what the Ghanaian revolutionary Kwame Nkrumah called 'jet propelled modernisation' fosters unstable amalgams of 'modern' and 'archaic'. Revolutionary situations emerge when the dual (geopolitical and economic) dependency of states becomes unsustainable, and when the amalgam of 'modern' and 'archaic' fosters state crisis. In these circumstances, revolutionary conditions surface when an opposition group emerges that espouses an alternative political ideology, holds sufficient capital to provide a credible challenge, and carries the support of significant social groups. This opposition is given space for manoeuvre by the 'expanded access' fostered by shifts in inter-social ties and the failure of regimes to cope effectively with these shifts (Tarrow 2012: 78–80). The result is the emergence of dual or multiple sovereignty (Tilly 1978; cf. Trotsky 1997/1932).

The first critical configuration within revolutionary situations is, therefore, intimately connected to changing inter-social relations. This is, in turn, linked to the type of regime that is in power and, in particular, its capacity to institutionalize dissent. Although revolutions are often a response to economic exploitation, they are more conditioned by political oppression than by concerns about poverty and inequality (Goodwin 2001). Poverty and inequality need to be turned into political projects. Protests are only likely to upscale into revolutionary uprisings if an opposition successfully associates poverty and inequality with regime practices: corruption, malfeasance, repression, and so on. Revolutionary movements are not, therefore, tied together by class-based solidarity (to the contrary, class-based antagonisms may hinder the formation of revolutionary coalitions), but through political exclusion (Goodwin 2001: 23; see also Brancati 2016). In short: injustice trumps poverty.[1] Unsurprisingly, therefore, states are the basic targets of revolutionary movements – they are the means by which everyday grievances are politicized and local uprisings reconfigured as general mobilizations.

Goodwin (2001: 177; see also Chehabi and Linz 1998) differentiates between authoritarian states, which contain a degree of autonomy from civil society, but not from core elites and, following Weber, sultanist regimes: personalistic, exclusionary rule in which power is vested in the

---

[1] Injustice is often context-dependent – what seems intolerable at one moment and in one setting may not be in another time and place.

hands of a single ruler.[2] Authoritarian states operate through 'protection pacts', which unite an elite through shared fear of an (often revolutionary) opposition (Slater 2010: 4–6). These protection pacts establish durable organizations, most notably political parties such as Vladimir Putin's United Russia, the Pinochet-supporting Unión Demócrata Independiente (UDI) in Chile, or the National Party in apartheid South Africa, which bind elites, mediate intra-elite disputes, and block opposition (Brownlee 2007: 2–3, 32–5, 42). Most authoritarian regimes permit a degree of pluralism, abide by the rule of law (even if constitutions usually serve as an extension of regime authority),[3] and fall short of the continuous mobilization that characterizes sultanist regimes, such as the deployment of a long-term state of emergency. Authoritarian states are, therefore, at least partially embedded in society – they foster sites of institutional connection that prevent opposition groups from developing concerted challenges to state authority. The partial incorporation of these groups tends to decompress revolutionary sentiments by providing outlets for negotiation, formalizing limited contestation, and delegitimizing revolutionary excess. The next chapter demonstrates the ways in which the Pinochet regime in Chile was able to decompress revolutionary unrest through just such a strategy of co-optation.

In the post-Cold War era, a range of states from Russia to Malaysia have combined authoritarian rule with a degree of electoral competition. These 'competitive authoritarian' states do not operate on the basis of 'level playing fields' – to the contrary, 'competition is real, but unfair' (Levitsky and Way 2010: 5; see also Karl 1995; Carothers 2002; Diamond 2002; Brownlee 2007). Despite claims in earlier scholarship that such 'halfway houses' were insecure (Huntington 1991: 174–5), hybrid regimes are often stable. They endure because they skew incumbent power through strong party organizations, superior spending power, control of the media, and, occasionally, outright coercion (Levitsky and Way 2010: 13, 62–6, 72). However, these regimes also recognize

---

[2] As a term, sultanism carries with it the whiff of Eurocentrism. I use it here for two reasons: first, because it is an established term-of-art in the literature, which allows me to build on previous scholarship; and second, because it highlights an excessive personalism that prompts state instability. There is no sense in which sultanism is limited, as it was for Weber, to states outside the modern West. To the contrary, in the next chapter, I use sultanism to describe the 'modernizing' English state of the seventeenth century. The use of the term in this book is analytical rather than normative.

[3] Regardless of the inequality of authoritarian legal systems, their adherence to a basic constitutionalism can prompt challenges to their authority. Augusto Pinochet, for example, was ousted in Chile after holding (and losing) a plebiscite required by the constitution, while the apartheid regime in South Africa was challenged regularly through the courts. For more on these cases, see Chapters 4 and 5.

a legal opposition. And this opposition can be successful through the ballot box, as was the case in Serbia, Ukraine, and Georgia during the 2000s. Elections, therefore, serve as dangerous moments for competitive authoritarian regimes, particularly under three circumstances: when Western states and international organizations enjoy a high degree of leverage over a polity (Levitsky and Way 2010: 71–2); when a crisis emerges, for example through a sudden economic downturn or a constitutional impasse; and when a well-organized opposition runs a concerted electoral campaign, often with international support (Bunce and Wolchik 2011: 33–4, 215–16). However, opposition to competitive authoritarian regimes is made difficult by the state's deliberate weakening of civil society. As such, competitive authoritarian states often enjoy a relative immunity from revolutionary situations. And on the occasions that revolutions do occur in these states, opposition movements tend to engender only limited changes to the status quo. Chapter 6 illustrates this dynamic by examining the outcomes of the 2004 and 2013–14 uprisings in Ukraine.

Personalistic regimes are more fragile. For Weber (1978/1922: 231–2; also see Adams 2005: 3–4, 16), patrimonialism represents a form of rule in which political power is seen as the personal property of the ruler. Typically, officials and bodies recognized and/or sponsored by the ruler share the prerogatives of power, enabling rulers to accumulate resources in return for elites sharing the spoils of office.[4] For Eisenstadt (1973), neo-patrimonial regimes combine this system of shared rule with a degree of legal-rational functioning. As noted above, sultanism marks an extreme form of neo-patrimonialism in instances where personalized rule is linked with arbitrary power (Weber 1978/ 1922; also see Thompson 1995). Modern usage of Weber's original concept associates sultanism with four main characteristics: personal rulership; the securing of loyalty through a mixture of fear and rewards; the deployment of unencumbered, arbitrary power; and the use of the state as a nepotistic vehicle for gain (Chehabi and Linz 1998: 7). Like other ideal-types, neither neo-patrimonialism nor sultanism exists anywhere in reality. However, neo-patrimonialism has been applied to post-colonial states in which inter-social asymmetrical power relations combine with weak civil societies to form 'strongman' states (Vu 2010; for a critique see Mkandawire 2015). And many twentieth-century regimes displayed

---

[4] Weber based his idea of patrimonialism on systems of Early-Modern household governance. The relationship between patrimonialism and patriarchy, and their amalgamation within 'familial states', is explored in Adams (2005). For a wider discussion of the relationship between household governance and social scientific categories, see Owens (2015).

sultanist tendencies, including Cuba under Batista, Nicaragua under Somoza, Iran under the Shah, and the Philippines under Marcos. Others became more sultanist over time – Egypt, for example, shifted from an authoritarian system under Sadat and Nasser to sultanist rule under Mubarak. The link between sultanist regimes and revolution should be clear from the above list – Cuba, Nicaragua, Iran, the Philippines, and Egypt have all undergone revolutions over the past half-century, albeit of different character and intensity.

Both neo-patrimonial and sultanist regimes are stabilized through the centralization of power within the office of the ruler. This power, in turn, rests on the strength of the relationship between the ruler and elites. Because neo-patrimonial and sultanist regimes enjoy only a weak social base, they often rely on a combination of coercion (the state of emergency in Egypt ran from 1981 until 2012) and patronage, both domestic (by co-opting rival sources of power) and international (such as the support offered by the United States to Egypt, Cuba, Nicaragua, Iran, and the Philippines). At the same time, because they lack formal channels of independent authority, such as a meritocratic civil service, the policies of such regimes can be unpredictable, resting on the whim of rulers and their coteries. This makes neo-patrimonial and sultanist regimes particularly vulnerable to fluctuations in social ties, whether this stems from economic shocks, defeat in war, or the weakening of patron–client networks. Such regimes can be stabilized through political parties, which manage intra-elite conflict and regulate access to the spoils of office (Geddes 1999). They can also be stabilized through political ideologies, such as nationalism, that articulate a sense of collective resonance and promote elite coherence (Hanson 2010: 77). However, some arbitrary rulers, including the Shah and Hosni Mubarak, attempt to institutionalize their rule beyond these political ideologies by fostering familial dynasties. But even if elites and opposition groups are relatively stabilized by the rule of a particular individual, this does not mean that the system will survive a succession. On the contrary, succession calls into question both future *and* current conditions. In this way, opposition groups such as Kefaya, which served as an irritant to the Egyptian regime during the late 2000s, had two aims: first, to end Mubarak's rule; and second, to deny *tawreeth* (inheritance of power) to his son, Gamal.

Regimes most susceptible to revolutionary situations are, therefore, those that combine an excessively neo-patrimonial form of rule with subordination to foreign powers – hence the vulnerability of Iran in 1979 and the Philippines in 1986. These states are 'suspended in a void', polarized between an 'arbitrary state' and a 'quicksand society'

(McDaniel 1991: 100, 229). Neo-patrimonial and sultanist regimes incubate grievances by foreclosing opportunities to reform the political order – their exclusionary rule turns moderates into radicals and unifies opposition forces (Goodwin 2001: 47, 177–8). When alternative voices are excluded from the political process, all forms of opposition serve to weaken the state's legitimacy. During times of state weakening, such as an economic downturn or succession crisis, these regimes often deploy their despotic power in erratic ways. However, the use of arbitrary state violence tends to escalate tensions. Because the state is disembedded from both civil society groups and alternative elites, opposition forces are able to mobilize beyond its reaches. Depending on when they take place, reform programmes initiated by the old regime may hasten rather than slow the emergence of revolutionary situations. Thereafter, if the ruling elite fractures, for example through the evident corruption of a personalistic regime, revolution becomes a plausible scenario.[5]

The development of a revolutionary situation, however, is not axiomatically correlated with regime type, nor is it a necessary consequence of state ineffectiveness. Some apparently weak regimes last for a long time, while others experience coups or undergo 'authoritarian upgrading' (Heydemann 2013). Only a few experiences sustained revolutionary challenge. Crucial in this respect is the role of the coercive apparatus in supporting or undermining state effectiveness (Chorley 1943; Huntington 1968; Russell 1974; Moore 1978; Tilly 1978; McAdam and Sewell 2001; Slater 2010; Chenoweth and Stephan 2011; Nepstad 2011; Bellin 2012; Mann 2012; Talmadge 2015; Barany 2016; Levitsky and Way 2016). Alliances between political elites and the coercive apparatus produce party-state complexes. When faced with sustained contention, the crucial factor in testing the durability of party-state complexes is the internal cohesion of the coercive apparatus, particularly the relative harmony between services, elite and regular forces, and officers and rank-and-file (Barany 2016: 40, 168–73; also see Slater 2010; Levitsky and Way 2016). In neo-patrimonial and sultanist regimes, the coercive apparatus is contained within a single command structure. In these circumstances, the withdrawal of support for the regime by the armed forces is an act of unmatchable illegitimacy. For example, as the protests against the Mubarak regime escalated in early 2011, the Egyptian military initially pursued a double game: permitting protests to continue (so as to weaken

---

[5] The importance of elite fracture is often traced to Plato, who argued in the *Republic* (1997/420BC: 262) that, while a united ruling class could resist popular threats, a disunited elite opened up the space for opposition to emerge and mobilize: 'the constitution cannot be upset so long as that class [the ruling class] are of one mind'.

the position of state officials vis-à-vis the military), while simultaneously containing them (so as to restrict the capacity of the protests to radically reshape military prerogatives) (Stein 2012: 24). However, the close association drawn by protestors between their struggle and the military, as in the notion of the 'one hand' shared by the people and the army against the regime, pushed the military closer to the protests. At first, the military refused to fire on the protestors and protected them from state-sponsored violence, albeit selectively. As the protests escalated, the military publicly endorsed the people's 'legitimate demands'. Mubarak resigned shortly afterwards.

If neo-patrimonial and sultanist regimes are particularly susceptible to the withdrawal of support from the coercive apparatus, authoritarian regimes in which coercive power is parcelled out between agencies (usually some combination of the armed forces, the police, the intelligence services, and paramilitaries) can also be fragile. Although, as discussed above, political ideologies such as nationalism and enduring political parties help to stabilize authoritarian regimes, processes ranging from corruption scandals to contested elections can prompt elite defections, particularly if these processes weaken the patronage system propping up the coalition (Hanson 2010; see also Beissinger 2002; Thompson 2004; Robertson 2010). In this way, authoritarian leaders sow the seeds of their own demise by dispersing authority in institutions that are subsequently converted into power bases for rival factions (Slater 2010: 140–1). In similar vein, autocrats often seek to coup-proof their regimes by constructing security apparatuses that can counter-balance the military. However, even as it reduces the likelihood of coups from above, this strategy makes autocrats vulnerable to popular mobilization from below by reducing the stake of the military in the regime. This was the case in Egypt in 2011, where the spoils of the military economy were unevenly distributed. While high-ranking officers benefited from their close relationship with state and corporate elites, junior officers and the rank-and-file were left out of the spoils. This allowed popular protests to both widen and deepen. The capacity to sustain a contentious movement over the long term erodes support for authoritarian coalitions, inducing 'loyalty shift' within elites and strengthening international support for the uprising (McAdam and Sewell 2001: 115; Chenoweth and Stephan 2011: 44, 220–1). Sultanist, neo-patrimonial, and authoritarian states that have been weakened by elite fracture are increasingly forced to rely on high-intensity coercion – visible, violent repression ranging from imprisonment to assassinations (Levitsky and Way 2013: 11). This, in turn, radicalizes the opposition, often making revolution more rather than less likely.

Overall, there are three ideal-typical sequences that act as critical configurations in the development of revolutionary situations. First, changing inter-social ties act as the principal field within which revolutionary change takes place – hence the rapid increase in revolutions after the collapse of empires, at the end of inter-state wars, and in the midst of shifting client–patron relations. Second, some regimes are more vulnerable than others to any instability in inter-social ties, most notably sultanist and neo-patrimonial regimes that are based on the authority of a single ruler. Authoritarian states are less vulnerable, but can be destabilized by the emergence of rival sites of institutional authority, elite fracture, and concerted opposition, particularly around crisis points: elections, referendums, successions, corruption scandals, and so on. Crucial here is the role of the coercive apparatus and whether it is cohesive enough to either contain or widen elite fracture. The third critical configuration emerges from a combination of: a political-coercive crisis in which the legitimacy of the old regime collapses and a viable alternative is offered; a symbolic crisis in which alternative ideas, a widespread perception of failure, and a belief that things are getting intolerably worse induces the possibility of revolutionary conflict; and a relative economic crisis, which presents a challenge to secure standards of living (Lawson 2004: 71).

On this latter point, consider the case of Iran. In general terms, Iran during the 1970s was not a poor country: its GDP per capita was 60 per cent higher than Turkey, 300 per cent higher than Egypt, and 500 per cent higher than Indonesia (Kurzman 2004a: 85, 93). However, during the mid 1970s, a mini-recession exposed the reliance of the regime on oil rents. Dependency on oil meant the drawing of capital and labour away from other sectors of the economy. A relative decline in economic performance resulted in the withdrawal of a number of welfare programmes, the freezing of wages, the suspension of state subsidies to the clergy, and increased taxation demands. At the same time, the regime established price controls and passed an Anti-Profiteering Act that reduced the capacity of merchants to keep prices in line with inflation. During 1977, over 100,000 shopkeepers in Tehran (half of all the shopkeepers in the city) were investigated under price control and/or anti-profiteering legislation, while over 20,000 *bazaaris* were deported from Iran's major cities to remote areas (Parsa 2000: 206). In Iran, as in other revolutionary situations, protestors mobilized through reference to previous protests, such as the 1906 Constitutional Revolution, the 1953 coup against President Mosaddeq, and the White Revolution of the 1960s. These repertoires were augmented by the emergence of a revolutionary coalition in the form of an accommodation between the Freedom Movement (a moderate Islamic-nationalist organization), the pro-Moscow Tudeh Party, guerrilla organizations, and the Coalition of Islamic Societies. During 1977 and 1978, transformative events like the 'Black Friday massacre' in which police killed hundreds of protestors and suddenly imposed grievances, such as the removal of state subsidies to the clergy, amplified opposition voices (McAdam and Sewell 2001: 119). By the time the regime attempted to deploy its despotic power, in early 1979, it was too late – its legitimacy and authority had been critically undermined.

Revolutionary Trajectories

As with revolutionary situations, the development of revolutionary trajectories has a close relationship with the type of social order in which the revolution takes place. In democratic orders, radical polarization is constrained by the presence of institutional sites for the resolution of conflicts. Where there are few institutional sites to manage conflict, social orders are compelled to accommodate rival movements – as Trotsky (1997/1932: 17) notes, 'the history of revolution is first of all a history of the forcible entry of the masses into the realm of rulership over their own destiny'. As discussed above, early reforms by an incumbent regime can decompress revolutionary pressures by fragmenting opposition and isolating extremists. This was the strategy pursued by a number of regimes in North Africa and the Middle East during the 2011 Arab uprisings, most notably Saudi Arabia and Morocco. But, as Alexis de Tocqueville (1999/1852) argued over 150 years ago, reform programmes are a risky strategy, providing space for opposition movements to thrive – hence the escalation of protests against Syrian and Yemeni rulers following measures intended to defuse demonstrations. For those who have been fighting for scarce resources with little chance of success, the chance to operate in more amenable circumstances means an opportunity to spread messages, organize resistance, and build alliances more widely. In such conditions, if a strong revolutionary movement exists alongside a weak regime, repression may escalate rather than decrease protests, something that Hosni Mubarak discovered to his cost. It is not reform per se, but the *timing* of reform that governs its success or failure.

Revolutions are targeted at breaking the state's claimed monopoly on the legitimate use of physical force. This tends to take place in three ways: first, by delegitimizing the authority of the old regime to such an extent that the coercive apparatus will no longer employ violence against its own people, as was in the case in Iran in 1979 after mass protests paralyzed the armed forces; second, by seizing power and, thereby, generating a condition of dual sovereignty, as in Russia in October 1917; and third, by using a regional stronghold as a base by which to conduct long-term guerrilla campaigns, as the Chinese communists did in Yan'an and Cuban revolutionaries did in the Sierra Maestra. However, these are not hard and fast laws. In 1989, the electoral victory of Solidarity in Poland, negotiations in Hungary, and the opening of the Berlin Wall appeared as 'a chain of spectacular transformations' that made revolutions in neighbouring states appear to be inevitable (Lévesque 2010). The decision by Polish, Hungarian, and East German leaders not to call in the military contrasts starkly with the decision by the Chinese politburo to employ the army against student protesters in Tiananmen Square in June 1989, a policy that helped to defuse large-scale opposition to the regime.[6] In East Germany, Erich Honecker came close to deploying the armed forces against protesters, until Mikhail Gorbachev, amongst others, persuaded him otherwise.[7] In Romania, Nicolae Ceausescu's elite force, the Securitate, failed to defend the leadership against a determined uprising. In each case, it was a combination of elite action, opposition strategies, and inter-social relations that shaped the path of the insurrection.

Crucial to the development of revolutionary trajectories is the formation of a close-knit identity within the revolutionary movement. These identities are syncretic blends of the local and the transnational: Haitian 'vodou' incorporated symbols from Africa, the Americas, and Europe; protestors in Tehran in 1979 wore Che Guevara t-shirts, just as revolutionaries around the world sang local variants of the 'Internationale' or, more recently, donned Guy Fawkes masks. In each case, revolutionaries had 'one eye on global revolution and another on local outbreaks' (Sohrabi 2002: 72). These eclectic tropes are the building blocks of repertoires that legitimate and sustain the revolutionary struggle. Revolutionary repertoires take many forms, ranging from rallies to strikes, petitions to marches, occupations to armed confrontation. Music is central to revolutionary repertoires, providing the 'affectual fixing' to revolutionary struggles (Clover 2009: xiii). Often, revolutionary actors use music in

---

[6] Chinese leaders saw the 'spectacular transformations' in Central and Eastern Europe as a transnational wave that had the potential to spread well beyond the region. The deployment of the military against protestors in Tiananmen Square was closely bound up with the fear of revolutionary contagion, not least because China was already witnessing protests linked to rising prices and the death of the reform-minded Party General Secretary, Hu Yaobang. On the reaction of Chinese leaders to the events of 1989, see Sarotte (2012).

[7] Honecker and Gorbachev drew opposing conclusions from the Tiananmen massacre (Kramer 2011). For Honecker, Tiananmen made clear that decisive action by the coercive apparatus was necessary if the regime was to survive. For Gorbachev, Tiananmen demonstrated that the legitimacy of socialist orders could not rest on the barrel of a gun. They were both right.

innovative ways. For example, during the 2011 Syrian uprising, the protest movement appropriated a song ('Yalla irhal ya Bashar') written by
Ibrahim Qashoush, a singer murdered by the regime. This proved so
popular that the regime re-appropriated the song for its own purposes,
using its version in official propaganda videos. Such examples of innovation and counter-innovation run to non-musical repertoires as well.
After hundreds of people were murdered by the Syrian regime in Homs
near the city's clock tower, protestors began to carry replicas of the tower.
When the authorities claimed that the uprising was being staged at Al-
Jazeera's studios in Qatar, protestors built a traffic sign pointing the way
to Doha.

Revolutionary repertoires tend to be drawn from existing sets of
performances – they are 'learned clusters of historically situated actions'
(Tilly 2008: 4–5). Demonstrations, strikes, and occupations, for example,
are well-established rhythms of revolutionary protest. However, as noted
above, revolutionary performances are also frequently innovative. For
example, the creative use of religious rituals for political purposes was
a striking feature of Iran's protest movement in 1978–9. Leading clergy
appropriated rituals, such as the Eid-e Fitr festival, and turned them into
opportunities for demonstrations against the Shah. The emergence and
institutionalization of innovative repertoires illustrates the ways in which
protests both draw upon, but also go beyond, existing repertoires. The
most successful of these repertoires have transnational appeal, becoming
deployed in a range of settings (Beissinger 2007: 74–7; Bunce and
Wolchik 2007: 96; Khalili 2007: 13). Repertoires diffuse transnation-
ally through impersonal networks, such as forms of print, broadcast, and
social media,[8] and also through the personal connections fostered by
revolutionaries (Bunce and Wolchik 2007: 93–7; Tarrow 2012: 174). For
example, former leaders of the Serbian revolutionary movement, Optor!,
subsequently set up an organization, the Centre for Applied Non-
Violence Action and Strategies (CANVAS), which has trained thousands
of individuals in techniques of people power. Transnational networks cir-
culate models of unarmed protest in the post-Cold War world just as

---

[8] It is important to remember that forms of media are crucial not just as a means of
dissemination, but also as a means of organization that unites, or at least coordinates,
dispersed activists. Similarly, revolutionary ideas are not free-floating – they are
produced and distributed via available technologies. In short: ideas need hardware.
Social media tends to generate short-term micro-circuits rather than the deeper, collectivist milieu sustained by print. In this sense, what social media appears to make
easier through the cheap, immediate circulation of ideas is actually harder, at least in
terms of generating an enduring revolutionary consciousness. I come back to this point
in Chapter 7.

previous networks circulated ideas of guerrilla war, vanguardism, and the mass strike.

Revolutions are also settings in which words – comrade, *citoyen*, *revolucionario* – denote who is inside and outside the revolutionary struggle. These words are often mobilized beyond their original context, changing in meaning as they travel. Patriot, for example, changed from being a subversive term to one denoting loyalty to the French revolutionary regime. Words, like practices, are modified as they make sense of new settings. Terms with particular resonance combine 'symbolic resonance' (their meaning translates to multiple contexts) with 'strategic modularity' (their associated practices work in different settings) (Tarrow 2013: 17). Revolutionaries systematically borrow from each other, sharing ideas, slogans, and tactics across borders (Sohrabi 1995; Markoff 1996; Bunce and Wolchik 2007; Khalili 2007; Kurzman 2008; Weyland 2012).

These symbolic tools are underpinned by revolutionary stories that, as Eric Selbin (2010: 3) puts it, serve as 'tools of connection' between everyday life and collective protest. Revolutionary stories are vital to cohering the disparate groups that make up a revolutionary movement. Selbin highlights the role of four such narratives: 'civilizing and democratizing revolutions', such as the American War of Independence; 'social revolutions', including France, Russia, and Cuba; 'freedom and liberation revolutions', like Haiti and Mexico; and 'lost and forgotten revolutions', such as the Green Corn Rebellion of Oklahoma. The first two narratives are 'elite histories', foundational narratives told by the victors; the latter two are 'stories from the periphery', representing the struggle of slaves, *campesinos* (peasant farmers), and the disenfranchised to free themselves from bondage. Because revolutions are polarizing processes featuring mutually incompatible claims over a particular polity, revolutionary adversaries are locked into apparently irreconcilable narratives. The establishment of these exclusive narratives provides the central frame for revolutionary events. Stories are used to legitimize both sides of the conflict – they are the social technologies of revolutionary struggles.

Revolutionary movements, therefore, are coalitions of diverse social groups, often with disparate interests and identities, which are held together through common social technologies: stories, songs, chants, slogans, and, most importantly, the act of struggle itself. Crucial to mobilizing this struggle are injustice frames, actualized in practices such as chanting and singing, which generate a sense of 'we-ness', and the burning of hated symbols and effigies, which cultivate a sense of shared indignation (Aminzade and McAdam 2001: 31–3, 43). For example, the fraternization between protestors and members of the armed forces in

Egypt in 2011 was fostered by slogans, photographs, and visual cues, such as the mounting of military vehicles (Ketchley 2017: 5). In similar vein, the placing of flowers in the barrels of military rifles in the 1974 Portuguese Carnation Revolution served to simultaneously unite the opposition and divide the regime. These repertoires serve as emotional triggers that decrease fear of the regime, and heighten feelings of hope and solidarity within the opposition (Bellin 2012: 136). Emotional triggers often include the occupation of sites of symbolic importance, such as the area around the Berlin Wall in 1989, Tiananmen Square the same year, or Midan al-Tahrir in Cairo in 2011. The symbolic importance – or 'spatial agency' – of these sites serves as a means of generating a collective revolutionary identity (Sewell 2001: 88), making clear that this is an area occupied by the people rather than the regime.

Despite the potency of these repertoires, and despite increasingly high numbers of demonstrators taking part in people power protests in recent years, most members of the public do not take part in revolutions. It is estimated that 10 per cent of the Iranian population were involved in demonstrations, strikes, and other organized protests during the 1978–9 revolution, even though these were some of the largest protests in world history (Kurzman 2004a: 121). This corresponds favourably to the French and Russian Revolutions, where the figures are closer to 2 per cent and 1 per cent respectively, but still stops short of constituting a sizeable minority, let alone a majority.[9] In Egypt in 2011, the term 'hizb al-kanaba' ('the party of the sofa') was used to describe – and denigrate – the many millions who watched the revolution unfold on television.

Whether or not they are based on high levels of popular support, leadership is crucial to the fostering of a shared identity within a revolutionary movement. Conceptions of revolutionary leadership tend towards dispositional statements that link leadership to certain core attributes, such as relative levels of charisma or pragmatism. Jack Goldstone (2001), for example, differentiates between people-oriented leadership, which is based on the capacity to inspire through charismatic vision, and task-oriented leadership, which is rooted in strategic capabilities (also see Selbin 1993). Jeff Colgan (2013: 662–3) claims that revolutions select for risk-taking, ambitious leaders who are, in turn, more likely to lead states into war. The relational commitments of this book lead away from these attributional statements towards an understanding of the positional

---

[9] It is worth pointing out that taking part in revolutions where transgressive action is risky is not the same as voting in consolidated democracies where the threat of repression is low. One million people on the streets forcibly confronting a regime is not the same as one million people voting through the ballot box.

features of revolutionary leadership. Central to revolutionary leadership is the capacity for brokerage – the ability to close a gap between competing coalitions through the effective use of organizational resources and rhetorical strategies (Aminzade et al. 2001; Goddard 2012). Successful brokerage relies less on force of personality than on the position individuals occupy within networks. Revolutionary leaders need the social skills to connect fragmented opposition groups. They also need to occupy positions that endow trust and legitimacy. Successful brokerage means linking revolutionary struggles with influential allies, both local and international. The social ties fostered by revolutionary leaders are deepened in struggle. As the revolution develops, it forges connections of solidarity that strengthen commitment to the struggle: revolution revolutionizes the revolution. Paradoxically, just as the revolution deepens ties within the opposition, so it can also work to strengthen regime solidarity: the revolution revolutionizes the counter-revolution. Both incumbents and challengers rely on the strength of social ties that are forged in the revolution itself.

Revolutionary trajectories are chronically uncertain fields of action bound up with high levels of risk, audacious action, and a considerable degree of guesswork. Although revolutionaries often claim after the fact to have controlled the revolutionary process, revolutionary struggles are a cacophony of unruly practices (Scott 2012b: 138–9). The Bolshevik Revolution was a monumental event, yet it was one that almost no one foresaw. In January 1917, Lenin commented that: 'we, the old, may not live to see the decisive battles of the coming revolution'. Just three days before the fall of the Tsar, the British ambassador in Moscow cabled London in apparent ignorance of the worsening situation: 'some disorders occurred today, but nothing serious' (in Kuran 1995: 28). This example warns against 'retroactive prediction' – the tendency to find an event inevitable after the fact (Kurzman 2004a: 5–11; Kurzman 2004b: 340–1). Revolutions are not choreographed events, even if official narratives often retell them as such. Rather, they are the result of considerable confusion, in which the collapse of the old order generates uncertainty about both present conditions and future prospects. During revolutions, what was unthinkable can quickly become viable, and move just as swiftly to inevitability. Yet there is rhyme to the revolutionary unreason. Central to understanding their trajectories are two critical configurations: first, the ability of a state elite to limit fracture and maintain the loyalty of the coercive apparatus as the revolution develops; and second, the capacity of the opposition to generate a cohesive revolutionary movement through effective leadership and social technologies that mobilize – and unite – diverse coalitions. Crucial here is the capacity to turn fear into a combination of anger and hope – demonstrations, music, and chants serve to unite a movement and foster a divide between publics and regimes. So too does the act of struggle itself. The willingness of revolutionaries to die for their cause best illustrates the transgressive character of revolutionary trajectories.

Revolutionary Outcomes

If revolutions represent a generalized crisis in existing fields of action, their outcomes are marked by the re-establishment of order through new institutional formations: constitutions, legislation, political parties, holidays, and so on. The minimum condition of revolutionary success is the takeover and establishment of state power or its equivalent by revolutionaries – in other words, when institutions are sufficiently embedded as to appear unbreakable (Hobsbawm 1986: 24; also see Stinchcombe 1999). John Foran (2005: 5) puts this well: revolutionary success is defined by a revolutionary party 'coming to power and holding it long enough to initiate a process of deep structural transformation'. Successful revolutions are those instances where a revolutionary regime takes control of a society's principal means of violence, production, and information. By this reckoning, the immediate condition of revolutionary success is when the new regime is no longer directly challenged by domestic rivals, marked, for example, by the end of the civil war in Russia in 1921 and the successful defeat of a CIA-funded and trained invasion force by Cuban revolutionary forces at the Bay of Pigs (Playa Girón) in 1961.

The maximum condition of revolutionary victory is the institutionalization of a new political, economic, and symbolic order – in other words, a 'new framework for historical development' (Hobsbawm 1986: 24). There have been a number of 'reversed revolutions' that assumed power, but did not generate such a framework, including Guatemala in 1944, Bolivia in 1952, and Grenada in 1979 (Foran 2005: 7). Only if the principal institutions within a social order are systemically transformed can a revolution be considered fully successful. This means the institutionalization of novel means of economic, political, and symbolic relations, ranging from programmes of redistribution to the advent of new constitutions, the development of new education systems and legislative environments, major changes to gender relations, and so on.[10] It is, therefore, necessary

---

[10] The story of women and revolution is not, on the whole, well told. This book is, to its detriment, no better in this regard, saying little about the role of either female revolutionaries (such as Olympe de Gouges, Alexandra Kollontai, and Celia Sánchez) or rank-and-file (such as the 30 per cent of female Sandinistas or the even higher proportion of female revolutionaries in contemporary Rojava). Very often, women have

to wait at least a generation after the end of the revolution – until the 'children of the revolution' emerge onto the public scene – to assess the success, or otherwise, of a revolution. As Chapter 1 illustrated, not everything changes after revolutions. Some institutional features of the old order are so embedded that they cannot be altered, while other measures are blocked by surviving members of the regime, and there are some things that revolutionaries do not attempt to change. No revolution has attempted, let alone succeeded, in wiping the slate clean as if institutions, habits, and norms were tabula rasa.

Revolutionary regimes are often durable: the Soviet and Mexican revolutionary regimes lasted for 74 and 83 years respectively, while the Cuban, Chinese, and Vietnamese revolutions are all over 60 years old and counting (Levitsky and Way 2013: 6).[11] Of course, quantity should not be mistaken for quality – survival is no indicator of virtue and being a successful revolutionary offers few lessons for running a successful state. Nevertheless, revolutionary regimes tend to be resilient. In the case of Cuba, the regime has withstood the loss of its patron (the Soviet Union), two leadership successions (first from Fidel to Raúl Castro, and then from Raúl to Miguel Díaz-Canel), and an economic crisis (including a 40 per cent decline in GDP after the collapse of the Soviet Union). One reason for the relative longevity and resilience of revolutionary states is the closeness of the relationship between revolutionary outcomes and state coercion – more often than not, revolutions lead to the formation of 'garrison states' (Gurr 1988: 57). Revolutionary states have constructed mass surveillance projects, such as the Soviet human archive project, which registered, catalogued, and classified potential 'enemies of the people' – those considered to be contaminating the purity of the revolution (Holquist 2003: 27; Weiner 2003: 186; Losurdo 2015: 199–206). Some 'enemies of the people', a term that became a legal category after 1936, were sent to camps in Siberia and Central Asia where they were 're-educated'; others were killed. In France, more than one million people died in the revolution and the wars that followed; in Cambodia, nearly a

---

been at the forefront of revolutionary uprisings, only to see their post-revolutionary role heavily circumscribed. The Jacobins, for example, banned female clubs, women from attending political assemblies, and even discussing politics. Readers interested in the role of women and the construction of gender in revolution should begin with: Hunt (1989, 1992); Moghadam (1997, 2008); Diamond (1998); and Rowbotham (2013).

[11] Counter-revolution is equally durable – just consider the long-term sanctions regime instituted by the United States against the Cuban revolutionary state, or the development of alliance structures, such as the Gulf Cooperation Council (GCC), which was initially set up to counterbalance the post-1979 revolutionary state in Iran and which remains in place today.

third of the population died in violence following the seizure of power by the Khmer Rouge (Goldstone 2014a: 40).[12]

However, it is not only through despotic power that states increase their authority after revolutions. States are also the principle vehicles for projects of social transformation, ranging from policies of nationalization and collectivization to land reform and redistribution. The French revolutionary regime transformed provinces into webs of départements, districts, cantons, and communes. It also introduced a new penal code, trial by jury, and the metric system. In Cuba, Revolutionary Instruction Schools and Committees for the Defence of the Revolution embedded the revolution deep into the country's social fabric. The revolutionary state ran mass programmes, such as its highly successful 1961 literacy drive, and nationalized almost the whole economy over the course of just a few years. Material transformations of this kind are reinforced by symbolic transformations. Revolutionaries use symbols, images, and rituals such as festivals in order to socialize publics in the revolutionary message (Ozouf 1991). This socialization even extends to spheres as apparently humdrum as holidays. In Cuba, for instance, the regime replaced the 'imperial' figure of Santa Claus with the more 'authentic' character of Don Feliciano, replete with *guayabera* shirt and revolutionary beard (Thomas 2001/1971: 851). Of course, not all revolutionary states are equally transformative. Indeed, one of the complaints often made about revolutionary states is that little has changed. As discussed in Chapters 6 and 7, the failure of many contemporary revolutions to deliver systemic transformation has led to discussion over whether they should be seen as revolutions at all.

For its part, the inter-social effects of revolution endure long after the initial promise of revolution has faded. The Bolshevik Decree on Peace in November 1917 called for revolution throughout Europe and Asia, and was sustained by a substantial fund to support world revolution. Although the short-term success of the Bolsheviks in fostering revolution was slight, by the 1970s a third of humanity lived under regimes that took their inspiration from the Russian Revolution (Strayer 2015: 442); a Tsarist empire covering one-sixth of the size of the globe had been disbanded and put back together. Maoism too was a transnational force. Mao's international theory began with the notion of 'intermediate zones' (*zhongjian didai*), a term intended to characterize those countries, like China, that were 'in-between' the United States and the Soviet Union,

---

[12] Despite being so violent, the Khmer Rouge did not last long – they were ousted by a Vietnamese intervention four years after coming to power. Extreme brutality is not a proxy for regime stability.

and that needed to unite in order to throw off the shackles of imperialism (Frazier 2015: 110). Mao later reworked this concept into his 'Three Worlds Theory' (*san ge shi jie*), which called for the 'exploited countries' to lead a global revolution against their oppressors. Mao provided aid, equipment, and infrastructural support to a range of anti-colonial movements in Africa and Asia, and fostered links with African American groups, including the Black Panther Party and the Revolutionary Action Movement. Cuban internationalism extended even further than the examples set by the Soviet Union and China. During the 1960s, Cuba provided military assistance to revolutionary groups in virtually every Latin American country. In the 1970s, attention turned to Africa: 12,000 troops were sent to Ethiopia in 1974 and more than 50,000 Cuban soldiers served in Angola in a mission that lasted over a decade. In the 1980s, Cuba actively supported revolutionary groups in Nicaragua and El Salvador. In the 1990s and early years of the twenty-first century, considerable assistance was provided to Hugo Chavez's Bolivarian Revolution and South America's 'pink tide' movement. Over the past 60 years, the Cuban regime has sent thousands of teachers, professionals, and engineers throughout the global south, and offered free training in Cuba to many thousands more.

Beyond the material support offered by revolutionary states to like-minded groups is their role as exemplars. For instance, after the 1688 Glorious Revolution in England, the Treasury stood at the heart of a system of public finance that provided predictable, secure, reliable revenue and credit. In 1689, a Bill of Rights was passed, forbidding taxation through royal prerogative and royal interference in elections. The National Debt was instituted in 1693, to be managed the following year by the newly created Bank of England. Such policies, along with the 'hidden sinews' of public administration (Brewer 1990: 89), constructed a means of revenue raising and credit provision that gave Britain a decisive advantage over its competitors: between 1688 and 1697, annual tax revenues in England doubled; they doubled again from 1697 to 1714 (Ertman 1997: 214; Hui 2005: 126; Harris 2006: 491). An interlocking system of parliamentary oversight, public finances, and credit markets operated as a 'structural check' on monarchical power, turning parliament from an event into an institution (Ertman 1997: 200–1; Pincus 2012). In this way, a 'non-proprietary fiscal-military bureaucracy' presided over an efficient state administration with considerable infrastructural reach (Ertman 1997: 187: Harris 2006: 492). Whereas French absolutism and the Dutch Republic served as models for sixteenth- and seventeenth-century states, it was the English 'fiscal-military juggernaut' that served as a model to eighteenth-century states and, indeed, to eighteenth-century revolutionaries, not least those in North America (Bailyn 1967; Brewer 1990: 251).

Despite the impact of revolutionary regimes on inter-social dynamics, such effects rarely match the rhetoric of either supporters or opponents. On many occasions, it is revolutionary states themselves that nation-alize the international dimensions of their struggle (Halliday 2008). In 1920, the Soviet leadership laid down 21 conditions for membership of Comintern; in 1928, fidelity to the Soviet Union became a requirement of membership: 'an internationalist is one who unreservedly, unhesitatingly, and without conditions is prepared to defend the Soviet Union because it is the basis of the world revolutionary movement' (in Stern 1967: 47). During the 1930s and 1940s, the Soviet Union instituted a policy of 'socialism in one country', dissolving both the Third International and Comintern. Trotsky started a Fourth International in 1938, although without much success. In the early part of the twenty-first century, the Movement for a Revolutionary Communist International attempted, with even less success, to form a League that could stand as a Fifth International. Communist internationalism, therefore, has been uneven in both design and impact. Indeed, splits within the left often arose pre-cisely over the issue of internationalism, whether seen in Soviet distaste for Cuban 'adventurism' or in specific debates over Soviet non-intervention in the Spanish Civil War and the 1968 invasion of Czechoslovakia (under the guises of the Warsaw Pact). The weakness and pragmatism of revolu-tionary states on the one hand, and the strength of counter-revolutionary forces on the other, inhibits the spread of revolution. At the same time, the attempts by revolutionary states to control the spread of revolution can provoke disquiet. As discussed in Chapter 6, the attempt by Iranian revolutionary forces to spread their brand of militant Shi'ism has helped to polarize the Muslim world.

There are, therefore, three main critical configurations associated with revolutionary outcomes. First is the relationship between sticky, embedded patterns of behaviour and emergent fields of action. The latter do not completely replace the former. Rather, revolutions produce melded orders in which novel fields of political, economic, and symbolic action are embedded alongside established social ties. Second, local configurations are, in many ways, forged through inter-social interactions, whether these take the form of the export of revolution or the combating of counter-revolutionary forces. Third, the outcomes of revolutions are realized unevenly – their direction is not predetermined, but forged through dynamics of contention that take place long after the immediate seizure of power. These outcomes are neither the sole result of volitional action taken by revolutionary actors, nor are they the predetermined outcome of macro-social forces. Rather, revolutionary outcomes are dependent on situational logics that arise from purposeful action taken in contested social fields. The nesting of revolutionary orders, as with other revolutionary anatomies, is sensitive to contestation, sequence, and process.

From Analytics to Empirics

This chapter has used a range of revolutionary episodes to construct a composite picture of how revolutions begin, endure, and end. The preceding sections are not rooted in a substantialist understanding of social reality that associates causation with regularity-determinist statements. Rather, analytical narratives have been presented that simplify historical clutter in order to identify the principal causal configurations through which revolutionary events can be ordered across time and space. The result is a synthetic picture of revolutionary situations, trajectories, and outcomes – a picture intended to identify not finite properties of a single revolutionary entity, but confluences of different revolutions that, together, can be used to construct robust, logically coherent causal configurations. The success of this enterprise must be measured in both theoretical and empirical terms. As Max Weber (2004/1903–17: 90, 94) puts it:

Historical research faces the task of determining in each individual case the extent to which this ideal-construct approximates to or diverges from reality ... we comprehend reality only through a chain of intellectual modifications.

In an attempt to foster just such an organic link between theory and history, the next three chapters examine the ways in which the ideal-typical anatomies of revolution presented in this chapter comprehend distinct, yet comparable, revolutionary situations, trajectories, and outcomes.

Part II

Histories

Part II is made up of three chapters, each of which contains two historical illustrations: England and Chile (revolutionary situations); Cuba and South Africa (revolutionary trajectories); Iran and Ukraine (revolutionary outcomes). These illustrations have two main purposes: first, to elaborate the relationship between concrete episodes of revolutionary situations and the ideal-typical anatomies outlined in Chapter 3; and second, to explore the substantive utility of the causal configurations charted in the previous chapter. In each case, revolutionary events are filtered into an analytical narrative that represents idealized causal pathways. These narratives are tools of simplification in that they emphasize certain sequences of events, and downplay others. But they are also systematically constructed and logically coherent, producing explanations of specific instances of revolutionary change while, at the same time, providing insights into a wider corpus of revolutionary processes.

These illustrations have been chosen in order to cover as wide a group of revolutionary episodes as possible. They range from the seventeenth century to the present day, include cases from Europe, West Asia, the Americas, and Africa, and feature examples of both successful and unsuccessful revolution, as well as one or two cases that lie in-between. When paired, they tease out the ways in which revolutionary dynamics are simultaneously singular and comparable. They are singular in that, even when the 'right' structural ingredients appear to be in place, events unfold in a way that is reliant on time, place, and history. They are comparable in that, even allowing for different contexts, it is possible to draw out causal configurations that act as portable insights across diverse settings. This interplay between singularity and regularity lies at the heart of this book. So too does an emphasis on historicity – as the following chapters make clear, timing and sequence are more important to the unfolding of revolutionary dynamics than any checklist of necessary conditions or essential properties. The three foundations of this book – historicism, relational social action, and an inter-social approach – provide a means by which to unravel the development of revolutionary situations, trajectories, and outcomes.

4 Revolutionary Situations
England and Chile

Revolutionary Situations

This chapter is concerned with revolutionary situations. It begins with an examination of two revolutionary situations in England during the seventeenth century, often seen as embodying the first revolutions of the modern era.[1] The second section assesses an instance when the critical configurations associated with revolutionary situations appear to have been present, but a full revolutionary situation did not emerge: Chile in 1973 and 1983–6. In the case of the former, a military coup immobilized revolutionary polarization; in the case of the latter, the junta saw off a wave of popular protest and carried out a programme of authoritarian upgrading. In neither instance did a combination of inter-social openings, regime vulnerability, and systemic crisis develop into a revolutionary situation. Rather, in 1988, a plebiscite on military rule in Chile unintentionally established a timetable for a transition to democracy.

Each illustration is composed of an analytical narrative, which orders the events through which revolutionary pressures built up over time, and that directs its attention towards three main configurations. First, as the last chapter argued, changing inter-social relations acted as the overarching field within which revolutionary situations emerged, providing openings through which protest movements rearticulated their positions.[2] In England, the pressure afforded by two different models of statehood, represented by the Dutch Republic and France, acted as stimulants to the build-up of revolutionary pressures; so too did the deepening of transnational trading networks and heightened geopolitical

---

[1] The chapter treats the whole period from the 1640s to the 1680s as 'the first modern revolution'. In this sense, it follows the periodization established by Harris (2005) rather than the more restricted focus on 1688 followed by Pincus (2009).

[2] The point here is to highlight a critical component of inter-social relations rather than bracket inter-social relations from other revolutionary dynamics. As the discussion in subsequent sections shows, inter-social relations were also central to issues of regime type and systemic crisis.

competition. In Chile, a range of factors, from shifts in US policy to the example effect of democratization in neighbouring countries, were critical to how revolutionary pressures ebbed and flowed. Second, as noted in the previous chapter, some regimes are more vulnerable than others to changing inter-social configurations, most notably sultanist and neo-patrimonial regimes that are based on the authority of a single individual. England during the seventeenth century is a useful illustration of the vulnerability of such regimes. The case of Chile, a regime that, after 1973, combined sultanist and neo-patrimonial tendencies with authoritarianism, illustrates that, although such regimes can be vulnerable, they are also capable of resisting the onset of revolutionary situations. Finally, the previous chapter argued that revolutionary situations emerge from a combination of: a political-coercive crisis in which the legitimacy of the old regime collapses and a viable alternative is offered; a symbolic crisis in which alternative ideas, a widespread perception of failure, and a belief that things are getting intolerably worse induces the possibility of revolutionary conflict; and a relative economic crisis, which presents a challenge to secure standards of living. England exhibits well this sense of systemic crisis. In Chile, however, the military was able to contain the scale of the crises in 1973 and 1983–6. This exemplifies the need to historicize the relationship between inter-social relations, regime type, systemic crisis, and revolutionary situations. Timing and process are central to any assessment of how, when, and where revolutionary situations emerge.

The First Modern Revolution: England

In Early Modern Europe, political conflicts were religious conflicts – 'heresy in the Church was tantamount to sedition in society' (Malia 2006: 59). Given this, it is not surprising that revolutionary movements in Early Modern Europe were religious in character: religion and politics were codetermined. From the fifteenth-century Hussites in Bohemia to the sixteenth-century Anabaptists in Münster and the Huguenots in France, radical movements began – even if they did not end – with the issue of religious reform. Perhaps the most widespread of these revolts – those of the United Dutch Provinces in 1566 – was simultaneously a movement oriented around freedom from Spanish rule and one sustained by a radical form of theology: Calvinism. The success of the Dutch Revolt had significant ramifications for the international relations of the region. Over the next century, the Dutch Republic pioneered novel commercial relations, practised at least relative political tolerance, and embraced scientific rationalism in a way that was to prove as attractive to

European reform movements as it was threatening to existing forms of absolutist rule (Wilson 1968; Israel 1998; Adams 2005).[3]

Towards a Revolutionary Situation: The 1640s

Perhaps the most striking echo of the Dutch Revolts took place in England, curiously so in that this was a country that existed, to some extent at least, outside the continental European experience of radical Reformation (Nexon 2009). Beyond England's distinct experience of the Reformation, England was unusual in two further ways: first, parliament was more deeply embedded within governance structures than in most other European states through its role in financial oversight, justice, and state administration; and second, England contained a form of local government that tied together counties, shires, boroughs, and towns into a common legal framework and tax-collecting network.

This 'shared rule' was threatened by three processes: war, shifts in political economy, and the patrimonial tendencies of the Stuart dynasty. Although the British Isles experienced less inter-state war during the sixteenth century than most continental European states, intra-elite competition within the 'multiple kingdoms' of England, Wales, Scotland, and Ireland often turned into armed conflict (Russell 1990). These wars were, more often than not, the product of dynastic struggles played out between ruling families. These families claimed sovereignty based on genealogical claims rather than an 'organic unity' of state, territory, and people (Schroeder 1994: 8). The personalization of sovereignty meant that claims of inheritance and succession often led to war – 'private' issues of 'dynastic nuptials' served as the source of 'public' conflicts (Teschke 2003: 229–31). The 'composite monarchies' of Early Modern Europe, therefore, were frequently destabilized as territories were redistributed through war. In many respects, England was a peripheral figure in these geopolitical struggles. Britain relied on militias rather than a standing army – until the last quarter of the seventeenth century, Britain's army was a quarter of the size of the Swedish army, an eighth the size of the Dutch army, and a tenth the size of the French army (Brewer 1990: 8; also see Kennedy 1976). The British navy was reliant on privateers – of the 197 vessels that sailed against the Spanish Armada in 1588, only 34 were crown ships (Brewer 1990: 10–11). British weakness, therefore, left it susceptible to stronger powers. Attempts by the monarchy to overcome

[3] Examples of Dutch tolerance include the sanctuary given to figures as diverse as (the Catholic) Rene Descartes, (the Jew) Baruch Spinoza, and the (liberal) John Locke during the seventeenth century.

this weakness and modernize its armed forces required funds. This, in turn, led to confrontation with parliament, which was unwilling to deliver these funds without limiting claims to personalized sovereignty. Shared rule, therefore, was destabilized by the monarchy's attempts to take part in European geopolitical practices and, in particular, by its attempts to 'catch up' with more 'advanced' states.

In terms of political economy, the seventeenth century marked the beginning of the shift from agriculture to manufacturing. Whereas in 1600, agriculture made up 80 per cent of the English economy, by the end of the century, this figure was 60 per cent; by 1700, manufacturing constituted a third of the English national product (Pincus 2009: 52). The rise of manufacturing went hand-in-hand with the commercialization of agriculture. Between the last quarter of the sixteenth century and the last quarter of the seventeenth century, the number of rural labourers depending on the market doubled. These changes were, in turn, enabled by the rise of long-distance trade (De Vries 1976). Between 1640 and 1688, England's merchant shipping doubled its tonnage; between 1660 and 1700, imports rose by a multiple of six and exports by a multiple of seven (Pincus 2009: 83). Colonialism played a substantial role in this growth: tobacco imports from North America increased from 50,000 pounds per year in 1615 to 13 million pounds per year in 1700; by 1700, India provided nearly a third of English imports; and during the 1690s, three times as many English products were exported to the colonies as were sent to the continent (Acemoglu et al. 2005). The extension of transnational trade circuits meant the development of new sectors, such as insurance, and presaged shifts in England's economic topography. The rise of extractive industries, including tin in Cornwall, coal in Newcastle, and lead in Derbyshire, heralded the formation of new commercial centres. By 1700, 40 per cent of people in England lived in towns, compared to 10 per cent at the beginning of the century, while London was more heavily populated than Paris, had twice the population of Amsterdam, and four times the population of Madrid (Pincus 2009: 60). The extent of these changes in England's political economy fuelled the rise of antagonisms between town and country, and between the monarchy and an incipient commercial elite.

These antagonisms were exacerbated by the patrimonial tendencies of the Stuarts. In 1625, Charles I inherited a throne where authority was sanctioned by divine right. The throne vested personal sovereignty on Charles as an individual and on the Stuarts as a dynasty – it was a quintessentially patrimonial system. As noted in Chapter 3, patrimonialism is a form of rule in which political power is seen as the personal property of the ruler. In Early Modern England, this meant that political power was bestowed in the monarch. Rather than embed personalized rule with a degree of legal-rational functioning (as in neo-patrimonial regimes), Charles used personalized sovereignty to construct a system of proprietary patronage. Under Charles, as much as a third of royal income was raised through practices ranging from the sale of offices to the imposition of feudal rights (Anderson 1974: 141; Aylmer 1974: 248). Fees and reversions were charged in return for posts; the sale of offices went hand in hand with the sale of charters and trade monopolies. During the 1620s and 1630s, wars with Spain and France led to a deepening of Charles' proprietary system. By 1640, there were twice as many peers as there had been in 1603 (Hill 2002/1961: 69). The result of these sales was an extension of patrimonial rule and a diminution of the role of parliament. Although the 1628 Petition of Right granted parliamentary levies to the crown in exchange for royal recognition of limits to its tax prerogatives, Charles continued to raise money through arbitrary practices. A number of disputes took place between the crown and parliament over entitlements to customs revenue, as well as over the crown's use of feudal tenures, wardships, and purveyance. In 1629, Charles attempted to collect taxation without parliamentary authorization. When merchants refused to pay, and parliament supported them, Charles dissolved parliament. As a result, royal debts increased and credit became hard to come by – the crown was faced with a fiscal shortfall.

The long-term roots of the crown's fiscal troubles stemmed, in part, from demographic changes. As noted above, during the seventeenth century, England's political economy was beginning a major transformation, one that included rapid population growth and urbanization. In the century leading up to 1640, the population of London increased by 650 per cent; between 1600 and 1640 alone, the city's population doubled (Goldstone 1991: 84, 100). This demographic bulge meant that goods became scarce and prices rose – food riots were common in the years leading up to 1640. Higher prices for staples impoverished many ordinary people, leading to sporadic disturbances and, between 1628 and 1631, more general unrest. Some, however, thrived on the opportunities opened up by increasing trade and high prices. Favoured nobles were granted state monopolies, such as Sir Edmund Verney (tobacco), the Earl of Salisbury (silk), and the Earl of Northampton (starch), while industrialists took advantage of improvements in manufacturing – by 1640, England produced three times as much coal as the rest of Europe put together (Hill 2002/1961: 20). Industrialists and gentry alike sought greater influence within the state. However, during the 1620 and 1630s, the crown's extended use of titles, offices, and reversions made it difficult to translate wealth into political power (Goldstone 1991: 114–15).

It also created networks that served as the basis for intra-elite faction-alism. Individual malfeasance added to the sense of elite friction. Often, this friction assumed ideological form, particularly given that the 'culture of discipline' associated with the 'middling sorts' associated them with congregational movements rather than episcopal orders, putting them at odds with the High Anglicanism favoured by Charles I and William Laud, the Archbishop of Canterbury (Downing 1992). In effect, reli-gious belief acted as a surrogate for political competition.

During the 1620s and 1630s, therefore, Stuart administration became dominated by the 'three P's': patronage, patrimony, and purchase (Aylmer 1974: 89). At the same time, the monarchy sought to centralize powers within the court rather than the parliament. During Charles' period of personal rule after 1629, the Star Chamber and Privy Council worked as tools of executive prerogative. Charles also introduced a number of new levies, most notably 'Ship Money', an attempt to extend a wartime charge on ports into a nationwide system applicable in peace-time. Several national figures, including John Hampden and William Fiennes (Viscounts Saye and Sele, respectively), refused to pay the tax on the basis that parliament had not issued consent for it. Nevertheless, in 1639, Charles I demanded further levies for a war with Scotland, forcing him to recall parliament. When parliament rebuffed Charles' demands, a fiscal shortfall turned into a political crisis. In the summer of 1640, Scottish forces invaded England, capturing Newcastle and Durham, and forcing Charles to summon parliament again. The 'Long Parliament' that assembled in November proved just as hostile to the king as its prede-cessor. Parliament impeached several advisers to the king, abolished the Star Chamber, demanded the release of political prisoners, and forbade the royal collection of tonnage and poundage. Parliament also issued a 'Grand Remonstrance', indicting Charles both for his defeat to the Scots and for breaching the trust of his subjects. The crisis worsened during 1641 when the king attempted to raise an army to put down a revolt in Ireland. Around the country, officials refused to pay tithes and rents, and riots against enclosures and Catholics became widespread. At the same time, merchants, shopkeepers, and craftsmen in London rebelled, forcing the king to flee to Oxford. In early 1642, both Charles and parliament raised their standards – a condition of dual sovereignty had emerged.

As noted in the previous chapter, a revolutionary situation is defined by a regime and an opposition advancing competing, but exclusive, claims to the same polity. During the early 1640s, a number of factors combined to form a revolutionary situation in England. First, as discussed above, the geopolitical system of Early Modern Europe was inherently destabilizing. Territorial claims based on dynastic claims generated unstable alignments and, as a result, regular conflict. At the same time, the emergence of transnational, often colonial, trade expanded access to wealth even as the crown restricted political authority to the court. Second, these inter-social dynamics (the constancy of conflict and shifting patterns of trade) strained England's system of shared rule. After 1629, Charles attempted to rule without parliamentary consent. The elaboration of patrimonial practices meant that the monarchy was increasingly sultanistic, combining personalized rule, the securing of loyalty through fear and rewards, the deployment of unencumbered, arbitrary power, and the use of the state as a nepotistic vehicle for gain. Chapter 3 argued that such orders are particularly vulnerable to fluctuations in social ties. During the 1620s and 1630s, Charles' acceleration of proprietary rule constructed patronage networks that were personally accumulated rather than deeply embedded. This, in turn, fuelled intra-elite competition, generating factions that could be mobilized during periods of state weakness. The crisis of 1639–41 demonstrates how quickly such mobilization can take place. Finally, although the court was the centre of English despotic power, its authority was restricted by the monarchy's weak infrastructural reach. It could neither fully immobilize rivals nor decisively quell popular contention. Alternative power centres such as parliament were able to compete for state power. It was not structural conditions per se, whether understood as geopolitical weakness, the increasing sultanism of Charles I, or the beginnings of agrarian capitalism, which generated a revolution situation in England. Rather, it was the temporal ordering of these dynamics that led to a condition of dual sovereignty. Dual sovereignty led, in turn, to civil war.

From Civil War to Glorious Revolution

The English Civil War took place in two phases that, together, lasted nearly a decade. The decisive step was the formation of the New Model Army in 1645 under the leadership of Oliver Cromwell and Thomas Fairfax. After winning a crucial battle at Naseby, the army forced the king's surrender. The king fled to Scotland, only to be handed over to parliamentary forces by the Scots. A second, briefer, civil war reignited during 1647–8 after Charles escaped from imprisonment. In the aftermath of the victory by the New Model Army, there was considerable debate over how to treaty with the king. In December 1648, an intervention by Colonel Thomas Pride ('Pride's Purge') prevented over 100 (mostly Presbyterian) MPs considered to be 'enemies of the army' from entering the palace of Westminster. Pride's Purge opened the way to Charles' trial. The king was charged with tyranny, making war on his own people, the plunder of towns, and the torture of prisoners of war. He was publicly executed on 30 January 1649. In May, the 'Rump Parliament' (those MPs who remained following Pride's Purge) declared England to be a Commonwealth. The office of the king was abolished, along with the Privy Council and the House of Lords. Parliamentary standing committees were established to oversee government departments and reforms were initiated in key spheres of activity, from tax collection to ordnance. English, rather than French or Latin, became the official language of governance. Adultery and incest were made capital offences, and there were attempts to ban public drinking and dancing. A diverse range of groups made use of cheap, portable printing presses to take part in vigorous, often raucous, public debates (Thomas 1971; Hill 1975; Harris 2005: 16–20).

By any measure, these were revolutionary changes. And that was certainly how they were seen at the time (Harris 2015: 29–30). However, not for the last time, revolutionary transformation did not produce a stable settlement. To the contrary, attempts by Cromwell to centralize power, as well as his need for funds to subdue revolts in Ireland and fight wars on the continent, led to further polarization.[4] Between 1640 and 1660, 85,000 people died in conflicts in England (Tilly 2004: 135). Cromwell faced opposition from both recalcitrant monarchists and radical members of his own coalition, including the New Model Army, which was a hothouse of political debate. The Army, along with groups such as the Levellers, took part in discussions ranging from the supremacy of parliament to the possibility of confiscating gentry estates, instituting universal suffrage, and extending rights to freedom of speech and conscience (Hill 1975; Robertson 2007). Leveller documents such as the Agreement of the People called for political representation based not on property requirements or historical precedence, but on natural rights. As one of their number, Colonel Thomas Rainsborough (in Robertson 2007: 69), stated during the 1647 Putney Debates, 'I think that the poorest he that is in England hath a life to live as the greatest he … and I do think that the poorest man in England is not at all bound in a strict sense to that government that he has not had a voice to put himself under'.[5] These

---

[4] The conflict in Ireland was particularly bloody. The scorched-earth campaign waged by Cromwell's son-in-law, Henry Ireton, killed 40 per cent of the Irish population (Tilly 2004: 136). Ireton's campaign had a dramatic effect not just on population size, but also on land ownership. In 1641, Catholics owned 60 per cent of the land in Ireland; in 1660, this figure was closer to 20 per cent (Foster 1989: 115–16).

[5] There were, however, limits to the franchise proposed by Rainsborough – beggars, servants, and, perhaps unsurprisingly, women.

groups took part in a revolution within the revolution, lobbying for a halt to enclosures and the return of communal property, universal suffrage, and the disestablishment of the Church (Hill 1975: 15).

Cromwell, however, was no Leveller. He purged the New Model Army of its 'Agitators' and dealt severely with mutineers. During the 1650s, Cromwell (now known as the Lord Protector) also dissolved a number of parliaments and instituted a major overhaul of the armed forces. As noted in the previous section, before the civil war, Britain's army was one of the smallest in Europe and its navy was reliant on privateers. Cromwell added over 200 new naval vessels and extended the capacities of the New Model Army – England was divided into 11 regions, each of which was presided over by a Major General. His government sold over £2 million worth of crown lands and rents, and a similar amount of Church property (Hill 2002/1961: 146). The estates of 700 royalists were sequestered; many more were forced to pay compensation. Commercialization was actively pursued – a number of royal forests were turned over to cultivation, while monopolies held by nobles were opened to competition from the City of London and its merchants. The Navigation Acts extended British interests over a burgeoning Atlantic trade in slaves, tobacco, and sugar, while an aggressive foreign policy saw England acquire territories as diverse as Jamaica and New Brunswick. By the time of Cromwell's death in August 1658, a considerable transformation of English state and society was underway.

But the transformation of England begun during the Commonwealth was not deeply embedded. Indeed, in the short term, it did not last beyond Cromwell's death. In 1660, after a short period of rule by Cromwell's son, Richard, Charles II was restored to the throne amidst widespread desire for a return to normalcy (Hutton 1985). Charles was awarded a grant of £100,000 per year by parliament, which also sought to pay off the army. An Act of Indemnity pardoned all but the worst offences committed during the civil war, some land was restored, and church courts were reintroduced. The restoration of the Stuarts also meant the restoration of the royal prerogative. Charles and his Lord Chancellor, the Earl of Clarendon, revived the traffic of offices, grants of reversion, and fee-taking (Aylmer 1973; Chandaman 1975). The Treasury, Ordnance, and Admiralty were removed from the hands of independent commissioners and returned to the status of private gifts. Many of the weaknesses of the administration of Charles I returned: factionalism based on competing networks, extravagance, and malfeasance. Attempts by parliament to limit the king's income forced Charles into the hands of city financiers just as he sought to raise funds to fight wars against France and the United Provinces. Both wars went badly and, in 1667, the Dutch fleet celebrated its victory by sailing up the Thames.

These defeats prompted Charles to 'rationalize the irrationalization' of patrimonial rule (Ertman 1997: 322). The Treasury gained powers of supervision, regulation, and oversight over state finances and administration. Other reforms sought to develop a professional civil service, while Charles began an overhaul of the navy and army. However, a reversion to arbitrary rule was never far away. In January 1672, the 'Stop of the Exchequer' repudiated state debt outside specific acts of parliament. The Lord Treasurer, Sir Thomas Osborne, streamlined state borrowing to a narrow band of financiers and made liberal use of the Treasury discretionary fund. Increasingly, Charles' court sought to emulate the style and practices of Louis XIV, the 'Sun King' (Roi Soleil), Europe's leading exponent of absolutism. In 1670, Charles signed a secret treaty with Louis XIV in which he promised to become a Catholic. Charles also announced a Declaration of Indulgence for Catholics and dissenting Protestants. Concerned at these developments, parliament passed an Exclusion Bill, seeking to ensure the succession of the Duke of Monmouth, Charles' illegitimate son, rather than James, the son of Charles I.[6] Two years later, the Rye House Plot – an attempt to assassinate both Charles and James – was discovered. The plot presaged a full-blown attempt at rebellion in 1685 under the leadership of the Duke of Monmouth. Although a failure, the rebellion hardened, and appeared to legitimate, James' drive towards absolutism. It also illustrated that elite fracture was deepening and that English social order was polarizing.

In February 1685, Charles died, declaring himself a Catholic on his deathbed. He was succeeded by James II. Although James promised to hold elections to parliament, uphold the rule of law, and maintain property rights, his policies extended the patrimonial rule of his predecessor. Even more so than Charles, James envisaged an English monarchy based along French lines. This vision combined personalized sovereignty premised on the divine right of monarchs with state centralization – in short: absolutism. The centralization of state power in the royal court included assuming control of an enhanced military. James increased the size of the army from 9,000 to 40,000 between 1685 and 1688, and raised the budget for the navy by a third (Pincus 2009: 144, 149). He also removed the army from its dilapidated garrisons, positioning it in requisitioned houses, inns, taverns, and coffeehouses around the country. When James'

---

[6] The Exclusion Bill was passed in the aftermath of public hysteria surrounding the 'Popish Plot', a fictitious conspiracy claiming that there was a Catholic plot to assassinate Charles II.

request for parliamentary funds to support a standing army was denied, he prorogued Parliament. From this point on, James attempted to 'live of his own' (without parliamentary funds). However, this could not be achieved without the raising of customs, excise, and hearth taxes. And such policies did not find favour amongst commercial elites.

Not only was James patrimonial, he was also draconian. Networks of spies kept watch on his opponents, while James seized printing presses and proscribed pamphlets. He also carried out purges of the Privy Council, judiciary, armed forces, and local administrative offices to ensure their loyalty. The king's Catholicism deepened levels of polarization.[7] Between 1686 and 1688, there was a marked increase in Catholic places of worship, schools, and texts. The king attempted to repeal the Penal Laws and Test Acts,[8] and established a Commission for Ecclesiastical Causes. Several leading bishops, including Henry Compton, the Bishop of London, refused to recognize the legality of the Commission. The subsequent trial of these bishops mobilized opposition to James. In 1687, James became involved in a feud with the fellows of Magdalen College, Oxford over their refusal to appoint the king's (Catholic) nominee as president, a process that, again, rallied opposition to James. The birth of an apparently Catholic heir, Edward, in June 1688 was, for many, a step too far, engendering the possibility of a Catholic monarchy that stretched far into the future, something that British elites and publics had opposed for at least a century, sometimes violently. Leading figures defected and prominent bankers refused to lend to the king. Several dignitaries wrote to William of Orange, asking him to intervene. William landed with his army on Guy Fawkes Day 1688 – his arrival was met by anti-Catholic riots in London and widespread desertions amongst James' troops.[9] The arbitrary patrimonialism of James had served to unify opposition to the crown. An anti-coalition of Whigs, Tories, Anglicans, Dissenters, and Catholics loyal to the Pope took up arms against the attempted imposition of Catholic absolutism (Pincus 2009: 187, 209). In December 1688, James fled from London. In February 1689, William and his wife, Mary, became king and queen of England.

---

[7] James' Catholicism was inspired by the French courts' elevation of national Catholicism over allegiance to Rome. This put James at odds with both the Pope and many influential Catholics within England. On this point, see Pincus (2009: 139–41).

[8] The Test Acts subjected civil and military officials to an oath of supremacy and allegiance to the Church of England, as well as a declaration against transubstantiation. Along with the Penal Acts (the requirement that everyone in the country attend Church of England services), the Test Acts acted as the main barrier against 'popery'.

[9] Pincus (2009: 234) estimates that around half of William's invasion force was made up of deserters from James' army.

Assessing the Glorious Revolution

There are three main ways that the 'Glorious Revolution' of 1688 is usually interpreted. For Marxists (e.g. Moore 1966; Anderson 1976; Hill 1980; Callinicos 1989; Brenner 1993; Wood 2000; Teschke 2005; Davidson 2012), 1688 is usually seen as a bourgeois revolution, arising from the onset of agrarian capitalism and prompted by a new class of yeomen and merchants whose commercial interests were at odds with those of the crown. However, there was little sense of a united bourgeois class of agrarian capitalists during the revolution (Trevor-Roper 1953; Stone and Stone 1986; Stone 1988; Goldstone 1991). Nor did merchants collectively oppose the crown – to the contrary, agrarian capitalists, manufacturers, and colonial traders relied on the crown for offices and privileges (Goldstone 1991: 68–9). A second group of scholarship sees the English Revolution as premised on the ineptitude of the ruling elite, particularly the court of James II (e.g. Elton 1974; Rose 1999). But this view neglects the widespread nature of the uprising and the extent to which it was genuinely popular (Harris 2005, 2006; Pincus 2009). Third, there is a tradition of thought that associates 1688 with a short-term constitutional crisis caused, in turn, by the conflict between Catholics and Protestants (e.g. Tawney 1926; Stone 1966). However, these accounts overplay the continuities between pre-revolutionary and post-revolutionary periods. The Glorious Revolution was not a blip within a history of gradual, moderate reform, as argued by Whig historians: Burke, Macaulay, Trevelyan, et al. It was a bloody conflict that reshaped both English social order and the country's relations with other polities. At the same time, as noted above, religion was the form through which political competition was articulated in Early Modern Europe. It was not Catholicism or reform ideologies per se, but the use of these belief systems as political distinctions around which factions could mobilize that explains the hardening of polarization. The revolutionary situation of 1688 was a systemic crisis that took place through a combination of inter-social changes and regime vulnerability.

Inter-Social Changes   The main inter-social dynamic associated with the 1688 revolution was the draw exerted by two competing visions of modern statehood. The first, articulated by the Dutch Republic, combined representative government with commercial strength, military power, and religious tolerance. The second, associated with absolutist France, linked state centralization, Catholicism, and personalized sovereignty sanctioned by divine right. Both of these models had their adherents in England. And for much of the seventeenth century, it was not clear which of the two was the more potent (Scott 2000). If anything, in the late seventeenth century, French absolutism looked more secure than the Dutch Republic. Both Denmark and Sweden had become more absolutist, while even the United Provinces had shifted from republic-anism towards a quasi-monarchical regime. There was nothing inevit-able, therefore, about the English embrace of parliamentary sovereignty and public finances along Dutch lines. To the contrary, it was the com-petition between French and Dutch visions of modern statehood that polarized the country so sharply, helping to facilitate the formation of a revolutionary situation. Elites in England took part in transnational learning from both France and the Dutch Republic (Israel 1991; Ertman 1997: 321).

Beyond these attempts to learn from more 'advanced' states, there were three main forms of inter-social interaction between England, France, and the United Provinces. First were personal ties, particularly between elites, but also those forged by Dutch settlers in East Anglia and French Huguenots in London. Second was geopolitical conflict – all three states were involved in a number of wars with each other during the second half of the seventeenth century. Third were the denser connections that emerged from burgeoning trade, itself imbricated with colonialism and the globalization of European geopolitical competition. In each of these spheres of activity, England was the junior partner. This meant that English elites did most of the borrowing, whether this meant importing notions of high culture, military organization, or trading practices. These appropriated ideas and practices were conjoined with local conditions in new, often unstable, amalgams. For example, James' attempt to import French absolutism to England heightened state instability. It paid little attention either to England's history of shared rule or its experience of the Commonwealth. Nor did it heed deep-rooted anti-Catholic senti-ment. The result was the draining of James' support amongst elites – the importation of French absolutism to English state–society relations fostered an anti-coalition that was simultaneously anti-absolutist, anti-French, and anti-Catholic.

In terms of inter-social relations, therefore, England's relative 'back-wardness' provided elites with the opportunity to learn from more 'advanced' states. Defeats in war underlined the superiority of the French and Dutch models, as did the relative wealth of these states, itself enabled by colonial trade. Attempts to emulate these continental powers were unsuccessful. To the contrary, they destabilized existing forms of social order, fostered intra-elite competition, and deepened polariza-tion. Inter-social relations acted as the overarching field within which the revolutionary situation emerged, exacerbating existing tensions and providing the space through which alternative elites rearticulated their positions. This opening was intensified by the patrimonialism and, at times, sultanism of both Charles and James.

Regime Type   As was the case in the 1640s, patrimonialism on its own was not enough to generate a revolutionary situation in England in 1688. As noted above, during the seventeenth century, the most powerful state in Europe – France – was an absolutist state presided over by Louis XIV. Yet France experienced regular defeats in war during the seventeenth century. At the same time, French absolutism was more parasitical than its English equivalent: taxes were higher, debts were greater, and the state more exorbitant (Hui 2005). As John Brewer (1990: 17) puts it, venality was the 'white noise' of French administration. As a result, France suffered regular bouts of domestic turbulence, including a civil war (La Fronde) between 1648 and 1653. These conflicts took place for similar reasons as those in England – the resistance by nobles, local administrators, judicial bodies, and publics to the exertion of arbitrary authority, personal appropriation, and malfeasance by the crown. But at no point did French resistance – or state vulnerability – prompt the emergence of a full-blown revolutionary situation.

It was not, therefore, patrimonialism per se that caused a revolutionary situation to emerge in England in 1688. Rather, it was a specific sequence of regime ineffectiveness, elite dissatisfaction, and political oppression that weakened the state and unified opposition. Under both Charles and James, personalized rule was conjoined with arbitrary power. Most notably, their policies were unpredictable, resting on whim rather than effective governance. As a result, commercial elites had no predictable governance structure through which to support their activities, while the state lacked a reliable source of credit. The succession of James II was a crucial moment in this respect. Although initially willing to give James a chance, the arbitrary nature of James' rule, from the appointment of Catholics to high offices to the re-establishing of legal bodies illegitimated by the Commonwealth, alienated elites and unified opposition. At the same time, James' emulation of French absolutism estranged members of his social base, including ecclesiastical officials and a number of prominent Catholics (Miller 1973). Their desertion, along with the defection of both officers and rank-and-file members of the army, turned intra-elite competition into a general crisis.

Systemic Crisis   In two instances during the seventeenth century in England, systemic crises turned into revolutionary situations: the 1640s and 1688. This was, as Tim Harris (2015: 40) puts it, England's 'century of revolution'. The first crisis resulted in a revolutionary civil war, establishing a Commonwealth that was overturned in the restoration of 1660. The second crisis resulted in a revolution that established parliament rather than the monarchy as England's sovereign body. This helps to make clear the lack of a fixed relationship between inter-social relations, regime type, and systemic crisis. Many states go through systemic crises without this developing into a revolutionary situation. Many states, because of their regime type, are vulnerable to such crisis. And just as many take part in transnational learning, generating unstable amalgams of 'advanced' and 'backward', without descending into revolutionary crisis. None of these factors on their own are sufficient to prompt a revolutionary situation. Nor does the presence of all three *require* a revolutionary situation to emerge. These configurations are not indispensable conditions or essential properties, but idealized constructions of the causal pathways through which revolutionary situations emerge. Actual history is, by necessity, more complex and more context-dependent than such constructions allow. The task, therefore, is to use the casual sequences that cohere in particular revolutionary situations like England to probe the utility of these configurations.

Seventeenth-century England yields three insights in this regard. First, shifting inter-social relations, including elite attempts to learn from the French and Dutch models, the extension of trading circuits, and the spread of radical ideas, destabilized English social order and fostered the repositioning of intra-elite competition and state–society relations. This instability acted as the overarching field within which the two revolutionary situations emerged. Second, Stuart patrimonialism, allied to venality and malfeasance, sharpened elite competition and deepened polarization. Third, systemic crisis in the 1640s and 1688 were exploited by opposition elites, who seized the opportunity to radically recast social order. By the end of England's revolutionary century, political authority rested primarily in parliament rather than in a patrimonial monarchy – parliament had morphed from 'an event into an institution' (Pincus 2012). From this time on, parliamentary control was exerted over government debt, which was, in turn, underwritten by London financiers. The capacity of the state to borrow without insolvency and the embedding of parliamentary sovereignty became the core ingredients of modern statehood. Many of the ideas contained in the American Revolution, such as representative government, an end to arbitrary taxation, freedom of speech and conscience, and an independent judiciary, were products of the English Revolution (Bailyn 1967). At the same time, revolutionaries in France at the end of the eighteenth century were well aware of the debts they owed to their English predecessors. Writing in the second quarter of the nineteenth century, François Guizot, the French historian and statesman, named the events of the 1640s to 1688 as the world's first modern revolution. He was right.

Crisis Without Revolution: Chile

The discussion of the revolutionary situation that emerged in England in the seventeenth century illustrates the sequence of causal configurations that lie behind the formation of revolutionary situations: changing inter-social relations, regime type, and systemic crisis. This section uses two periods of state crisis in Chile in order to demonstrate the ways in which systemic crisis does not necessarily engender a full-blown revolutionary situation. Rather, in Chile, systemic crisis in 1973 was met by a military coup; in 1983–6, it resulted in authoritarian upgrading. This analysis illustrates that it is not contextless attributes, but situational logics, that explain why revolutionary situations emerge in some settings, but not in others.

A Revolutionary Situation?

In 1964, Eduardo Frei, candidate of the centre-left Partido Democratica Cristiano (PDC), won Chile's presidential election. Frei instituted a programme – 'Revolution in Liberty' – centred around the 'Chileanization' of industry, land reform, and the inclusion of previously marginalized groups into policy-making processes. But Frei's reforms only served to polarize the country. Large landowners opposed the break-up of *latifundia* (large estates), just as big business was opposed to nationalization. For their part, many on the left, particularly those influenced by the Cuban Revolution, pressed for more radical reforms, including land and factory seizures (*tomas*). These cleavages engendered a split vote in the 1970 presidential elections: Salvador Allende, representing Unidad Popular (UP), a coalition party of the left, took 36.2 per cent of the vote, narrowly defeating the candidate of the right, Jorge Alessandri, who polled 34.9 per cent. Allende, the first democratically elected Marxist head of state in the world, declared in his victory speech (in Bethell 1993: 157):

We shall abolish the pillows propping up that minority which has always condemned our country to underdevelopment. We shall abolish the monopolies, which grant control of the economy to a few dozen families. We shall abolish the large estates, which condemn thousands of peasants to serfdom. We shall put an end to the foreign ownership of our industry and our sources of employment ... I won't be just another president. I will be the first president of the first really democratic, popular, national and revolutionary government in the history of Chile.

Allende promised a 'peaceful road to socialism' through a range of radical social, economic, and political reforms. Despite opposition from an often-hostile Congress, the president pushed through a number of major changes: 500 firms were nationalized; over two million hectares of land was expropriated; some 2,000 land seizures were tolerated; substantial wage increases were granted to public sector workers; the franchise was extended to include illiterates; and the age restriction for voting was lowered to 18. Initially, these policies appeared to be both popular and successful. GDP rose by around 8 per cent, industrial production rose by over 10 per cent, unemployment halved, and wages increased by a third in 1971 (Bethell 1993; Hickman 1998). In April 1971, the UP vote climbed to almost 50 per cent in municipal elections. But Allende faced opposition from a myriad of domestic sources. Revolutionary groups like the Movimiento de la Izquierda Revolucionaria (MIR) called for armed struggle to defend the revolution and ensure the victory of the *pobladores* (urban poor) and *campesinos* (peasant farmers) from counter-revolutionary forces. But some peasants who had become smallholders for the first time under Frei were unhappy at plans to turn their land into state farms. Both big and small business felt threatened by nationalization, particularly the *gremio* movement of guilds and professional associations. The rationing of goods, including staples like beef, cigarettes, and toilet paper led many housewives to protest against government policies. In December 1971, thousands of women took part in a March of the Empty Pots in Santiago, beating saucepans to highlight the shortage of food. Far-right paramilitary groups like Patria y Libertad (Fatherland and Liberty) caused blackouts by blowing up electricity pylons.

Internationally, attitudes to the UP regime were mixed. Allende's foreign policy was pragmatic, but internationalist: he retained Chile's membership of the Organization of American States (OAS), hastened Chilean full membership of the Non-Aligned Movement, and stepped in to host the third meeting of the United Nations Conference on Trade and Development (UNCTAD) in Santiago as a symbol of his commitment to 'Third World' emancipation and global economic restructuring. Allende received an enthusiastic welcome from Cuba – his long-standing friend, Fidel Castro, was the first foreign head of state to visit Chile – and more lukewarm support from the Soviet Union and other Eastern-bloc states (see Gustafson and Andrew 2018 on the covert support provided by Soviet and Cuban intelligence services to Allende). In Western Europe, socialists and social democrats tended to regard Allende as an exemplar of peaceful, but radical, change.

The main international opposition to Allende came from the United States. Under Frei, Chile had been a showcase for the American government's Alliance for Progress Programme, receiving the highest per capita sum in the hemisphere. The US government, most notably the influential '40 Committee', was deeply hostile to Allende's brand of democratic socialism, which it saw as the forerunner to a Marxist seizure of power – a new Cuba in the making. Nixon's Secretary of State, Henry Kissinger, argued that Allende's victory via the ballot box was more dangerous to the United States than a Cuban-style revolution as it was a model that could be emulated by both Latin American and European leftists (Harmer 2011: 63). As he commented, 'I don't see why we have to let a country go Marxist just because its people are irresponsible' (in Jervis 2010: 33). The US government enacted a two-track policy designed to pressurize the Allende regime. Track I attempted to push Christian Democrat deputies into using a loophole in the Chilean constitution that would allow Frei to challenge Allende in a presidential run-off. When Frei and other Christian Democrat Senators refused to go along with the plan, Track II was stepped up. Track II sought to hasten a military coup through funding for opposition factions, propaganda, and the provision of arms to paramilitary groups. In October 1970, CIA weapons were used in a botched attempt to kidnap General René Schneider, head of the army.[10] After a period in which US attention had been drawn away from the Americas, policy towards Allende's Chile became the barometer of a renewed counter-revolutionary surge throughout the continent (Harmer 2011: 64–72).

During 1972 and 1973, Allende's Chile began to implode. US policy hardened following the nationalization of the copper industry and Allende's refusal to compensate US corporations. Short-term credits were denied and aid cut off in an attempt to follow through President Nixon's instructions to 'make the Chilean economy scream' (in Andrew 2010: 424).[11] Nixon's policy of détente towards international socialism

---

[10] The attack turned out to be counterproductive. Schneider was fatally wounded in the attack, dying days later and becoming a martyr to the constitutionalist faction in the armed forces.

[11] The Senate Select Committee on Intelligence Activities later established through a special investigation – the Church Report – that the CIA funnelled $7 million into Chile between 1970 and 1973. However, the report concluded that this had not been sufficient on its own to destabilize the Allende regime. For detailed analysis of the role of the United States in Chile during this period, see: Hickman (1998); Haslam (2005); Gustafson (2007); and Harmer (2011).

did not apply to Chile. Large increases in public sector investment and extensive money printing led to a sharp rise in public debt, a widening fiscal deficit, and soaring inflation. The black market exchange rate for the peso was 30 times its official value, while the budget deficit ran at 25 per cent of GDP (Zeitlin 1984; Constable and Valenzuela 1991). On the left, MIR called for radical, extra-constitutional action that could hasten a revolutionary takeover, and met with sibling revolutionary groups from the region in order to build links and discuss shared objectives (Harmer 2011: 185). On the right, a lorry owners' dispute turned into a general 'Bosses Strike' (Fishwick 2014). Doctors, dentists, and lawyers shut their practices; shopkeepers closed their stores. In response, groups of workers occupied their workplaces and came out on strike. Both sides prepared for violent confrontation. Allende appealed for compromise, appointing three military advisers to his cabinet, including General Carlos Prats, head of the armed forces. He also set off on a tour to the United States, the Soviet Union, and Cuba, hoping to ease Chile's financial situation and shore up his position. Speaking at the UN in late 1972, Allende received a standing ovation after laying out the full extent of Chile's 'financial strangulation'.

Although the UP performed well in congressional elections held in March 1973, it failed to achieve the outright majority that would have seen the party take over Congress. Vigilante groups from both the left and right took to the streets, creating a level of disorder that threatened to pull Chile into a revolutionary situation. As *Punto Final*, a left-wing journal, put it, 'for Chile, the cards are on the table. It will be either socialism or fascism – there is nothing in between' (in Cooper 2001: 22). In June, an attempted coup by army officers was successfully dispersed by Prats. In August, after a group of officers' wives had publicly berated him as a 'chicken' (Harmer 2011: 227), Prats resigned, to be replaced by his apparently loyal deputy, Augusto Pinochet. Later that month, Congress voted the actions of the government to be unconstitutional and invited the military to defend the nation.

If a revolutionary situation is defined by a regime and an opposition advancing competing, but exclusive, claims to the same polity, by September 1973, Chile was heading towards just such a moment. The modernization programmes initiated by Frei and extended by Allende hoped to overturn deeply embedded socio-economic formations. Yet the political authority of the presidency was eroded by opposition in parliament, including radical voices from within his own party, who favoured confrontation rather than negotiation. The hostility of private actors ranging from large corporations to small businesses added to the sense of siege. As a result, the regime became reliant on the armed forces to maintain order and defend democracy. But in early September, the navy, backed by the air force, upped plans for a coup. After considerable vacillation, Pinochet joined the plotters on 9 September.[12] Overnight, the navy took control of the port at Valparaiso. At 8.30a.m. on the morning of 11 September, the plotters publicly announced their intentions. After defending the palace from attack, Allende ordered his personal guard, friends, and colleagues to leave La Moneda. When the army entered the palace, Allende was found dead with a shotgun, a present from Fidel Castro, lying by his side (Gil et al. 1979; Garcés 1990).

There were two main reasons why the events of September 1973 did not prompt a revolution. First, although both sides of the conflict had international support, the most powerful state in the region – the United States – favoured authoritarian stability rather than revolutionary instability (Sigmund 1993; Haslam 2005). This support was crucial to the success of the coup. Second, Chilean democracy acted as a brake on revolutionary mobilization. Although there were figures around Allende who supported a revolutionary seizure of power, the president himself was committed to constitutional processes. At the same time, leftist movements could not match the firepower available to the Chilean coercive apparatus. The only armed resistance to the coup came in parts of Santiago, a handful of factories, and isolated gunfights between the military and MIR activists. When the military 'rattled their sabres', many Chileans welcomed the restoration of order (Zeitlin 1984).

Revolutionary Situation or Authoritarian Upgrading?

Under military rule, Chile became a laboratory for neoliberal experimentation.[13] In the late 1970s, it appeared as if the policies of a group of monetarists from the Economics Faculty of La Pontificia Universidad Católica de Chile, nicknamed 'the Chicago Boys' because they had previously trained at the University of Chicago, had stoked a bull market. The economy recorded 8.6 per cent growth in 1977, 6 per cent in 1978, and 8.5 per cent in 1979 (Silva 1995: 102). In 1979, Pinochet outlined seven areas that would be the focal points of radical reform: health care, social security, labour, education, justice, agriculture, and the regions. A new phase of 'popular privatization' was initiated, featuring the sale of

---

[12] Pinochet's loyalty to the government seemed so firm that Allende, on seeing the ultimatum to resign signed by the four coup leaders, was heard to say, 'poor Pinochet, he's been captured' (in O'Shaughnessy 2000: 56).

[13] The exception to neoliberal experimentation was the military, which continued to enjoy subsidized access to housing, education, transport, and health facilities.

state assets ranging from kindergartens to swimming pools. At the same time, the state was largely removed from social provision. State spending on welfare was sharply reduced, becoming the province of regional planning offices that determined eligibility for payments through ownership of household appliances rather than income. In 1986, government expenditure on health was $11 per person; in 1973, it had been $28 per person. The combined totals of the housing, health, and education budgets in 1988 were less than that spent on the military alone (Martínez and Díaz 1996: 52). The concentration of resources at the top was in stark contrast to life for most Chileans: nearly half of the population lived below the poverty line and a quarter were indigent (Huneeus 2011). World Bank figures calculated that Chile was the seventh most unequal country in the world.

By the early 1980s, the Chilean experiment in neoliberalism had begun to unravel. The consumer boom had been based on credit, engendering a sizeable debt that was, to a large extent, underwritten by bad loans. A number of companies were sold off to state backers for a fraction of their real value and several major companies declared bankruptcy. In 1982, GDP dropped by 14 per cent and a third of the workforce became unemployed; 62 per cent of jobs in construction, 44 per cent in mining, and 30 per cent of factory work were lost in a single year (Constable and Valenzuela 1991; Bethell 1993). GDP per capita dropped to levels below those of the early 1970s (Valenzuela and Valenzuela 1986). Over half-a-million Chileans were forced onto state emergency schemes, which paid a fraction of the minimum wage for menial work or manual labour (Angell 1995: 188–9). The peso, previously pegged to the dollar, was allowed to float freely, rapidly losing 40 per cent of its value. Despite an $850 million rescue package from the IMF, the government was forced to take over nine key banks and financial institutions in an $8 billion bailout.

The economic crisis punctured the government alliance. The regime was home to two main camps: *los duros* ('the tough ones'), who favoured largely hardline policies, and *los blandos* ('the soft ones'), who sought the eventual return of (partial) democracy. Each had their own media outlets, periodicals, and policy institutes. In the first decade of the military's rule, an alliance between the two principal strands of duros – the Chicago Boys and the *gremialistas* – saw them dominate policy-making. But the crash of the early 1980s gave *blandos* an opportunity to reassert their position. In 1983, nine former National Party congressmen came out publicly against the dictatorship, setting up a new political party that could stand as a centre-right presence in any transition to democracy.

Gremialistas responded by starting their own party, the Unión Demócrata Independiente (UDI), to defend the interests of the regime.

Opposition to the regime took many forms. From May 1983, monthly demonstrations were held around the country, most prominently in shantytowns around Santiago (Schneider 1995). A new opposition coalition, La Alianza Democrática, initiated by Christian Democrats and moderate socialists, called for a gradual return to democracy. A more radical group, the Movimiento Democrático Popular, advocated mass action and the forcible overthrow of the regime. In 1985, the church sponsored a talking shop, El Acuerdo Nacional para la Transición a la Plena Democracia, to foster common principles, goals, and tactics among the disparate groups. The result was the Manifesto for Democracy, signed by 21 leading politicians on behalf of 11 political parties ranging from socialists to the centre-right. The Manifesto called for a lifting of the state of emergency, the legalization of political parties, and a peaceful transition to democracy. Half-a-million people joined a demonstration in Santiago to hear the leader of the Christian Democrats, Gabriel Valdés, exclaim, 'the people are on their feet, saying enough dictatorship, enough decay, enough repression' (in Constable and Valenzuela 1991: 286). At the same time, radical opposition groups escalated their actions. Over 1,000 bombings took place in 1984 alone. In 1986, El Frente Patriótico Manuel Rodríguez (FPMR), the armed wing of the Communist Party, attempted to assassinate General Pinochet.[14] Their failure and the discovery of a substantial arms cache including 3,000 M-16 rifles, 150 rocket launchers, 2,000 hand grenades, and two million rounds of ammunition imported from Cuba became a propaganda coup for the regime (Vidal 1995).

At first, the regime pursued a twin-track approach to the opposition. An official *apertura* (opening) saw Minister of the Interior Sergio Jarpa begin negotiations with opposition leaders. From 1984, thousands of exiles were allowed to return home, while a proliferation of media outlets exploited the more open environment. But at the same time, the regime arrested thousands of people and imposed a general curfew. Demonstrations were (often brutally) dispersed and a campaign of murder begun, centred on the poorer areas of Santiago. In 1986, La Asamblea de la Civilidad, a grassroots movement, published a list of demands calling for the return to democracy. When the government refused, La Asamblea called for a general strike. The two-day stoppage was met by repression. In one infamous incident of state brutality, two

---

[14] The assassination attempt, Operación Siglo XX, killed five presidential bodyguards and injured 12 others; Pinochet escaped with minor wounds.

young students, Rodrigo Rojas de Negri and Carmen Gloria Quintana, were set on fire by a military patrol.[15] After the attempted assassination of General Pinochet, a state of siege was announced in which a number of opposition leaders were denounced and arrested.

At the same time, inter-social relations worked to reduce state effectiveness. Under the dictatorship, Chile was as geopolitically isolated as it was geographically remote. Although few governments pursued a policy of consistent, outright opposition to the regime, even fewer actively engaged with it. No foreign head of state visited Chile between 1973 and 1981. In 1980, a planned state visit to the Philippines by General Pinochet backfired when President Marcos, under American pressure, cancelled the visit at the last minute. Pinochet's plane was forced to stop, refuel, and turn around at Fiji, where his entourage was pelted with eggs and tomatoes. At the same time, democratization throughout Latin America, starting in Ecuador in 1979, acted as a spur to opposition groups. Civilians assumed political authority in Peru (1980), Bolivia (1982), Argentina (1983), Uruguay (1984/5), and Brazil (1985). For its part, the Reagan administration was torn about how to approach the dictatorship – its stance was one of 'constructive ambiguity' (Morley and McGillion 2015: 113). At times, Reagan in particular, and his administration in general, saw Pinochet as the least-bad option for Chile. At other times, they favoured democratization. Following the mobilization of the early 1980s, the latter view took precedence. In 1985, the State Department issued a statement describing Chile's human rights record as 'the greatest disappointment in the Western hemisphere' and the United States sponsored the annual UN resolution reproaching Chile for the first time. A number of government level loans were refused and Ambassador Harry Barnes was encouraged to establish links with opposition groups (Tulchin and Varas 1991; Sigmund 1993; Foot 2010; Clark 2015; Morley and McGillion 2015).

Between 1983 and 1986, Chile once again appeared to be moving towards a revolutionary situation. First, inter-social changes, ranging from the slippage in US support to regional democratization, helped to stimulate opposition movements. Second, the state was weakened through factionalism. As noted in the previous chapter, quasi neopatrimonial regimes such as Chile are highly susceptible to fluctuations in social ties, whether this stems from economic shocks or the weakening of patron–client networks. Because these regimes are acutely exclusionary, even moderate opposition is destabilizing. In Chile, there was no

---

[15] Rojas, a US resident, died from his wounds but Quintana survived, becoming a powerful opposition symbol.

effective political ideology that could unite the regime beyond an intra-elite protection pact, which was stabilized through fear of the opposition, itself refracted through Cold War anti-leftism and a commitment to relatively loose ideas such as 'modernization'. These ideals were undermined by elite fracture, the removal of 'moderate' support for the regime, and the economic crisis of 1983–6. Third, the Chilean opposition was more united in 1983–6 than it had been for a decade. Opposition groups, ranging from the church to social democratic parties, fostered the possibility of successful democratization, one that sought to banish public qualms about leftist extremism and democratic 'anarchy' (Drake and Jakšić 1995; Roberts 1998).

For all this, the regime survived. Jarpa's overtures to the opposition were, for the most part, ignored, leading to his resignation from the government. Higher copper prices and a partial retreat from neoliberalism helped the economy to register renewed growth, averaging 5 per cent between 1986 and 1988 (Bethell 1993). Inflation and unemployment fell as tariffs were increased and the budget deficit allowed to rise. A new finance minister, Hernán Büchi, secured over \$1 billion in loans from the World Bank, supporting sensitive sectors of the economy, while keeping a tighter rein on the conglomerates and banks.[16] The certification of the regime by private and public actors served to stabilize the state. Although Chile under Pinochet contained both neo-patrimonial and sultanist tendencies, it combined these tendencies with authoritarianism. For example, although the state fostered neoliberal economic policies, it left much of the management of the economy to private actors. As long as these private actors remained supportive of the regime, its collapse was unlikely to take place. Even more importantly, the coercive apparatus remained squarely behind the regime. Although coercive power was parcelled out between the armed forces, the Ministry of the Interior, and the Dirección de Inteligencia Nacional (DINA),[17] Chile's notorious secret police, these potential sites of autonomy did not seek to fundamentally either erode or challenge Pinochet's authority. Nor did they become rent-seeking in their own right. Rather, the coercive apparatus retained its unity, serving to contain opposition mobilization and prevent it from becoming fully transgressive. When this opposition did

---

[16] This is indicative of a broader split between political agencies, like the UN, that regularly condemned the dictatorship, and economic agencies like the IMF and World Bank, which provided the resources to prop up the regime. In contrast, the World Bank approved no loans at all to the Allende government.

[17] In the aftermath of its murder of Orlando Letelier, Allende's former Defence Minister, in Washington, DC in 1976, DINA was shut down and replaced by La Central Nacional de Informaciones (CNI).

employ extra-constitutional measures, such as the assassination attempt on General Pinochet, the coercive apparatus lined up behind the regime. As a result, there was no collapse of the state and no condition of dual sovereignty.

If relative state stability – even in the face of crisis – was one reason why Chile did not descend into revolution in the early-to-mid 1980s, a second factor was the strategy pursued by opposition groups, most of which favoured constitutional challenge rather than revolutionary mobilization (Tulchin and Varas 1991; Schneider 1995; Roberts 1998). As discussed in the previous chapter, this is not unusual in regimes that partially co-opt opposition groups. After the crisis of the early-to-mid 1980s, opposition groups directed their attention towards the 1988 plebiscite on the dictatorship required by the 1980 constitution. In February 1988, 14 political parties joined the Concertación de Partidos por el "No" (Coalition of Parties for "No"). In August, the junta confirmed Pinochet as the official candidate of the regime. In the weeks leading up to the vote, both sides were given 15 minutes per day on state television to publicize their views. The opposition's slick bulletins stressed positive images of moderation and reconciliation, in contrast to the state broadcasts that portrayed the Concertación as covert communists. 'What is truly at stake is the freedom of Chile' claimed Pinochet. The opposition preferred a more optimistic message: 'La alegría ya viene' (joy is coming).[18] On polling day, 5 October, seven million Chileans voted 'No': 55 per cent of voters nationwide and 10 out of 12 regions came out against the regime. The junta met overnight and persuaded Pinochet to accept the result. At the same time, the Chilean ambassador to the United States was invited to the White House and told of the need to abide by the decision of the Chilean people, a point reiterated by the US ambassador in Santiago (Garretón 1980; Sigmund 1993). After 15 years, the dictatorship was drawing to an end.

Chile's dictatorship did not fall at a time of dual sovereignty, but in a period of relative strength with a growing economy and a secure grip on the coercive apparatus. An almost accidental process saw the regime collapse through self-inflicted constitutional defeat. Like many other dictators who believe in their own popularity, Pinochet felt secure in office – he was sure that he would win the plebiscite and that, in turn, the plebiscite would entrench his rule. Again like many before him, Pinochet was wrong. In this sense, the 1988 plebiscite was not the action of an

---

[18] This message was popularized through an extensive marketing campaign, examples of which can be found online: www.youtube.com/watch?v=IFAMpW0hPNY, accessed 3 October 2018.

embattled regime. What followed was a legal transition, not an extra-constitutional revolution. During the plebiscite campaign, opposition groups demonstrated considerable bravery and political acumen. Their victory was very much against the odds. But even popular mobilization, followed by a landslide victory in the 1989 elections, failed to give Concertación a free hand. Rather than seeking to overturn the system as a whole, the opposition accepted substantial parameters of the regime's system of rule. Economically, the opposition broadly maintained the policies of the regime, albeit with an increased emphasis on redistribution. In the field of symbolic relations, they persuaded Chileans that there could be an end to repression without a descent into anarchy. Politically, by proceeding through a series of pacts with the country's main power brokers, Concertación guaranteed the maintenance of order and, to some extent, safeguarded the position of incumbent elites. After 1988, Chile became a partial democracy, one in which the hands of the opposition were 'atado y bien atado' (well and truly tied up) (Roberts 1998; Cooper 2001; Loveman 2001; Lawson 2004: ch. 5). Precisely because Chile's dictatorship did not end through revolutionary mobilization, it took an entire generation to undo core aspects of Pinochet's legacy and construct a fully democratic order (Richard 2018).[19]

The Utility – and Limits – of Ideal-Types

The two illustrations outlined in this chapter demonstrate the utility – and the limits – of the ideal-typical anatomies of revolutionary situations outlined in Chapter 3. On the one hand, these analytical constructs have stood as a means by which to examine both the emergence and avoidance of revolutionary situations. On the other hand, these constructs have, on their own, proved to be inadequate. They have delivered neither indispensable conditions, nor have they served to display the essential attributes of revolutionary situations. Rather, causal configurations have been shown to be approximations, drawn from particular sequences of historical events, which fail to completely capture the singularity of concrete instances of revolutionary crisis.

However, the analytical narratives outlined above have also helped to yield commonalities between apparently distinct revolutionary processes. By examining the relationships between events and the fields of practice

---

[19] One example of this is the ongoing attempt to try agents involved in Operation Condor, a transnational counterinsurgency network that operated in several South American states, including Chile, from 1975 to 1981. Operation Condor oversaw the murder, disappearance, and torture of thousands of activists.

within which they take place, and by ordering these sequences into analytical narratives, it is clear that some causal configurations are robust
across dissimilar settings. First, inter-social relations, ranging from the
push of more 'advanced' polities (France and the Dutch Republic) in
seventeenth-century England to shifting relations between Chile and
the United States, have served as the overarching field of revolutionary
situations, providing critical antecedents for the articulation of revolutionary sentiments. Second, English patrimonialism proved to be more
vulnerable than the Chilean blend of sultanism, neo-patrimonialism, and
authoritarianism, largely because of the loyalty of Chile's coercive apparatus to the regime. Third, the role of an opposition has been shown to
be less important than the type of regime within which this opposition
operates. Those who fought against the Stuarts and Pinochet were cour-
ageous and committed. But they could not hope to win absent a range
of more important factors: an opening in inter-social relations, elite fracture, a split in the coercive apparatus, and a systemic crisis. Although
one or more of these conditions transpire from time to time, it is a rare
occurrence that sees them all appear together as a single conjuncture.
This helps to explain why full-blown revolutionary situations are rare.
It also points to the need to see revolutionary situations both as contextually located events that contain situated logics *and* as idealized
constructs with causal pathways that contain wider analytical purchase.
This point is further exemplified through a discussion of revolutionary
trajectories.

5   Revolutionary Trajectories
Cuba and South Africa

Revolutionary Trajectories

This chapter examines the revolutionary trajectories of two quite different episodes: the Cuban Revolution and the struggle to end apartheid in South Africa. The Cuban case is the exemplar case of revolution being made in unpromising circumstances through a concerted armed struggle. The ending of apartheid illustrates how radical transformations can take place through negotiation rather than a fight to the finish.

Discussion consists of an analytical narrative oriented around two causal configurations. First is the ability of a state elite to remain united and maintain the loyalty of the coercive apparatus as the revolution develops. In Cuba, support for Fulgencio Batista eroded during the mid-to-late 1950s to such an extent that, by mid 1958, former loyalists were seeking his overthrow and substantial numbers of troops were refusing to fight. In South Africa, by contrast, although there were splits within the apartheid state, these did not pose an existential threat to the regime. Similarly, although opposition groups mounted a full-spectrum assault on the apartheid state, from civil disobedience to force of arms, at no point did they threaten the primacy of the state's coercive apparatus. The second causal configuration is the capacity of the opposition to generate a coherent revolutionary movement through effective leadership and social technologies. Both Cuba and South Africa boasted high-quality leadership and wide-ranging revolutionary coalitions, which had developed over decades of mobilization. Both also legitimized their struggle through vibrant melds of local–transnational stories, songs, and symbols, from the beards and combat fatigues of Cuba's guerrillas to the *toyi-toyi* dances of the townships and the black, green, and gold of the African National Congress (ANC) flag. Yet, while Cuba's revolution ended in a dramatic social transformation, South Africa's outcome was more circumscribed. The contrast between the two cases, whether of time and place or in terms of their sequence of events, tells us much about the causal configurations that lie at the heart of revolutionary trajectories.

Cuba

On 25 November 1956, 82 revolutionaries set out from Tuxpan in Mexico on board a yacht, the *Granma*, intending to sail over 1,000 miles across the Gulf of Mexico to Cuba. Their intention was to overthrow the government of General Fulgencio Batista. The group planned to coincide their landing with an uprising in the southern city of Santiago. However, bad weather delayed their arrival. By the time they landed, the uprising in Santiago had been defeated and their position had been given away. Popular legend has it that just 12 people (the actual number was almost certainly higher), including Fidel Castro, Raúl Castro, Che Guevara, and Camilo Cienfuegos survived and regrouped in the nearby Sierra Maestra mountains. Over the next two years, this small band of revolutionaries, part of a wider coalition of urban insurgents and exile groups, forged the most unlikely of revolutions. When Batista fled Cuba, on New Year's Day 1959, the state faced no endemic crisis – it had not experienced, let alone lost, a recent war, nor was it suffering a pronounced economic downturn. Cuba was a largely urban, middle-income country that ranked in the top five states in Latin America across a range of social indices, from life expectancy to infant mortality (Dunn 1972: 199). Next to Batista's 40,000-strong military, armed with bombers, tanks, and helicopters, the guerrillas in the Sierra Maestra could muster only 2,000–3,000 *rebeldes* (rebels), many of whom had joined only in the final months of the conflict, and most of whom were lightly armed. Yet, in 1959, Cuba experienced the first successful socialist revolution in the Americas. Sixty years later, it remains a socialist state.

So what happened? First, support for the regime was not as strong as it appeared. In 1958, under pressure from domestic audiences alarmed by Batista's repression and corruption, and influenced by positive reports of Cuba's 'freedom fighters', the Eisenhower administration halted arms shipments to Batista. Given the long shadow held by the United States over many aspects of Cuban life, the weakening of US support was a major shift in inter-social relations. Second, although Batista's coercive apparatus was large, loyalty to him was thin on the ground, both amongst an officer class that had faced repeated purges and a rank-and-file that had little affection for a distant dictator who appeared to be primarily concerned with enriching himself and his coterie. Third, if the guerrilla movement was small, it had shown its mettle by surviving for two years against Batista's forces and then advancing from its stronghold in the Sierra Maestra to open multiple fronts. Finally, the broader movement that toppled Batista was genuinely popular – it was a cross-class coalition of urban and rural groups that was embraced, at least initially, by

Cubans from across the political spectrum.[1] Cubans had a long tradition of unruly politics from which to draw. If there was something novel about the 1957–9 struggle, it was that this particular uprising both succeeded in seizing power and, more surprisingly, held onto it. As Fidel put it in a speech in Santiago on 3 January 1959, 'It will not be like 1895 … it will not be like 1933 … We will have no thievery, no treason, no intervention. This time, it is truly the revolution'.[2]

Towards the Revolution

In the late eighteenth century, Cuba was largely a service colony for Spanish fleets carrying bullion from South America to Spain. It had some tobacco farms, cattle ranches, and sugar plantations, but fewer slaves per capita than most other islands in the region (Thomas 2001/ 1971: 23).[3] During the early part of the nineteenth century, Cuba was the only Spanish colony in Latin America that did not experience a successful independence movement. To the contrary, after the revolution in Saint-Domingue at the turn of the century, Cuban elites rallied behind Spanish imperial rule. In Cuba, Saint-Domingue's revolution was seen as a warning – in response, there was a hardening of both slavery and the plantation system (Gott 2005; Ferrer 2014). It was also seen as an opportunity – the Cuban government began a conscious attempt to emulate Saint-Domingue's sugar economy. The expertise of the 30,000 or so refugees from Saint-Domingue who fled to Cuba helped to raise both the quantity and quality of its sugar mills in the first two decades of the nineteenth century. During the same period, coffee production boomed. Increasingly, Cuba was to Spain what Saint-Domingue had been to France – its most important colony.[4]

---

[1] Although a majority of Cubans supported the revolution, a minority did not. This minority has subsequently grown. Since 1959, more than a million Cubans have left the island, some through legal channels, others by more unconventional means. Many have settled in Florida, particularly around Miami, where they have formed a powerful counter-revolutionary lobby.

[2] Available at the Castro speech archive (last accessed 13th September 2018): http://lanic. utexas.edu/project/castro/db/1959/19590103.html.

[3] Cuba's slaves were subject to a different legal regime than that found in the United States and most of the Caribbean: slaves could marry, enjoyed some legal protections, and had more possibilities to buy their freedom (Dunn 1972: 208–9).

[4] Cuba was nearly a US colony. President Jefferson attempted to buy Cuba from Napoleon during the French occupation of Spain. Jefferson's proposal was that the United States would give France a free hand in South America in return for Cuba. Although he was turned down, this was not the end of attempts by US administrations to purchase Cuba; doing so was a persistent theme within US political circles during the nineteenth century.

Independence movements therefore appeared relatively late in Cuba. There were a number of slave revolts during the nineteenth century. But these did not become full insurgencies, mostly because elites, particularly the settler sugar planters (*colonos*), were concerned that a successful slave revolt would bury them (Blackburn 1963: 55). It was only in the second half of the nineteenth century that sustained rebellions challenged Spanish rule. A decade of fighting between 1868 and 1878 killed over 300,000 people, many in Spanish concentration camps, while large areas of sugar and tobacco cultivation were destroyed. Reforms over subsequent years abolished slavery, but left most sources of discrimination in place – in the early 1890s, 90 per cent of sugar remained in the hands of white settlers (Thomas 2001/ 1971: 251). A second war from 1895 to 1898, initially led by the nationalist writer José Martí, was just as destructive and bloody (an estimated 15 per cent of the population were killed), but this time led to Spanish defeat, prompted in large measure by US intervention in 1898. After the war, the United States occupied Cuba and, even after Cuba became formally independent in 1902, restricted Cuban sovereignty. Under the Platt Amendment, the United States maintained a right of intervention in Cuba, a right that was taken up several times during the first two decades of the twentieth century. Cuba was also forced to cede the naval base at Guantánamo Bay in the south of the island. By 1929, US investments in Cuba represented over a quarter of all US investments in Latin America (Blackburn 1963: 58). By the 1950s, the United States controlled 40 per cent of sugar production, 90 per cent of telephone and electrical services, and 50 per cent of Cuba's railways (Blackburn 1963: 60). If the US ambassador was considered to be the second most important person on the island, the only question was whether this underestimated their importance.

During the first half of the twentieth century, Cuba experienced frequent periods of turbulence. Chief amongst these was the 1933 uprising against the administration of Gerardo Machado, a former cattle rustler turned businessman, who was notorious for corruption, criminality, and repression – a 'tropical Mussolini' (Gott 2005: 130). The revolution was an alliance of students, led by Eduardo Chibás, the clandestine ABC group, led by Joaquín Martínez Sáenz, and non-commissioned officers, who rallied around Fulgencio Batista, a young Mulatto stenographer. The actions of the latter gave the uprising its name: The Sergeants' Revolt. In the aftermath of the uprising, a revolutionary government, ostensibly led by Ramón Grau, a university professor, but in reality dominated by Antonio Guiteras, who represented the radical wing of the protests, embarked on a period of considerable reform: the nationalization of some US interests, the introduction of an eight-hour working day, the granting of autonomy to the University of Havana, and more. But in January 1934, General Batista, with US support, ousted Grau, installing Carlos Mendieta as president and propping up support for his regime by securing agreement from the United States to abrogate the Platt Amendment.

The period 1934–40 saw a number of civilian governments come and go. Behind the scenes, however, things were more stable – Batista pulled the strings and the army emerged as the most significant force in Cuban politics (Gott 2005: 142). Batista constructed a coalition made up of the military, wealthy Cubans, and some leftist groups, most prominent amongst them the Communists and the Confederation of Cuban Workers (Confederación de Trabajadores de Cuba – CTC), which agreed to cooperate with Batista in exchange for formal recognition and higher salaries for workers. In 1940, on the back of a reformist constitution that promised land reform, a rollout of public education, the introduction of a minimum wage, and the establishment of an independent judiciary, Batista won an election to become president. He subsequently governed as a 'pan o palo' ('bread or the stick') president, combining elements of social provisioning with high levels of autocracy.[5] Four years later, Grau returned as president, defeating Batista's favoured candidate, Carlos Saladrigas. Grau claimed to represent the legacy of the 1933 revolution; in reality his presidency represented an 'orgy of theft' as the administration engaged in systematic looting (Thomas 2001/ 1971: 462). In response, a number of opposition action groups were established – shootings, bombings, and assassinations became commonplace. A splinter party, the Ortodoxos, under the leadership of former student activist, Eduardo Chibás, split from Grau's Auténticos, running on a platform of clean government – their symbol was a broom. Chibás, however, lost the 1948 election to Grau's Minister of Labour, Carlos Prío. Bar the odd surface-level reform, little changed under Prío; Cuba remained polarized, corrupt, and violent. In March 1952, Batista again seized power, this time without a shot being fired, claiming that parliament had failed to maintain order and safeguard property. Many Cubans welcomed the restoration of order. However, opposition to Batista, including those willing to take up arms, grew at pace during his period in office. They fed into a broader public distaste for the venality and disorder that had characterized Cuba's parasitic political class for several decades.

---

[5] My thanks to Eric Selbin for this point.

If Cuban governance during the first half of the twentieth century was a story of malfeasance and greed, the country's economy fared little better. The Cuban economy was doubly dependent: first on sugar, second on the United States. The sugar industry employed over a quarter of the workforce, provided 80 per cent of exports, and was responsible for nearly a third of GDP (Pérez-Stable 2012: 1, 3). Over half of the cultivatable land on the island was given over to sugar; at its height, Cuba's share of the world sugar market reached around 50 per cent (Foran 2009: 18). If sugar dominated the Cuban economy, US interests dominated sugar. Cuban sugar enjoyed a duty concession and a fixed, guaranteed quota within the US market in exchange for preferential access for US firms operating in Cuba. Beyond sugar, US corporations contained deep interests in infrastructure and utilities, while American criminal figures ran a number of casinos and hotels in Havana, turning parts of the city into the seediest of playgrounds. By 1958, US companies had over one billion dollars invested in the country, up a third from pre-1952 levels (Foran 2009: 18).

The Cuban and US economies were, therefore, integrated, but unequally so. The result was that the biggest issue facing the island was not poverty, but inequality. Around 0.5 per cent of the population owned one-third of the land, while approximately 8 per cent of farms controlled three-quarters of the available land (Defronzo 2011: 211). In rural areas, rates of illiteracy were four times those found in the cities, while school enrolments ran at half the rate of urban areas; nearly half of Cuba's doctors were located in Havana (Pérez-Stable 2012: 12, 13). In contrast to most urban households, few rural homes had running water or electricity, while a large proportion of rural Cubans were reliant on seasonal work, particularly the short sugar harvest season. Dependence on the United States, and the resentment this provoked, allied to inequalities between rich and poor, and city and countryside, provided the backdrop to the revolution. Cuba's wealthy elite drove around in Cadillacs, while some *campesinos* were forced to eat bark and locusts (Foran 2009: 18). During the 1950s, growth averaged around 1.4 per cent per year, less than the rate of population growth. Even though 1957 represented something of a boom year, standards of living hovered between flat and declining. And all the while, Batista and his supporters were becoming increasingly – and conspicuously – wealthier.

Discussion of the opposition that emerged to Batista during the 1950s is the subject of the next section. For now, it is worth noting that, by the summer of 1957, Cuba was experiencing sustained civil unrest, if something short of a condition of dual sovereignty. All of the country's major cities experienced regular demonstrations, strikes, and explosions.

All were subject to severe police brutality. In the summer of 1958, a major offensive against the guerrillas in the Sierra Maestra failed. Batista's forces were beset with refusals to fight, defections, and, sometimes, mutinies. When the rebels attacked, frequently the army retreated (Domínguez 1998: 130). As a result, the Rebel Army was able to mobilize along several fronts, breaking out of the Sierra Maestra and Sierra Cristal regions of Oriente to central regions, effectively cutting the island in half. Thirty battles were won in ten weeks (Sweig 2002).[6] The red and black flag of the M-26–7 was increasingly publicly displayed, while periodicals such as *Revolución!* and radio stations like Radio Rebeldes carried up-to-date news from, and magnified the success of, rebel victories. In November and December, the Rebel Army made decisive advances as Batista's army all but disintegrated. On 31 December, Santa Clara, one of Cuba's largest cities, was taken. The following day, Batista fled to the Dominican Republic, taking a considerable chunk of his fortune with him. A week later, Fidel Castro, following a triumphant tour of the island, stood at the head of a Rebel Army convoy that swept into Havana.

Elite Unity and the Role of the Coercive Apparatus

Batista's regime combined autocratic-paternalism with high levels of corruption and nepotism – it was a classic 'mafiacracy' (Wickham-Crowley 1992; Domínguez 1998). For large parts of his presidency, Batista operated via a state of emergency – his regime was 'an apparatus of terror and extortion' (Blackburn 1963: 72). Paramilitary groups such as Los Tigres, which operated in Oriente, were given a free hand, while characters like Amadeo Barletta, who had served on Mussolini's military council, held a monopoly on Havana's Cadillac concession. Gangsterism was formalized. The suspension of constitutional guarantees and often high levels of media censorship were allied to overtly violent tactics: intimidation, arrest, torture, and assassination, including that of high-profile figures like Frank País, the most important figure within the opposition's urban underground.

These tactics did much to alienate Cuba's middle class. So too did Batista's theft of state coffers, whether from the national lottery or through bodies such as the Sugar Stabilization Institute, which became vehicles for embezzling funds and rewarding supporters (Pérez-Stable 2012: 61). At the same time, many aspects of Batista's behaviour were both arbitrary, such as the inconsistent ways in which censorship was

---

[6] Crucial to the military advance was the role played by female combatants, particularly the all-woman Mariana Grajales platoon. On this, see: Puebla (2003); Espín et al. (2012).

applied, and irrational, not least his insistence on spending days playing canasta and watching horror films (Domínguez 1998). During the 1940s, Batista's coalition had been institutionalized through agreements with conservatives and communists alike. This time around, Batista's regime was more personalistic and clientelist. Being loyal brought rewards. Those considered to be threats, including many of Cuba's most experienced military officers, were purged. No wonder that Batista's summer offensive against the *rebeldes* in 1958 failed. With elite units kept close to the president in Havana, those sent to fight in the mountains were raw recruits with little by way of operational experience (Brown 2017: 19). They also had little motivation to fight.

The quasi-sultanist nature of Batista's regime meant that it was weakly institutionalized – he had no political party, no social base, and no legitimating ideology (Domínguez 1998). Batista also alienated those who should have been part of his power apparatus, partly through the personalization of rewards, partly through the personalization of punishments. The result was considerable opposition from within the coercive apparatus. In April 1956, a group of officers rebelled. The following year, there was a naval mutiny in Cienfuegos. In 1958, General Francisco Tabernilla, chair of the Joint Chiefs of Staff, held talks with US officials about replacing Batista, while General Eulogio Cantillo, head of operations in Oriente, opened direct talks with Fidel Castro. The March 1958 decision by the Eisenhower administration to stop sending arms shipments to Cuba was crucial to the withering away of the military's morale. In late 1958, US Ambassador Ed Smith began to actively approach alternatives to Batista. Inter-social shifts, elite fracture, and the loss of support from within the coercive apparatus meant that, during 1958, Batista's regime was reduced to little more than a hollow shell. As the rebels advanced, it imploded.

The Revolutionary Movement

If there were many larger-than-life figures within Cuba's revolutionary movement, there is no doubt that its most important figure was Fidel Castro. Fidel's initial politicization was not as a revolutionary, but as a prospective candidate for the Ortodoxo Party in the 1952 elections. When Batista seized power, Fidel turned to more radical options. On 26 July 1953, he led a raid on the Moncada barracks in Santiago, hoping to steal weapons and incite a general uprising. The raid failed and Fidel was imprisoned on the Isle of Pines, where he served a little under two years before being freed in an amnesty. Fidel's trial made him a national figure – his long, powerful defence speech was an early indication of his oratory skills.[7] After his release, Fidel formed the M-26–7 movement, named to commemorate the date of the Moncada raid. Fidel emerged as the leader of the revolution not at once, but gradually, during the course of the struggle. His elevation had less to do with any innate qualities on his part than with his capacity to connect with multiple audiences. Positive reporting, particularly by Herbert Matthews in the *New York Times*, who interviewed Fidel in the Sierra Maestra in early 1957, portrayed Fidel as a patriot fighting a just war against a corrupt, brutal dictatorship.[8] At home, Fidel was widely seen as a nationalist and revolutionary in the Martí mould, an honourable figure who stood for social justice and Cuban self-reliance. Relatively few Cubans saw him as a communist, and he denied this association in several interviews and speeches. Rather, Fidel was a Cuban 'David' standing up to the American 'Goliath' (Gleijeses 2009: 5).

The M-26–7 movement that Fidel led was more of a 'loose amalgam' than a cohesive party (Foran 2009: 19). The movement is usually seen as comprising two main groups: La Sierra (the mountain) and El Llano (the plain), with the former representing the guerrillas of the Sierra Maestra, and the latter representing the urban underground. Classical views, propagated by Cuba's revolutionary elite as well as early histories of the revolution, valorized the former and downplayed the role of the latter (e.g. Huberman and Sweezy 1961; Franqui 1968; Gerassi 1968). This view is more exaggerated than wrong. More often than not, both worked together: the Llano channelled people, money, arms, medicine, and provisions to the Sierra, while the publicity gained by the Sierra helped to legitimate a range of actions by the Llano, including arson, the sabotage of infrastructure, and bombings. There was, no doubt, tensions between the two, particularly after a failed general strike in April 1958. But, for the most part, Sierra and Llano represented two parts of the same revolutionary movement.

If M-26–7 was the central force in Cuba's uprising, it was a long way from constituting the whole of the revolutionary movement. In the cities, particularly Havana, the Student Revolutionary Directorate (Directorio Revolucionario Estudiantil – DRE) played a key role. The DRE favoured armed confrontation; their most direct, if foolhardy, mission was a failed assault on Batista's palace in March 1957. A more secondary role was played by Cuba's communists. On the one hand, the communist party

---

[7] The speech, usually known as 'History will absolve me', is available at: www.marxists.org/history/cuba/archive/castro/1953/10/16.htm, accessed 14 September 2018.
[8] The first of Matthews' articles can be found here: www.nytimes.com/packages/html/books/matthews/matthews022457.pdf, accessed 14 September 2018.

(after 1943, the Popular Socialist Party – PSP) was well-established, and communists had a strong presence within labour organizations, particularly the CTC. On the other hand, many Cubans were anti-communist, while a number of revolutionaries found it difficult to forgive the PSP's opportunism that had seen it cooperate with Cuban regimes going back two decades. It was only in March 1958 that the PSP came out in favour of guerrilla war and the general strike as the twin elements of a 'patriotic united front'. Third, there was the mainstream political parties: the Ortodoxos and the Auténticos, some of whom favoured *politiquería* (politicking), while others were prepared to take up arms. The Society of the Friends of the Republic (SAR), led by the 83-year-old Don Cosme de la Torriente, called for negotiations with Batista in order to restore electoral democracy. For their part, exiled politicos, including Prío and Grau, vacillated over whether to support armed insurrection. Some met with Fidel, sent him money and arms, and offered public support. Others continued to seek a return via electoral politics. Beyond these formal bodies could be found a myriad of civil society groups, some of which formed the Conjunto de Instituciones Cívicas (Joint Civic Institutes), which represented over 200 groups, many of them made up of middle-class professionals (Sweig 2002: 25).

All in all, the anti-coalition mustered against Batista was a plural, heterogenous, decentred movement (Sweig 2002: 9, 15). It was able to foster a consistent pulse of mobilization, from demonstrations and strikes to arson and bombings (Cushion 2016; Guerra 2018). Yet the opposition, plural as it was, united around several common themes: national sovereignty rather than dependence on the United States; clean government (along the lines of the 1940 constitution) rather than Batista's mix of corruption and extra-constitutional despotism; a viable economy that was diversified rather than reliant on sugar; and social justice rather than inequality. Similarly, both the working classes and wealthier Cubans were supportive of many aspects of the revolutionary agenda: diversification of the economy, industrialization, and tax reform (Pérez-Stable 2012: 69). Opposition groups put differences of emphasis aside to issue joint communiqués, most notably the July 1957 Sierra Maestra Manifesto, which called for a united 'civic-revolutionary front' oriented around armed insurrection,[9] and the July 1958 Pact of Caracas, which argued that armed insurrection should go hand in hand with popular mobilization.[10] Over time, M-26-7 assumed the leading role within the

---

[9] Available at: www.latinamericanstudies.org/cuban-rebels/manifesto.htm, accessed 17 September 2018.

[10] Available at: www.latinamericanstudies.org/cuban-rebels/caracas.htm, accessed 17 September 2018.

revolution, in part because of the weaknesses of other groups (Sweig 2002; Gott 2005). The DRE had failed to assassinate Batista, the PSP was tainted by its association with previous regimes, and exiles found it difficult to sustain credibility from outside the country. To some extent, M-26–7 was the only group left standing.

The repertoires deployed by Cuban revolutionaries were, as with other revolutionary groups, a combination of the time-honoured (e.g. strikes, stayaways, work stoppages, sabotage) and the novel (e.g. the *foco*, discussed below). The slogans of the revolution were largely familiar refrains, if no less powerful for this familiarity: 'Patria o Muerte' (Country or Death); 'Cuba Libre' (Free Cuba); 'Venceremos!' (We will win); 'Con Cuba o Contra Cuba' (With or Against Cuba); 'Las Armas, la Unidad, y las Masas' (Weapons, Unity, and Masses) (Castañeda 1993: 61). The terms used for counter-revolutionaries and exiles were stark: *ladrones* (thieves), *gusanos* (worms), *escoria* (scum). In the aftermath of the revolution, large crowds chanted 'al paredón' (to the execution wall) for the 'war criminals', 'imperialists', and 'international oligarchies' who stood in a 'state of siege' against the revolution (Thomas 2001/1971: 851; Brown 2017: 11). Visual points of reference included the green military fatigues worn by Fidel and the other *rebeldes*, and the revolutionary beard, which even became the name of a tongue-in-cheek 'revolutionary' baseball team – Los Barbudos (The Bearded Ones).

The main innovation of the revolution was the *foco*. This was an approach distilled largely from the writings of Che Guevara (1963, 1968; also see Anderson 1997) and, some years after the revolution, the French activist, Régis Debray (1967). The main message of the *foco* was the centrality of struggle itself to making both the revolution and revolutionaries. Put simply, the duty of a revolutionary was to make the revolution (Guevara 1963). As Fidel put it in his Second Declaration of Havana in 1962, revolutionaries should not 'sit in the doorways of their houses waiting for the corpse of imperialism to pass by'. Rather than wait for objective conditions to be ripe, revolution could be made in apparently unpromising circumstances. Instead of forging a revolutionary consciousness gradually through the work of a Leninist-style vanguard party, the guerrilla army served as the immediate crucible of both revolutionary consciousness and revolutionary action (Guevara 1968: 4). In other words, it was not the revolutionary that made the revolution, but the revolution that made the revolutionary. In this understanding, guerrilla war fostered the nucleus of both a people's army and a future revolutionary state: the military and political sides of revolutionary struggle were of one kind. The theory of the *foco* envisaged mobile strategic forces, located in rural areas, which served as clandestine, independent units under conditions of 'constant vigilance, constant mistrust, constant mobility' (Debray 1967: 43). As the revolution developed, insurgents forged connections of solidarity that strengthened commitment to the struggle – the revolution revolutionized the revolution. The *foco* was a 'total war' against the enemy, ranging from ambush to propaganda patrols, which sought to convince *campesinos* to embrace the struggle. The result was an organic alliance of workers, peasants, and intellectuals that, together, constituted a militarized vanguardism. There was to be no waiting and no compromise; the *foco* required immediate armed insurrection.

Both Guevara and, particularly, Debray gave the *foco* more coherence than it had enjoyed during the revolution. And it is fair to say that, wherever the *foco* was exported, it resulted in failure, from Congo to Bolivia. In contrast, when the exporting of Cuba's revolution succeeded, it was either through massive military commitments, such as the 50,000 plus troops sent to Angola in a mission that lasted more than a decade, or humanitarian, as in the hundreds of thousands of teachers, health professionals, and engineers sent by Cuba to states throughout the global south. Nevertheless, for some time after the revolution, the *foco* appeared to stand for a new form of revolutionary practice. The theory and practice of *foquismo* was taken up by groups as diverse as the Weather Underground, the Sandinistas, the Red Army, and Fatah (Prestholdt 2012: 524). This is as good an example as any of the ways in which, as detailed in Chapter 1, the theory and practice of revolution has consistently adapted to novel conditions. It is also a pertinent example of how a revolution is rationalized after the fact as it shifts from the unthinkable to the inevitable.

A Big Revolution in a Small Country

One leading historian of Cuba argues that: 'Cuba's role in the world since 1959 is without precedent' (Gleijeses 2011: 327). It is difficult to argue with this assessment. Regardless of political persuasion, and regardless of judgement about relative success or failure, there is no doubting the radical transformation that has taken place in Cuba over the past 60 years. At minimum, and against all odds, Cuba's revolution has survived. In the short term, the revolutionary regime defeated a counter-revolutionary insurgency in the Escambray mountains, as well as an invasion force of 1,300 exiles funded and trained by the CIA. In the long run, the revolutionary regime has remained in place despite a sustained offensive from the United States: an economic embargo worth billions of dollars in lost revenue, diplomatic isolation, sabotage campaigns, and assassination attempts on Cuban leaders, most notably Fidel Castro, who was reported to have survived over 600 such attempts (Castañeda 1993).

It is easy to forget that, in 1959, the world seemed amenable to Cuba's brand of Third World internationalism (Westad 2007; Byrne 2016). The Cuban Revolution was sandwiched between the French withdrawal from Indochina in 1954 and Algerian independence in 1962. From 1957 to 1962, decolonization saw the emergence of 25 new states. In 1960, OPEC was formed: a symbol of Third World strength and solidarity. The following year saw the emergence of the Non-Aligned Movement (NAM), a grouping that represented over half of the world's population. Underpinning these events was a sense that imperialism, racism, and underdevelopment were shared problems that required shared, revolutionary solutions. The Cuban Revolution symbolized this moment of global southern insurrection, when the revolutionary imaginary shifted from the industrialized first world to the insurgent 'Third World', when the revolutionary agent changed from the proletariat to the peasant, and when the vanguard party was transformed into the vanguard guerrilla. No wonder that the United States acted as it did. If the Cuban Revolution was not overturned, so the argument went, other states were bound to follow. Yet the world failed to turn. Bar Salvador Allende's brief period in office in Chile in the early 1970s, only the Sandinista Revolution in Nicaragua in 1979 and the Bolivarian Revolution ushered in during the early years of the twenty-first century by Hugo Chavez in Venezuela offered the Cuban regime much in the way of revolutionary solidarity. At home, the regime stumbled, but survived, a number of existential moments: the immediate period of post-revolutionary consolidation and contestation, which ended with the 1962 missile crisis that nearly led to thermonuclear war (an option favoured by Castro), and the collapse of much of the socialist bloc between 1989 and 1991, which induced the so-called 'Special Period' of austerity.

In retrospect, the US counter-revolutionary strategy, a full-spectrum programme that ranged from propaganda campaigns to paramilitary training, stands as a testament of counter-revolutionary excess, not just as an attempt to generate regime change in Cuba, which it has self-evidently failed to do, but also in terms of its underlying rationale (Gleijeses 2009). US concern about the spread of a Cuban-style revolution brought with it alliances with a range of unpalatable dictators. In this sense, Cuba sparked not a revolutionary wave, but a counter-revolutionary wave. There were only four dictatorships in Latin America at the time of the Cuban Revolution (Nicaragua, the Dominican Republic, Haiti, and Paraguay); only Colombia and Venezuela had escaped military rule by the end of the Cold War (Brown 2017: 453). As the previous chapter showed, the United States often favoured the apparent stability offered by authoritarianism over a democratically elected left-wing government. If the history of counter-revolution prompted by the Cuban Revolution is not a happy one, the challenge represented by the revolution remains profound. It remains the quintessential instance of a big revolution in a small country.[11]

South Africa

The struggle against racial domination in apartheid South Africa took many forms: an initial movement for political rights developed into a widescale demand for civil rights in the post-Second World War period, diversifying into a still broader struggle that incorporated mass action, international diplomacy, and armed resistance. By the end of the 1980s, increasing international pressure on the apartheid regime, domestic unrest, high levels of political violence, and economic stagnation combined with a facilitative international environment to generate a systemic crisis in the country. Out of positions of mutual weakness, combatants on both sides turned to negotiation. Several years of negotiations between state leaders and former revolutionaries led eventually, although by no means inevitably, to South Africa's first fully democratic elections in April 1994.

The Long Walk

The politics of racial domination in South Africa have a long history (Guelke 2005: 3–4, 24–5; also see Rich 1996). South Africa's colonial experience was bound up with racial discrimination and separate development. Formal urban segregation by race began as early as 1834, in the aftermath of the abolition of slavery. After South Africa became a sovereign state in 1910, a raft of legislation institutionalized this experience: in 1911, the Mines and Works Act imposed a colour bar in the workplace; the Native Land Act of 1913 restricted black ownership of land to designated reserves; in 1923, the Natives Urban Areas Act introduced residential segregation in cities; and the Native Administration Act of 1927 brought in separate political structures for blacks and whites. But it was not until the election of the National Party government led by

---

[11] This expression was used by Fidel to describe the 1979 revolution carried out by the New Jewel Movement in Grenada. The revolution in Grenada was overturned by a US intervention during a period of civil unrest in 1983. For more on this, see Selbin (2009).

D. F. Malan in 1948 that racial policies took on a cohesive form. The Malan administration's doctrine of 'apartheid' (separateness) sought to make race 'relevant to every sphere of life' (Hendrik Verwoerd, Minister of Native Affairs, in Westad 2007: 208). The Population Registration Act divided South Africans into four categories – 'white', 'coloured', 'Asiatic' and 'native';[12] the Group Areas Act decreed that all residential areas should be made separate with non-whites forced, if necessary, to relocate into racially designated areas; public amenities such as restaurants, cinemas, and hotels were required to keep races apart. In 1950, the Malan government's Suppression of Communism Act banned the South African Community Party (SACP) and listed racial equality as a 'communist doctrine'. From then on, the *swart gevaar* (black peril) was equated to the *rooi gevaar* (red peril). Advocating racial equality became the equivalent of being pro-communist.

If apartheid built upon a well-established set of practices and attitudes, opposition to racial stratification had an equally long history, reaching back into the late nineteenth and early twentieth centuries. Originally formed in the early twentieth century, by 1948, the African National Congress (ANC) was the predominant opposition movement in South Africa. The launch of the 1949 Programme of Action and the 1952 Defiance Campaign further raised the ANC's status and capabilities, demonstrating the movement's capacity to generate and guide protest on a large scale. The ANC used tried and tested methods of mass action (boycotts, stay-at-homes, strikes, etc.), while urging supporters to disobey curfew restrictions and refuse to carry passes. However, protests only served to harden state oppression. Most of the opposition leadership was put on trial for treason in a case that ran for five years. Although unsuccessful in terms of securing prosecutions, the Treason Trial quietened influential opposition voices for the duration of the hearings. In 1959, the government began the first steps to establishing so-called 'independent homelands' for blacks and, the following year, declared that membership of political parties should be restricted to one race.[13] In 1960, police in Sharpeville killed 69 unarmed protestors, many of them shot in the back

---

[12] These categories were set up to discriminate between: Afrikaners and other descendants of European settlers (white); the descendants of indentured labourers from the Indian sub-continent (Asiatic, then Indian); people of 'mixed race' (coloured); and South Africa's indigenous communities (native, later Bantu, then black).

[13] The government envisaged 'independent' black homelands for each 'ethnic tribe' in South Africa. The first of these to begin the path to independence was Transkei, which became self-governing in 1963. By the end of 1972, eight homelands were self-governing entities. Transkei became an 'independent republic' in 1976, followed by Bophuthatswana in 1977, Venda in 1979, and Ciskei in 1981.

as they tried to flee. A further wave of repressive legislation gave the police powers of detention without charge and banned both the ANC and the Pan-African Congress (PAC), an Africanist organization that emerged after some ANC members broke away from the organization, in part because of the presence of non-black members.

In response, both of the main opposition groups set up armed wings: Umkhonto we Sizwe (MK) for the ANC; Poqo (later the Azanian People's Liberation Army – APLA) representing the PAC. A number of ANC and PAC leaders escaped to exile in Zambia and Tanzania. The APLA's policy was straightforward: 'One settler, one bullet'. For their part, MK units took part in joint campaigns with the Zimbabwe African People's Union (ZAPU) and their armed wing, the Zimbabwean People's Revolutionary Army (ZIPRA) in Rhodesia – the Wankie and Sipolilo campaigns – in 1967–8. MK also used its underground networks to run sabotage campaigns within South Africa, primarily targeting transport, communications, and industrial facilities, less as a means of confronting the apartheid state than in order to increase the costs of apartheid and spread 'armed propaganda' (Seekings 2000: 8; Lodge 2011: 215). The external wing of the ANC, based initially in Lusaka, assumed broad control of the liberation movement: diplomats lobbied key states and multilateral organizations; the Soviet Union and East Germany supplied military training, arms, and funds;[14] African states from Algeria to Mozambique provided ideological and logistical support. Camps to train revolutionaries were set up in the 'Frontline States' around South Africa (Angola, Botswana, Mozambique, Tanzania, Zambia, and Zimbabwe), drawing national defence forces deep into regional conflicts.

During the 1970s, South Africa's economy began to stutter. Faced with a global downturn as a result of the 1973 oil crisis, opposition militancy at home, and a wave of liberation struggles on its borders, the South African state again cracked down on dissent. In 1976, police opened fire on children in Soweto protesting against legislation demanding that half pupils' instruction be conducted in Afrikaans. Protest spread around the country; hundreds of people were killed. The government was further weakened by a corruption scandal in the Department of Information that led to the resignation of several leading figures, including the Prime Minister, John Vorster. Vorster's successor, P. W. Botha, announced

---

[14] After 1956, the Soviet Union recognized the ANC as the only legitimate liberation movement in South Africa. The Soviets preferred the ANC to the SACP because they saw the latter as independently oriented Euro-communists, and also as too white to be able to mobilize and sustain grassroots support (Westad 2007: 216).

that white South Africans must 'adapt or die'. Botha promised both to reform apartheid and crackdown on dissent: a hearts-and-minds campaign backed up with an iron fist. Botha's 'total strategy' included the removal of many symbolic aspects of apartheid: public amenities in large cities were no longer obliged to be segregated; the Mixed Marriages Act was repealed; some private schools became multi-racial; pass laws were abolished; some moves were made to reduce the policy of job reservation for whites and formally recognize black trade unions. Botha also restructured the political system, introducing a tricameral constitution that established distinct parliamentary bodies for whites, Indians, and Coloureds. Black South Africans were excluded from proposals as, ostensibly, the Black Local Authorities Act already gave power over their own affairs to township community councils. Neither black-run municipal councils nor the new parliamentary assemblies for Indians and Coloureds carried any legitimacy with the wider public: only 13 per cent of Indians and 18 per cent of Coloureds voted in the 1983 elections, while just 12 per cent of black South Africans turned out to vote in municipal council elections held the same year.

The other side to Botha's 'reform apartheid' was a significantly increased role for the security apparatus to combat what Botha described as the 'total communist onslaught' waged by forces both inside and outside the country (Guelke 2005: 10). In the late 1970s, 'Third World' socialism appeared to be in the ascendancy. Successful revolutions in Vietnam, Ethiopia, Yemen, Afghanistan, and Nicaragua spoke to a new confidence within leftist movements. In 1980, Robert Mugabe, a self-declared communist, came to power in Zimbabwe. At the time of the death of Soviet leader Leonid Brezhnev in 1982, the Soviet network stretched to 31 component states: states run by Soviet clients (e.g. Cuba and Vietnam); states oriented towards socialism (e.g. Ethiopia and Nicaragua); independent communist states (e.g. China and the Democratic People's Republic of Korea); a group of what the Soviets considered to be 'less advanced states of socialist orientation' (e.g. Algeria and Iraq); and several more marginal cases (e.g. Ghana and Surinam) (Halliday 2010: 118–19). In South Africa, there was a major expansion in leftist activism. Between 1976 and 1981, there were over 100 attacks and explosions organized by opposition groups, including bombs at three oil-from-coal refineries. In response, a new National Security Management System was set up. At its pinnacle was a State Security Council responsible for formulating policy and advising the cabinet on all matters relating to state security. The system was an interlocking web that spread throughout the country via 11 regional Joint Management Centres (JMCs), 60 sub-JMCs, and 350 mini-JMCs.

Reform apartheid did little, however, to combat the deep-rooted structural weaknesses facing South Africa's economy, ranging from a relatively low consumer base as a result of the exclusion of non-whites from the marketplace to the lack of skilled and semi-skilled workers because of decades of job reservation for whites. The weaknesses of 'racial Fordism' were deepened by the costs of administering the apartheid bureaucracy, which meant maintaining multiple departments of health, welfare, education, and finance (Nattrass 2013: 69). In August 1985, a much-trailed speech by Botha seemed to dispel any hopes of further reforms as he refused to 'take the road to abdication and suicide', railing against the 'barbaric agitators' who sought to overturn apartheid (in Guelke 2005: 106). As a result, Chase Manhattan Bank declined to roll over short-term loans. As the vast majority (around 85 per cent) of government loans were due to be repaid within a year, any run on them posed a significant threat to an already unsound economy. Other banks followed suit: $400 million was withdrawn from the country in August 1985 alone. The rand lost 60 per cent of its value, and currency dealing was temporarily suspended. Capital flight worsened as big business, along with leading pension and investment funds, pulled out of the country.

In January 1989, Botha suffered a stroke. F. W. de Klerk won an election to become leader of the National Party and, therefore, president. De Klerk's right-wing credentials seemed impeccable. His father, Jan de Klerk, had been a cabinet minister under Hendrik Verwoerd and president of the Senate. His uncle was the former president J. G. Strydom, 'the lion of the North', a man dedicated to *baaskap* – white mastery. But De Klerk understood that apartheid as a system was failing. After a series of minor concessions, De Klerk secured the agreement of his cabinet for more far-reaching steps at a two-day *bosberaad* (bush conference) in December. Two months later, on 2 February 1990, he announced that 'the time for negotiation had come'. De Klerk revoked the ban on the ANC, the PAC, and the SACP, eased emergency regulations, abolished media restrictions, and announced the release of a number of political prisoners, including Nelson Mandela. He also began to dismantle Botha's National Security Management System and gave permission for protest marches to take place.

In truth, the government had little choice. By the end of the 1980s, South Africa faced a mounting crisis. The decade as a whole had seen a significant upsurge in opposition activity. In 1983, a new coalition, the United Democratic Front (UDF) was formed, initially as a multi-racial forum to protest against the tricameral constitution (Seekings 2000; Van Kessel 2000). The UDF formed part of a parallel people power structure, including courts, civics (community organizations), and media outlets (Suttner 2012: 732). The Mass Democratic Movement (MDM) incorporated around 700 civics, students, youth and women's organizations, religious bodies, trade unions, and professional associations. At the same time, rising unemployment heralded a wave of labour militancy, spearheaded after 1985 by the Congress of South African Trade Unions (COSATU). In 1985, COSATU announced that the political and labour struggles were 'inseparable' (Lodge 2011: 221). Between 1985 and 1990, COSATU membership more than doubled, reaching around a million members (Schock 2005: 65). Over 200,000 days were lost because of non-cooperation. Labour mobilization was part of a general climate of militancy. In 1984, violence in the Vaal Triangle near Johannesburg erupted into mass demonstrations. The government called in the military to quash the unrest – the first time they had done so in over two decades (Lodge 2011: 216). Oliver Tambo, president of the ANC, called for South Africa to be rendered 'ungovernable'. The government announced a partial state of emergency in July 1985, extending this over the whole country in June 1986. Over the next three years, approximately 5,000 people were killed in political violence, while tens of thousands were detained under emergency regulations. Several hundred attacks were made on police and military targets; teargas, explosions, fire-bombs, and 'necklacing' became everyday components of life in black South Africa.[15] To all intents and purposes, South Africa was in a condition of dual sovereignty.

South Africa's crisis was given its final momentum by the collapse of communism in Eastern and Central Europe. Between 1987 and 1989, Soviet advisers encouraged the ANC to move towards a political settlement rather than continue the armed struggle. By this point, the armed struggle had become a symbol of resistance rather than an existential threat to the apartheid state. Frontline States, with the exception of Zimbabwe, had stopped allowing the ANC to use their countries as transit points for the movement of weapons and guerrillas. The 1989 revolutions in Eastern and Central Europe marked the end of Soviet bankrolling for the ANC, as well as Moscow training for MK operatives. They also stripped the last vestiges of legitimacy from an apartheid state that had long claimed to be a bastion against communism. The winding down of the Cold War altered the strategic interests of the United States.

---

[15] Necklacing, placing a car tyre filled with petrol around someone's neck and setting it alight, was used by ANC activists to discipline suspected informants. Necklacing represented one of the ways in which, as Raymond Suttner (2012: 733) observes, 'the difference between activism and gangsterism became blurred'. For more on this, see Manganyi and Du Toit (1990).

Backing, or what US Assistant Secretary of State for African Affairs Chester Crocker called 'constructive engagement' with white-run South Africa, could no longer be justified through anti-communist rubric. Neither the government nor the ANC could win an outright victory, and international actors were no longer willing to pay for, or prop up, their clients. For all parties, negotiations promised a way out of what Chris Landsberg (2001: 197) calls 'armed equilibrium'.

Negotiations

The government's principal demand was for a new constitution to be drafted by a convention representing all of South Africa's minority groups. The government rejected what De Klerk called 'simple majority rule', arguing that the new constitution should be drawn up along conso-ciational principles, safeguarding group rights and allowing for a minority veto on important issues. The government believed that, through an alliance with the Zulu Chief Mangosuthu Buthelezi and other groups hostile to the ANC, they could isolate the ANC and preserve their hold on institutional levers of power. The ANC, particularly its caucus of SACP members, was considered to have been severely weakened by the removal of Soviet support.[16] Many government advisers felt that ideological and generational cleavages within the ANC could be exploited. The government therefore moved quickly to control the agenda. In 1990, the legis-lative pillars of apartheid were repealed, the homelands programme was abandoned, and the National Party was opened to people of all races. Later that year, De Klerk made a visit to Soweto, where he was warmly received. Such steps also generated international rewards – on a foreign tour, De Klerk was fêted as the man who had single-handedly abolished apartheid. Initially, at least, it appeared like the government was control-ling the pace, flow, and direction of change.

For their part, the ANC, much concerned over the 'balance of forces' within the country, accepted the need for 'consensus' and a 'two-stage strategy', which would see the movement negotiate a transfer of power in the first instance, followed by a programme of radical reform once

---

[16] As an assessment, this made a lot of sense. After 1989, South Africa quickly became a non-issue for the Soviet Union. Although the ANC proposed that Nelson Mandela visit the Soviet Union on his first foreign trip following his release from jail, the Soviets refused, not wanting to jeopardize their relationship with the National Party. Instead, Soviet Foreign Minister Edward Shevardnadze met F. W. de Klerk and South Africa's Foreign Minister, Pik Botha, in March 1990 to secure much-needed credits, loans, and investments. In contrast, the Soviets (after 1991, the Russian Federation) refused to offer any support to the ANC up to and including the 1994 elections.

in office. In May 1990, the ANC signed an agreement with the government – the Groote Schuur Minutes – that secured the release of political prisoners, the return of exiles, and several amendments to security legislation. In August, the movement unilaterally suspended the armed struggle. But it was not easy to transform the ANC from a liberation movement into a political party (Suttner 2012). The ANC had to restructure its internal systems and develop a party line on the nature of negotiations, as well as the future shape of the country. Nelson Mandela was elected president and Cyril Ramaphosa, leader of the National Union of Mineworkers, became Secretary General. Mandela travelled to the annual Davos meeting in early 1991, where he was advised by Li Peng, the Chinese premier, to embrace economic liberalization (Nattrass 2013: 64). In September 1991, a National Peace Accord was signed, paving the way for multi-party talks.

The first Conference for a Democratic South Africa (CODESA 1) was held at the World Trade Centre in Johannesburg in December 1991. Proceedings got underway with a confrontation between De Klerk and Mandela after the president publicly accused the ANC of reneging on a deal to disband MK. Despite the turbulent start, a Declaration of Intent was agreed by all parties – that South Africa should be undivided and undergo peaceful constitutional change to multi-party democracy featuring universal suffrage, the separation of powers, and a codified bill of rights. Five working groups were set up. The first, on freeing the political process and establishing the conditions for free and fair elections, made little progress. The second, on the future political shape of South Africa, fared even worse. The government wanted major decisions in parliament to require 75 per cent of MPs' support, to institutionalize power sharing through mechanisms like a rotating presidency, and to set up an upper chamber representing provinces and minority groups with the power to veto legislation. The ANC, by contrast, sought a quick move to free elections with MPs responsible for drafting a new constitution and forming a government. Although the third and fourth working groups on the nature and role of transitional arrangements and the future of homeland states were both largely successful, their work meant little next to the ruptures that emerged from the first two groups. The final working group, convened to approve time frames for the transition, hardly met at all because so little had been agreed. In the end, CODESA collapsed with all parties blaming the others for its failure.

In May 1992, the ANC conference, dominated by radicals, called for a 'Leipzig option' of rolling mass action in order to prompt the collapse of the government. Senior officials agreed out of a need both to repair links with grassroots members and to remind the government of the extent of their popular support. On 16 June, the anniversary of the Soweto uprising, rallies, demonstrations, and stayaways took place around the country. The following day, a group of Zulu hostel-dwellers massacred 45 people in Boipatong. Mandela formally suspended all talks, accusing the government of collusion in the attack and outlining 14 demands that had to be met before negotiations could resume. On 3 August, a general strike saw millions of workers stay away from work. In early September, a march led by Ronnie Kasrils, a former MK Chief of Intelligence, to Bisho, capital of the Ciskei, led to 28 ANC supporters being shot dead by homeland defence forces.

Despite these setbacks, hopes for a peaceful settlement had not been extinguished. First, the government appeared to have secured white South Africans' approval for negotiations. After two by-election defeats to the Conservative Party in November 1991 and February 1992, the government held a referendum in March 1992 asking whether it should proceed with negotiations. Over two-thirds of the white electorate voted yes, shoring up the position of reformers. Second, lines of communication between the ANC and the National Party remained open. Within the National Party, moderates led by Roelf Meyer argued for direct negotiations with the ANC. For three months Meyer met regularly with Cyril Ramaphosa, forging a personal relationship and common set of understandings that formed the basis for talks. Third, international actors helped to keep discussions alive. The UN sent a team of observers to support the transition on the ground. The United States applied pressure on the government to abandon its call for a minority veto.

In September 1992, the ANC made a range of concessions to the government, reducing its 14 demands to three: the release of political prisoners, government policing of hostels, and the prohibition of dangerous weapons, including 'cultural weapons' like Zulu spears. The ANC also agreed to reign in extremists. For their part, the government set up an independent review of police malpractice and carried out a mini-purge of Military Intelligence and the army: 13 generals were retired, and reform of the security forces hurried through. On 26 September, both sides signed a Record of Understanding, committing themselves to future talks. In March 1993, 26 groups reconvened at the World Trade Centre. Although talks ostensibly embraced all parties, big decisions were increasingly taken bilaterally by the ANC and the National Party, together making up what they called a 'sufficient consensus' for agreement. In May 1993, 23 parties signed up to a Declaration of Intent; in November, terms for the interim constitution were concluded, with both the government and the ANC securing important concessions. Four hundred elected MPs were to be responsible for drawing up a new constitution, as the ANC demanded, but the process was to be jointly carried out with a Senate made up of 10 members per province, a concession to the government. Any political party with 80 seats (20 per cent) had the right to a deputy president, and each party with 20 MPs (5 per cent) would have a minister, forming a Government of National Unity that would run for the first term of parliament: five years. Although this was less than the ten years the government had hoped for, it was hardly the rupture with the past the ANC had called for. Cabinet decisions were to be made in a 'consensus seeking spirit', headed by a president elected by the National Assembly. In April 1994, South Africa held its first free and fair elections, and Nelson Mandela became its first post-apartheid president.

Elite Fracture and the Role of the Coercive Apparatus

Between 1999 and 2001, a gruesome story was relayed in court by Wouter Basson, former head of the apartheid government's Chemical and Biological Warfare programme. Basson, on trial for multiple counts of murder, recalled how his remit had included murder, germ warfare, money laundering, and drug trafficking. Basson's testimony was a reminder of the despotic power of the apartheid state. The South African Defence Force (SADF) was made up of over 70,000 personnel. In addition, six homeland armies were trained and staffed by the SADF. The SADF and homeland armies were joined by a militarized police, *kitskonstabels* (special constables), *skietkommandos* (paramilitaries), *impimpis* (informants), and *askaris* (police officers who had once been ANC activists). The result was a powerful coercive apparatus: battle-hardened, well-equipped, and professionally trained. This apparatus used both constitutional sanctions, such as banning and banishment, alongside extra-constitutional techniques, including murder, torture, and rape (Sanders 2006).

South Africa's coercive apparatus was sustained through both domestic counter-insurgency and foreign wars. The apartheid state's aggression abroad was designed to generate a buffer zone between the white-controlled south and the black-run continent to the north. The government occupied South-West Africa (Namibia), administering it as a fifth province and allowing its white voters to be represented in the South African parliament. South African units were first sent to fight the South-West Africa People's Organization (SWAPO) in 1965. This was followed by action against rebels in Rhodesia in 1967–8. Covert military aid was provided to the Portuguese dictatorship to help it fight insurgents in Angola and Mozambique until its overthrow in 1974.

After 1978, Botha's 'total strategy' included intervention in a number of southern African states. Botha authorized military support for Resistencia Nacional Mocambicana (RENAMO) and União Nacional para a Independência Total de Angola (UNITA). Ruth First, a high-profile anti-apartheid campaigner, was assassinated in Maputo in 1982. In 1986, Botswana, Zambia, and Zimbabwe were bombed during a high-profile visit to South Africa by a Commonwealth Eminent Persons Group. The bombing, authorized by Botha and Malan, was a public relations disaster, which led to the imposition of mandatory sanctions by the Commonwealth, including apartheid South Africa's long-time supporter, Great Britain. In 1988, the SADF were fought to a stalemate by a coalition of Cuban, ANC, and MPLA forces at Cuito Cuanavale, prompting the withdrawal of SADF troops from Angola. In March 1990, after years of protracted violence, Namibia attained independence. The country's subsequent peaceful transition to democracy and the victory of SWAPO in elections served as an example of what could be achieved through dialogue.

By 1992, it was clear that South African security forces were complicit in civil unrest, using black-on-black violence as a means of legitimating white rule. Evidence emerged of a secret war being waged against the ANC by units of the security services, including Vlakplaas, a cell run by Eugène de Kock responsible for the murder and torture of hundreds of suspected ANC sympathizers. De Klerk instigated a commission under General Pierre Steyn, chief of the Defence Force, to investigate. Steyn found that the SADF had provided funds, arms, and training covertly to the Inkatha Freedom Party (IFP), and had actively initiated violence between Inkatha and the ANC. A further investigation headed by Judge Richard Goldstone uncovered an edifice of corruption and collusion between the government and Inkatha. Senior politicians, including Magnus Malan, were forced to resign, although De Klerk denied any personal involvement. Mandela refused to believe the president's protestations, publicly denouncing De Klerk as 'a totally different man than we thought' (in Meredith 1994: 37). Both at home and abroad, South Africa's coercive apparatus was being undermined.

The undermining of the coercive apparatus was augmented by elite fracture. The National Party had long been divided into moderates (*verligtes*) and hardliners (*verkramptes*). In 1982, 17 right-wing MPs led by Andries Treurnicht, unhappy with Botha's reforms, left to form the Conservative Party. At the same time, leading moderates in politics, business, and academia called for more radical reforms. In 1986, Pieter de Lange, chairman of the influential Afrikaner Broederbond, announced that 'the greatest risk is not to take any risks'.[17] Later that year, a group of businessmen flew to Lusaka for talks with senior ANC officials. Willie Esterhuyse, a prominent Afrikaner academic, led a delegation to England to meet senior ANC figures like Thabo Mbeki and Jacob Zuma, establishing a group that was to meet many more times over the next three years. Other influential figures in the apartheid regime like Niel Barnard, the head of the National Intelligence Service, also met with ANC officials. Frederick van Zyl Slabbert, former leader of the Progressive Federal Party, arranged a meeting in Dakar between Afrikaner intellectuals and the ANC. Scenario forecasters at major companies invited ANC officials to seminars and briefings, which made the case for negotiations. Behind the backs of hawks like Botha and Malan, what Allister Sparks (1995: 17) describes as a 'roundtable of informal talks' was taking place.

The period of negotiations further undermined both elite unity and the role of the security services. In May 1990, a mass demonstration of over half-a-million people took place at the Voortrekker Monument in Pretoria. Far-right groups like the Afrikaner Weerstandsbeweging (AWB), led by Eugène Terre'Blanche, proudly displayed swastikas and showed off their weapons; banners and slogans promised a race war, claims that were backed up by a spate of bombings and murders, including that of Chris Hani, MK Chief-of-Staff and SACP politburo member. The Afrikaner Volksfront (AVF), an amalgamation of 21 Afrikaner groups led by Constand Viljoen, a former chief of the SADF, opposed all negotiations. In March 1994, Lucas Mangope, leader of the Bophuthatswana homeland, asked Viljoen to help him quell civil unrest. But the AWB got there before Viljoen, careering round the streets in pickup trucks and shooting randomly at black passers-by. Mangope turned on his former allies and ordered homeland defence forces to attack the AWB. The subsequent scenes of violence, including the live execution of AWB members, were relayed around the country. Pik Botha and Mac Maharaj, leading members of the National Party and the ANC respectively, were dispatched by the transitional government to Mmabatho, where they convinced Mangope to step down.

These incidents aided F. W. de Klerk's attempts to dismantle the security state. Under De Klerk, expenditure was reduced from 4.2 per cent to 2.6 per cent, military service was cut from two years to one, and a number

---

[17] The Broederbond was a secret association founded in 1918 whose members were 'devoted to service to the Afrikaner nation'. All prime ministers and the vast majority of cabinet members from 1948 were Broederbond members, as were the heads of Afrikaner universities, churches, corporations, media, industry, etc.

of military bases were closed. In 1991, the government destroyed its nuclear weapons and, in 1993, abandoned its chemical weapons projects. Between 1992 and 1994, attempts were made to depoliticize the police service. The Security Branch was merged with CID to form a new crime-fighting division. An Internal Stability Division was established to deal with political violence. Eleven apartheid-era agencies were moulded into a single South African Police Service (SAPS). In 1994, General Siphiwe Nyanda, former MK Field Commander and Chief of Staff, became Chief of the Defence Force Staff of the newly formed South African National Defence Force, an amalgamation of the SADF and MK. In the years to follow, South Africa's Truth and Reconciliation Commission (TRC) heard applications for amnesty from both former police commissioner, Johan van der Merwe, and Defence Minister Joe Modise, who had served as MK Commander-in-Chief for over two decades. If nothing else, their testimony demonstrated the ways in which a security apparatus deployed in the service of apartheid was being transformed into a post-independence defence force. The ANC could not defeat an apartheid state that rested on a powerful, united coercive apparatus. Indeed, in many ways, South Africa was a 'constitutional police state' – its constitution served to enable rather than constrain the excesses of the security state (Guelke 2005: 106). A crucial part of the destruction of apartheid, both leading up to and during negotiations, was the delegitimating and weakening of this apparatus.

The Revolutionary Movement

If the dismantling of the apartheid security apparatus marked one side of South Africa's negotiated transformation, the transition of the ANC from revolutionary movement to political party represented the other. Like many other radical groups in southern Africa, the ANC was deeply influenced by the Cuban Revolution, in part because of its successful use of asymmetrical warfare, in part because of its transition from a grassroots, nationalist insurgency into a people's war, and in part because of the organic link made by Cuban revolutionaries between its political and military wings (Westad 2007: 208). However, the ANC pursued both armed and unarmed strategies simultaneously. Indeed, the ANC possessed diplomatic networks that were in many ways superior to those of the apartheid state. The ANC maintained offices and headquarters in over 20 countries, while its lobbying of international organizations helped to establish the movement as a government in exile (Schock 2005: 67). Many aspects of this lobbying were successful. In 1973, a UN convention on apartheid first declared the system 'a crime against humanity'; in

1977, an international arms embargo was imposed on South Africa; in 1985, member states were urged to suspend new investments in South Africa and impose sanctions; in 1986, all leading investors in South Africa imposed sanctions ranging from bans on the import of South African steel, iron, coal, textiles, and agricultural products to the withholding of key exports like oil and sensitive computer equipment. Sanctions had a profound impact on the South African economy – the oil embargo alone cost South Africa refineries around $6 billion per year (on the often ingenious ways used by the regime to circumvent sanctions, see Van Vuuren 2017).

As with other revolutionary movements, South Africa's contentious repertories featured a mixture of the time-honoured and the novel. Campaigns included common methods of civil disobedience like consumer and rent boycotts, strikes, and stayaways. Many of these were effective – rent boycotts cost the state millions of rand per month (Schock 2005: 61–2). More innovative were dances like *toyi-toyi*, which blended drills from ANC training camps (themselves learned from ZAPU/ZIPRA) with liberation theology and township routines (Kasrils 1998: 192; Michie and Gamede 2013; Macmillan 2017: 191–2). Major events, such as the funerals of activists, saw thousands of black South Africans *toyi-toyi* their way to police lines where they faced off with the security services. A popular struggle song, 'Ayesaba Amagwala' ('The Cowards are Scared'), included the lines 'aw dubul'ibhunu (shoot the boer), amagwala (the cowards), dubula dubula (shoot shoot)', often later shortened to: 'Kill the Boer, kill the farmer'. Coffins were draped in the ANC flag, while protestors held images of banned figures, such as Mandela, and sang about the virtues of exiled leaders, such as Tambo. As the trumpeter Hugh Masekela put it in the 2002 documentary, *Amandla!*, if popular protests could not hope to defeat apartheid security forces militarily, they could still 'scare the shit out of them'.

The difficulty was that the ANC was split along various axes: between exiles and those who fought apartheid from within South Africa, between self-declared communists and more moderate figures, between those who advocated armed struggle and those who favoured a negotiated solution, and between those who called for unconditional transformation and those who advocated 'sunset clauses' for some apartheid-era practices, personnel, and institutions (for an illustration of these splits, see the debate between Cronin (1992), Jordan (1992), Nzimande (1992), and Slovo (1992) over ANC/SACP strategy during the negotiations). At the same time, the difficulty of converting the ANC from a mass movement geared at revolutionary change to one engaged in secret negotiations was far from straightforward (Suttner 2012: 733). However, the ANC was deeply embedded in civil society, partly because of its close links with community organizations and trade unions, partly because of the underground networks it sustained over many decades (Suttner 2008). In addition, it enjoyed a well-established culture of debate, accountability, and participation (Lodge 2011: 229). This organizational legacy held a number of advantages, amongst them a well-established institutional infrastructure, an engaged membership, and an experienced leadership (Kadivar 2018: 392–4). This meant that the ANC functioned as the central node within the broad opposition coalition that emerged in the 1980s. If the UDF was a decentralized organization with a diverse membership, it was steered, if not controlled, by the ANC.

If leadership within the opposition movement served as a central part of the ANCs status, they also had to convince white South Africans that they could make the move from opposition to government. In 1988, after much internal debate, the ANC took a decisive step in cementing this status by accepting the need for a mixed economy. Previously, the nationalization clause in the ANC's Freedom Charter and the prominent role of the SACP within the movement had allowed opponents to claim that the ANC was a front organization for communists. The acceptance of the need for a mixed economy was a message reiterated by ANC negotiators in meetings with business leaders. At the same time, the 1990 Harare Declaration outlined the ANC's terms for the suspension of the armed struggle and the onset of negotiations: commitment to a united, democratic and non-racial South Africa; universal suffrage; a codified bill of rights; the release of political prisoners; a lifting of the ban on the ANC and other opposition groups; the removal of troops from the townships; an end to the state of emergency; and the repeal of proscriptive legislation. Again, these moves helped to reposition the ANC, particularly for white South Africans, as a government in waiting.

However, the opposition was not completely united. The main barrier to unity came from Chief Buthelezi's Inkatha movement, restructured as a political party – the Inkatha Freedom Party – after 1990. Buthelezi was a former member of the ANC Youth Wing who had been denounced as a 'snake' and a 'puppet' by the movement because of his compliance with the apartheid regime and opposition to sanctions.[18] By 1990, Inkatha had 1.7 million members, and its networks spread beyond its homeland of KwaZulu, most notably to the hostels of the Reef area of the East and West Rand. Tensions between Inkatha and ANC supporters ran

---

[18] In contrast, Buthelezi enjoyed a fine reputation abroad, not least in the UK, where he was championed by Sir Laurens van der Post, an Afrikaner writer (and fantasist) who had the ear of both Margaret Thatcher and Prince Charles.

high. During the 1980s, approximately 3,000 people were killed in political violence in Natal alone. From July 1990 to June 1993, on average 100 people died each month in Natal and nearly 5,000 were killed in Transvaal. In all, around 16,000 people were killed in political violence between Inkatha and ANC supporters from 1990 to 1994, much of it stoked by the security forces (Lodge 2011: 227). On many occasions, violence threatened to derail talks, and the inclusion of the IFP in the 1994 elections was only secured a week ahead of polling day. The central role played by Nelson Mandela in the negotiations once again underlined the centrality of the ANC to the opposition movement. It also heightened the status of the ANC as the pre-eminent political force within South Africa.

From Trajectories to Outcomes

As Asmal et al. (1997: 2) write, 'Apartheid was not ended by military defeat but through sustained resistance and peaceful negotiation'. Unlike Cuba, there was no moment when the revolutionary army swept triumphantly through the capital. The heads of the old regime did not roll, nor were they forced into exile. To the contrary, the TRC offered amnesty for anyone who came forward and made a full disclosure about their role in gross violations of human rights. The post-apartheid South African state was deeply constrained by the settlement it reached with the old regime. For many observers, this dilution of revolutionary aspirations marked a betrayal of the anti-apartheid struggle. Its outcome was not only a failure to meet the maximum condition of revolutionary transformation (the establishment of a new social and legal framework, and the institutionalization of a new political and economic order), but also the minimum criteria (the takeover and establishment of state power).

The status of negotiated transformations like the one in South Africa is discussed in Chapters 6 and 7. For now, it is worth noting two points relating to revolutionary trajectories that emerge from both Cuba and South Africa. First, when it comes to elite unity and the loyalty of the coercive apparatus, neither the Cuban nor South African regimes faced existential defeat, even if in Cuba's case, this was not far from being the case. In South Africa, the apartheid regime, although split in important ways, retained a secure hold on the coercive apparatus. In Cuba, by contrast, Batista faced extensive defections by both officers and rank-and-file. Both countries had seen a significant erosion in the support of their most powerful geopolitical allies. However, if neither state was fully stable, nor were they primed for revolution. Until late 1958, the United States continued to work with Batista in the hope that his regime, or something like it, was salvageable. In South Africa, negotiations were far from sure of generating an agreement. In both cases, revolutionary trajectories conjoined elite fracture to a significant degree of revolutionary agency.

Second, both revolutionary movements were effective bodies that deployed social technologies in creative, innovative ways. However, both were also quite different. In Cuba, the movement was a wide-ranging coalition, albeit one in which M-26-7 guerrillas played the leading role, both symbolically and substantively. The notion of the *foco* in particular, and the ideology of Cuba's revolutionary leaders more generally, were of unflinching commitment to the armed struggle. In many ways, the leading role played by M-26-7 in the revolutionary coalition emerged as a *result* of this commitment. Where others compromised, they remained steadfast, and when other militant movements failed, they not only survived, but thrived. In South Africa, by contrast, the ANC refashioned itself as a moderate, if still leftist, political party – its legitimacy arose, at least in part, from its *abandonment* of the armed struggle. This illustrates a central tension within revolutionary movements, particularly those unable to win military conflicts. On the one hand, these movements need to mobilize as wide a cross-section of the population as possible – much of their strength comes from the power of numbers. On the other hand, revolutionary movements require leadership and coherence, as well as a clear sense of what will happen if they win. In the case of the ANC, its programme had been forged through decades of struggle – it was as far away from a spontaneous movement as it is possible to find. This stands in contrast to many contemporary movements that emerge in response to immediate crisis points: a stolen election, a succession, an uprising in a neighbouring state, etc. These movements, for all their capacity to generate mass mobilizations, often struggle to establish a clear sense of leadership and purpose. The following chapter examines this tension in depth.

6 Revolutionary Outcomes
Iran and Ukraine

Revolutionary Outcomes

Along with China and Cuba, the post-revolutionary history of Iran represents the starting point for analysis of how revolutionary dynamics continue to influence contemporary world politics – the impact of the Iranian Revolution has been central to the development of core strands of contemporary international order. After examining the causal configurations that have shaped revolutionary outcomes in Iran, the chapter turns to the 2004 and 2013–14 uprisings in Ukraine, in which popular impulses towards radical change have been curtailed. If Iran provides a window onto the continuing challenges presented by major social revolutions, Ukraine serves as an indicator of how core aspects of revolutionary anatomies are changing in the contemporary world. This provides a segue to the next chapter, which explores this shifting configuration in more detail.

Analytical narratives of each revolution are followed by examination of three critical causal configurations. First, the production of melded social orders in which novel political, economic, and symbolic fields are embedded alongside established social ties. In Iran, this is exemplified by debates over the relationship between spiritual and temporal sovereignty, as captured by the construction of a specifically *Islamic* Republic, the notion of *velayat-e faqih* (guardianship of the jurist), and the role of the Leader and Supreme Jurist, Assembly of Experts, and Guardian Council. In Ukraine, it is visible in a political system that combines weak democratic institutions with fierce intra-oligarchical competition. Second is the generative capacity of inter-social interactions, whether seen in the ongoing dynamic between Iranian attempts to export its revolution and counter-revolutionary forces seeking to contain it, or in the ways in which Russia and the West have loomed large over Ukrainian protests. Finally, there are the ongoing contestations that lie at the heart of post-revolutionary orders: in Iran, over issues ranging from its nuclear programme to young people's dress sense; in Ukraine, over the extent to which two major mobilizations have yielded anything truly revolutionary.

Iran

Since its revolution in 1979, Iran has been a major force in world politics. In part, Iran's impact derives from its resources: Iran holds 10 per cent of the world's proven oil reserves and 15 per cent of its natural gas reserves. In part, Iran matters because it is a central actor in a region that has experienced decades of turmoil. Finally, analysis of Iran matters because, like many other revolutionary states, it has punched above its weight in international affairs, as witnessed by the multi-faceted challenges it presents to liberal international order, ranging from its alliances with a range of illiberal states to its nuclear programme. For all its bluster, however, the Iranian state exerts only partial control over an animated, unruly public that contests state authority through grassroots activism and via the ballot box. Its development since the revolution has been one of fierce contestation, both between elites, and between elites and publics.

The Revolution

The story of why and how the Iranian Revolution came about is well told elsewhere (e.g. Abrahamian 1982; Halliday 1982; Foran 1993b; Parsa 2000; Keddie 2003; Kurzman 2004a; Harris 2017). The narrative here begins with Mohammad Reza Shah Pahlavi's flight from Iran to Egypt in mid-January 1979, where he waited in the hope that he would be restored to power by the military. Ayatollah Khomeini, a central figure in the opposition to the Shah, returned to the country on 1 February; an estimated three million Iranians took to Tehran's streets to welcome him.[1] Although protests had built up over a 16-month period, the actual period of dual sovereignty lasted less than two weeks. Early February saw the emergence of two parallel governments: the first led by Shahpour Bakhtiar, a member of the moderate opposition who had been appointed by the Shah as prime minister; the second, recognized by Khomeini and the opposition, led by Mehdi Bazargan. The loyalty of the armed

---

[1] The Shah exiled Khomeini in 1964 – he fled first to Turkey before settling in Najaf in Iraq, a major seat of Shi'a learning. Khomeini stayed in Najaf for 13 years. In spending so long outside his home country, Khomeini joined a long list of exiled revolutionaries, including Louverture, Bolívar, Marx, Lenin, Trotsky, Ho Chi Minh, Fanon, Cabral, Castro, and a good many Salafists in the contemporary world.

forces to the former was not assured. During the early part of February, some rank-and-file refused to fire on protestors; others, perhaps as many as 1,000 military personnel a day, deserted (Parsa 2000: 243). Many members of the armed forces openly fraternized with the protestors, who gave them flowers and urged them to stand down. Other sections of the opposition directly engaged forces loyal to the government. On 9 and 10 February, units of the Imperial Army were defeated by a coalition of revolutionary forces and mutinied air-force personnel. Protestors prevented reinforcements from mobilizing and took control of key military bases and police stations, seizing weapons and distributing them widely. On 11 February, the Chiefs of Staff officially announced their neutrality. Revolutionaries occupied government buildings and media outlets; Bakhtiar fled the country. During the revolutionary period as a whole, around 3,000 people were killed, the vast majority of them in the last two months of the revolution (McDaniel 1991: 222).

Once in power, the programme ushered in by the post-revolutionary regime was highly ambitious. In this sense, it sits squarely within the legacy established by the French, Russian, and Chinese revolutions. It also sits within their legacy by virtue of the way in which a cross-class, heterogeneous movement became monopolized by a particular faction. The means through which the faction around Khomeini defeated its opponents was brutal. Some of its opponents were placed under house arrest; others fled or were exiled; many were killed. Iran's revolution was born under the sign of coercion.

Coercion at Home and Abroad   As noted in Chapter 3, revolutions often lead to an increase in a state's despotic capacity, in large degree because the post-revolutionary period is one of considerable tumult as the anti-coalition that generated the revolution fractures and the revolution coalesces around a particular faction. Iran was no exception to this pattern. In 1979, there were violent clashes between Mujahidin-e Khalq (MEK) (The People's Warriors) and Khomeini's Islamic Republican Party (IRP), including bombings and assassinations. The response of Khomeini and his allies was either to establish or retool several coercive bodies: the Islamic Revolutionary Guard Corps (IRGC) (Sepah-e Pasdaran-e Enghelab-e Eslami) and, within the Guard, an elite Quds (Jerusalem) Force; the Sepah-e Basij (Mobilization Army); and Hezbollah (Party of God). These bodies, forged in part because of a distrust of old regime institutions, in part in the midst of intra-elite competition, and in part as a vehicle to direct revolutionary energies, were to be central actors in post-revolutionary Iran (Harris 2017: ch. 3). At the same time, several thousand military officers were purged, including a large number of senior officers and half of all air force pilots (Walt 1996: 239, fn. 35). A number of leading figures within Sazeman-e Ettelaat va Amniyat-e Keshvar (SAVAK), the Shah's secret police, were tried in revolutionary tribunals, and subsequently convicted and executed. SAVAK was formally disbanded, then reconstituted as the Ministry of Intelligence (SAVAMA), with responsibility for ensuring domestic stability. This was a far from straightforward task. In June 1981, an explosion carried out by The People's Warriors caused the death of 74 leading members of the IRP. The response by state forces was severe. Around 2,600 leftists were executed in November 1981 alone; all in all, between 1981 and 1985, around 12,000 Iranians were killed in post-revolutionary violence, a third of whom were students (Walt 1996: 217; Parsa 2000: 106). Not for the last time, those who had been in the vanguard of the revolution became its victims.

The post-revolutionary regime was also militant in its dealings with external foes. In June 1979, Iran refused to recognize the US ambassador designate. In August, the regime cancelled a major arms deal with the United States. These were preludes to a more serious deterioration in US–Iran relations that followed the Shah's arrival in New York for medical treatment in October 1979, which heightened fears of a US-sponsored coup. Even as Prime Minister Bazargan met with the US National Security Advisor, Zbigniew Brzezinski, 450 student militants seized the US embassy where they held 66 officials and demanded that the United States return the Shah to Iran. Having condemned the actions of the hostage takers, Bazargan resigned. The United States responded by freezing Iranian assets, deploying additional military forces in the region and organizing an international embargo of the country. In April 1980, President Carter attempted a rescue of the hostages. Operation Eagle Claw was a disaster. Three out of eight helicopters malfunctioned, leading to the mission being aborted. The remaining 52 hostages (13 African-American hostages were set free in November 1979, along with one unwell individual in July 1980) were released after 444 days of captivity, just minutes after the swearing-in of US President Reagan (Sick 1985; Cottam 1988; Houghton 2001; Beeman 2008; Kamrava 2014).[2]

Even more serious was the invasion of Iran by Iraq in September 1980. Saddam Hussein's invasion, following months of inflammatory rhetoric, represented the breaking of the 1975 Algiers Agreement that had pledged mutual non-interference and agreed on a division of the Shatt al-Arab waterway. Saddam gambled that post-revolutionary Iran

---

[2] In return, Iran secured the release of some of the country's assets and the promise of US help in extraditing the Shah's funds.

was weakened by civil unrest, both from the conflict between leftists and Islamists noted above, and also following uprisings by Kurdish and Azeri minorities. At minimum, Saddam hoped to capture Shatt al-Arab. At maximum, he hoped to incite rebellion amongst the Arab population of the southern Iranian province of Khuzestan which, allied to other sources of domestic turmoil, would prompt the overthrow of the revolutionary regime (Walt 1996: 240). Both assumptions were misplaced. The inhabitants of Khuzestan remained loyal and the regime was able to see off its domestic enemies in a 'rally around the flag' effect sustained by patriotic fervour. The patched-up army, IRGC, and Basij, including volunteers ranging in age from 13 to 65 (Axworthy 2013: 218–19), first forced a stalemate and then launched a counter-offensive.

Just as Saddam thought that an invasion would incite domestic rebellion, so the Iranian regime thought that it could provoke an uprising amongst Iraq's majority Shi'i population. Like Saddam, they were wrong. Although some Iraqi Shi'a did rise up against the Ba'ath regime, nationalism trumped religious solidarity. Many thousands of Shi'i Iraqis were deported, while some of those loyal to Tehran were arrested and executed. Following the Iraqi withdrawal to their pre-invasion border position in May 1982, the war became one of bloody attrition. Both sides carried out extensive air campaigns on the other's cities, while Iraq deployed parts of its chemical arsenal, most infamously against Iranian and Kurdish forces at Halabja. From 1984, the war was extended to the Gulf. A 'tanker war' saw Iran threaten to attack oil shipments from Saudi Arabia and Kuwait, while the United States provided naval escorts for their ships and reflagged many of them as US vessels (Halliday 2005: 181). A series of skirmishes followed between US and Iranian forces. Most seriously, in early July 1988, US forces mistakenly shot down a civilian Iranian airliner. Rather than lead to further escalation, the incident was followed by a ceasefire. With a weak economy (GDP per capita in 1988 was around two-thirds of its 1979 level) and an increasingly war-weary population, Khomeini agreed to end the war, even as he claimed that doing so was 'more deadly than drinking poison' (in Keddie 2003: 259; also see Razoux 2015).

If the war with Iraq was, at least initially, defensive, the revolutionary regime also possessed expansionist tendencies. In the aftermath of the revolution, the regime was quick to display its internationalist aspirations. As Khomeini put it: 'Muslims are one family ... we have no choice but to overthrow all treacherous, corrupt, oppressive, and criminal regimes ... we will try to export our revolution to the world' (in Walt 1996: 214–15). The Iranian regime used the *hajj* as a means of spreading its message and provoked demonstrations in Kuwait, Bahrain, and Saudi Arabia. This provoked a response from a number of its regional rivals, most notably Saudi Arabia. Most notably, the Saudis played a leading role in the creation of the Gulf Cooperation Council (GCC), which was formed as a counter-revolutionary response to Iranian subversion. The animosity between Iran and Saudi Arabia subsequently became one of the central axes of competition and conflict in the region.

Iran's longest lasting, and most successful, revolutionary alliance has been with Lebanon's Hezbollah, which it created and subsequently trained, financed, and armed (Norton 2009). Not only was the Lebanese Hezbollah forged into a fighting force, it was also provided with funds to establish schools, clinics, and hospitals – the foundations of 'social Islam'. In return, Iran gained a Shi'i ally and found a partner willing to carry out terrorist attacks on Iran's behalf. Some of these attacks were highly successful. Most notably, Hezbollah's bombing of a US marine barracks in 1983 led to US withdrawal from Lebanon, an event that acted as a spur to Islamist groups around the region. Beyond Hezbollah, the regime allied with Islamic Jihad and Hamas,[3] as well as regimes in South Yemen and Syria. The latter was Iran's only Arab ally during its war with Iraq. But it was a valuable one, allowing Iran to use its airspace, as well as helping with intelligence, logistics, and training. Since the revolution against Bashar al-Assad in 2011, Iranian support for the Syrian government has been extensive, including the use of the Quds Force, the IRGC, and Hezbollah, and encompassing ground troops, special forces, arms, funds, technical assistance, logistical support, and intelligence (Ansari and Tabrizi 2016: 5). In this way, Iran has forged alliances not just with Shi'i allies such as Hezbollah, but also with Sunni (Hamas) and Alawite (Syria) groups.

Iran's stance has not always been confrontational. Indeed, the post-revolutionary regime has oscillated between a combative, oppositional stance on the one hand, and a reformist, even 'normalizing', position on the other (Saikal 2010: 121; Fawcett 2015: 648). Despite claims of being in the vanguard of a global Islamic revolution, Iran supported the Armenians rather than Shi'i Azeris during their conflict in Nagorno-Karabakh, the Indians rather than the Pakistanis in Kashmir, and secular Chinese communists rather than Muslim insurgents in Xinjiang. During the Iran–Iraq war, Iran received weapons from 41 different countries, including Israel and the United States (Walt 1996: 265, fn. 176). The former, described by Khomeini as a 'cancerous tumour' (in Kamrava 2014: 157), hoped that arms sales would protect Iran's 90,000 Jews

---

[3] Financial support for the latter was halted in July 2015.

and keep two of its regional rivals occupied. For its part, the United States sold arms to the post-revolutionary regime and provided intelligence on Iraqi military deployments in exchange for Iranian help in freeing American hostages in Lebanon. The Iran–Iraq war was not the only example of collaboration between Iran and Western powers. Iran remained neutral during the 1991 Gulf War, and provided both intelligence and logistical support for US forces in Afghanistan in 2001. It also pledged $530 million for Afghani reconstruction in the aftermath of the war (Takeyh 2006: 123). In recent years, Iran has supported Western attempts to curtail the threat of Islamic State. Although Mahmoud Ahmadinejad's confrontational language, including Holocaust denial and a claim that Israel should be 'wiped off the map', stand as the prototypical form of Iranian enmity for Western audiences, foreign policy rhetoric and practice in post-revolutionary Iran is more complex than such caricatures depict, representing a kaleidoscope of views and policies (Ehteshami 2009: 119).

Political Order   The key issue facing post-revolutionary Iran was whether clerical rule was to be temporary or permanent. On 1 April 1979, a referendum on whether Iran should become an Islamic Republic saw 98 per cent of the public vote yes on an 89 per cent turnout. The new constitution that was passed in November 1979 melded a number of influences. The separation of powers between the executive, legislature, and judiciary bore a close resemblance to the constitution of the French Fifth Republic. So too did the stipulation of two-term maximum presidencies and presidential authority over both the prime minister and parliament (*Majlis*). As Akbar Hashemi-Rafsanjani, the first speaker of the post-revolutionary *Majlis*, put it: 'Where in Islamic history do you find a Parliament, President, Prime Minister, and Cabinet of Ministers? In fact, 80% of what we now do has no precedent in Islamic history' (in Abrahamian 1993: 15).

Equally unprecedented was the leading role for clerics stipulated by the constitution. Some of the institutional authority of the clerics arose from popular mandate – members of the Assembly of Experts, for example, were elected rather than appointed. Other aspects of the constitution, however, were 'quasi-absolutist' (Marrat 1993: 95). Two aspects in particular stood out. First was the vesting of the Leader and Supreme Jurist as the single 'source of emulation' (Matin 2013: 137). This gave Khomeini, whom the constitution named as Leader and Supreme Jurist for life, wide-ranging political authority, ranging from serving as Commander in Chief of the Armed Forces to appointing the heads of state media. Article Four of the constitution made clear that the Leader possessed divine authority and was accountable only to God. Interpretations of the role and mandate of the Supreme Jurist have been regular sources of debate – and disquiet – in the post-revolutionary period. The second illustration of the 'juristic-theological' hold over central sites of political authority was the Guardian Council, which was a cross between a Supreme Court and a super-legislature (Marrat 1993: 83, 88). Six members of the Council were religious jurists chosen by Khomeini; six were religious jurists elected by parliament. Either way, the leading position of the jurists was secured. The Guardian Council held extensive powers, including responsibility for screening all legislation (to ensure that it was compatible with Islam and the constitution) and, later on, vetting all candidates for the presidency (to ensure that they would serve the interests of the Islamic Republic). Its vetoes on the former and its disqualifications on the latter have, as with the role and mandate of the Leader, been sources of considerable tension in post-revolutionary Iran.

These tensions were well illustrated by the 1988 constitutional crisis. The crisis began when Khomeini intervened in a standoff between the president, parliament, and Guardian Council over the capacity of the latter to block and reject legislation. Khomeini argued that the needs of the state outweighed those of Islamic law. The result was a strengthening of the position of the executive and legislature, which used the Leader's clarification to argue that political expediency could trump religious authority. A new body was established, the Expediency Discernment Council, in order to arbitrate cases of deadlock between the Majlis and the Guardian Council. Following Khomeini's death in 1989, several constitutional amendments were introduced that sought to further rationalize the system of governance (such as abolishing the role of prime minister) and specify the powers of the Leader (by making clear that the Leader was to have wide knowledge of social and political issues) (Keddie 2003: 261). The latter made it possible for President Khamenei to be appointed as Leader in the aftermath of Khomeini's death.

By the early 1990s, a more pragmatic air had set in – the model for the Rafsanjani administration in the early part of the decade was China: politically autocratic, economically successful, and (within reason) culturally tolerant (Takeyh 2006: 40). Rafsanjani attempted to increase the technical acumen of the regime – only four out of 22 ministers in his administration were clerics (Harris 2012a: 256). If these steps were met with opposition (in 1992, the Guardian Council disqualified a third of the candidates standing for election to the Majlis and, in 1996, disqualified 40 per cent of Majlis candidates), then the election of Mohammad Khatami as president in 1997 promised to accelerate reform. Khatami's programme included deepening representation, fostering civil society, and respecting rights. Khatami promised not only to nurture civil society, but also to moderate foreign policy. The president issued a statement recognizing the sovereignty of Iran's neighbours, including the Gulf States. As part of the president's 'good neighbour policy', Khatami became the first sitting Iranian president to visit Riyadh, where he signed agreements on drug trafficking and money laundering (Takeyh 2006: 69). On a visit to the United States, itself a statement of purpose, Khatami called for a 'dialogue of civilizations'.

Yet neither Khatami's attempt to normalize Iran's foreign relations nor his domestic reforms were successful. Grassroots activism stimulated a conservative backlash: as many newspapers were closed as opened; dissidents who spoke up were attacked, arrested, and in some cases, murdered. The Guardian Council vetoed legislation aimed at reducing gender discrimination. Vested interests ensured that economic reforms were similarly constrained. As moderates either retreated or were forced out of politics, conservatives won municipal elections in 2003 and parliamentary elections in 2004. In 2005, the conservative mayor of Tehran, Mahmoud Ahmadinejad, succeeded Khatami as president. Ahmadinejad oversaw a consolidation of conservative power. His campaign was based on a return to the 'roots of the revolution': self-reliance, self-sufficiency, and social justice (Takeyh 2009: 223). For Ahmadinejad, Iran needed to be saved from the 'betrayal' of Rafsanjani's 'crony capitalism' and the 'decadent reformism' of Khatami (Ansari 2007: 19–20). Forged by grassroots groups from war veterans to Qur'an reading groups, a 'new right' mobilized around the 'victimization' of Iran and the 'betrayal' of the revolution. War veterans were venerated – 'martyrs' were reburied in prominent public places, while the regime sought to mobilize patriotism through the commemoration of 'heroic victories' such as the capture of the al-Faw Peninsula in 1986. Scores of NGOs were shut down and vigilante groups were used to attack student gatherings; thousands of people were arrested. The commander of the IRGC, Yahya Rahim Safavi, went on record to state that 'when I see conspirator cultural currents, I give myself the right to defend the revolution' (in Takeyh 2006: 52).

Yet the emergence of the new right served to heighten factionalism. If the conservative coalition became known as the Principlists (Osoulgarayan),[4] there were many sub-factions within this broad grouping. Ahmadinejad's 'Sweet Scent of Service' was one. Others formed around Mohammad Baqer Qalibaf, the mayor of Tehran,

---

[4] The term Osoulgarayan literally means 'fundamentalist'. However, aware of the connotations this term would have in the West, leading figures in the faction translated the term as Principlists (Harris 2017: 157).

and Ali Larijani, a former nuclear negotiator who had fallen out with Ahmadinejad. These groupings became concerned with reaffirming the supremacy of *velayat-e faqih*. *Velayat-e faqih*, developed in Khomeini's (1970) *Islamic Government*, linked temporal and spiritual sovereignty – the interpretation of Islamic law by suitably qualified jurists served as the basis for rightful state authority. The only legitimate form of government was one that was Islamic, not in the sense of rulership *over* a Muslim society, but in the sense of being governed *by* the *faqih*-approved state in accordance with Islamic legal and behavioural codes. In opposition to the Principlists were Reformists, who argued that God delegated sovereignty to the people, granting them the capacity to choose and form their own government. Reformists sought to move away from the notion – and practice – of a 'religious jurisprudence state' (Takeyh 2006: 47). Between the polarizing visions of the Principlists and Reformists could be found a Pragmatist faction, led by Rafsanjani, who acted as a broker through his roles as Chair of both the Assembly of Experts and the Expediency Council.

The period 2005–9 saw an erosion in public support for the Principlists. In part, this arose from dissatisfaction with the way that Ahmadinejad delivered jobs and sinecures for his cronies. In part, it arose through the eccentric nature of Ahmadinejad's views, which included the conviction that, when the president spoke at the United Nations in 2005, he had been accompanied by an orb that held his audience spellbound. As the 2009 presidential elections approached, Reformists mobilized behind Mir-Hussein Mousavi, a former prime minister. Mousavi's campaign was primarily formulated within rather than against the revolutionary legacy – his main slogan was 'renewal' and he made ample use of the revolutionary slogan: 'Estiqlal, Azadi, Jomhuri-ye Eslami!' (Independence, Freedom, Islamic Republic!). Some aspects of the campaign were more transgressive, such as the use of the colour green in banners, clothing, prayer rugs, and face-paint. However, much was familiar, particularly to those who had observed Khatami's campaign a decade earlier (Harris 2012b: 439–40).

The theft of the 2009 elections by Ahmadinejad, the protests that followed, and the severe repression by the state that followed are discussed below. For now, it is worth noting that the election and its bloody aftermath prompted further factionalism amongst conservatives. On the one hand, Ahmadinejad sought to reaffirm his regime's anti-Western credentials, instituting a programme to ward off 'Westoxication' (*Gharbzadegi*).[5] On

---

[5] The term 'Gharbzadegi' was popularized in 1962 by the writer Jalal al-e Ahmad. By using this term, Ahmadinejad was mobilizing a well-worn trope used to denounce Western immorality and accentuate Iranian victimization.

the other hand, some leading conservatives distanced themselves from the president. For his part, Khamenei began to reposition his office from that of the 'benevolent guide' who was 'above the fray' of everyday political cut-and-thrust to being a more assertive, direct participant in policy-practice (Sadjadpour 2009). Conservative factionalism stood in marked contrast to Reformist unity. In 2013, Reformists gathered around the figure of Hassan Rouhani, a former national security adviser and chief nuclear negotiator. Much of Rouhani's campaign repeated themes that had animated those of earlier reformers: an extension of rights at home; normalization abroad. Rouhani won the election. This time around, there was no repression.

Despite his victory, Rouhani was faced with the same structural constraints that had faced his predecessors: the same Leader and Supreme Jurist, and the same institutionalized forces in the coercive apparatus, the judiciary, and the media (Milani 2015). The Leader remained in command of the armed forces, the Revolutionary Guard Corps, state media, and the judiciary. Given these constraints, it is not surprising that relatively few major reforms have been instituted since Rouhani came to power. A number of leading Reformists, including Mousavi, remain under house arrest. Institutional sites of reform are closely monitored. In many ways, the death of the ultimate revolutionary survivor, Akbar Hashemi-Rafsanjani, in January 2017, marked the end of an era. But in ways that go beyond the scope of any one individual, Iran's post-revolutionary political order is deeply institutionalized; it will not be either reformed or overturned easily. The unyielding force used by the regime against those protesting high food prices and economic hardship in 2018 shows the ongoing despotic capabilities possessed by the post-revolutionary Iranian state.

Economic Order The immediate post-revolutionary period was one of considerable adversity, partly because of extensive capital flight, partly because of the war with Iraq, and partly because of the sanctions regime imposed on Iran in the aftermath of the hostage crisis. The war alone cost an average of $250 million per month, with each offensive requiring an extra $500 million (Moshiri 1991: 132). High unemployment and inflation were met by rationing. Khomeini spoke of the virtues of austerity and renunciation, lowering the material expectations of the population and arguing that the revolution had not been conducted in order to provide the people with 'cheap melons' (Halliday 2003a: 226, fn. 42). But Khomeini also divided society into two main forces: the oppressed (*mostazafin*) and the oppressors (*mostakberi*), arguing that 'Islam belongs to the oppressed, not the oppressors' (in Abrahamian

1993: 31). Khomeini's rhetoric pictured a utopian Islamic society free from want, hunger, and unemployment. The first post-revolutionary constitution promised free primary and secondary education, extensive welfare, and economic development. Despite these promises, between the mid 1970s and mid 1980s, GDP per capita declined by around a third (Moshiri 1991: 131–2). Economic hardship threatened the legitimacy of the regime.

In the early years of the post-revolutionary government, extensive debates took place over the introduction of land reform, labour laws, and the nationalization of banks and insurance companies. The former was particularly contentious. The constitution included provisions to safeguard both the private sector and home ownership. Khomeini himself called for the protection of private property in his Eight-Point Declaration in December 1981. Parliamentary attempts to push through land redistribution were blocked repeatedly by the Guardian Council. Between 1981 and 1987, the Guardian Council vetoed around 100 reform bills covering not just land reform, but also labour legislation, income tax, and the nationalization of foreign trade (Abrahamian 1993: 55). It was not incidental to these vetoes that the *ulema* were conservatively minded on issues of private property and contract law. Nor was it incidental that the regime needed the support of the *bazaari*: the network of merchants and traders that supported a wider ecosystem of craft industries, teahouses, mosques, and schools. Yet the blocking of significant reforms led to considerable antagonism. There were riots against forced evictions and the demolition of shelters. Those working in the informal economy, including thousands of street vendors, complained bitterly of police harassment.

Filling the gap between state and society were the many foundations (*bonyads*) that emerged after 1979: The Imam's Relief Committee, The Construction Crusade, The Foundation of Martyrs, and more. Perhaps most important was the Foundation of the Dispossessed (Bonyad-e Mostazafin), which inherited both the remit and resources of the Shah's vast Pahlavi Foundation. Collectively, these foundations provided the basis for social Islam – they built schools and health clinics, and provided electricity, sanitation, welfare, aid, and networks of support (Bayat 2013: 68). Many of these programmes have been highly successful. So too has been the state's role in rural welfare delivery. In 1978, Iranian life expectancy was 56; in 2015, it was 75.[6] The 2015 literacy rate was 93 per cent; in 1977 it was 32 per cent. Whereas 60 per cent of Iranians did not finish primary school in the mid 1970s, in 2015 half of all young Iranians

---

[6] This figure, like those below, come from data provided by the Iran Data Portal hosted at Princeton University: www.princeton.edu/irandataportal/, accessed 15 March 2019.

went to university. A family planning initiative saw population growth fall from 3.2 per cent in 1989 to 1.2 per cent in 2015; during the same period, the fertility rate dropped from 7 to a little under 2. One of the hallmarks of post-revolutionary Iran has been the centrality of welfare to strategies of institution building, whether this has been carried out by the state or other sites of political authority (Harris 2017).

Alongside the *bonyads* and state institutions that deliver social Islam can be found parastatal organizations, such as the IRGC, which have become vast conglomerates with interests that stretch from telecommunications to energy, and from pension funds to military organizations (Ostovar 2016). They sit within a complex web of state, quasi-state, semi-public, and private bodies, many of which are linked through political offices and personal ties. Given the political clout and wealth of these bodies, it is not surprising that attempts at sustained economic reform have been stymied. At the same time, extensive sanctions, which began after the revolution and were extended both in the 1990s and more recently in response to Iran's nuclear programme, continue to restrict growth.

Symbolic Order   Since 1979, the Islamic state has sought to combine orthodoxy (correct belief and rituals) with orthopraxy (correct conduct) (Halliday 2003a). The result has been an attempt to 'Islamicize' Iranian society. The earliest indication of this was the 1979 Cultural Revolution, which saw streets renamed and towns revert to their pre-Pahlavi designations. Ties were discouraged for men and, in 1981, all women were required to wear 'Islamic Dress' in public. The state assumed control of print media, radio, and television. Universities were closed on the grounds that they were dens of vice, immorality, and depravity (i.e. Western thought). When they reopened three years later, they were placed under close supervision; over half of the country's professors lost their jobs in the five years following the revolution (Moaddel 1993: 265). The school system was also Islamicized – new textbooks were introduced and gender segregation enforced. Western films, music, and writing were banned. Several thousand Islamic associations were established in villages where they worked with the *bonyads* to Islamicize everyday life (Moaddel 1993: 229). Some minorities, particularly the Baha'i, faced a range of discriminatory practices. New punishments were introduced including flogging, amputation, and stoning. Sodomy became subject to capital punishment. An anti-narcotics campaign led to hundreds of executions.

Since the Cultural Revolution, the symbolic sphere in Iran has been characterized as one of acute repression, punctuated by moments of relative openness. The position of women helps to illustrate these tendencies.

Women were conspicuous participants in the revolution. Yet the immediate aftermath of the revolution saw the repeal of the 1967 Family Protection Act and the introduction of a range of discriminatory legislation and practices, including the revival of polygamy and the loss of a woman's right to initiate divorce. Women also lost the right to be judges, and faced discriminatory quotas in education and employment. They were barred outright from studying certain subjects, including agriculture and engineering (Moaddel 1993: 264). A range of groups, such as the Women's Association of the Islamic Revolution and, after 1992, a state Bureau for Women's Affairs, fostered demands for women to be seen as public as well as private actors (Bayat 2013: 89). In some respects, their campaigns were successful: literacy rates amongst women doubled in the two decades after the revolution; by 1998, more women than men were attending university, and a state-sponsored birth control campaign lowered the population growth rate dramatically (Bayat 2013: 89–92). In 1992, Shirin Ebadi, Iran's first – and only – pre-revolutionary female judge was allowed to restart her practice; in 2003, she was awarded the Nobel Peace Prize for her work. Magazines such as *Zanan* (Women) debated controversial issues, such as domestic abuse and cohabitation, even as it faced regular sanctions by the authorities (Keddie 2003: 294). In 2007, prominent female campaigners began a 'million signature campaign' that sought to repeal post-revolutionary legislation around marriage, child custody, educational inequality, and related issues. Much of this legislation was subsequently either amended or repealed. In 2017, an online campaign using the hashtag #whitewednesdays sought to oppose mandatory dress codes through posting pictures and videos of Iranian women wearing either white headscarves or pieces of white clothing. All in all, gender relations stand as a potent source of contention in contemporary Iran.

The same is true of 'youth'. In contemporary Iran, political dissent amongst young people often takes place in the symbolic sphere: over hair, clothes, music, and related issues. The attitudes of this Iranian counter-culture represent a direct challenge to the Islamic Republic: 70 per cent of young people say that the government is the source of their problems, 80 per cent don't trust politicians, and although 90 per cent of young Iranians believe in God, far fewer conform to the behavioural codes that the state requires as accompaniments to their belief (Bayat 2013: 116). Levels of drug use are high (Axworthy 2013: 364). Unsurprisingly, state attacks on the 'degenerate behaviour' practised by the 'hooligans' within the Iranian counter-culture are frequent (Ansari 2007: 92; Bayat 2013: 132). The Iranian state has attempted to assume close control over both the Internet and other forms of media. Regular crackdowns by the state on 'depravity' include the closure of a large number of restaurants and cafes. Special units are tasked with arresting women who wear their scarves too high on their heads, stop cars blaring out loud music, and prohibit the drinking of alcohol. Iran has the highest execution rate of minors in the world. Yet despite this repression, forms of 'micropolitical defiance' stand as everyday forms of contention that, in turn, erode the legitimacy of the regime (Milani 2015: 58–60). These sites of everyday contention are not going away.

Critical Configurations

Chapter 3 introduced three critical configurations through which to examine revolutionary outcomes: first, the production of melded social orders in which novel political, economic, and symbolic fields are embedded alongside established social ties; second, the generative capacity of inter-social interactions; and third, the ongoing contestations that lie at the heart of post-revolutionary orders. These three configurations are assessed in turn.

Melded Orders The post-revolutionary Iranian state is a quite different – and much more resilient – entity than its predecessor. If Pahlavi Iran was a 'patrimonial absolutist' regime that was 'suspended above its people' (Skocpol 1994: 244), the contemporary Iranian state has considerable infrastructural power – it is deeply embedded in and through society. The size of the public sector doubled in the decade after 1976 (Harris 2012a: 156); by 2005, Iran had more than one million civil servants (Abrahamian 2008: 6). At the same time, and as discussed in the previous section, a proliferation of organizations in post-revolutionary Iran delivers forms of social Islam: welfare, education, housing, health care, insurance, and loans. Many of these organizations are not official state bodies, but complex entities that have been appropriated by elite factions (Harris 2012a: 132). The development of this system was not planned. Just as the Foundation of the Dispossessed assumed the role of the Pahlavi Foundation in 1979, so the Basij assumed responsibility for the coupon programme that distributed basic goods during the Iran–Iraq war. In rural areas, the Imam Khomeini Relief Committee took responsibility for providing interest-free housing loans, health insurance, and stipends for the elderly poor (Harris 2017: 105–10). Together, the state and the foundations control 80 per cent of Iran's economy (Abrahamian 2008: 6). And, together, they have been responsible for dramatic interventions into Iranian society – a developmental project that links intra-elite competition with state formation.

As well as being infrastructurally strong, the post-revolutionary state is also despotically strong. Here there are both similarities and differences with the Pahlavi state. On the one hand, both the pre- and post-revolutionary regimes contained extensive coercive apparatuses, which were – and are – despised and feared by the public. On the other hand, as with the state more generally, the post-revolutionary coercive apparatus is far more deeply embedded than its Pahlavi predecessor. In part, this is because of the continuing hold of the Iraq war, which remains a potent source of legitimacy. In part, it is because, for all of the size of the Shah's military, it was mobilized less frequently than its post-revolutionary counterpart, which has fought one major inter-state war and taken part in several smaller-scale operations. At the same time, elements of the coercive apparatus, particularly the IRGC and Basij, have become major players in a 'warfare-welfare' complex that has translated coercive power into infrastructural capacity (Harris 2017: 14). Both have used their gains from war to become central providers of social Islam and major stakeholders in revolutionary Iran's developmental state.

Yet, if the post-revolutionary state is a more robust body than its predecessor, it still contains several weaknesses. First is its factionalism. No sustained political parties have emerged during the post-revolutionary era. Rather, factions are loose alliances held together by personal ties and opportunism, with a veneer of ideological solidarity. This produces a chronically fluid political order, one that generates both intense intra-elite competition and weak ties with wider publics. Second is the sense in which the Islamic Republic is 'divided against itself' (Takeyh 2006: 6). This division comes from the attempt to combine 'Islamic' with 'Republic'. The former has led to the vesting of considerable power and authority in unelected bodies such as the Leader and the Guardian Council, which as the previous sections make clear, claim their authority not from the will of the people, but from God. The latter has engendered the formation of elected presidents, parliaments, and municipalities, along with a public that has shown itself to be quick to rise. Far from being an unyielding dictatorship, Iran is a polity stuck in a condition of virtual multiple sovereignty in which diverse sites of authority are occupied by particular factions. This generates a highly competitive system, but also an unstable one in which parallel forms of authority have been constructed, each with their own systems of patronage.

Far from being a patrimonial autocracy, therefore, contemporary Iran is a web of multiple sites of authority. Even the most powerful individual in Iran, the Leader, is circumscribed by other branches of government and a constitution that owes as much to French republicanism as it does to Shi'a ideology and practices. There are many within the *ulema* who would like to see the power of the Leader further circumscribed and the latter word in the conjunction Islamic Republic take on greater salience. At the same time, the post-revolutionary regime is far more deeply embedded than that of the Shah, even if this embedding is not always carried out by the state, but achieved through a diverse set of institutions and actors. This settlement has yielded two interconnected sources of tension: first, within the elite; and second, between the state and wider publics. The relative openness of these conflicts distinguishes the post-revolutionary Iranian state from its predecessor. It also speaks to the likelihood of ongoing contention in years to come.

The Generative Capacity of Inter-Social Relations   For many years leading up to the revolution, Khomeini (1981: 57, 294) railed against the 'world plunderers' (imperial powers) and sources of 'vice and corruption' (the regional monarchs) who 'looted' Islamic lands. Revolutionary Iran has maintained this hostility to existing international order and, in particular, the 'world arrogance' of Western powers. One potent illustration was the *fatwa* (ruling) imposed on the British writer, Salman Rushdie, whose book, *The Satanic Verses*, was denounced by Khomeini as representing 'world blasphemy'. The punishment for Rushdie's apostasy was death, and a bounty of $2.6 million was offered to an Iranian assassin and $1 million to a foreign assassin for his execution. Although Rushdie survived, others associated with the book's publication were murdered. Many other enemies of the state have also been murdered abroad, while the post-revolutionary state has been responsible for extensive terrorist activities around the world. These activities have been consistently legitimized by anti-Western and anti-imperialist rhetorical tropes. The regime used both the hostage crisis and the war with Iraq as a means of sidelining its domestic rivals, radicalizing its mission, and consolidating its authority (Westad 2007: 296). More recently, such tropes have been used both to condemn Western policies and generate ties with other illiberal polities, including Venezuela, Bolivia, Russia, Syria, and China (Fawcett 2015: 649). Over the past decade, China has become Iran's biggest trading partner, while Russia and Iran have signed an oil-for-goods agreement worth well over $1 billion per year (Vatanka 2015: 64). If the Shah's Iran was a central node within the Western alliance system, post-revolutionary Iran has been one of this system's most persistent opponents.

Such dynamics are especially evident in debates over Iran's nuclear programme. The Shah's nuclear programme was shelved in the aftermath of the revolution, but reactivated following the war with Iraq thanks to aid from Russia and, in particular, Abdul Qadeer Khan's network in

Pakistan (Dabashi 2010: 22). In 2002, it became clear that Iran was carrying out uranium enrichment. The following year, Iran agreed to suspend uranium enrichment and adhere to the Additional Protocol of the Nuclear Non-Proliferation Treaty (NPT). Yet many inside the country, particularly amongst the new right, saw these moves as akin to 'nuclear imperialism', an attempt by Western powers to inhibit the country's independence and self-sufficiency (Bowen and Moran 2015: 687; also see Moghaddam 2008). In 2006, Ahmadinejad confirmed that Iran possessed 160 centrifuges and was also carrying out plutonium enrichment. A series of International Atomic Energy Agency (IAEA) resolutions condemned Iran's conduct, particularly its refusal to allow IAEA inspectors access to certain areas of interest. The IAEA referred Iran to the UN Security Council. UN Resolution 1929 (2010) included sanctions targeted at military commercial holdings and the IRGC, as well as travel restrictions and the freezing of assets. In 2010 the Stuxnet worm was directed against Iran's nuclear facilities, with the US and Israel widely held to be its likely initiators. Inside Iran, these steps were depicted as a foreign conspiracy, an affront to Iranian independence. In 2012, the IAEA provided evidence that Iran had stockpiled 20 per cent enriched uranium, a level close to weapons grade. New, more punitive, sanctions were introduced. Oil exports declined by a quarter and, in turn, government revenues declined by a third.

In 2013, a Joint Plan of Action saw a short-term freeze of Iran's programme, including the halting of construction on a number of new facilities and complexes. Stop-start negotiations continued over the next two years. By the time of the April 2015 Framework Agreement between Iran, the EU, and the P5+1 (the five permanent members of the UN Security Council, plus Germany), the country possessed 19,000 centrifuges and was planning an expansion of its programme, mostly through Russian assistance (Bowen and Moran 2015: 689). The subsequent Comprehensive Plan of Action signed in July 2015 was a wide-ranging agreement that maintained Iran's 'low level latency' while containing both its 'breakout' (a 'dash for the bomb') and 'sneak-out' (a circumvention of the agreement) capacities. In return, nuclear-related sanctions were to be lifted once Iran had taken initial measures stipulated in the agreement. US sanctions related to human rights abuses and terrorism were to stay in place. In Iran, the agreement was greeted with joyous public celebrations. For his part, the Leader provided cautious, ambiguous support for the agreement. Others, including elements of the Principlist coalition, condemned Iran's 'capitulation' towards its foreign enemies. These denunciations took on greater force after President Trump's repudiation of US backing for the deal in May 2018.

Such dynamics illustrate well the connections between inter-social relations and domestic sources of legitimacy. The post-revolutionary elite has consistently tied domestic affairs to external influences: Western immorality, plans by Western states to foster a 'velvet revolution' inside the country, the branding of enemies as 'spies' for foreign powers, and so on. The notion that the Iranian Revolution is anti-imperialist in character and an act of defiance against foreign intervention remains potent. So too do appeals to sovereignty, as in debates around the nuclear issue. At the same time, it is difficult to overemphasize the centrality of the Iraq war to the contemporary political landscape – the veneration of veterans and 'martyrs', along with the commemoration of key battles and the rhetorical force of the conflict, remain central to Iranian political rhetoric. At the same time, Iran's interventionist stance around the region have begun to face a popular backlash – protests in early 2018 were in part motivated by what is widely seen to be excessive state spending overseas. Inter-social dynamics have been, and continue to be, generative of the outcomes of the revolution.

Ongoing Contestation   As the above discussion makes clear, there were no predetermined outcomes to the Iranian Revolution. After the revolution, many actors, both domestic and international, assumed that leftist forces would seize control of the uprising (Halliday 1982; Keddie 2003). For various reasons, many of them chronicled earlier in this chapter, this did not happen. But even with the advent of an Islamic Republic, it was not clear that Khomeini's faction would triumph over others – at the time of the revolution, his was a minority position and he was just one of a number of prominent clerics. In this sense, it was not the inevitable logic of history, nor the particular cunning of Khomeini, which produced an Islamic Republic. Rather, it was political contestation, as seen in the conflict between Islamists and leftists, debates within the *ulema*, the hostage crisis, the Iraq war, deliberations around the constitution, the Cultural Revolution, discussions over economic reconstruction, the disputed roles of the Leader and Guardian Council vis-à-vis parliament, the presidential elections of 1997 and 2009, the mass street protests that accompanied the latter, and the nuclear negotiations, which have produced the post-revolutionary order.

Two examples illustrate the importance of ongoing contention to the outcomes of the revolution. The first is the 2009 elections and its aftermath. The official result of the election saw Ahmadinejad achieve the largest victory of any candidate since 1979. Yet it did not take long for opposition groups to contest the result.[7] Despite widespread scepticism about the results, the Leader endorsed them. In response, an estimated three million people gathered on the streets of Tehran in the largest protests since 1979. As protests spread, they became oriented around the slogan: 'Where is my vote?' and memes such as 'You are the Media'.[8] Amidst talk of a 'velvet revolution' being plotted by 'foreign conspirators' in cahoots with a 'Western-educated, North-Tehrani elite', the regime countered with massive police deployments (Ansari 2010: 24–5; Ritter 2015: 188; Harris 2017: 196–211). Most of the international media were expelled and both cell phone networks and the Internet shut down for long periods. Several thousand arrests were made and around 100 people were killed (Ritter 2015: 186). As protestors, including a number of dissenting clerics, were denounced in increasingly strident tones, Kahrizak detention centre and Evin Prison in Tehran became sites of systematic abuse and torture (Ansari 2010: 68–9).

A second example is provided by ongoing contestation over the state of the Iranian economy. Iran continues to combine weak growth with high inequality, in part because of the multi-layered institutionalism that fosters intra-elite competition, in part because of rent-seeking, and in part because of sanctions. In 2011, the economy contracted by 5.8 per cent; in 2012, it contracted by another 2 per cent. During the same period, export revenues fell by a third and oil exports by a half. Car production, worth around 10 per cent of GDP, fell by 70 per cent; inflation in 2014 reached 30 per cent. It was not lost on some members of the political elite that this mini-recession, following on the back of average per annum growth of 5 per cent during the 2000s, was the type of relative decline that had precipitated the fall of the Shah. As was the case during the mid-to-late 1970s, contemporary Iran is a middle-income country. But this presents its own problems, not least those arising from the presence of a sophisticated, knowledgeable middle class with a long history of mobilization. Indeed, many of those hurt by the mini-recession of the early 2010s are what Asef Bayat (2013: 264–5) describes as the 'middle class poor' – professionals with degrees who, despite their qualifications and high-status jobs, are insecure and have a precarious standard of living (also see Harris 2017: ch. 5). High food prices are ongoing sources of unrest, most recently

---

[7] A detailed analysis of the vote, which illustrates just how unlikely the outcome was, can be found at: www.personal.umich.edu/~wmebane/note29jun2009.pdf, accessed 20 March 2019.

[8] These memes also spread through transnational networks, including social media. For two weeks after the election, #iranelection was the highest trending hashtag in the world, only dropping its position after the death of Michael Jackson.

when protests by workers and teachers turned into a country-wide mobilization in 2018. The economic gains that were supposed to be realized by the nuclear deal have not reached the middle-class poor, let alone those who are worse off. The result is that large sections of the population are willing to protest, both violently and non-violently, against the regime.

These points of contention sit alongside regular, but still potent, sources of unrest, whether these take place around gender relations, dress and behavioural codes, or the rights of street vendors. Far from being some kind of 'totalitarian' regime in which the people have been cowed by 'mad mullahs', post-revolutionary Iran has been formed by contestation within highly competitive elites and between these elites and a consistently unruly public. Only through examining these contentious dynamics does the shape of post-revolutionary Iran become evident.

Legacies of the Iranian Revolution

There are three ways in which the Iranian Revolution marked a sea-change in revolutionary practice. First, the revolution broke the notion that revolutionary insurgencies must be Marxian in inspiration, or even leftist at all. Revolutionaries in Iran emphasized their independence from both superpowers. One of the slogans of the revolution was 'neither East nor West'. As Khomeini put it in September 1980, 'We have turned our backs on the East and the West, on the Soviet Union and America, in order to run our country ourselves' (in Westad 2007: 296). Second, Iran is the only successful social revolution of the twentieth century that has not produced a one-party state (Harris 2017). Rather, post-revolutionary Iran is home to a complex state–parastatal–*bonyad* apparatus that features multiple, overlapping sites of political authority. This is augmented by the question of where ultimate political authority resides in the Islamic Republic: Leader or President, Guardian Council or Parliament, cleric or technocrat. The result is a system that fuels intense intra-elite competition. Third, the repertoires employed in the revolution, particularly its use of mass, non-violent protest, have been emulated in many subsequent movements. The use of non-violence may have been tied to a long-standing Iranian tradition of peaceful protest (Abrahamian 2011), but its influence has outgrown this tradition. Non-violence has become the preeminent form of protest in the contemporary world.

Ukraine

The opening years of the twenty-first century saw a wave of revolutions, from Serbia in 2000 to a number of states in the Middle East and North

Africa in 2011. This section concentrates on two episodes that took place in Ukraine: the first, in the midst of this wave, in 2004; the second, a little after its highpoint, in 2013–14. Like other waves, these revolutions shared a modular character: a foundation in youth movements, from Otpor ('Resistance') in Serbia to Pora ('It's Time') in Ukraine; an ethos of non-violent protest based around the occupation of squares and major streets; the linking of dissent with a carnivalesque atmosphere; the identification of supporters with clearly distinguishable symbols, such as the orange clothes, flags, and banners used in the 2004 uprising in Ukraine; an organizational structure that was decentralized; a form of leadership that was fluid; a symbolic repertoire oriented around nation-alist renewal and other, time-honoured ideals – freedom, justice, dignity; and international support, whether from state agencies, international organizations, NGOs, or foundations. Rather than being oriented around the social question, notions of left and right, or vanguard parties, these were mass movements that mobilized, at least in part, through marketing campaigns, music, and pranks. As one of the leaders of Otpor put it, a central part of its strategy was an ethos of 'laughtivism' – the idea was to 'make regime change fun' (Popovic 2015).

Early twenty-first-century revolutions therefore departed from pre-vious revolutionary configurations in a number of ways, most obvi-ously in terms of the movement's tactical repertoires and organizational structure. These issues are discussed in the following chapter. In other ways, however, these revolutions were familiar processes, requiring inter-national support, elite fracture, the desertion or neutrality of the coercive apparatus, the construction of a unified opposition, and the emergence of a condition of dual sovereignty. Also like previous revolutions, they were catalysed around an event, such as a stolen election or a constitutional crisis, which provided the impetus for mobilization. The ambiguous relationship between these revolutions and previous instances of revo-lutionary change speaks to a shift in revolutionary outcomes, from the claims of total victory that marked social revolutions over the past two centuries to the more limited settlements represented by early twenty-first-century revolutions. This section explores this shifting configur-ation; the next chapter takes it up in earnest.

From the Orange Revolution to the Maidan

During Soviet times, Ukraine was the second largest and second most populous republic within the USSR; with Russia, Ukraine constituted 60 per cent of the Soviet population. Ukrainian agriculture and industry were central to the Soviet economy. The country also loomed large in Soviet collective memory, mostly because of its frontline role during the Second World War, but also because it was the birthplace of a number of influential Soviet leaders, most notably Nikita Khrushchev (Mitchell 2012: 18). The Ukraine 'clan' represented one of the most important power centres in the Soviet Union (Zygar 2016: 85–6). Ukraine was also geopolitically important, partly because of the size of its population and economy, and partly because of its 2,000-kilometre border with Russia, its ports on the Black Sea, and its links to Eastern and Central Europe via borders with Poland, Romania, Hungary, and Czechoslovakia. At the time of its independence following the collapse of the Soviet Union in 1991, Ukraine was the world's third largest nuclear power (Krushelnycky 2006: 6).

The post-Soviet state that emerged in the 1990s was headed first by Leonid Kravchuk and then, from 1994, by Leonid Kuchma. Both Kravchuk and Kuchma were former Soviet apparatchiks. They managed a kleptocracy in which 'virtually every government and economic transaction was viewed as an opportunity to steal money' (Mitchell 2012: 31). Oligarchs controlled the economy, while elections were little more than internecine squabbles between elites. In 2004, Kuchma, unable to run for a third term in office, endorsed Viktor Yanukovych, who, like Kuchma, had close ties to Russia and whose main support came from the eastern region of Donbas. The election, widely seen as fraudulent, saw Yanukovych defeat opposition leader Viktor Yushchenko. Protestors took to the street, many of them wearing orange to signify their support for Yushchenko. After a standoff that lasted several weeks, an agreement between Yanukovych, Kuchma, and Yushchenko was brokered by European and Russian negotiators. A rerun of the election was held, which Yushchenko won easily.

Although Yushchenko became president, little changed. Intra-elite wrangling and public dissatisfaction at the slow pace of change saw support drain away from the president. At least part of it returned to Yanukovych, who became prime minister in 2006 and president in 2010. With Yanukovych back in power, crowds returned to the streets in November 2013. This time, mass mobilization began as a protest against Yanukovych's refusal to ratify an Association Agreement and establish a Deep and Comprehensive Free Trade Area (DCFTA) with the European Union. It soon turned into a general uprising against the regime. Although successful (again) in removing Yanukovych from office, mass mobilization (again) did little to change Ukraine's political, economic, and symbolic order. Worse, Russia used the opportunity presented by the removal of Yanukovych, which it denounced as an illegal coup orchestrated by the West, to annex Crimea and fuel an insurgency in Donbas. Ukraine became a state divided. This section details the outcomes of Ukraine's two revolutionary episodes and assesses what they tell us about contemporary revolutionary anatomies.

Political Order   Ukraine, like many other states that experienced revolutions during the 2000s, combined competitive authoritarianism with a high degree of personalism. The post-1994 Kuchma government operated via networks that ran throughout political and corporate life. The nodal point of these networks resided in the presidential office. Kuchma used the secret services, tax inspectorate, and courts as vehicles for extending his power and enhancing the wealth of his coterie. Kuchma's interests, and those of his associates, spread from steel to timber and from coal to natural gas, the proceeds of which were funnelled through insider privatizations. When investigators, such as the journalist Georgiy Gongadze, shed light on these practices, they were intimidated or, in Gongadze's case, kidnapped and beheaded.[9] To all intents and purposes, Kuchma's regime was a mafia state – it was a system that combined 'patronage, harassment, media bias, and fraud' (Levitsky and Way 2010: 117).

That said, Ukraine's oligarchical class was not unified. To the contrary, competing clans maintained a degree of independence, both because they operated from different regions and also because they held distinct corporate interests. This made Ukraine at least partly pluralist in that competition, including violent clashes, took place between rival clans. Leading figures tended to be drawn from this wider class of oligarchs. Yulia Tymoshenko, who has been deeply immersed in frontline politics since the 1990s, made her fortune from gas. Petro Poroshenko, who became president in 2014, is nicknamed 'The Chocolate King' because of his confectionery business. During the early 2000s, the most important opposition faction was Viktor Yushchenko's Our Ukraine. Yushchenko was a former governor of the Central Bank, who had helped to construct a series of reforms that stabilized the Ukrainian economy at the turn of the century. Seeing Yushchenko as a threat, Kuchma sacked him in 2001. Yushchenko responded by forging an alliance with Tymoshenko. Our Ukraine came first in the 2002 parliamentary elections, taking around a quarter of the seats. These provided the foundations for a run at the presidency in 2004.

---

[9] Kuchma was directly implicated in Gongadze's murder through the 'Melnychenko tapes', recorded by a former bodyguard, which appeared to show Kuchma ordering Gongadze's kidnapping. It remains unclear whether the tapes were genuine; they have not been admitted as evidence in subsequent court cases. In 2013, General Olexey Pukach, a former senior official in the Interior Ministry, was found guilty of Gongadze's murder and sentenced to life imprisonment.

As noted above, Kuchma favoured Viktor Yanukovych, the governor of Donetsk, who had a reputation for criminality, including serving a period in jail as a young man for assault and robbery. The endorsement of the president was, if anything, counterproductive – Kuchma's approval ratings on the eve of the election stood at 8 per cent (McFaul 2007: 54). Ukrainians had more trust in astrologers than the president. In part, this was because of endemic corruption, in part because of the parlous state of the economy – on the eve of the election, three-quarters of Ukrainians said that the economy was either in a 'bad' or 'very bad' state (Kuzio 2006: 55; Bunce and Wolchik 2011: 118, 125). Leading oligarchs such as Tymoshenko, Poroshenko, and the speaker of the parliament, Volodymyr Lytvyn, broke with Kuchma. Although intra-elite competition was the principal form of political contestation, publics and NGOs also organized against the regime. From 1999, Freedom of Choice acted as an umbrella NGO; it was harassed by Kuchma, but not closed. Freedom of Choice, along with The Committee of Voters of Ukraine, followed the example of movements around the region by focusing on elections. They delivered leaflets, opened a helpline, and took out advertisements in an attempt to increase voter education and reduce the possibilities of fraud. A youth movement, Pora, acted as a vanguard of popular protest.[10] Many of these groups had their origins in earlier protests, particularly those that followed the Gongadze murder, when protestors occupied Kiev's main shopping street (Kreshchatyk) and square (Maidan Nezalezhnosti). Although the protest was broken up by police, the solidarities forged and the tactics used served as forerunners to the 2004 protests.

The 2004 election campaign was fraught. Opposition groups oriented their meetings, rallies, and concerts around the slogan: 'I believe, I know, We can do it' (Viryu, Znayu, Mozhemo). For his part, Yanukovych sought to portray Yushchenko as a stooge of the West, dubbing him 'Bushchenko'. Not only was Yushchenko attacked personally, he was also attacked physically. Most extreme was his poisoning with dioxin following a dinner with officials from the state security services. The incident left Yushchenko badly pockmarked. Other coercive techniques included the arrest of several hundred Pora activists, along with raids on their headquarters in which explosives were said to have been discovered. The election itself was marked by intimidation, the stuffing of ballot boxes, and the electronic manipulation of results. When Yanukovych was announced as the winner, only 13 per cent of Ukrainians said that they

---

[10] Pora was split between 'Black Pora', which saw itself as operating largely outside mainstream politics, and 'Yellow Pora', which maintained ties to formal political factions. On this, see Demes and Forbring (2006).

believed the result (Kuzio 2005: 31). As one opposition joke ran: 'One of Yanukovych's staff comes to him and says: "I have bad news and good news for you. The bad news is that Yushchenko won the election. The good news is that you are the President"' (in Collin 2007: 116).

Following the announcement of the result, a tent city was established as a 'quasi-permanent presence' in downtown Kiev, centred around Maidan Nezalezhnosti (McFaul 2007: 64). Other tent cities were set up around the country. The occupation of the Maidan was 'part Glastonbury, part Paris Commune' (Collin 2007: 136). Hundreds of thousands of Ukrainians chanted, sang, and danced, many of them wearing orange, the colour of the Our Ukraine campaign. An auxiliary network provided logistical support, including food, water, and shelter. Attempts were made by protestors to co-opt the coercive apparatus; as one popular chant had it: 'The police are the people'. An increasingly feisty media, including websites such as Maidan.org and Ukrayinska Pravda, television stations like Channel 5, and journalists who had defected from mainstream media outlets, operated outside state control. Government buildings were blockaded. On 23 November, Yushchenko staged a ceremony in front of nearly 200 parliamentarians in which he declared himself president. Ukraine was in a condition of dual sovereignty.

Negotiations, mediated by European and Russian officials, were held between Kuchma, Yanukovych, and Yushchenko. Yushchenko agreed that the powers of the president should be curbed, and those of the prime minister and parliament increased. For their part, Yanukovych and Kuchma agreed to changes in the electoral law that reduced the possibilities of fraud. This paved the way to an agreement. On 3 December, the Supreme Court officially annulled the election. On 26 December, a new poll was held – the official result saw Yushchenko beat Yanukovych by a margin of 52 per cent to 44 per cent. In a sign of the regional divisions that were to intensify in years to come, four out of five voters in western and central Ukraine voted for Yushchenko, while a similar proportion in the east and south voted for Yanukovych. Yushchenko was sworn in as president on 23 January 2005. The Orange Revolution, it seemed, had been a success.

Soon after Yushchenko's election, the revolutionary coalition began to unravel. Pora was dissolved, although a section of the organization took part in the 2005 parliamentary elections, receiving 1.5 per cent of the vote. More damagingly, accusations of corruption divided Yushchenko and his Chief of Staff, Oleksandr Zinchenko, from high-profile Orange figures such as Tymoshenko and Poroshenko. The personal feud between Yushchenko and Tymoshenko was particularly sharp, reflecting deeper tensions over where political authority lay (Arel 2013: 128–9). As a result of the negotiations, constitutional powers were not clearly demarcated. While the president had the power of decree, only parliament could legislate. Although the president nominated foreign ministers, only parliament could dismiss them. A tug of war between individuals and factions fostered a highly volatile setting (Arel 2013: 133).

Like Iran, post-revolutionary Ukraine was home to multiple political factions that regularly changed both personnel and name. Deputies switched frequently between factions, whether to boost their power or their wealth. Poroshenko, for example, was a member of Kuchma's inner circle and central in the creation of the Party of Regions, before becoming Foreign Minister under Yushchenko, then Economic Development and Trade Minister under Yanukovych. In the meantime, he became spectacularly rich through his interests in confectionery and television. Such cronyism was, at least in part, a product of a voting system in which seats were organized via a list system. To be near the top of a list for one of the major factions was to secure parliamentary office. This incentivized personal connections rather than public loyalty (Mitchell 2012: 120; also see Fedorenko et al. 2016). Not only did serving in parliament offer legal immunity, it also provided access to lucrative contracts and rents. Two-thirds of Rada (parliament) deputies were dollar millionaires (Aslund 2006: 21). Factionalism was also fostered by regional clans. Chief amongst these was the Donetsk group. The interests of the Donetsk clan sprawled from coal to breweries. They also had effective control of one of Ukraine's biggest companies: System Capital Management. The Donetsk clan provided a formidable local organization for the Party of Regions, which tended to take around three-quarters of the vote in the Donbas, the region formed around the Donets Basin, which included the Donetsk and Luhansk administrative regions (*oblasts*).[11]

Elite in-fighting, allied to the slow pace of post-revolutionary change (no oligarchs were tried, few suspect privatizations were revisited), generated a sense of public malaise in the run-up to the 2006 elections. The Party of Regions joined forces with former communists and the Socialist Party in an Anti-Crisis Coalition, which was advised by foreign consultants, amongst them Paul Manafort, who had previously worked for Mobutu Sese Soku and Ferdinand Marcos, and who would later act as Donald Trump's campaign manager during the 2016 presidential elections in the United States. The Party of Regions received the largest

---

[11] In many ways, parties were façades that covered up intra-clan divisions. For example, Rinat Akhmetov, the richest figure in the Donetsk clan, shifted from supporting to opposing Yanukovych, most notably in the impeachment vote against Yanukovych in February 2014.

share of the vote, Tymoshenko's bloc came second, Our Ukraine was a distant third. The result saw Yanukovych become prime minister. The man who had been ousted as president through forceful mass mobilization in 2004 was, two years later, back as one of the leading figures in Ukrainian politics. 'Revolutions always disappoint', writes Andrew Wilson (2014: 38), 'but few have disappointed more comprehensively than Ukraine's once famous "Orange Revolution" of 2004'.

Yanukovych used his position as prime minister to stymie Yushchenko's policies. In response, Yushchenko tried to dissolve parliament. Tymoshenko removed her bloc from parliament, and troops surrounded government buildings. Emergency elections saw Tymoshenko return as prime minister. Once again, Ukrainian politics became captured by personal vendettas and horse-trading. So severe was the animosity between Yushchenko and Tymoshenko that the president increasingly saw Yanukovych as the lesser of two evils. In March 2010, Yanukovych defeated Tymoshenko to become president for a second time. Yanukovych restored the pre-2004 constitution and instituted a number of legal reforms, which allowed him to hire and fire officials, and place his own candidates in key posts (Kudelia 2014: 21). Yanukovych's control of law enforcement meant that he could imprison Tymoshenko, ostensibly for 'abuse of office', along with a number of other high-profile officials. It also meant that he could institutionalize the power of the Party of Regions, which became over-represented in government and executive agencies. Yanukovych pressurized independent media outlets, using tax audits as a means of disrupting their activities. Corruption was reintroduced on a grand scale. A number of parliamentarians defected to the Party of Regions, in part because of the substantial sums on offer: $450,000 as a one-off sum, plus a retainer of $25,000 per month (Wilson 2014: 50). A company owned by Yanukovych's son, Oleksandr, became the fastest growing business in Ukraine (Kudelia 2014: 22). Along with two other oligarchs, Rinat Akhmetov and Dmytro Firtash, Oleksandr won nearly half the state procurement contracts that were tendered in 2012 and 2013 (Kudelia 2014: 26). Holdings of the Yanukovych 'family', embracing both his immediate family and wider coterie, ranged from banking to construction, and from real estate to winemaking. The system of 'patronal power' instituted under Kuchma (Hale 2011), in which an elite worked through a central patron and constructed a highly hierarchical order, was back with a vengeance.

The centralization of power through Yanukovych's office and the Donetsk clan worked to revitalize opposition, in part because of the exclusion of other factions from the patronal system. In the 2012 parliamentary elections, despite high levels of fraud, the Party of Regions received nearly two million fewer votes than it had gained in 2007. New parties, including Svoboda (Freedom) and the Ukrainian Democratic Alliance for Reform (UDAR), fronted by the former boxer Vitali Klitschko, did well. As Yanukovych's approval ratings fell, he sought to consolidate his base in the eastern parts of the country. In the summer of 2012, he introduced a law permitting local governments to officially recognize second languages in regions with a minority population of at least 10 per cent. Half of the country's regions, almost all of them in the east and south, recognized Russian. In response, there were protests in parts of western and central Ukraine.

On 21 November 2013, Yanukovych decided not to ratify a proposed Association Agreement and free trade agreement with the EU. Following a tweet by Mustafa Nayem, who worked for Ukrayinska Pravda, the website established by Giorgiy Gongadze, a group of protestors converged on the Maidan under the slogan: 'For a European Ukraine'. The 'Euromaidan' protests were born. Over the next few days, the protests grew in both size and intensity. Yanukovych ordered a crackdown; attacks followed from the police, Berkut (a special police housed within the Ministry of Internal Affairs), and titushky (militias who acted as shock troops for the police and security services). Repression served to deepen polarization and heighten protests. Several city council and trade union buildings were occupied. Opposition politicians, including Klitschko, attempted to control, or at least direct, the crowds. But Euromaidan had its own systems of governance, entertainment and educational programmes, food distribution networks, medical clinics, and self-defence units (Way 2014: 37). The latter were the province of football ultras, along with Svoboda and another right-wing group: Pravy Sektor (Right Sector). These groups set up barricades and armed supporters with slingshots and Molotov cocktails.

As with the 2004 uprising, the Euromaidan protests morphed into a general mobilization; from 1 December, it was simply referred to as the Maidan, or 'The Revolution of Dignity'. Parallel movements sprang up around the country – by early December, there were around 800,000 protestors on the streets of Ukraine's major cities (Onuch 2014: 45). On 17 December, Russia and Ukraine agreed an Action Plan in which Russia promised debt relief and a discount on the price of natural gas. The following month, Yanukovych introduced legislation, amounting to a 'dictatorship package' (Leshchenko 2014: 52), which prohibited gatherings of more than three people, groups of more than five cars, and the erection of tents and stages in public spaces. 'Off screen violence' saw activists seized, often at night, beaten and, sometimes, tortured (Wilson 2014: 86). Once again, repression only served to intensify protests. Numbers swelled and government buildings were seized. In mid-February, a march in Kiev turned violent, and the headquarters of the Party of Regions and House of Trade Unions were set on fire. The state responded with a violent storming of the Maidan on 18 February, which led to several days of battles on and around the square. On 20 February, snipers opened fire from a range of locations around the Maidan. Nearly 100 people died during this period, including some snipers; many hundreds were injured. Thirty parliamentarians from the Party of Regions defected, and a hastily convened parliamentary vote agreed to release Tymoshenko. Troops from the Ministry of Internal Affairs responsible for guarding the presidential compound and government buildings abandoned their posts. On 21 February, after negotiations brokered by three EU foreign ministers, Yanukovych agreed a return to the Orange constitution, new presidential elections, and investigations into state-sponsored violence. Although the politicians who relayed details of the negotiations to the crowds in the Maidan were jeered, the Maidan Public Council voted to support them. Yanukovych promptly fled Kiev, via Kharkiv and Crimea, to Russia, taking with him millions of dollars in cash, paintings, icons, books, and ceramics (Wilson 2014: 93).

After a period of Fatherland–UDAR coalition following Yanukovych's flight, in May 2014, Petro Poroshenko defeated Tymoshenko in presidential elections. The 'Heavenly Hundred' who had died during the final stages of the mobilization were given the titles 'Hero of Ukraine', and 20 February became a day of national commemoration. Poroshenko formalized the Association Agreement and DCFTA with the EU. An anti-corruption office was established; so too were lustration policies. Yet it was questionable how deep these reforms went. As discussed below, anti-corruption investigations were disrupted and activists targeted. Following corruption allegations, the prime minister, Arseniy Yatsenyuk, resigned in 2016, to be replaced by a close associate of the president, Volodymyr Groysman. Several other top jobs went to Poroshenko allies. Despite trialling a range of electoral systems, Ukraine remains a volatile political order in which a range of factions fuse corporate and political power through the use of bribes, kickbacks, and rents (Fedorenko et al. 2016: 628).

Two themes stand out when assessing the outcomes of changes to Ukrainian political order since 2004. The first is marked, like Iran, by intense intra-elite competition. In some ways, Ukraine supports a pluralist politics in that diverse factions compete against each other. This competition takes place within a media ecology that is at least partly open and a civil society that is, if not vibrant, at least active. Despite this, and unlike Iran, formal politics is cut off from society. Only occasionally, whether through elections or major mobilizations, does mainstream politics interact in a significant way with publics. Ukraine functions in part as a competitive authoritarian state and, in part, as a low-intensity democracy (Levitsky and Way 2010: 355). Second, Ukraine serves to demonstrate what can be called a *protest spiral*, in which militancy from one side prompts an escalation from the other.[12] Until either the state or opposition de-escalates or is defeated, there is a ratcheting up effect that intensifies militancy. On the one hand, this means that state repression does not always work, as was the case in 2013–14. On the other hand, it means that, once a protest spiral is underway, the outcome is likely to be increased militancy. The deaths that formed part of the 2013–14 uprising take place within a wider pattern observable not just in Ukraine, but also in the 2011 Arab Uprisings. I return to this issue in the next chapter.

Coercion at Home and Abroad   The post-Soviet Ukrainian military was big but weak, with low levels of cohesion (Levitsky and Way 2010: 214–15). It was, however, loyal. As such, it was a surprise that Kuchma's order to use force against protestors in late November 2004 was not followed through (Wilson 2011). Kuchma did use agents provocateurs against protestors, as did Yanukovych in 2013–14. For their part, protests in 2004 were predominantly non-violent; this was also how the 2013–14 mobilization began. As noted above, however, it was not how they finished. As with other revolutions, the actions of the coercive apparatus played a crucial role in determining the outcomes of the two revolutionary episodes. In both 2004 and 2013–14, key elements of the coercive apparatus either abandoned their posts or assumed a position of neutrality. Those elements loyal to the regime in 2013–14, such as the Berkut, were dissolved following the uprisings.[13]

As discussed in the following chapter, one of the ways in which contemporary revolutions are distinguished from previous revolutions in that they do not result in the formation of a state with enhanced coercive capacities. In part, this is because revolutionaries do not come to power through sustained violent campaigns. In part, it is because revolutionaries do not seek to overturn the core features of liberal international

---

[12] The concept of 'protest spiral' differs from Tarrow's (1998) 'protest cycle' in that it is not linked to notions of political opportunity structure, makes no claims about levels of diffusion or innovation, and focuses on contentious escalation rather than a general intensification of challenger–regime interactions. Its focus is on increased militancy by both sides. In this sense, it shares some resemblances with the notion of 'backfire' developed by Hess and Martin (2006), who analyse the public outrage, and increased mobilization, that flows from state repression.

[13] Some units defected to Russia and were repurposed as a police force in Crimea.

order. Ukraine was no exception to these rules. Many of those taking part in the revolutions wanted to become more Western – as noted above, the 2013–14 uprising began as the 'Euromaidan'. Political leaders in both 2004 and 2013–14 made much of Ukraine's European heritage. And both uprisings deployed overtly liberal slogans: justice, freedom, dignity. However, the experience of Ukraine points to a significant tweak within this story. Ukraine's pivotal geopolitical position, and the pro-Western symbolic framing of its major mobilizations, meant that it became part of a broader tug of war between Russia and the West.

Historically, politically, and culturally, Ukraine is seen as lying at a crossroads between Russia and the West – its name is usually translated as 'Borderlands'. This is reflected in everyday practice: most eastern Ukrainians speak Russian as a first language; those in the West speak primarily Ukrainian. After 2013–14, these tensions deepened. On 27 February 2014, with a backdrop provided by Berkut fighters and Russian armed personnel, the government of Crimea, a peninsula that was transferred from Russia to Ukraine in 1954, passed a motion of secession. On 16 March, a hastily organized referendum sanctioned the secession. Two days later, Russia annexed Crimea and the autonomous city of Sevastopol, the first formal territorial annexations in Europe since the Second World War. In parallel, Russia amassed a sizeable force on Ukraine's border, and provided supplies, fighters, and weapons for separatist movements in Kharkiv, Donetsk, and Luhansk. Russia was expelled from the G8, cooperation in a number of international organizations was suspended, and sanctions were introduced. After the shooting down of a Malaysia Airlines flight over Donbas in July, the United States and EU extended sanctions. Russia responded with tit-for-tat penalties, including the introduction of import bans from a number of Western states. A ceasefire signed in September 2014, Minsk I, failed to hold. A second agreement, Minsk II, signed in February 2015, contained, but did not stop, the fighting. In 2017, Russia recognized the Russian ruble as legal tender in two self-declared breakaway republics: the Donetsk People's Republic (DPT), and the Luhansk People's Republic (LPR).

Since 2014, Ukraine has followed a long-established tradition of revolution turning into civil war. At the time of writing, the war in eastern Ukraine continues to simmer. Russia is fighting a hybrid conflict that combines conventional warfare with false flag operations, targeted assassinations, the subversion of state institutions, cyberwarfare, disinformation campaigns, and more. For their part, the Ukrainian military has fought to a stalemate, but cannot force a victory. Private militias and volunteers, many of them funded by oligarchs, fight on both sides of the conflict. By mid-2018, over 10,000 people had died in the conflict;

many more have fled the region. It is difficult to see how the stalemate can be broken. Russia's leadership considers the Ukrainian government to be anti-Russian neo-fascists. The Ukrainian state sees Russia as a neo-imperial power seeking to subvert its territorial sovereignty. Although the two countries are deeply entwined – the three million Ukrainians living in Russia provide remittances of around $10 billion per year (Sakwa 2015: 77) – they have rarely seemed so far apart.

Economic Order   Like many other former Soviet states, independent Ukraine instituted wide-ranging shock therapy programmes in the 1990s. Privatizations of swathes of the economy were enacted and public provision rolled back. As a result, unemployment rose and GDP declined sharply. There were shortages of basic goods and runaway inflation: 2,000 per cent in 1992, 10,000 per cent in 1993, 400 per cent in 1994 (Menan and Rumer 2015: 17, 26; also see Krushelnycky 2006). Those in a position to take advantage of liberalization became spectacularly rich, assuming control of key industries, from gas to steel. State credits and loans acted as subsidies that helped the construction of monopoly companies that paid little-to-no tax, legally or otherwise. Complex systems of trade and arbitrage built-in incentives for rent-seeking. Profitable firms were taken over, by force if necessary. The result was a deeply stratified economy in which a corrupt oligarchy presided over an impoverished population (Cheterian 2013: 26). Those living in poverty increased from 15 per cent in 1989 to 50 per cent in 1992; real wages during the same period declined by 63 per cent (Menan and Rumer 2015: 26).

The 2004 revolution was intended to correct the failures of the 1990s, in particular the corruption that fuelled the rise of the oligarchs. Ukraine's GDP in 2005 stood at just 59 per cent of its 1989 level (Lane 2008: 526). However, moves to stabilize the economy and restore growth preceded the Orange Revolution. In 1996, a new currency – the hryvnia – was introduced, helping to control inflation. Between 1999 and 2004, Ukrainian GDP nearly doubled. The economy grew by an average of 9 per cent during this period; real wages increased by 24 per cent in 2004 alone (Aslund 2006: 25). Yet this did not translate into support for the government. To the contrary, as Ukrainians watched an elite become fantastically wealthy, dissatisfaction with existing conditions intensified; by the time of the 2004 presidential elections, one-third of Ukrainians said that they wanted to emigrate (Kuzio 2006: 51).[14] Output continued to expand after the revolution, albeit at a reduced rate: 2.5 per cent in

---

[14]   Many of them did. From a population of c. 52 million in 1991, Ukraine's 2018 population was around 44 million.

2005 and 5.5 per cent in 2006. Levels of FDI also increased, reaching $3.5 billion in 2006. In 2008, Ukraine became a member of the WTO. The country stabilized its currency, saw incomes rise, and sustained a manageable budget and current account deficit.

Growth, however, was replaced by contraction following the 2008 financial crisis. In 2009, GDP fell by 15 per cent. In 2010, Ukraine agreed a $15 billion loan from the IMF. However, this was suspended in 2011 after the Yanukovych regime failed to fulfil its conditions. Yanukovych preferred to walk a tightrope between the EU and Russia; his stated policy was 'non-blocness' (*pozablokovist*) (Charap and Colton 2017: 113). With the former, he tried to keep open the possibilities of association and free trade agreements. With the latter, he ratified the Kharkiv Accords, which gave Russia the right to place their Black Sea Fleet in Crimea until 2042, and publicly maintained an interest in joining a Eurasian customs union. However, Yanukovych held a weak hand, and in the end, energy dependency forced him to play it. In a context in which two-thirds of the country's natural gas was provided by Russia, Yanukovych agreed to a Russian gas discount worth several billion dollars (Menan and Rumer 2015: 77). He also looked further afield for help. At the height of the 2013–14 mobilization, Yanukovych leased over seven million acres of land to China, an area roughly the size of Belgium (Wilson 2014: 16). In part, these policies acted as camouflage for a bigger story going on behind the scenes – the systematic looting of state finances. Corruption during Yanukovych's second term of office may have been worth $100 billion, at a time when GDP was $150 billion per year and total tax revenue worth $17.8 billion per annum (2013 figures, cited in Wilson 2014: 53). After the uprising of 2013–14, the scale of this robbery was laid bare. Yanukovych's residence, Mezhyhirya, was revealed as a 137-hectare modern Versailles. After being abandoned by its owner in February 2014, Ukrainians were able to gaze, whether in awe or disgust, at the 70 cars Yanukovych had acquired, his customized greenhouses, personal yacht club, zoo, helipad, hunting grounds, and even a golden loaf of bread (Wilson 2014: 59). Never had the corruption of Ukraine's elite been more conspicuously displayed.

Unsurprisingly, the war in eastern Ukraine has done further damage to Ukraine's economy: GDP fell by 6.6 per cent in 2014 and 9.8 per cent in 2015. By 2017, a degree of stability had been restored. The economy grew by a little over 2 per cent in both 2016 and 2017; central bank reforms and currency restabilization helped control inflation from a high of 60 per cent to a more manageable, if still considerable, 13–14 per cent. In 2016 and 2017, real wages rose and some FDI returned, while spending cuts and higher tax returns reduced the deficit. A major IMF loan helped to restructure debts, even if parts of the payment were delayed following a failure to meet conditionalities, most notably in anti-corruption measures. This was despite the introduction of an electronic system for state procurement tenders, an e-declaration system for the assets of state officials, and the formation of a number of anti-corruption bodies, including the National Anti-Corruption Bureau of Ukraine (NABU) and the National Agency for the Prevention of Corruption (NAPC). However, both the judicial system and police have actively hindered the work of these organizations. In 2017, the Security Service of Ukraine (SBU) opened charges against both bodies and targeted anti-corruption activists. Perhaps unsurprisingly, fewer than 10 per cent of Ukrainians say that they trust the government (Ash et al. 2017: 61).

Over the past generation, Ukraine's economy has gone backwards. In 1989, Ukrainian GNP per capita was higher than Russia's; in 2012, it stood at a third of Russian levels (Menan and Rumer 2015: 49). When measured in terms of power purchasing parity, from a position of relative equivalence in 1989, Ukraine's GDP per capita in 2017 was a third of Polish levels (Ash et al. 2017: 40). Ukraine is one of only two post-Soviet states to have a GDP below its pre-independence level (the other is Kyrgyzstan) (Sakwa 2015: 72). There are fewer schools, students, and teachers in the country than there were in 1990 (Aslund 2015: 221). Since 1991, Ukrainians have experienced only one period of sustained growth, from 1999 to 2007. There are many reasons for this poor performance. The story starts with the sham privatizations of the 1990s. Next comes the corruption – in 2017, Ukraine placed 130th in Transparency International's ranking of states around the world, little better than its 144th placing before the 2013–14 uprising. And then there is the war, which has deepened the enmeshing of political and economic power. If Ukraine under Yanukovych was little more than a 'rent-seeking oligarchy' (Aslund 2015: 4), it is doubtful whether anything substantial has changed since he was ousted.

Symbolic Order As with other features of Ukrainian society, symbolic relations have been a polarizing force in post-independence Ukraine. As with most other post-communist countries, nationalism has been a potent source of this polarization, serving as a tool of both legitimation and contestation. Central to this dynamic is memorialization of the 'Holodomor' – the famine of 1932–3 in which three to four million Ukrainians died of starvation as a consequence of Soviet policies of industrialization and collectivization (Snyder 2010). For some, particularly those in the western and central parts of the country, the Holodomor has become a symbol of Ukrainian suffering at the hands of Russia. In 2006, President Yushchenko introduced a law defining the

Holodomor as a genocide and making its denial unlawful. It has assumed a central place in school curricula and the country now observes a Holodomor Memorial Day each November. A museum commemorating its victims opened in 2008. Yet for others, particularly in the eastern and central parts of the country, the Holodomor should be seen as a general tragedy rather than as a genocide targeted specifically at Ukrainians. Memorialization divides rather than unites Ukrainian society.

Similarly polarizing are figures like Stepan Bandera, who fought first against the Poles in the 1930s and then against the Soviets during the Second World War, at times with the support of the Nazis. For Russians and separatists, Bandera is regarded as a fascist war criminal. For his supporters, Bandera is a central figure within a longer-term history of heroic Ukrainian resistance to Russian imperialism. In 2010, Yushchenko decreed that Bandera was a 'Hero of Ukraine'. Bandera also became an important symbol during the 2013–14 protests. Marches were held in his honour, and self-defence units established in his name. Both Svoboda and Right Sector self-consciously styled themselves as inheritors of the Organization of Ukrainian Nationalists (OUN) and the Ukrainian Insurgent Army (UPA), groups responsible for the murder of tens of thousands of Jews and around 100,000 Poles during the 1930s and 1940s. Bandera was a leading figure in both organizations.

Since the Orange Revolution, memorials to OUN and UPA figures, including Bandera, have been established in many parts of Ukraine. In 2016, Kiev city council agreed to change the name of Moscow Avenue to Stepan Bandera Avenue. The result is an intensification of existing cleavages (Kulyk 2016). Russian nationalists and separatists refer to the south and east of Ukraine as Novorossiya (New Russia), the imperial Russian name for the territory north of the Black Sea. Those in the western and central parts of the country are increasingly nationalistic in their outlook and politics. What started as fissures have become schisms. When parliament voted to give greater autonomy to separatist regions in August 2015, right-wing nationalists clashed violently with police in Kiev, killing three officers. President Poroshenko denounced the violence. But just a few months earlier, he had signed into law a proposition that honoured the OUN and UPA, and which made it a criminal offence to publicly question their legitimacy as freedom fighters. By engaging in this toxic politics, Ukrainian leaders are playing a dangerous game.

Critical Configurations

As with the first part of this chapter, this section uses three critical configurations in order to assess revolutionary outcomes: first, the production of melded social orders; second, the generative capacity of inter-social interactions; and third, the ongoing contestations that lie at the heart of post-revolutionary orders.

Melded Orders   Beginning with the Rukh movement that held large demonstrations between 1989 and 1991, the post-Soviet era saw repeated instances of popular mobilization in Ukraine. There were mass protests in 1996 after constitutional reforms awarded new powers to the president. And there were demonstrations, including an occupation of the Maidan, in 2000–1 oriented around the slogan: 'Ukraine without Kuchma'. These experiences provided many of the symbolic repertoires for the 2004 and 2013–14 movements. They also helped to construct networks and foster know-how that was put to use in later mobilizations. As ever, these mobilizations blended established tropes, such as freedom and dignity, with novel repertoires, from the use of Internet sites (such as yanukovich.info) to twitter handles (such as #Euromaidan). Like other movements during this period, protestors aimed to foster a welcoming, fun spirit – music, comedy, and other performances played central roles in the uprisings.

However, alongside this history of protest can be found equally strong histories of elite negotiation, whether this takes the form of formal pacts or informal corridor politics (Wilson 2011: 351). In both 2004 and 2013–14, elites negotiated settlements far removed from the Maidan. These settlements reflected a shift in revolutionary anatomies towards a model of 'negotiated revolution', which originated in Eastern and Central Europe in 1989, and became an influential strand within post-Cold War uprisings (Lawson 2004, 2005). The next chapter discusses this model in depth. For now, it is worth simply noting the ways in which negotiated revolutions moderate outcomes rather than enable one side of the revolutionary fissure to secure ultimate victory. As the first half of this chapter showed, in Iran, the victory of militant Shi'a clerics enabled a social order to emerge that was quite distinct from that of the Shah – Iran since 1979 has experienced a social revolution. This is not the case with negotiated revolutions. As the example of Ukraine shows, the outcomes of the two post-independence revolutionary episodes has resulted in a rotation between elites rather than a 'world turned upside down' (Cheterian 2013: 28). In both 2004 and 2013–14, the leaders of the revolutionary mobilization were drawn from existing elites, even if these elites were, at the times of the uprisings, outside the exclusive regime that ran the state. Their goal was to inherit rather than change the system – alternative elites used popular mobilizations to oust incumbents and take control of the state. It is not surprising, therefore, that post-revolutionary elites did not close the gap between state and society. This was never their intention. The result is likely to be further mobilizations, or at least sustained volatility, for some time to come.

The Productive Capacity of Inter-Social Relations Inter-social dynamics have been, and continue to be, central to unravelling the outcomes of both 2004 and 2013–14. Western support for the revolutions and post-revolutionary regimes has been substantial. Funds were made available for opposition campaigns, election monitoring, and observers – the United States alone spent $18 million on election assistance from 2002 to 2004 (McFaul 2007: 48). Private foundations such as George Soros's Open Society Foundation supplemented funding channelled through state bodies. This support was extended for the post-revolutionary regime. Between 2014 and 2017, the EU provided over $100 billion in aid for Ukraine; its delegation to the country was its second largest anywhere in the world (Ash et al. 2017: 31). As Mark Beissinger (2006) puts it: 'Fostering democratic revolution has become an international business.'[15]

Western support for its candidates and causes was counterbalanced by Russian support for its allies – Russian provided both advisers and considerable funding for Yanukovych. The result was – and is – polarization. On the one hand, there was the push from the West, as exemplified by the EU's proposed Association Agreement and DCFTA. On the other hand, there was the pull from Russia, as typified by its threat to hike gas prices and restrict trade if Ukraine signed these agreements. Events since 2014 have only exacerbated this polarization. When the DCFTA came into operation in 2016, Russia responded by placing an embargo on Ukrainian agricultural imports and suspending preferential trade between the two countries. Ukraine responded in kind. The result has been a revolutionary–counter-revolutionary tit-for-tat, played out in part rhetorically, in part through sanctions, in part through political manoeuvring, and in part through armed conflict. Both geopolitics and geo-economics form the backdrop to a multi-faceted revolutionary–counter-revolutionary dynamic.

Inter-social relations have also been crucial to the spread of the revolution. As noted at the beginning of this section, Ukraine formed part of a wave of revolutions that began in Serbia in 2000, and that spread around many parts of the region, and beyond, over the next 15 years

---

[15] The exemplar is Georgia. The United States provided Georgia with $700 million in aid between 1995 and 2000; in 2000, USAID delivered aid worth $200 per person – the fourth largest per recipient sum in the world (Jones 2006: 41).

or so. In part, revolution spread through conscious emulation, in part through analogous reasoning: 'if it happened there, it can happen here'. As in Ukraine in 2004, these revolutions were often catalysed by a stolen election. Elections allowed for preparation, whether around procedural issues such as election monitoring, or more strategic purposes, such as the construction of a unified opposition (Bunce and Wolchik 2007: 96; also see Brancati 2016). They also acted as focal points for international support. However, as the events of 2013–14 indicate, elections are not the only way to galvanize protests; a catalytic event can take many forms.

Ongoing Contestation The Orange Revolution was a tightly coordinated affair – preparations were long in the making, there was a unified opposition around Yushchenko, and the protests were oriented around a few central demands. In contrast, the 2013–14 coalition was more diverse than 2004 in terms of its personnel and politics, more dispersed around the country, and more decentralized in terms of its leadership (Onuch 2014; Onuch and Sasse 2016). In general, diverse movements like 2013–14 are more difficult to control than centrally organized movements like 2004. Not only do they produce divergent claims and make the formation of a collective identity difficult, they also allow minority positions, particularly militant flanks, to assume an exaggerated role (Onuch and Sasse 2016: 558, 561, 563). During the 2013–14 mobilization, for example, militants constituted 10–20 per cent of protestors, organized loosely into two coalitions of convenience: Svoboda and Right Sector (Onuch and Sasse 2016: 578). Because these groups were in the frontline of clashes with state forces, they received a level of attention that outweighed their actual support. This was demonstrated once the mobilization ended. Oleh Tyahnybok, the leader of Svoboda, received a little over 1 per cent of the vote in the presidential elections of 2014, while nationalist parties performed poorly in parliamentary elections held later that year.

This indicates something important about both organizational structure and revolutionary tactics. On the one hand, both the 2004 and 2013–14 mobilizations can be considered successful if success is measured by the removal of a targeted autocrat. However, if this constitutes success, it is a conspicuously limited definition of success. In Ukraine, political order has remained endemically corrupt, the state has collapsed into civil conflict, economic growth is anaemic, and nationalism functions as a polarizing force. Defining revolutionary success is, therefore, not a straightforward matter. This is particularly important given that some contemporary revolutions, because of their negotiated nature, often struggle to right the wrongs that prompted the uprising in the first place. By failing to foster the creation of a single revolutionary subject, mobilizations not only leave existing cleavages in place, they may exacerbate them.

At the same time, those who study mass participatory movements tend to concentrate on the actions of protestors without carrying out a similarly forensic examination of the actions of state elites (e.g. Chenoweth and Stepan 2008, 2011). This elides the ways in which autocrats learn to repress and, sometimes, emulate these movements. Vladimir Putin, for example, responded to uprisings in post-Soviet spaces by encouraging the establishment of a pro-government youth movement – 'Ours' ('Nashi') – replete with catchy slogans and identifiable colours, and organized through a party apparatus that made widespread use of information and communication technologies (Beissinger 2006). In a number of authoritarian states, counter-revolutionary tropes mobilize publics against 'Western-inspired velvet revolutions'. This helps to explain why the wave of revolutions that began in Serbia in 2000 has seen more failures than successes. At times, authoritarian regimes have carried out preventive repression, as in a number of states in the Middle East, Africa, and Central Asia. At other times, movements that have emerged have been violently suppressed, as in Iran in 2009 and 2017–18. Almost every revolution generates a counter-revolutionary backlash, one that fosters ongoing contestation between unruly publics and authoritarian states. This dynamic is well captured by the experience of Ukraine since independence. It is a dynamic that many other states will experience in years to come.

The Revolutionary Coup

The form of revolution epitomized by Ukraine's two mass mobilizations in 2004 and 2013–14 is, perhaps, best captured by the notion of a 'revolutionary coup' in which revolutionary mobilization has led to the replacement of one elite by another (Lane 2008: 529). The result of Ukraine's two revolutionary episodes has been changes in elite personnel rather than the systemic transformation associated with Iran's social revolution. The limited outcomes of these revolutions mean that they are weakly embedded. This is not just the case in Ukraine. The leader of the Tulip Revolution in Kyrgyzstan, Kurmanbek Bakiev, became the subject of mass protests that forced him to flee the country in 2010. Mikheil Saakashvili, the leader of Georgia's Rose Revolution, was charged in Georgia for a range of criminal offences. Having been granted Ukrainian citizenship by President Poroshenko, this was subsequently revoked after the two men fell out. In Ukraine, as this chapter has chronicled, support for Viktor Yushchenko dwindled quickly after 2004. For his part, Viktor Yanukovych was thrown out of office not once, but twice. He currently resides, a very rich man, in Russia. Few of the issues that caused Yanukovych to be removed have been effectively tackled, let alone resolved.

To some extent, these outcomes are a result of a shift in revolutionary tactics that this chapter has begun to outline – the formation of mass participatory coalitions that are largely committed to non-violence and usually decentralized, with power changing hands not through revolutionary violence, but via elite negotiations. What holds these movements together is not strong ties of shared struggle, political ideology, and kinship, but weak ties oriented around a single goal: removing the dictator. These movements are influenced less by the social question that unified revolutionary movements in the twentieth century than by short-term political goals, most notably the rejection of an incumbent and a fairer redistribution of political authority. This has led some observers to question whether contemporary revolutions are 'real' revolutions. They are in that they present an existential challenge to a regime that is extra-constitutional in nature and that arises from a condition of dual sovereignty. They are not in that they do not seize the state in order to instigate programmes of systemic transformation. To the contrary, they are deliberately self-limiting in that protest mobilizes around narrower goals: the removal of an autocrat, an end to corruption, and constitutional reforms. This presents a considerable shift in anatomies of revolution. This shift may be unsurprising – after all, as this book has argued, revolutions are adaptive, evolving practices. But it is a crucial change, one that forms the basis for the next chapter.

From Revolution to Regime Change?

Similarities between post-revolutionary Iran and Ukraine range from the incidental, such as the coincidence of both regimes having experienced the shooting down of civilian airliners, to the structural. Of the latter, three stand out. First is the construction of fluid factional alliances rather than enduring political parties, resulting in fierce, volatile intra-elite competition. The second, partly related, theme is ongoing contestation between states and publics. As this chapter has chronicled, both Ukraine and Iran have seen the emergence of protest spirals that point to the likelihood of ongoing, likely militant, mobilizations in years to come. Finally, both post-revolutionary Iran and Ukraine have been hindered by weak economic performance. In part, this is the result of extensive corruption, which is closely linked to the formation of personalistic networks and rival sites of authority that serve as the basis for state-validated graft. In part, it is because opposition movements have failed to craft a systemic alternative to the economic status quo. The most that opposition groups in Iran and Ukraine offer are tweaks to the existing order.

Alongside these similarities can be found two important points of divergence. The first is inter-social. In many ways, Iran stands as an exemplar of revolutionary sovereignty – the regime blends interventionism abroad with claims to domestic autarchy. Iran has sought to export its revolution, which it sees as offering a root-and-branch challenge to liberal international order, both regionally and further afield. Iranian foreign policy since 1979 is one of revolutionary expansionism, tempered by pragmatism. Post-revolutionary Ukraine, in contrast, has become a tool of more powerful actors, a reflection of contested views within Ukraine about its international position. Second is the type of state that has emerged in the post-revolutionary period. Since 1979, the Iranian state has become both despotically and infrastructurally more powerful. This stands in contrast to Ukraine's post-revolutionary state, which is weaker in both regards. The reason for these divergent outcomes stems from the securing of final victory by Iranian revolutionaries as opposed to the elite negotiations that brought the 2004 and 2013–14 mobilizations to an end. Where the former legitimizes radical transformation, the latter points to institutionalized moderation. The next chapter explores the wider ramifications of this shift to 'negotiated revolution'.

Part III

Prospects

It often appears that the meaning of revolution has become lost in the contemporary world – 'the god that failed' as Krishan Kumar (2008) puts it. Critics assign revolution to the dustbin of history, even as they associate revolutions with the worst crimes of the past two centuries. Hence, Alfred Cobban (1971) and François Furet (1999) argue that totalitarian terror was a natural product of the French Revolution, just as Richard Pipes (1991) and Orlando Figes (2014) see gulags and purges as the inevitable consequence of the Russian Revolution.[1] At the same time, many on the left have shifted from advocacy of class-based, vanguardist revolution to support for leaderless social movements and revolutionary assemblies, given their backing to new big-faith projects such as non-violent protest and climate justice, or shifted towards a view of revolution as a singular 'Event' rather than a collective project. Where once there were dreams of universal revolutionary emancipation, now there is only 'cynical reason' – the idea that fundamental change is impossible, even if it was desirable (Jameson 2010). At the same time, in many contemporary societies, it seems that there is no need for revolutionary utopias when 'the future is now ... in market economies, democratic governance, and scientific progress' (Gordin et al. 2010: 12). In such an environment, 'revolution has no future and an increasingly attenuated past' (Haynes and Wolfreys 2007: 6).

Yet revolutions persist. The increasingly personalistic tendencies of many states, from Russia to China, and from Turkey to Saudi Arabia, speaks to a vulnerability that could, in time, yield revolutionary pressures.

---

[1] Domenico Losurdo (2015: 5, 31) argues that these 'revisionists' build on earlier attempts by Tocqueville, Burke, and Arendt to 'liquidate the revolutionary tradition' of 1789 and 1917 by associating the French and Russian revolutionaries with 'a rabid psychopathological zealotry and an exotic fanaticism'. For Losurdo, far from carrying out programmes divorced from concrete events, both French and Russian revolutionaries reacted rationally to particular, if extreme, historical circumstances. In this sense, they share considerable common ground with the English and American revolutionaries that revisionists often exult.

Militant Islamism represents a challenge to international order that has its roots in a miscellany of revolutionary heritages. Around the world, authoritarians deploy nationalism both as an assertion of state power and as a defensive shield against globalization, Westernization, and neo-liberalism. Even as this move seeks to legitimize state power, it also serves to rouse revolutionary sentiments. In many parts of the world, a range of radical movements contest ongoing injustices: corruption, inequality, racism, sexism, austerity, climate justice, and more. Many of these mobilizations have produced mass movements, sometimes even political parties, which directly challenge the authority of state managers, corporate elites, and other power brokers. Uprisings in Iran, Venezuela, Armenia, Algeria, Sudan, and elsewhere during 2018 and 2019 speak to the continuing hold – and adaptation – of revolutionary practices. As one astute observer puts it, 'revolution has a future, even if many theoretical definitions of revolution do not' (Paige 2003: 19).

The final two chapters of this book explore the ambivalent place of revolution in the contemporary world. Chapter 7 outlines the contours of a new modal form of revolution, 'negotiated revolution', tracing its emergence in the 1989 revolutions in Central and Eastern Europe, and exploring its development during the first two decades of the twenty-first century, paying particular attention to the 2011 uprisings in the Middle East and North Africa. The final chapter examines three strands of contemporary revolution: social-movements-come-revolutionary-movements (such as Occupy Wall Street), militant Islamism, and populism. The chapter also considers the prospect of 'realistic utopias', which combine a revolutionary ethos of contestation, solidarity, and commitment with a concern for pluralism, criticality, and egalitarianism. Realistic utopias have two main characteristics: a concern for the improbably possible rather than the probably impossible, and the pursuit of multiple small 'r' revolutions rather than a single big 'R' Revolution. It may be that these two features best capture the theory and practice of revolution in the contemporary world.

7   Revolutions in the Contemporary World

Revolution Today

What are the prospects for revolution in the contemporary world? Chapter 3 outlined three critical configurations that lie behind the emergence of revolutionary situations: changes in inter-social relations; the vulnerability of certain types of regime, particularly neo-patrimonial and sultanist regimes, which are based on the authority of a single individual; and a systemic crisis rooted in a conjuncture of political, (relative) economic, and symbolic crises. All three dynamics are present in the contemporary world. The (re)emergence of authoritarian global powers such as China and Russia, the relative decline of the United States and the EU, capitalist volatility, and the rise of populism have brought a heightened sense of instability to international affairs (Buzan and Lawson 2014). Such an uncertain environment provides a volatile and, therefore, amenable context for revolution. At the same time, there are considerable numbers of personalistic regimes around the world, relying on an unstable mixture of despotic power and patronage. Russia under Putin, China under Xi, and Turkey under Erdogan all display these characteristics. The uprisings in the Middle East and North Africa during 2011 provide the latest example of the vulnerability of these regimes to revolutionary pressures. Finally, there is an assemblage of challenges to state authority: mass, predominantly unarmed protests, secessionist struggles, terrorist networks, issue-based movements, and more. The continuing presence of these transgressive repertoires and the circulation of contentious scripts around rights, social justice, dignity, and autonomy make it likely that the twenty-first century will see just as many, perhaps more, pressures for radical change than previous periods in world history (Beck 2011, 2014; Goldstone 2016).

However, revolutionary situations rarely lead to successful revolutions. Crucial to revolutionary success are two critical configurations: levels of elite loyalty, particularly within the coercive apparatus; and second, the capacity of an opposition to generate a cohesive revolutionary movement through effective leadership and social technologies that mobilize – and unite – diverse coalitions. Here lies the rub. Although the first of these remains commonplace, the second has changed markedly – there appears to be little adhesive within contemporary revolutionary ideologies that can act as the binding agent of a new social order (Dunn 2008: 25). This means that, for all the amenable conditions for revolution in the contemporary world, and for all the willing capacity of many people around the world to demand radical change, there is little sense of what an alternative order would look like once such trajectories are underway. To the contrary, contemporary revolutionary movements are often diffused rather than centralized in character.[1] These movements promote self-organization and autonomous action, eschewing the need for a centralized party that will organize protest and an ideology that will sustain a project of state transformation. Contemporary revolutionary movements are usually established as a means of resistance to existing conditions. But few have a sense of how this resistance is to be realized or what would happen if their mobilizations were successful. In other words, the dilemma facing revolutionary movements in the contemporary world is not *whither* struggle, but to what *end* these struggles lead. In short: what happens if these movements win?

On the one hand, therefore, revolutionary sceptics are mistaken: there is considerable scope in the contemporary world for revolutionary challenges to take place. On the other hand, these sceptics are on firmer ground when it comes to identifying a shift in anatomies of revolution: many contemporary movements lack a sense of how social relations could – and should – be re-ordered. This chapter explores this shift in the meaning of revolution in two main sections. First, it examines one of the central modes of contemporary revolution – the negotiated revolutions that marked the end of the Cold War in Central and Eastern Europe, and that characterized the two mobilizations in Ukraine discussed in Chapter 6. Second, it explores the extent to which the 2011 Arab uprisings sit within, or offer a challenge to, this tradition, arguing that there is a family resemblance between the events of 2011 and negotiated revolutions, if also important differences around levels of negotiation and the use of violence. Particular attention is paid to the ways in which information and communications technologies (ICTs) impact on revolutionary trajectories. In contrast to cyber-utopians who see ICTs as exerting independent causal agency, the chapter argues that they do little

---

[1] The obvious exceptions are the revolutionary strand of militant Islamism, exemplified by al-Qaeda and Islamic State and populism. I discuss these movements in the following chapter.

to disturb existing revolutionary trajectories. This links the analysis of this chapter with the next, concluding chapter, which explores the ways in which revolutions, albeit in amended form, will continue to constitute core features of contemporary world politics.

Negotiated Revolutions

The first point to note about revolutions in the contemporary world is the continuing presence of self-declared revolutionary states, including China, Iran, and Cuba. These states use the rhetoric of revolution in order to legitimize many of their domestic and foreign policies. They also use the trope of revolution in order to build alliances, such as the 'anti-imperialist united front' promoted by Venezuela and Iran during the presidencies of Hugo Chavez and Mahmoud Ahmadinejad. Such alliances have a long heritage. The first state to recognize the Soviet Union was the monarchy of Afghanistan. For their part, the Soviets promoted anti-imperialist movements against Western empires in Asia, such as the campaigns waged by militant Muslims against British and Dutch forces. The Congress of the Peoples of the East, held in Baku in 1920, included calls by Bolshevik leaders for jihad against the British (Halliday 2008). Not only was jihad considered to be a legitimate form of anti-imperialist struggle, Islam was seen as embracing, at least to some extent, a nomadic form of collective production. Formal alliances between Islamists and socialists existed in the six Muslim republics of the Soviet Union. And, although many Islamists viewed socialism as a form of Western apostasy,[2] many rhetorical tropes used by Islamists were borrowed from socialist movements. Hence the familiar claims by figures as diverse as Ayatollah Khomeini and Osama Bin Laden that Muslim lands were under occupation, their resources were being plundered, and that corruption had infected the rulers of Muslim territories.

These self-declared revolutionary states, all of which were either formed during the Cold War or which take their inspiration from pre-1989 experiences, conform fairly closely to existing revolutionary anatomies. So too does the existence of branches of militant Salafism, which ably illustrate the long-term potency of the relationship between revolutionary ideologies, hierarchy, and violence. The goals and strategies

---

[2] It is worth recalling that, for the most part, Islamists and leftists were on opposite sides of twentieth-century history. In Turkey, Algeria, Sudan, Oman, Indonesia, Afghanistan, and elsewhere, alliances of convenience were constructed between conservative governments and Islamic groups against left-wing movements, often with US support. For more on this history, see Halliday (2008).

of these groups have been considered at length in previous chapters; I return to them in the next chapter. The focus of this chapter lies elsewhere, in excavating a second strand of contemporary revolution, one associated with the negotiated revolutions that marked the collapse of state socialism in Central and Eastern Europe in 1989 (Bruszt 1990; Karl 1992; Adam and Moodley 1993; Sparks 1995; Tökés 1996; Lawson 2004; Armbruster 2010). The claim is not that negotiated revolutions are the *sole* vector of contemporary revolutions. Rather, it is that negotiated revolutions are one of the principal vectors through which to understand contemporary revolutionary anatomies.

The events of 1989 are often considered to mark a breakthrough to a new form of 'unarmed' (Ritter 2015), 'color' (Beissinger 2007), 'self-limiting' (Staniskis 1984), 'democratic' (Thompson 2004), or 'electoral' (Wilson 2011) revolution.[3] Although some scholarship is concerned with differentiating these categories (e.g. Nepstad 2015), this chapter sees them as synonymous. If the events of 1989 are considered to be the principal breakthrough to this new form of revolution, their origins are rooted in earlier streams of thought, movements, and events. In terms of streams of thought, the next chapter argues that negotiated revolutions, which are oriented around political injustice rather than the social question, occupy a well-established, if latent, tradition in the study of revolutions. In terms of preceding movements, some features of negotiated revolutions can be found in twentieth-century civil rights campaigns, in particular their advocacy of non-violent protest (Ackerman and DuVall 2001; Karatnycky and Ackerman 2005; Nepstad 2011, 2015). In terms of events, repertoires associated with negotiated revolutions can be detected in earlier movements, not least the 1974 Carnation Revolution in Portugal, which ousted the Estado Novo (Goldstone 2003), and the 1986 Philippine uprising, which deposed Ferdinand Marcos (Thompson 1995). However, if their origins can be traced to earlier traditions, movements, and events, 1989 represents the archetypal articulation of negotiated revolutions.

Negotiated revolutions 'scrambled the revolutionary inheritance, mixing past, present and future in novel, yet incoherent ways' (Kumar 2008: 227). They did so in five main ways. First, like previous revolutions, negotiated revolutions stemmed from systemic crisis in which the existing order could not continue in the same way. But at no point did

---

[3] Bunce and Wolchik (2011: 27) also focus on elections, but prefer not to use the term revolution, seeing this as setting unreasonable expectations about degrees of transformation. Instead, they label these processes 'democratising elections', or instances of 'electoral turnover'.

the old regime collapse. There was no process to mirror the French defeat in the Seven Years War, or Russian traumas over its defeat to Japan in 1904–5 and its losses during the First World War. These events were critical antecedents in the slide towards a revolutionary situation. But in negotiated revolutions, it was the weakness of both sides that compelled them to negotiate. The legitimacy of state elites was undermined by two dynamics: first, the removal of the Soviet guarantee by Mikhail Gorbachev, following the announcement that each state would be left to go it alone; and second, the long-standing vulnerabilities associated with autocratic regimes in which few intermediate associations stand between state and society. These weaknesses meant that states in Central and Eastern Europe were chronically vulnerable to revolutionary pressures. However, although state socialism contained inherent frailties, it is not the case that the system had to fail when or where it did so (Halliday 2010). Indeed, in many cases, particularly East Germany, it was a close-run thing as to whether elites chose to deploy coercive force against protestors (Sarotte 2012). If they had done so, the regimes may well have endured for some time. This was the path taken by both the Burmese junta and the Chinese politburo in 1989. It has also been the path taken by Syria's president, Bashar al-Assad, since the 2011 uprising against his rule. In all three cases, regimes managed to hold onto power.

If most state elites in Central and Eastern Europe disavowed coercion as a policy tool, so too did their opponents. There was no opposition movement in the region that saw armed confrontation as a viable option, with the partial exception of Romania. Rather, violence was considered to be an illegitimate strategy, partly because of the role of the coercive apparatus in suppressing protests in the region (including in Hungary in 1956 and Czechoslovakia in 1968), and partly because of the routinized coercion associated with state security forces. This not only served to weaken the collective capacity of opposition movements, it also weakened the viability of violence as a transformative tool. In this sense, both sides of the conflict approached the crisis from a position of mutual weakness. And both sides sought a settlement of previously irreconcilable differences primarily through non-violent means. While the central motif of past revolutions was linked closely to armed confrontation, negotiated revolutions took on an explicitly non-violent character.

Second, because negotiated transformations were relatively non-violent processes in which deals were struck between revolutionaries and their adversaries, they were conducted through a distinct set of mechanisms: roundtables replaced guillotines (Garton Ash 1989). During almost all of the 1989 revolutions, members of the old regime sat across the table from revolutionaries in order to negotiate their surrender. Negotiations also dealt with the immediate aftermath of this surrender: the make-up of transitional bodies, the rules by which elections would take place, the role and function of constitutional committees, and so on. For the most part, negotiations were restricted to questions of political and symbolic relations. The main demands of the students, intellectuals, white-collar workers, professionals, and labour representatives who made up the revolutionary coalition were oriented around political injustice rather than economic equality, and their main ideological tool was nationalism rather than class (Goldstone 2009: 29–30). Although all revolutionary movements are anti-coalitions that share a negative goal (to oust the old regime) rather than a common transformative programme (Dix 1984: 433), negotiated revolutions represent an extreme form of this configuration, deliberately disavowing hierarchical organization, and containing no economic programme beyond a basic desire to liberalize. At the same time, negotiations circumscribe the potential for radical change, thereby reducing the transformative impact of the revolutions.

This leads to a third difference between negotiated revolutions and past revolutions: rather than engender the creation of a stronger, more bureaucratic state, negotiated revolutions produce a relatively weak state constrained both in terms of its despotic authority and its infrastructural capacity. As previous chapters have shown, in order to shore up their regime from opposition at home and abroad, modern revolutionaries built vast bureaucracies and armies, exerting domestic authority through extensive mechanisms of surveillance and control. As a result, post-revolutionary states possessed a dual strength: a considerable infrastructural capacity and a despotic potency. These strengths often spilled over into tyranny. This pattern was not repeated by negotiated revolutions. Those who conducted negotiated revolutions sought to 'catch up' with liberal states. They signed up to a raft of international treaties and ordinances, even when these restricted their freedom of manoeuvre over fiscal and security policy. At the same time, because they faced neither major domestic or external opposition, revolutionaries had no need to build up mass armies or extend their control coercively. On the contrary, incoming governments sought to contain rather than expand the authority of the armed forces and security apparatus, seeing them as bastions of the old order – post-Soviet satellite states reduced the size of their militaries by an average of 44 per cent and reduced the percentage of GDP spent on their militaries by an average of 65 per cent (Carter et al. 2012: 452).

Fourth, the utopian vision associated with the excesses of revolutionary states was exchanged for a revolutionary ideology rooted in 'anti-politics' (Konrád 1984). By eschewing fidelity to a totalizing schema, negotiated revolutions avoided the patterns of domestic and international terror, counter-revolution, and war that characterized many previous revolutions. Negotiated revolutions sought to build a new order through tried-and-tested mechanisms: representative government secured through a liberal constitution; regular elections competed over by a range of political parties; the separation of the state from the military; and an active, supportive voice in liberal international organizations. Economically, negotiated revolutions adopted privatization and liberalization programmes that opened up domestic markets to foreign competition, and established an independent financial sector. Politically, negotiated revolutions favoured forms of reconciliation such as lustration and truth commissions. In terms of their social policies, negotiated revolutions adopted a relatively open environment secured by an independent media. In this way, the vision offered by negotiated revolutions was rooted in liberal principles, norms, and practices: a concern for representative government; marketization (even if there were stark differences within coalitions about how this was to be realized); and the securing of cooperation through international organizations. As a consequence, the outcome of negotiated revolutions was a strengthening of liberal international order rather than a challenge to it.

Finally, negotiated revolutions generated a shift in the relationship between revolution and counter-revolution. As previous chapters explored, revolutions have often generated new military and economic alliances that, in turn, induced a conflict between the revolutionary state and a counter-revolutionary coalition that sought to contain it. In contrast, because revolutionaries in 1989 did not seek to export their revolution and because they did not present a challenge to liberal international order, no counter-revolutionary force was unleashed to contain or overthrow the new regime. To the contrary, leading international actors welcomed negotiated revolutions. As long as revolutionaries agreed to abide by the rules of liberal international order (most notably, liberalization programmes and membership of international organizations), great powers accepted what had previously been outcast states into international society. As the last chapter showed, the support of the United States, the EU, and Western foundations was central to Ukraine's revolutionary mobilizations in 2004 and 2013–14. More generally, states in Central and Eastern Europe joined international organizations ranging from NATO to the WTO. And they were given assistance, both in normative terms (through recognition of the legitimacy of the uprisings) and in material forms (through aid packages, support for reforms, election monitors, and so on). Burkean suspicion of revolution was supplanted by Paine-like enthusiasm for revolution.

Negotiated revolutions, therefore, form a considerable amendment to existing anatomies of revolution, so much so that they have prompted debate as to whether they constitute revolutions at all (e.g. Garton Ash 1989, 1990; Habermas 1990; Lévesque 1997; Furet 1999; Goodwin 2001; Lawson 2004, 2005; Foran 2005; Kumar 2008; Goldstone 2009; Rupnik 2014; Bayat 2017). The five points noted above engender shifts in understandings of revolutionary situations, outcomes, and trajectories. In terms of revolutionary situations, negotiated revolutions arise less through acts of radical delegitimation such as defeats in war than through more contained shifts in patterns of international hierarchy, authority, and rule. In terms of revolutionary outcomes, negotiated revolutions focus more on political and symbolic fields than on programmes of economic transformation. At the same time, because negotiated revolutions are not fights to the finish that yield decisive victory, their transformative programmes are less rapidly instituted, and pursued with less zealotry, than was the case in many modern revolutions. As a result, they foster weak rather than strong states, particularly in terms of their despotic capacity. Beyond these shifts in revolutionary situations and outcomes, negotiated revolutions offer a considerable challenge to existing accounts of revolutionary trajectories. From a position of dual sovereignty, both sides seek recourse via a set of primarily non-violent repertoires: negotiations, demonstrations, occupations, petitions, strikes, rallies, and the like. At the same time, the 'post-ideological' commitment of negotiated revolutions rejects the use of grand narratives, embedded in state institutions, as vehicles for social transformation (Dabashi 2012: 13). Finally, although negotiated revolutions are sustained by organizations such as labour unions and social movements, the coalitions they mobilize are less hierarchical in structure and less premised on a notion of vanguard leadership than previous movements.

Negotiated Revolutions 2.0?

The post-Cold War world has seen a number of negotiated revolutions. Uprisings in Serbia, Georgia, Ukraine, Lebanon, Moldova, and elsewhere have resembled the experience of Central and Eastern European states, sometimes closely, at other times at more of a remove. The uprisings that took place in many parts of the Middle East and North Africa in 2010–11 also shared a family resemblance with negotiated revolutions, including horizontally organized movements promoting primarily non-violent protest, a formal ethos of democratization, and a focus on political and symbolic concerns rather than economic transformation.

However, the Arab uprisings departed from existing understandings of negotiated revolutions in four ways: first, there was little by way of negotiation between the old regime and protest groups; second, there was more violence than in previous instances of negotiated revolution; third, there were claims that the use of ICTs acted as a break from existing revolutionary trajectories; and fourth, the context in which they emerged was different. The pro-democracy, pro-capitalist movements of 1989 and after fit with a triumphalist post-Cold War narrative in which democracy and capitalism were seen to be the only games in town. By 2011, things had changed, in part because of the fallout from the 2008 financial crisis, in part because of the challenge presented by apparently stable authoritarian states. History, it seemed, did not move in only one direction. At the same time, the regional context in 2011 was unlike that of 1989. In Central and Eastern Europe, the Soviet Union was the sole metropole around which satellite states revolved. In the Middle East and North Africa, two regional powers – Iran and Saudi Arabia – were embroiled in a rivalry that was severe enough for both to intervene in support of their allies. On the ground, Islamists saw the uprisings as a way to make their societies *less* rather than *more* liberal. In this sense, the events of 2011 demonstrate well the ways in revolutionary anatomies adapt to new circumstances. In 2011, as in other revolutionary contexts, time, place, and history are crucial to explaining how, why, and where revolutions take place.

Revolutionary Situations

Although the 2011 uprisings were surprising, they were not out of keeping with previous revolutionary pathways. First, there was a weakening of the state afforded by inter-social relations. For example, the Egyptian regime's ties to the United States and Israel were deeply unpopular amongst the general public. In the years leading up to the uprisings, Egypt was the second largest recipient of US aid (worth around $1 billion dollars per year in military aid alone), one of the main sites for the torture and rendition of suspected al-Qaeda suspects, and a backer of Israeli policies in the region, including the blockade of Gaza. These policies generated a sense of alienation between the regime and the people. According to the 2010 Pew Global Attitudes Survey, 82 per cent of Egyptians strongly disapproved of the United States (up from 69 per cent five years earlier). Opposition to the regime's support for the United States and Israel found its way onto the street: there were large-scale protests in solidarity with the second Palestinian intifada in 2000 and even larger protests following the onset of the 2003 Iraq war. These protests helped to forge ties that, in turn, sustained the 2011 uprising (Gunning and Baron 2013; Cole 2014; Ritter 2015). Changes in inter-social relations also included a demonstration effect in that uprisings in one state acted as a stimulus for protest in others.[4] Indeed, the example of protests in Tunisia and Egypt spread around the region and beyond, spurring movements in Mauritania, Djibouti, and Sudan as well as those in Bahrain, Syria, Yemen, Oman, Libya, and Jordan.

Second, many of the regimes were neo-patrimonial in nature, combining personalized rule with a degree of legal-rational functioning. For many years, these regimes appeared to be stable, so much so that much of the literature on the region revolved around the resilience of authoritarianism in the Middle East (e.g. Bellin 2004). However, over time, neo-patrimonial rule, personality cults, and the use of arbitrary force failed to substitute for the lack of institutional buffers between exclusionary states and civil societies (Bellin 2004: 145–6). The lack of intermediate associations between state and society meant that elites were insulated from the people, finding few effective channels by which to meet grievances and institutionalize contestation. This served to hollow out state–society relations, making regimes vulnerable to surges of discontent from below. Such discontent, ranging from strikes to assassinations, was a regular feature of contentious politics in the region, even if its main effect was to strengthen the position of the security apparatus. States in the region could subjugate their people, but they lacked the institutional depth to regulate society efficiently. In short, they were 'fierce', but not 'strong' (Ayubi 1995: xii). Indeed, it was just these weaknesses that enabled revolutionary pressures to emerge during 2011.

Third, during 2011, a systemic crisis emerged in a number of Arab states. Unlike most of the revolutions surveyed in this book, this crisis did not emerge out of an act of radical delegitimation such as a defeat in war. And nor did systemic crisis lead to state collapse. Rather, as with other cases of negotiated revolution, systemic crisis produced a stalemate in terms of state power. The example of Egypt helps to illustrate these dynamics.[5] Before the 2011 uprising, the legitimacy of the Egyptian state

---

[4] The closeness of the ties between ruling families and their congeries also fuelled diffusion. As Roger Owen (2012) notes, the elites of the region had close ties – their similar modes of rule meant that they shared similar vulnerabilities. For an argument that these similarities can be overplayed, see Stacher (2012).

[5] This section concentrates on Egypt for two reasons: first, for reasons of space; and second, because Egypt is, for most observers, the pivotal case within the revolutionary wave. In this sense, Egypt is to the 2011 uprisings what France was to the 1848 Springtime of

rested on three main pillars: the 1952 revolution; the role of the military in freeing Egypt from Western hegemony (particularly the nationalization and subsequent conflict over Suez); and the (broadly) socialist development policies pursued by Nasser, during which the state took over the planning, coordination, and management of production. This had the effect of demobilizing social forces, including private landholders and the bourgeoisie, by using land reform and industrialization as tools for exerting state authority over economic activities (Dodge 2012: 6–7).[6] It also led to reasonable levels of state-led growth, fortified by price subsidies that made basic commodities affordable to the vast majority of the population. State income was further generated through aid, particularly from the United States, which paid handsomely in exchange for Egypt's recognition of Israel following the 1979 Camp David Accords, its opposition to Iran, the suppression of Islamists (including the execution of the 'Islamist Lenin' – Sayyid Qutb), and the regular passage of US warships through the Suez Canal.

The Egyptian state was, therefore, secured through a combination of state-led development and redistribution. However, under Sadat and Mubarak, this legitimacy was eroded as the state became constructed more through repression than by popular mandate. Both Sadat (in 1977) and Mubarak (in 1986) deployed the army against domestic protestors. After the assassination of Sadat by members of al-Jihad (Sacred Combat) in 1981, emergency laws made the state an everyday presence in people's lives. A vast security establishment, made up of police, state security, and state-sponsored gangs (*baltagiya*), was constructed on the back of two million informants. The result was an extensive despotic system that combined low-intensity coercion, such as harassment and surveillance, with high-intensity coercion, ranging from imprisonment to murder. Even as Mubarak increased the despotic power of the state, he reduced its infrastructural potential through engaging in a range of neoliberal reforms. During the 1980s and 1990s, the regime reduced tariffs, abandoned interest rate controls, and removed import quotas. This served to intensify state dependence on Suez, aid, remittances, and tourism, making the Egyptian economy more susceptible to international capital. A dip in commodity prices during the mid 1990s forced

---

Nations and Poland was to the 1989 revolutions in Central and Eastern Europe. For more on pivotal cases, see Bunce (2013).

[6] At the same time, the military became a powerful economic actor in its own right, controlling up to 15 per cent of the Egyptian economy (Varol 2012: 346). The military ran farms and factories (often using conscripts as free labour), and owned a considerable portfolio of real estate. Members of the armed forces also enjoyed privileged access to housing, transport, and health facilities.

the state to further leverage its debt and reduce public expenditure. The subsequent austerity measures prompted a decline in living standards for much of the population, even as a 'network of privilege' (many of whom were associated with Gamal Mubarak, the president's son) used personal connections with state brokers to secure lucrative contracts (Cole 2014: 36–42). The conspicuous consumption of this elite network meant that they were increasingly seen as a minority caste operating outside, or on top of, civil society. At the same time, worsening living standards stimulated opposition around the loss of dignity (*al-karama*) associated with the degrading of social conditions (Alexander 2011: 5–8).

Concurrent with these dynamics, demographic changes placed additional burdens on the state. By 2011, around one-third of the Egyptian population was aged 15–29 (Shehata 2011: 28). This exerted considerable pressures on job markets, just as the state was becoming more neoliberal, more personalistic, and more repressive. In 2009, unemployment in the region reached nearly 25 per cent; many more were in informal, insecure work (Gunning and Baron 2013: 149). Unemployment rates were even higher amongst young people and disproportionately felt within the middle class – college graduates in Egypt were ten times more likely to have no job as those with only a primary school education (Goldstone 2011: 12). Short-term triggers added to the sense of state failure. Between 2008 and 2010, food prices increased by over a third (Dodge 2012: 11). The simultaneous removal of food subsidies (the bread subsidy alone cost the state $3 billion per year) fuelled resentment against the regime: over two-fifths of Egyptians lived at or below the poverty line (Abdelrahman 2013: 574; Gunning and Baron 2013: 131). Despite the decline in its economic sovereignty after two decades of neoliberal reforms, the legitimacy of the Egyptian state was tightly bound up with its capacity to guarantee a secure standard of living. It was, therefore, particularly susceptible to such crisis. To most Egyptians, it seemed like the state had abandoned the poor for the sake of the rich.

By 2011, Egypt, like many other states in the region, was home to a neo-patrimonial state sustained by 'repression, payoffs, and elite solidarity' (Quandt 1998: 30). Networks of crony capitalists secured profits through personal connections, while the majority of the population had seen their living standards fall, often quite dramatically. State and society were held together only through an extensive security apparatus. Despite this vulnerability, the Egyptian regime was slow to respond to the threat posed by the December 2010 protests in Tunisia. Already under pressure following allegations of vote-rigging in the November 2010 parliamentary elections, Mubarak did not react to the escalation of protests in the early part of 2011, even after the Tunisian president, Zine Ben Ali, resigned in mid-January. On 25 January, protestors called for a 'Day of Rage', chosen because it was a national holiday (Police Day) marking the anniversary of a massacre of police officers by the British in 1952. The chants of the protestors were unyielding: 'al sha'b yurid isqat al-nizam' (the people demand the overthrow of the regime); or, more simply, 'Arhil!' (Leave!).

From this point on, protests spread in both breadth (reaching Alexandria, Suez, Ismailia, and other parts of the country) and depth (upscaling from tens of thousands to hundreds of thousands of people). Although protestors largely embraced non-violence (*silmiyya*), resistance was shown to state forces and the *baltagiyya*, not least in the popular quarters of Cairo, by Ultra football fans, and in the burning down of the headquarters of Mubarak's National Democratic Party (NDP) during a second Day of Rage on 28 January. Around the country, police stations, state security, and NDP buildings were burned, often after sieges that lasted several days (Ismail 2012; Ketchley 2017). Further confrontations, including the bloody Battle of the Camel in and around Tahrir Square on 2 February, illustrate that, although non-violence was a prescribed tactic of the protest movement, elements of it were willing to use force, whether in self-defence or, on occasion, to confront regime loyalists. Non-violence was more of a strategic choice than a normative commitment (Lynch 2012: 91–6).[7]

As protests intensified, so Mubarak's hold on power weakened.[8] Initial hesitancy turned into a dual strategy of concession and repression. The

[7] The balance to be struck between violent and non-violent protest was much debated within the protest movement (Lynch 2012: 91–6; Gunning and Baron 2013: 193–201; Cole 2014: 151). It is important to note that, in the Arab uprisings and elsewhere, there was no straightforward either-or between violent and non-violent action. As discussed in Chapter 1, violence and non-violence often exist simultaneously within the same protest movement or develop from one to the other. At the same time, these distinctions are in the eye of the beholder in that they rely on interpretations that are themselves linked to political position. In any assessment of this issue, the central issue revolves around whether there is a *formal* embrace of non-violence by the *main* strands of the opposition. This is the case for most, but not all, protest movements during the 2011 uprisings. For a discussion of the 'violent flank effect' generated by armed wings of predominantly non-violent movements, see Chenoweth and Shay (forthcoming). For a useful distinction between violent protest (i.e. hand-to-hand fighting and rock throwing) and armed protest (i.e. guns and bombs), see Tilly (2003). For an analysis that uses this distinction in relation to Egypt, see Ketchley (2017). For a fuller discussion of these issues, see Kadivar and Ketchley (2018).

[8] During the early stages of the protests, Mubarak was bolstered by US reluctance to fully endorse the protests. The initial message from the White House was that the United States supported a 'managed' or 'orderly' transition rather than a popular revolution (Holmes 2012: 400; Gerges 2013: 415–16; Tripp 2013: 99). Some other states in the region, particularly Israel and Saudi Arabia, argued that the United States should be *more* forceful in its defence of Mubarak, seeing the US abandonment of its former ally as a betrayal.

president promised to resign at the end of his term of office, while simultaneously ordering an escalation of violence against protestors. The strategy failed. To the contrary, they splintered the coercive apparatus, sapping Mubarak's support within the police, his party, and the military. Large numbers of police failed to show up for work, took off their badges, or went over to the protestors. On 5 February, the entire executive committee of the NDP was forced to resign, including Gamal Mubarak. As the protests escalated, the military pursued a double game: permitting protests to continue (so as to weaken the position of state officials vis-à-vis the military), while simultaneously containing them (so as to restrict the capacity of the protests to radically reshape military prerogatives) (Stein 2012: 24). However, the removal of Gamal Mubarak and his associates from formal positions of authority reduced the need for further intra-elite competition. At the same time, the close association drawn by protestors between their struggle and the military, as in the notion of the 'one hand' shared by the people and the army against the regime, pushed the military closer to the protests (Stein 2012: 24). At first, the military refused to fire on the protestors and protected them from state-sponsored violence, albeit selectively. On 10 February, the military publicly endorsed the people's 'legitimate demands'. Mubarak resigned the next day. The head of the General Intelligence Service, Omar Suleiman, oversaw a transfer of power to the Supreme Council of Armed Forces (SCAF), which opened negotiations on a new constitution and elections.

The principal events of the Egyptian uprising sit well within prevailing revolutionary anatomies. First, there was a crisis of the state fostered by inter-social relations: the closeness of elite ties to Israel and the United States, the dependence of the regime on international capital, and the demonstration effect of the Tunisian protests. Second, the neo-patrimonialism of the Mubarak regime made it vulnerable to both elite fracture and surges of discontent – it was despotically strong, but infrastructurally weak. The gap between rich and poor, and state and society, plus the everyday brutality of the security apparatus, made the regime susceptible to extended contention from below. For many years, the regime was held together through a combination of elite pacts and shared rents. However, the defection of key elites, particularly the military, made Mubarak's position untenable (Bellin 2012: 130).

Revolutionary Trajectories

Earlier chapters noted two critical configurations that lie behind a successful revolution: elite unity, particularly over the coercive apparatus; and the formation of a close-knit oppositional identity. By early

2011, elite fracture was common to many states in North Africa and the Middle East as a result of rising levels of inequality, corruption, cronyism, shifts in inter-social relations, and widespread contention. In this context, the defection of the armed forces was crucial. Where this took place (as in Tunisia and Egypt), autocrats were ousted. Where the military and the regime remained united, protests were either decompressed (as in the Gulf monarchies) or became bloody (as in Syria). The next section assesses this variation in outcome in more detail. This section concentrates on the second feature associated with successful revolutions – the organizational coherence of a united opposition.

The coalition that deposed Mubarak was made up of disparate forces: labour groups, urban youths, students, hardcore football fans, professionals, and religious groups, most notably the Muslim Brotherhood, who formally joined the uprising at the end of January and, thereafter, took a leading role in protecting the protestors against the police and *baltagiyya* (Gunning and Baron 2013: 175). Street demonstrations, particularly in solidarity with the Palestinian intifadas, were an established tradition in Egypt, while the neoliberal policies initiated by Sadat and Mubarak had been met by frequent strikes. During the 2000s, these protests intensified – between 2004 and 2008, over 1.7 million workers took part in nearly 2,000 strikes (Solidarity Centre 2011: 14; also see Chalcraft 2016: 506–11). Groups like the 6th April movement (formed in support of a strike by textile workers in the Nile Delta) and Kefaya ('Enough') were persistent irritants to the regime. Revolutionary entrepreneurs attempted to connect these disparate groups into a coherent coalition. These wired cosmopolitans, mostly young, well-travelled, technologically savvy professionals, coordinated opposition activities and translated local events for foreign media.[9] They also used ICTs to establish safety committees and other such bodies. This prompted claims that the use of ICTs was generating a shift in the basic modalities of revolutionary trajectories.

As discussed in the previous chapter, recent years have seen a shift in revolutionary theory and practice away from the hierarchical vision associated with vanguardist parties towards a flatter structure associated with popular coalitions (Foran 2003). During the 2011 uprisings, it is argued, ICTs served to unify these popular coalitions (e.g. Brooke 2011; Howard and Hussain 2011; Simmons 2011; Walgrave et al. 2011; Castells 2012; Howard and Hussain 2013). This is a crucial claim.

---

[9]   Three-quarters of the social media traffic around Egypt's revolution came from outside the region, while 90 per cent of the tweets about the uprising originated from outside Egypt. See: Aday et al. (2012: 11–13); Brym et al. (2014: 269–70).

Without such unity, popular coalitions are unlikely to influence the development of revolutionary trajectories. In short: opposition requires organizing. For some analysts and protestors, ICTs were this organizational vehicle during the 2011 protests, providing a means through which messages were shared, grievances were aired, and abuses were documented (Howard and Hussain 2011: 36; Cole 2014: 8–13). For ICT enthusiasts, new technologies have the capacity to perform several key functions: overcome collective action problems, connect previously fragmented sites of opposition, and mobilize publics to action (Ayres 1999; Bennett et al. 2008; Brooke 2011; Simmons 2011; Walgrave et al. 2011; Tufekci 2017). In this way, it is claimed, ICTs formed part of a new media environment that provided a direct interface between publics and elites. Satellite television channels, such as Al-Jazeera, fostered a 'transnational public sphere' that unified 'Arab issues' (Lynch 2011: 302; Lynch 2012: 10–11). Bloggers reported where the mainstream media could not, evading state capture and galvanizing new solidarities (Lynch 2011: 309). In some countries, independent media (such as the Egyptian newspaper *Al-Masry Al-Youm*) offered analysis untainted by association with the state. By fostering decentralized networks out of the reach of formal sites of political authority and by sharing information both immediately and without official sanction, ICTs helped to provide the 'digital scaffolding' for a new type of contentious politics (Simmons 2011: 590; Howard and Hussain 2013: 64).

Despite claims of newness, the connection between ICTs and mass protest goes back a long way.[10] Marshall McLuhan (1962) outlined the liberating qualities of ICTs over half a century ago. A generation later, Manuel Castells (1996) argued that ICTs were disrupting existing power relations and constituting new forms of network society. The constitutive impact of ICTs on protest movements is also something that has been stressed by a number of Western governments over the past 30 years. In 1989, Ronald

[10] So too does cyber-utopianism. Nineteenth-century ICTs were seen as game-changing technologies, including by Marx, who saw them as prompting 'the annihilation of space by time'. The breakthrough technology was the telegraph. Optical telegraphs capable of sending messages 400 kilometres per day were available by the late eighteenth century, albeit mainly for military purposes. By the late nineteenth century, telephones were replacing the telegraph, still relying on wires, but replacing coding and decoding process with direct voice communication. During the same period, radio technology made long distance communication possible at the speed of light. These developments impacted on many aspects of social life. Governments could find out about political and military developments almost as they happened, financiers had faster access to information about markets, and revolutionaries could spread their messages both more quickly and over greater distances. On this, see Buzan and Lawson (2015).

Reagan declared that 'the Goliath of totalitarianism will be brought down by the David of the microchip'. As the last chapter showed, the Internet helped to mobilize protests in Ukraine in 2004 and 2013–14. Social media began to be seen as a major influence on mass uprisings following the extensive use of YouTube during the 2007 Saffron Revolution in Burma, the 2009 uprising in Moldova, and the Green Revolution in Iran later that year. Such associations were given extra impetus by a high-profile speech by US Secretary of State, Hillary Clinton (2010), who argued that 'the spread of information networks is forming a new nervous system for our planet'. The Internet, Clinton claimed, provided the first ever 'global networked commons'. Comparing bloggers to dissidents and social media to *samizdat*, Clinton argued that the Internet 'is like Radio Free Europe on steroids'. She went on to announce a range of policies designed to break down 'virtual walls' and secure 'internet freedom'. Leading advisers were charged with pursuing this '21st century statecraft' (Cull 2013: 134). There were well-publicized visits to Iraq, where the retinue included Jack Dorsey, founder of Twitter, and Colombia, where officials met with Oscar Morales, the web designer who used Facebook to generate a campaign against FARC guerrillas.

The Arab uprisings, therefore, fit smoothly within existing understandings of the relationship between ICTs and democratization. But to what extent did such technologies impact on revolutionary trajectories in 2011? Once again, it is worth examining the case of Egypt. There is little doubt that Facebook played some role in organizing protests in Egypt. The Facebook group Kulina Khaled Said ('We Are All Khaled Said'), established in commemoration of a blogger murdered by Egyptian police in 2010, gathered hundreds of thousands of members, many of whom took part in demonstrations against the regime. The widely circulated autopsy photo of Khaled Said served a mobilizing function comparable to the video of Neda Agha-Soltan, the Iranian protestor shot dead by police during the 2009 Green Revolution, which became a potent point of connection between protestors inside the country and transnational networks. Such points of connection usually circulated outside formal media outlets, most of which were distrusted by Arab publics. These informally circulated videos, photos, and messages served as information cascades, highlighting regime brutality and fuelling a sense of outrage (Lynch 2011, 2012). They also acted as connecting nodes between otherwise disparate networks, energizing empathetic cascades that ratcheted up pressure on elites to 'do something' (Walgrave et al. 2011: 329). During major events, such as the removal of Hosni Mubarak, these cascades helped to foster sharp spikes in the use of digital media (Howard and Hussain 2013: 57; Brym et al. 2014: 270).

Such dynamics certainly worried Arab states. At the end of January 2011, the Egyptian government required the country's main Internet Service Providers (ISPs) to disable their networks. The government also asked Vodafone for details on subscribers and used the network to send out pro-regime texts. After five days, however, the government lifted its blockade, seeing the ban as igniting rather than suppressing dissent. In other words, more people came onto the streets once the Internet had been disabled. This is a puzzling outcome given claims about the necessity of ICTs in mobilizing protest. Some protestors may have been able to work around the blackout via smartphones or alternative means of communication (Lynch 2012: 90). For the most part, though, the shutdown worked. But if protestors are supposed to have *required* ICTs in order to solve collective action problems, connect disparate networks, and coordinate activities, it is curious that protests in Egypt intensified during the period.

Perhaps this is not such a puzzle. As even the most enthusiastic cyber-utopians accept, digital data leaves an audit trail, one that can be used for surveillance and censorship as well as for transparency and mobilization (e.g. Brooke 2011: 233–5; Lynch 2011: 306; Howard and Hussain 2013: 50, 60; Tufekci 2017: 226–41). Social media is often appropriated by authoritarian governments in order to trace protestors, spread propaganda, and monitor the activities of opposition groups. These forms of 'negative control' act as vehicles of suppression (Deibert et al. 2010; Gunitsky 2015), something that many activists also recognize. In January 2011, a pamphlet entitled 'How to Protest Intelligently' was circulated widely amongst protest groups in Egypt. The pamphlet explicitly asked protestors not to use Twitter, Facebook, YouTube, or other websites because, 'they are all monitored by the Ministry of the Interior'. At other times, protestors used ICTs as decoys, while real demonstrations were organized through word of mouth (Gunning and Baron 2013: 284). After the 2009 Green Revolution, the Iranian government formed a cybercrime unit charged with countering the 'American led cyber-war' and arresting those guilty of spreading 'insults and lies' about the regime through the Internet (Morozov 2011: 10). The Chinese government has constructed a Great Firewall around the Internet and has become adept at initiating online blockades. A number of authoritarian states are well versed in carrying out Distributed Denial of Service (DDoS) attacks, while the Internet has proved to be a valuable source of authoritarian propaganda. Vladimir Putin's United Russia party enjoys an extensive online presence. The Kremlin also sponsors cybersecurity networks that spread pro-Russian views and disrupt competitor states, just as the Chinese government uses online message boards to legitimate its policies and draw out dissenters. Authoritarian states are increasingly using ICTs not just as tools of monitoring and suppression, but in order to better articulate their position, mobilize their support base, gather information about publics, and attack their opponents (Gunitsky 2015: 42–3).

On the one hand, therefore, ICTs can help to coordinate revolutionary protests. On the other hand, they can be used to disrupt these very protests. The utility of ICTs depends on how they are embedded within wider fields of action. At times, ICTs serve as echo bubbles rather than tools of connection, amplifying in-group communication and reinforcing existing sentiments (Pariser 2011; Aday et al. 2012). This means that ICTs can foster a dialogue of the deaf as easily as they encourage a unifying narrative. And even this dialogue takes place unevenly. Internet penetration rates in North Africa and the Middle East in 2011 were not particularly high – only 10–20 per cent of people in the region could 'easily gain access to the internet' (Howard and Hussain 2011: 47). Fewer than 8 per cent of Egyptians were registered Facebook users in April 2011,[11] while 131,000 had active Twitter accounts (0.15 per cent of the population); fewer than 10 per cent of Egyptians say that Internet news sites or social media were their principal sources of information during the 2011 uprising (Brym et al. 2014: 269–70). This may be a strategically important minority (Howard and Hussain 2011: 47), but such figures still suggest that a digital divide is in operation which is a long way removed from hopes of fostering a virtual commons. Those who see ICTs as valuable instruments of mobilization would do well to concentrate less on social media (which is relatively rarely used) and more on cell phones (which are commonplace). And they would do even better to relax assumptions about the *requirement* of ICTs to revolutionary processes. ICTs are good at generating 'weak ties' – networks of acquaintances that 'likes' or 'shares' the same tastes. They are less good at fostering 'strong ties' – the durable connections of solidarity, emotional intensity, and commitment that sustain collective protest (Granovetter 1973: 1361; Della Porta and Mosca 2005; Gladwell 2010; Bennett and Segerberg 2013; Walgrave and Wouters 2014). This latter form of connection, best forged through personal ties of kinship and friendship, and in the midst of struggle, is not easily made. To the contrary, it costs. And it is not something that ICTs foster easily.

---

[11] It is worth noting that Facebook was only made available in Arabic in 2009.

The grander claims of cyber-utopians do not, therefore, stand up to scrutiny. As previous chapters have shown, revolutionaries are adept at making use of available social technologies: pamphlets, banners, songs, cartoons, graffiti, and posters that mobilize protest through affective cultural performances. Multiple mediums, from salons to taverns, and from ships to public squares, have carried revolutionary repertoires around the world. Sometimes these repertoires are articulated through words, slogans, and visual cues, at other times, they are articulated in song – the importance of the Egyptian guitarist Ramy Essam, the Tunisian hip-hop artist El Général, and the Syrian musician Ibrahim Qashoush to the Arab uprisings take place within a longer tradition of revolutionary protest music. Whichever form these social technologies assume, the key point is that analysts of revolution should direct attention to the message rather than the medium. During the Arab uprisings, it was not ICTs per se, but the integration of these technologies within wider communicative ecologies based on strong, personal ties of trust that enabled protests to cohere (Bennett and Segerberg 2013: 88, 196). Most often, protestors got their information face-to-face or through word-of-mouth, the most trusted mediums of all.

This analysis yields two points. First, like many contemporary revolutionary movements, including the 2013–14 protests in Ukraine examined in Chapter 6, the organizational character of the popular coalitions in North Africa and the Middle East was predominantly horizontal and decentralized. This made them highly participatory. But participation came at a price. Although good at galvanizing protests against incumbents, these movements were less successful at turning mass protests into coherent, enduring opposition forces. As a result, post-uprising pacts were made out of the reach of the popular coalitions that had been at the heart of the protests. Second, the use of ICTs had a range of effects, from connecting local and transnational networks to helping construct an 'ecology of dissent' made up of associations of activist networks (Bennett and Segerberg 2013: 19). Although ICTs helped to raise levels of participation and, to some extent, coordinate protests, they did little to foster coherent, sustainable oppositional movements that would allow protestors to maintain pressure on their respective regimes.

This speaks to a second issue – the balance to be struck between generating large, diverse opposition coalitions and the need for internal cohesion within the protest movement. The former helps to explain why some revolutionary movements in North Africa and the Middle East were able to oust authoritarian regimes – as with Viktor Yanukovych in Ukraine, the despots who led these regimes served as a common enemy and, thereby, a temporary point of unity around which diverse groups could cohere. The latter makes clear why, after autocrats had been ousted, many movements were unable to consolidate their victories. The diversity of the coalition that helped them succeed in the first phase of the struggle worked against them in the second – participants shared a common short-term goal (to oust the dictator), but not a long-term vision of how political, economic, and symbolic relations were to be reforged. As a result, even when autocrats were overthrown, the aftermath of the revolutions saw elites sidestep revolutionary coalitions, decompress their challenge, or engage them in violent struggle. The result, as the next section shows, was considerable divergence in the outcomes of the revolutions.

Revolutionary Outcomes

In many ways, it is too early to assess the outcomes of the 2011 uprisings. If the minimum condition of revolutionary outcomes is the period in which a revolutionary regime takes control of the principal means of production, means of violence, and means of information in a society, only Tunisia has reached this point. And even then, this has been a close-run thing, sustained by a diverse coalition of secularists, from employer organizations to labour unions, which have united – for now – against militant Islamists. This coalition has done little to appease young Tunisians concerned about ongoing inequality and heightened security – 90 per cent of those under 31 abstained from voting in the 2014 elections (Achar 2016: 164). Many continue to protest the slow pace of change. Nevertheless, despite concerns about gradualism and the precariousness of Tunisia's governing coalition, it is worth emphasizing the achievements of the post-2011 settlement: the Ben Ali regime has been ousted, a new constitution is in place, multi-party elections have been held, the military has been confined to barracks, the political police has been disbanded, and a range of commissions have been established to tackle corruption and related activities. These are no small measures. They also stand in stark contrast to Tunisia's neighbours.

In Egypt, events since the uprising have demonstrated the salience of 'old politics' over 'new politics' as the military and old regime elites have worked together to recapture the political landscape. The presidential victory of Mohamed Morsi, a leading figure in the Muslim Brotherhood, in June 2012, led to attempts to extend the power of Islamists and institute a range of repressive measures. This break-up of the revolutionary coalition stimulated widespread protests, spearheaded by Tamarrod (Rebellion), a group whose leadership had previously headed Kefaya. Tamarrod organized mass petitions against Morsi, which were followed by large-scale street protests. For their part, the coercive apparatus used

Tamarrod's mobilization as a means of further destabilizing the Morsi government (Ketchley 2017: 16, 110–13). Police withdrew from routine duties and failed to follow up attacks on the offices of the Muslim Brotherhood. Increased violence by militant Islamists in Sinai deepened the sense of crisis. In June 2013, the army deposed Morsi. Substantial repression followed, not just against the Muslim Brotherhood, but also against journalists, labour unions, human rights bodies, and student organizations. In May 2014, the representative of the military, Abdel Fattah el-Sisi, became president with a proportion of the vote (96.9 per cent) that would have made Mubarak blush. Sisi's counter-revolutionary coalition included Nasserists, trade unionists, and prominent business interests, brought together by their shared opposition to Morsi and Mubarak, and by the long-standing hold of a 'populist authoritarian' model of state-led development, which Sisi was thought to represent (Allinson 2019). The Saudis and other Gulf states provided huge sums to keep the Sisi regime afloat. Sisi also took out a loan from the IMF in order to prop up the Egyptian economy. In the 2018 presidential elections, he secured an even higher percentage of the vote than he achieved in 2014, albeit on a turnout of just over 40 per cent. Yet, despite Sisi's apparently iron grip, Egypt remains fragile. Commodities are in short supply, inflation is high, and subsidies are being cut. The combination of inequality and repression that fuelled the 2011 revolution remains a combustible blend.

In Yemen, although President Saleh was forced to resign in early 2012, demands for further concessions and, in some areas, secession produced a bloody civil conflict that has turned into a proxy war between Saudi Arabia, which backs the government, and Iran, which backs the insurgents. Libya too is undergoing a period of significant civil unrest following the 2011 multi-state intervention; the country has effectively fractured into warlordism. Yet neither Libya nor Yemen matches the scale of the bloodshed in Syria, where the failure of protestors to oust President Bashar al-Assad led to the onset of a brutal civil war, one that has once again been internationalized by foreign intervention. Taken together, these three conflicts amount to international wars, fuelled by transnational flows of money, arms, and people (Lynch 2016: 3).

Bahrain's uprising was crushed by a combination of monarchical obduracy and Saudi force. Through the vehicle of the GCC, the Saudis sent 2,000 troops into Bahrain in order to secure the regime against protest, following this with large supplies of petrodollars in an attempt to appease protestors. The Saudis redirected 8 per cent of their GDP, worth over $100 billion, to mollify protest both in the region and at home, including a $1 billion gift to Jordan and a $4 billion grant to

Egypt (Lynch 2012: 131; Matthiesen 2013: 129; Chalcraft 2016: 3; Gerges 2016: 18). The Sheikh of Kuwait gave every citizen a $3,500 gift (Bayat 2017: 217). GCC states also stoked sectarian identities in an attempt to divide opposition coalitions. This threefold strategy of repression, aid, and sectarian polarization decompressed protest, at least in the short term. Together, GCC states promised (even if they did not always deliver) billions of dollars of aid around the region, while simultaneously clamping down on opposition groups and mobilizing sectarian affinities in a counter-revolutionary strategy that acted as a brake on the uprisings.[12] A second strand of counter-revolution, led by Qatar, sought to strengthen the position of political Islamists, such as the Muslim Brotherhood, as well as some Sunni militant groups, most notably al-Nusra in Syria. Although initially successful, Qatar's counter-revolution has been supplanted, both by force of arms and money, by the Saudi project. The Saudi-led isolation and blockade of Qatar, which began in 2017, aptly illustrates this shift.

Overall, therefore, the short-term outcomes of the 2011 uprisings can be split into four main groups: first, successful revolution (Tunisia); second, mixed outcomes in which autocrats were deposed, but transformation has been either overturned (Egypt) or led to intensified conflict (Yemen); third, the decompression of protest through authoritarian upgrading and counter-revolution (Saudi Arabia, Bahrain, Kuwait, Morocco, Jordan); and fourth, the emergence of violent polarization (Libya, Syria). No state in the region bar Tunisia meets the minimum criteria of revolutionary change, let alone the maximum condition of revolutionary success, whether understood as the simultaneous transformation of economic, political, and symbolic relations associated with modern revolutions or the more contained programmes associated with negotiated revolutions. All in all, two-thirds of the region's autocrats survived the uprisings and even where they did not, as in Libya and Yemen, the outcome has been ruinous (Geddes et al. 2014: 326). In many cases, 'dissidents made the first noises, but soldiers had the last word' (Brownlee et al. 2015: 63).

There are three main reasons for this lack of success. First, revolutionaries in states outside the original onset of the crisis overstated the possibilities of revolutionary success. The uncertainty generated by the ousting of Ben Ali in Tunisia generated 'cognitive shortcuts': the propensity to place too much weight on dramatic news from elsewhere and the drawing of firm conclusions from relatively sparse information

---

[12] This brake is likely to be short-lived: by solving one problem (mass protests), states have generated a new one (the re-ascription of forms of categorical difference).

(Weyland 2012: 920–4). This is a common theme in revolutionary waves, but it was heightened in 2011 by two additional factors: the despotic character of states in the region, which meant that they had few institutional filters through which to channel information, and the relatively weak organizational capacity of the protest movements, as documented in the previous section. Second, once the wave had begun, regimes learned quickly. As noted in Chapter 2, revolutionary waves often become less successful the further they travel from their original point of instigation, because revolutionaries enact their protests in increasingly inhospitable settings, because authoritarian regimes learn how to demobilize their challengers, and because authoritarian state–society relations do not disappear overnight. In this sense, the Tunisian uprising was successful not because of its particular state–society complex, the role of inter-social factors, or the organizational coherence of its opposition, but because it was the *first* such struggle in the region. This suggests that revolutionary scholarship should be concerned less with the fact of the emergence of a revolutionary wave than with the timing of its emergence. Finally, although some uprisings succeeded in ousting autocratic rulers, none succeeded in taking full control of the state. Rather, in a number of states around the region, post-uprising pacts were made through deals out of the reach of the popular coalitions that were at the heart of the protests.

This final point provides two main insights for those working on contemporary revolutions. First, too much attention has been paid on ways to oust autocrats and not enough on what happens after rulers have been deposed. The divergent outcomes of the Arab uprisings make clear that just as much attention should be paid to developing post-conflict visions and strategies as there is on constructing opposition movements. It is one thing to oust a dictator; it is another to construct viable economies and systems of governance. Wendy Pearlman (2011) has noted the importance of organizational coherence to ousting dictators. But this is just as important to the post-struggle stage. In the aftermath of a successful revolution, diverse coalitions must be moulded into well-ordered movements that are able to govern. Key to their success is the articulation of a clear vision that is able to go beyond opposition and sustain a new government. Second, those protest movements operating once a protest spiral is underway must be aware that autocrats are sometimes fast learners. As a result, techniques and strategies that work in the early stages of a revolutionary wave are unlikely to work once the wave is underway. In these circumstances, rather than replicating earlier techniques and strategies of contention, protestors will need to innovate in order to keep pace with autocratic learning.

That the outcomes of the 2011 uprisings are, in the short-term, one of largely unsuccessful revolution, the general analytical point this chapter has addressed – the emergence and adaptation of a mode of negotiated revolution – stands. As noted in the previous section, most negotiated revolutions produce weak states, hemmed in domestically through their failure to deliver decisive victory and constrained internationally through their desire to join rather than challenge existing institutions. To date, the 2011 uprisings do not disturb this pattern. The region as a whole is stuck between fragile pacts, illiberal renewal, and unmet grievances. Throughout the region, the deep state that characterizes the connections between power brokers in the military, the state, the security services, and the private sector will not dissolve easily. However, these connections will have to cohabit with (at least partial) democracies and (at least partially) reformed monarchies in a volatile environment in which alliances are being renegotiated. At the same time, expensive wars and high levels of arms spending, major public spending commitments, low oil prices, and mobilized publics speak to the ongoing fragility of regimes in the region (Lynch 2016: 245). The outcomes of the 2011 uprisings will be unfolding for some time to come.

Beyond Negotiated Revolution?

The introduction to this chapter laid out five main components of negotiated revolutions: their origins in a relative rather than systemic state crisis; their recourse to elite pacts rather than armed confrontation; their rejection of the utopian commitments of past revolutions; their welcoming by leading international actors; and their fostering of weak rather than strong states. All five of these components have been present, albeit in varying degrees, in the 2011 Arab uprisings.

First, the personalistic character of regimes in the region made them vulnerable. What made the 2011 uprisings distinct from previous protests was the defection of the coercive apparatus – without the support of the military, figures like Ben Ali and Mubarak could not survive. In contrast, where the military remained allied to state elites, regimes were able to endure. Second, even though protestors in some states forcibly deposed their regimes, few opposition coalitions had the capacity to engage the state in armed confrontation. In part, this was because of the illegitimacy of violence through its association with the security apparatus. In part, it was because the opposition, with the exceptions of Libya, Yemen, and Syria, did not contain a faction willing to take up arms in a concerted way.[13] This, in turn, links to a third point – the formal association of the

---

[13] Crucial here was the extent to which revolutionaries, including Islamists, felt that their

movements with non-violence. This embracing of non-violent repertoires made the Arab uprisings more palatable to liberal international actors – the fourth characteristic of negotiated revolutions. As Barack Obama put it, echoing Martin Luther King, in the aftermath of Mubarak's removal from office, 'it was the moral force of nonviolence – not terrorism, not mindless killing, but nonviolence – that bent the arc of history'.[14] Although support for the uprisings varied from case to case, there was a general sense amongst liberal international actors that the uprisings were legitimate, both in terms of their goal of ousting despotic regimes and in their formal support for non-violence. Finally, because of the limited organizational capacity of opposition movements, even when depots were ousted, state transformation has been limited. If the robustness of authoritarianism in the region has been broken, the outlook for democratization is, at best, patchy.[15]

The Arab uprisings, therefore, share a familiar revolutionary heritage. In sociological terms, they sit broadly within the framework established by the 1989 negotiated revolutions that ousted state socialism in Central and Eastern Europe, even if they depart from this schema in their lower levels of negotiation and higher levels of violence, and even if the context in which they appeared was quite different from that of 1989. This reinforces the need to examine the singularity of revolutionary episodes alongside wider themes drawn from revolutionary theory and practice. In terms of these broader currents, the 2011 uprisings belong to a stream of thought that both reinforces the legacy of 1989 and pre-dates it. Both the Arab uprisings and the collapse of state socialism can be said to sit within a family of 'civilizing and democratizing' revolutions whose roots can be traced to the American Revolution of 1776 (Selbin 2010). This places them within a distinct revolutionary tradition, one associated not only with 1776, but also with the 1848 Springtime of Nations.

Mike Davis (2011: 7–8) makes an arresting comparison in this regard, examining parallels between the protagonists in each case: Egypt and France as the 'revolutionary vanguards'; Saudi Arabia and Russia as the

---

goals could be achieved through a one-off historic compromise, as was the case in Tunisia. Where radical secularists were pitched in exclusionary conflicts with militant Islamists, as was the case in Libya and Syria, such compromises did not take place. On this, see: Goldstone (2014b).

[14] The full speech is available via the *New York Times*: www.nytimes.com/2011/02/12/world/middleeast/12diplo-text.html, accessed 7 October 2018.

[15] Around 75 per cent of those polled for the 2014 Arab Barometer favoured democracy as a system of governance, including 85 per cent of Egyptians (Tessler 2014: 31). However, it is also clear that Arab publics are somewhere between suspicious and fearful of militant Salafism, hence the wide support for the restoration of order by authoritarian forces around the region (Lynch 2014: 5, 7). Also see Bellin (2012).

'counter-revolutionary powers'; Turkey and England as the 'models of success'; Palestine and Poland as the 'romantic lost causes'; and Serbia and Shi'a groups as the 'angry outsiders'. As Davis (2011: 8), following Marx, also notes, no revolution in Europe could succeed, whether liberal or socialist, until Russia was either defeated or revolutionized. The same may be true of Saudi Arabia and Iran in the Middle East and North Africa. This tradition has further historical echoes, not least in the constitutional revolutions that took place during the early part of the twentieth century in Russia, Iran, Portugal, Mexico, China, and the Ottoman Empire. In these cases, pro-democratic movements unseated imperial regimes, held competitive elections (albeit in franchises limited to propertied men), convened parliaments, and instituted civil freedoms. In the short term, the constitutionalists were overthrown by an alliance of military elites, business groups, and great powers, in most cases after extended periods of civil strife. However, even if the revolutions of 1848 and 1905–12 were defeated in the short run, their main rationale (political liberalization) was more successful in the long run. That may also be the case for the 2011 Arab uprisings.

8   Revolutionary Futures

Back to the Future?

The previous chapter argued that the revolutions of 2011 and 1989 share a family resemblance in that both take place within a broad context of negotiated revolutions. This chapter further traces the lineage within which the Arab uprisings (in particular) and negotiated revolutions (in general) are articulated, placing them within a longer tradition of 'civilizing and democratizing revolutions' (Selbin 2010). In this way, it is argued, contemporary revolutions owe more to the legacy of 1776, 1848, and 1905 than they do to 1789 or 1917. This helps to locate contemporary understandings of revolution not just alongside strains of revolutionary liberal thought, but also alongside contemporary social movements and, somewhat paradoxically, post-modern views of revolution. The second section of the chapter examines two strains of contemporary revolution – militant Islamism and populism – that speak more directly to the traditions of 1789 and 1917. The final section uses this analysis to explore the ways in which revolutions will continue to constitute core features of contemporary world politics.

Contemporary Revolutions

The mode of revolution within which the Arab uprisings sit is one that some observers have found preferable to the social revolutions associated with Haiti, France, Russia, China, Cuba, Iran, and elsewhere. Hannah Arendt (1963), for example, attempted to resuscitate a revolutionary genealogy that ran through America rather than France (also see Dabashi 2012). For Arendt, the French Revolution marked the beginning of attempts to solve the social question, which she understood as mass poverty, inequality, and deprivation. Once revolutionary states saw themselves as responsible for issues requiring fundamental social transformation, Arendt argued, they legitimized strategies, like the Terror, which prioritized the collective over the individual. On the other hand,

Arendt argued, the social question was irrelevant in the prosperous North American colonies. Here revolution was oriented around fair political representation rather than the reordering of society – as such, it was deliberately self-limiting, seeking to restrain revolutionary excess within constitutional limits. As a result, the *novus ordo seclorum* ('new order of the ages') promised by the United States was 'of the people' rather than 'for the people' (Arendt 1963: 74), avoiding the 'compassionate zeal' that legitimized despotism in its drive for collective emancipation. For Arendt (1963: 56), this alternative revolutionary tradition, captured not just in America, but also by revolutionary councils and soviets in the early years of the Russian Revolution, was insufficiently recognized: 'the sad truth of the matter is that the French Revolution, which ended in disaster, has made world history, while the American Revolution, so triumphantly successful, has remained an event of little more than local importance'.[1] Revolutions should seek 'liberty' (from oppression), but not 'equality' (from scarcity) (for more on this point, see Dabashi 2012: 60–3).

It may be that Arendt's alternative tradition was latent rather than lost. The events of 1989 and after appear to vindicate her vision of self-limiting revolutions that focus on individual liberty and democratic representation, while leaving the social question relatively untouched. The slogans of the Arab uprisings are familiar in this regard: Huriyyah, Adalah Ijtima'iyah, Karamah (Freedom, Social Justice, Dignity). And few movements in the region, successful or otherwise, have a notion of economic restructuring that goes beyond a general desire to liberalize.[2] In many ways, therefore, it could be argued that the world's most revolutionary force over the past two centuries has been liberalism itself. Democratization and the extension of capitalism have together produced a potent amalgam – democratic capitalism – that has been embedded in many states around the world and as a kind of common sense through which most international organizations work. In this sense, there is a potent strand of revolutionary liberalism, oriented around the (sometimes coercive) promotion of democratic capitalism, which functions as a global project.

---

[1] This is not to say that Arendt's view of the American Revolution was right. Practices of institutionalized racism, slavery, and the extermination of indigenous peoples can hardly be described as self-limiting. On this, see: Bailyn (1995); Losurdo (2015). On the wider influence of the American Revolution, see Israel (2017).

[2] The main exception is the Rojava region with its three self-governing cantons: Afrin, Jazira, and Kobane. In Rojava, egalitarian notions of democracy co-exist with cooperative forms of production and exchange. The constitution of the cantons can be found at: https://civiroglu.net/the-constitution-of-the-rojava-cantons/, accessed 7 October 2018.

But if we can still speak of a revolution *to* democratic capitalism, what are the prospects for revolution *within* democratic capitalist states? Contemporary democratic capitalist states appear to be insulated from revolutions in two ways: by 'solving' the social question through a mixture of growth and redistribution; and by institutionalizing points of contact between those with grievances and those in positions of authority. These points of contact promote compromise rather than confrontation. They also serve to delegitimize violent protest, regarding this as outside the bounds of legitimate contention. It is not that violent protest does not take place in democracies – it does, whether through riots or sometimes violent campaigns by dissident groups, including the world's longest ongoing armed struggle: the Naxalite rebellion in central and eastern India (Shah 2018). But this violence is seen by the majority of citizens within democratic capitalist states as illegitimate next to regularized, non-violent forms of contention: demonstrations, strikes, boycotts, petitions, occupations, etc.[3] In contemporary democracies, the state can be lobbied and, on occasion, pressurized. But it cannot be directly confronted. The rational-bureaucratic structure of democratic states, plus the institutional linkages they promote between state and society, serve to demobilize revolutionary movements (Goodwin 2001: 27, 299–300). In this sense, the infrastructural power exerted by democratically embedded states is far more effective in averting revolution than the despotic power yielded by sultanist or neo-patrimonial regimes. Democracy anaesthetizes revolution.[4]

Despite this, recent years have seen the rise of a number of groups within democratic capitalist states that blend social movement techniques with revolutionary rhetoric: Occupy Wall Street, Podemos, Syriza, and more. Most of these groups emerged in reaction to the austerity programmes instituted in Western states following the 2008 financial crisis. However, their critique goes beyond austerity to include the corrosive effects of neoliberalism as a system, focusing on what Wolfgang Streeck (2014: 5) describes as the 'splitting of democracy from capitalism'. These groups argue that contemporary capitalism has 'immobilized' publics, generating a 'banal conformity' of 'consumer-spectators' who find it impossible to imagine a future without capitalism (Fisher 2009: 2, 4). At the

---

[3] Except when these processes turn violent or contain violent flanks, which they sometimes do.

[4] One partial exception are states, like Ukraine, which combine low-intensity democracy with competitive authoritarianism. The more authoritarian these states become, the more personalistic they are, and the more dependent they are on foreign powers, the more likely they are to experience revolutionary pressures. In this sense, the degeneration of democratic capitalism can serve as a prelude to revolution.

same time, it is argued, corporations have captured the state apparatus, making neoliberalism appear to be a natural force rather than a policy practice, and a realm of depoliticized technical expertise rather than a site of political contestation (Krippner 2011: 145–6). This process has been enabled by extensive lobbying. Between 2006 and 2010, the IMF estimates that US firms spent $4.2 billion on political activities, of which the financial sector was the most prominent (Crouch 2011: 68). In part, this is simply a matter of scale – the four biggest banks in Britain have balance sheets that, when combined, are two-and-a-half times bigger than the country's GDP (Lanchester 2018: 6). This disparity in financial clout, allied to extensive lobbying, amounts to 'the annexation of democracy by the financial markets' (Streeck 2014: 161).

Much of this critique is not new. To the contrary, its origins lie in accounts of the rise of modern capitalism in the nineteenth century, most notably the disembedding of economics from politics through the advent of the all-purpose price mechanism in which personal exchange was replaced by faceless transactions via the 'symbolic token' of generalized money (Simmel 1978/1900: 332–3; Polanyi 2001/1944). Under these conditions, every product became exchangeable, including labour. Hence, for the first time, 'free labour' could be sold (as wages) according to market logics. The bracketing of a private ('free') sphere of market exchange had the simultaneous effect of generating a public sphere of political regulation. The economy became seen as the realm of civil society mediated by logics of market exchange ('the self-regulating market' organized through 'the invisible hand'), while politics became seen as the realm of the state governed by the national interest ('raison d'état'). The separation of states and capitalism that, from a contemporary viewpoint, appears new is, in fact, a long-standing feature of modernity itself (Giddens 1985: 135–6; Rosenberg 1994: 126; North et al. 2009: 72).

For its critics, both old and new, the vision of capitalist markets as self-regulating and autonomous obscures the fact that states and capitalism are mutually constituted. The 'free market' is a political condition, an ideal that can be extended or reversed. Since the early 1970s, it has been extended through the institutionalization of neoliberalism – competitive exchange rates, tight control of the money supply, inflation targeting, a reduction of capital and currency controls, lower rates of taxation, deregulation, and so on – around the world. These policies have been closely tied to financialization, understood less as the dominance of the financial sector than as the dominance of financial activities (Krippner 2011: 2). Whereas in 1970, the financial sector provided 4 per cent of US GDP and 10 per cent of its profits, by 2010, it was worth 8 per cent and contributed 40 per cent of total profits (Turner 2011: 18). During this period, financial services become far more profitable than productive activities. In 2009, oil futures trading was worth ten times the value of physical oil production and consumption, while foreign exchange trading ran at 73 times the value of global trade (Mulgan 2013: 19). Major manufacturers, such as Ford, generate more profits through financial instruments, such as the financing of loans to buy cars, than from selling cars (Krippner 2011: 3–4).

Key to the critique offered by Occupy Wall Street and like-minded groups has been the inequality fostered by neoliberalism and financialization. For some (e.g. Piketty 2014), capitalist inequality is the norm rather than the exception. For others (e.g. Milanovic 2016), current rates of inequality are peculiar to the hyper-mobile worlds of finance and technology, which are difficult to regulate and tax. Whichever view is right, the result is the same: three decades of wage repression for those on median incomes; a growing gap between rich and poor; and a structural stagnation in middle-class incomes – the richest 5 per cent of Americans now hold as much income as the entire US middle class (Muñiz 2017: 12). With extraordinary profits available from the money magic that sustains financialization, a caste of super-rich individuals has effectively sealed themselves off from the rest of the world. The world's richest 8 per cent earn half of the world's income, the richest 1 per cent own more than half its wealth, and the world's 1,000 or so billionaires hold twice as much wealth as the entire continent of Africa (Bregman 2017: 217). At the same time, the poorest two-thirds of the world's population owns just over 4 per cent of its wealth and nearly 650 million people around the world are undernourished (Therborn 2012: 14; Bull 2013: 15). During President Obama's first term, 90 per cent of US income growth took place within the richest 1 per cent of American society (Watkins 2016: 6); 37 per cent of new income occurred within the richest 0.1 per cent (Streeck 2014: 53). If we think of the world as an apartment block, over the past generation the penthouses at the top have got larger, the apartments in the middle have been squeezed, the basement has been flooded, and the elevator between floors has become broken (Subramanian and Kessler 2013: 21).

Occupy Wall Street's slogan – 'We are the 99%' – speaks directly to this inequality. It also speaks to a growing sense of insecurity felt by two groups: first, a 'precariat' of unemployed or underemployed, often well-educated, young people facing a future of low incomes, high housing costs, few career prospects, and reduced welfare provision (Della Porta 2015: 4–5, 51); and second, salaried professionals who have been mobilized by the loss of relative incomes, a decline in job security, and a reduction in pension benefits associated with austerity programmes in particular, and neoliberalism in general. If some of those protesting had previously been involved in anti-capitalist and global justice movements, many have been newly motivated by the 'immorality' and 'indignity', as well as the inequality, of austerity programmes (Della Porta 2015: 69). The embracing of horizontal forms of participation and deliberation, including the occupation of squares and the establishing of public assemblies and protest camps, is intended as a means of defending democracy against the corporate capture of formal levers of governance.

Occupy Wall Street, Podemos, Syriza, DiEm25, and like-minded groups are therefore united in their moral outrage against three interlinked dynamics: first, post-2008 austerity programmes; second, neoliberal globalization and related processes of financialization; and third, the depoliticization of politics under modern capitalism. In many ways, these movements have been successful. At its height in 2011, Occupy had a presence in 951 cities in 82 countries. Following two years of mass protests, Syriza won 27 per cent of the vote in the June 2012 Greek elections, while Podemos won 21 per cent of the vote in the December 2015 Spanish elections. Many of the views espoused by these groups have subsequently been adopted by figures such as Bernie Sanders, Jeremy Corbyn, and Jean-Luc Mélenchon. Two-thirds of British 16–25-year-olds voted for Jeremy Corbyn in the June 2017 British elections; they also voted in higher numbers than had been seen for a generation. All of these movements speak to a desire to make capitalism more egalitarian. All share a desire to institute broadly neo-Keynesian programmes of state-led growth oriented around infrastructure, housing, and green energy. All operate with the help of new, mostly online, media outlets; some groups, such as Anonymous, emerged directly from this sphere (Beyer 2014; also see Castells 2012). And all seek to make alliances with other forums of protest, whether oriented around race (e.g. Black Lives Matter), climate justice (e.g. the 350 movement, the transition network, the Zone à Defender occupations), sexuality (e.g. #MeToo), or other issues (e.g. the drive for food sovereignty pioneered by La Via Campesina), generating cross-sectoral alliances that have stirred, if not shaken, many Western states.

A third strand of radical thought in contemporary Western states is associated with post-modern work. For post-modern scholar-activists, revolution in the contemporary world is less oriented around collective acts of systemic transformation than spectacular 'Events' that disrupt the 'dreamtime of capitalist society' (Dunn 1979: 115–16). In this understanding, revolutionaries occupy multiple spaces of hope within the capillaries of communicative capitalism, spaces where strength can be accumulated and multitudes roused to action (Deleuze and Guattari 1987; Hardt and Negri 2001, 2012, 2017; Puar 2017). For figures such as Alain Badiou (2001, 2010), the problem with modern revolutions was that they sought to totalize their experience from a singular Event. For Badiou (2001: 3, 110), a new revolutionary ethics must be articulated that is premised on the symbolic-political force of multiple Events. In similar vein, Jacques Rancière (2006: 97) argues that revolution can only be 'traced here and now through singular and precarious acts'. From a Gramscian perspective, Ernesto Laclau and Chantal Mouffe (2000; also see Errejón and Mouffe 2016) argue that the fragmentation of capitalism has produced mobile, nomadic sites of struggle that, in turn, require 'chains of equivalence' to be established between diverse, particular revolutionary articulations. Over the past generation, there has been a turn towards thinking about revolutions not as vertical, hierarchical, and collectivist, but as transversal assemblages of subjectivities and events.

These views of revolutionary theory have their parallels in revolutionary practice, from the Zapatistas (EZLN) that have contested power in Chiapas since the mid 1990s to the global justice movement of the late twentieth and early twenty-first centuries. Not only are these movements self-consciously leaderless and horizontalist, they are also rooted in prefigurative politics – the notion that the ends of a revolutionary struggle must be united with their means (Foran 2014).[5] In other words, a just revolutionary movement cannot justify unjust means, whether out of principle or expediency. Rather, ideal societies are embodied in their acts of creation. Better procedures – inclusivity, deliberation, pluralism, participation – produce better outcomes.

In the contemporary West, therefore, there are three main understandings of revolution: first, a notion of self-limiting revolutions as characterized by negotiated revolutions and their antecedents; second, the cross-sectoral movements associated with Occupy, Podemos, and similar groups; and third, post-modern approaches that stress plural assemblages. For all their differences, each disrupts the relationship between revolution and systemic transformation, seeing the revolutionary utopias associated with much of modern world history as either passé (at best) or authoritarian (at worst). All three demonstrate the ways in which revolutionary thinking adapts to novel historical circumstances.

There are two main limitations to these views of revolution. First, they often lack a clear sense of the collective, whether as foe, agency, or

---

[5] The notion of prefigurative politics has its roots in anarchist thought and practice, particularly debates with other leftists over the ethics and strategy of revolution. On this, see: Breines (1982); Graeber (2011); Gordon (2018); Raekstad (2018).

goal (Halliday 2003b; Callinicos 2008; Žižek 2012; Errejón and Mouffe 2016). The adversary of contemporary revolutionary struggles is a smorgasbord of contemporary ills: globalization, neoliberalism, austerity, environmental degradation, inequality, racism, sexism, injustice, neo-imperialism, militarism, and more. Many of those who study and take part in these movements celebrate this diversity. Similarly, many of them revel in an ethos of autonomism – horizontalism, self-organization, individuation – that seeks not to seize state power, or even engage it in direct confrontation, but to mobilize outside its reaches (Holloway 2002). But without a clear answer to the questions 'emancipation from what', 'emancipation by whom', and 'emancipation to where', these movements are likely to have fleeting rather than enduring effects. Although it may be weak ties between acquaintances that help people succeed in the workplace, it is strong ties of affective solidarity that are required to sustain revolutionary movements. Often, the micro-solidarities that revolutionaries construct heighten in-group attachments, while simultaneously decreasing levels of solidarity with those outside the revolutionary cohort (Malešević 2017: 206–7). It is little surprise, therefore, that the cross-sectoral alliances that bind contemporary movements in the short term have not generated the collective solidarities that can maintain struggles over the long term. It may be that their affective arc is too fragmented to sustain a revolutionary struggle.

Second, the results of contemporary revolutions undertaken within such parameters are often disappointing. Whether revolutions have appeared as offshoots of social movements or as spectacular irruptions, they have failed to radically transform social orders. At times, activists seem to prefer the 'purity of defeat' to the 'messy reality' of institutional politics – in Gramscian terms, they focus on a 'war of position' that articulates counter-hegemonic alternatives without translating this into a 'war of manoeuvre' that commits these alternatives to projects of state contestation and transformation (Errejón and Mouffe 2016: 78–9). In part, this is a direct result of the character of these movements themselves. The other side of the ideal that 'without leaders, we all become leaders' (White 2016: 2), is that without leaders, there are no leaders.[6] Such a view is, as its advocates acknowledge, uncompromisingly voluntarist. On the one hand, as the last chapter showed, horizontal,

---

[6] This issue is taken up by Hardt and Negri (2017: 27, 228), who favour a division of labour: 'strategy to the movement, tactics to leadership'. In turn, the leadership should be 'a Prince of the multitude'. For a defence of a communist party that can bind together the unauthorized spaces occupied by revolutionary crowds, see Dean (2016). On this broader debate, see: Thomas (2013); Errejón and Mouffe (2016).

decentralized movements are highly participatory and, as a result, good at galvanizing protests. But they are less good at turning mass protests into successful revolutions. In part, this is because coalitions are brought together for a particular purpose; once this purpose has been achieved, the coalition tends to break up. In part, it is because these movements are committed to inclusive and deliberative processes that can work at the level of a square or camp, but are difficult to scale up.[7] To date, these movements have been more successful at shifting debate within existing political ecologies than in offering an alternative to them.

A similar assessment can be made of negotiated revolutions. The orientation of negotiated revolutions towards political justice rather than the social question has limited much of their impact. Oftentimes, a concentration on fair representation has enabled policies that have deepened levels of economic inequality. At the same time, the lack of a sense of final victory, in combination with an ethos of compromise, has provided the space for old regime networks and deep states to re-establish themselves. This tendency can be dubbed *the moderation curse*. Some two centuries ago, Robespierre warned against the notion of a 'revolution without the revolution' – in other words, the notion that revolutionary transformations could take place without excess, terror, and violence. With the exception of militant Islamism and, to some extent, populism, contemporary visions of revolution are no longer oriented around utopian schemas aimed at systemic transformation. To the contrary, contemporary revolutionary struggles offer political justice, but without a corresponding commitment to socio-economic transformation. The rights and wrongs of the transformative projects associated with modern revolutions have been much debated. A comparably judicious assessment of the strengths and shortcomings of negotiated revolutions is a central task for contemporary students of revolution.

The Return of Revolution

If negotiated revolutions, social-movements-come-revolutionary-movements, and post-modern understandings of revolution represent a blurring of the revolutionary tradition, two contemporary strands of revolution – militant Islamism and Populism – lie more straightforwardly

---

[7] This is not to say that some movements do not have such ambitions, particularly those concerned with climate justice and eco-socialism. See, for example: https://systemchangenotclimatechange.org/; https://thenextsystem.org/, accessed 9 October 2018.

downstream of the view of revolution espoused by Jacobinism, Bolshevism, and comparable currents, including fascism.

Militant Islamism

To understand the revolutionary components of militant Islamism, it is worth taking a step back, both analytically and historically. Analytically, it is important to see revolutions not only as 'progressive' projects with eyes fixed on the future, but also as defensive projects aimed at protecting a way of life. Peasants, weavers, and artisans have often taken part in revolutions not in order to rebuild society from scratch, but in the hope of containing the dislocating tendencies of capitalist markets and projects of state transformation. Some revolutionary uprisings, like the one that seized power in Iran in 1979, rest on belief systems that legitimate this sense of return rather than rupture. Such movements represent profound challenges to existing conditions, yet are rooted in ideals of renewal and community (Calhoun 2012; see also Hobsbawm 1959; Thompson 1963; Hill 1975). Historically, it is worth situating militant Islamism within this conservative strand of revolution. The obvious place to start is fascism.

Although containing a number of differences, for example between southern and northern European movements over the centrality of social Darwinism and anti-Semitism (Mann 2004: 6), inter-war fascism can be seen as a single revolutionary project in that it sought to quickly and forcibly overthrow existing regimes and carry out a simultaneous transformation across multiple domains of social life: a political revolution oriented around the development of a militarized, corporatist, police-state; an economic revolution centred around the construction of a command economy that could sustain total war; and a symbolic revolution instituted through the advent of rituals, vocabularies, and practices that sought to realign the emotional commitment of the ethnos to the demos (Tooze 2007; on fascist internationalism, see Herren 2017). In this way, fascism attempted to solve the 'crisis of modernity' through a toxic blend of transcendent ideology, militarization, and the creation of an indivisible state – as Mussolini put it: 'Everything in the state, nothing against the state, nothing outside the state' (in Mann 2004: 7).

Both during the inter-war years and more recently, it has been common to see fascism and Bolshevism as two sides of the same revolutionary coin. Hitler himself said in 1934 that 'there is more that binds us to Bolshevism than separates us from it' (in Strayer 2015: 446). It is true that both fascism and Bolshevism emphasized the primacy of the collective and that both were explicitly anti-liberal. However, the sources of social power and sanctioning ideology of fascism were quite distinct from Bolshevism. Whereas fascism relied on 'the cooperation of the throne [the monarchy], the altar [the church], and the sword [the military]', Bolshevism sought to subvert and overthrow these forms of order (Mayer 1971: 21–2). Whereas fascism safeguarded private property and maintained capitalist order (Tooze 2007), Bolshevism attempted to eradicate the power of the bourgeoisie through collective ownership and central planning. Whereas fascism was overtly anti-feminist (Mussolini thought that each family should have 12 children), the Soviets set up a Women's Department (Zhenotdel), which was responsible for educating women about their legal rights, promoting female literacy, establishing medical clinics, and more (Strayer 2015: 456–7). And whereas fascism depicted a society of fear and anxiety, which it promised to remedy through a reinstatement of hierarchy and privilege, Bolshevism sought to foster a new society resting on the emancipatory potential of the working class. In short, fascism stood for national-ethnic renewal – it was an attempt to purify the nation through ties of blood, which were seen as sacred, indelible, and permanent. In contrast, Bolshevism promised a radical break with existing conditions.

If fascism and Bolshevism contain different anatomies, this does not mean that fascism should not be seen as revolutionary. Clearly it was. The fact that it has not often been studied as such demonstrates a bias within the study of revolutions towards self-consciously progressive movements. Analysts of revolutions have not spent nearly enough time on radical-conservative transformative projects.[8] As noted in the Introduction to this book, only 15 per cent of volumes on revolution survey 'reactionary' cases, almost all of which are studies of the 1979 Iranian Revolution (Beck 2018). This is a serious shortcoming. Without study of these cases, a range of important category errors are made, including over the core components of militant Islamism.

As with fascism and Bolshevism, so it is with fascism and militant Islamism – both are seen as occupying the same family tree. Once again, the comparison does not stand up. Militant Islamism is a sprawl

---

[8] The partial exception to this rule is Gramsci's (1971, 1988/1929–33) notion of passive revolution. For Gramsci, passive revolutions occur when a revolutionary crisis yields not radical rupture, but a form of 'revolution-restoration' in which dominant classes and state elites combine to deploy crisis for their own ends. In these instances, Gramsci argued, social relations are reorganized, but in ways that are geared at sustaining rather than overturning existing power relations. Passive revolutions have been a major mode of state-led development, tying together processes as diverse as the Italian Risorgimento (Gramsci 1971, 1988/1929–33), Mexican development after the 1910 revolution (Morton 2010), German politics during the inter-war years (Broué 2005; Anievas 2013), and Indian party politics in the post-war era (Desai and Riley 2007).

of assemblages rather than a coherent movement: a bricolage of Salafi, Wahhabi, and Deobandi influences, blended with local contexts and contemporary technologies (Bhatt 2009: 4). These assemblages operate in multiple sites of struggle: a transnational conflict against *kafir* (disbelievers); various attempts to form regional *ummah*; and specific struggles in places as diverse as Pakistan, Bosnia, and the Philippines. These layered spatial complexes are matched by diverse intellectual lineages. A central figure in the development of al-Qaeda's strategy, Abu Musab al-Suri, conceived the group as an amorphous, cellular network rather than as a centralized political organization (Shatz 2008). Over time, al-Qaeda has shifted from operating as a centralized vanguard with a utopian vision of social transformation into a franchise or 'network of networks' (Devji 2005: 27; Burke 2007: 13; Gerges 2007: 34; Mendelsohn 2016). Indeed, al-Qaeda's organizational structure, along with many of its activities and rhetoric, blends post-modern understandings of individuated nomads carrying out spectacular acts of martyrdom with the sparsely connected, often virtually mobilized, networks associated with contemporary social movements (Devji 2005: 31–2). This network structure, sustained by self-supporting activist cells, improves the group's flexibility and its capacity to carry out terrorist activities undetected, whether these activities are major spectaculars or, more frequently, low-tech operations that create a media 'event' through suicide bombings at public places or attacks with swords, guns, and vehicles (Burke 2015: 164–5). This is a long way removed from fascist understandings of the organic, indivisible state.

In recent years, the model of scattered, self-organizing cells promoted by al-Qaeda has been modified by the rise of the Islamic State (IS, also known as ISIL and ISIS). Over the past few years, IS has taken part in sustained competition with al-Qaeda over leadership of militant Islamism, often seeking to incite an existing al-Qaeda affiliate to splinter so that it can enter a prominent theatre, as has been the case in Yemen, Libya, Somalia, and Nigeria. On the one hand, IS is an old-fashioned revolutionary group in that its core is deeply centralized and hierarchical. On the other hand, IS is a full-spectrum organization that sustains a range of branches and affiliates, some of which are closely connected to the core and affiliated as provinces of the Caliphate (e.g. Libya), others of which operate at more of a remove (e.g. the Philippines) (Byman 2016: 155–6). Beyond this can be found individuals and independent cells, often radicalized online or via a peer group, whose only links to IS are informal, often adding up to little more than a shared ideology. IS sees these diverse formations as an organic whole – the strength of its core stimulates affiliates and inspires actions in its name. Although there are similarities with al-Qaeda's organizational form, the top-down structure of IS, its willingness to incorporate often weak branches, and its concern for territoriality represent a novel blend – the latest example of the ways in which revolutionary groups adapt to new circumstances (Dixon forthcoming; also see: Kalyvas 2015; Walt 2015; Mendelsohn 2016).[9]

Although speaking to a longer tradition of Islamist militancy, one that embraces nineteenth-century anti-imperialist struggles as well as more recent conflicts in Asia (especially Afghanistan) and Europe (especially Bosnia), most IS recruits are Iraqi Sunnis whose formative experience has been the bloody aftermath of the 2003 invasion. Its primary aim is to use state power as a vehicle of social transformation. IS administers social services, education, and cultural programmes in its territories, which it funds through oil rents, extortion, taxation, the sale of antiquities, private donations, and the spoils of war. Rarely has Charles Tilly's (1985: 169) quip about states being 'protection rackets' seemed more apt.

Whereas inter-war fascism concerned itself with national fascisms and making alliances between like-minded nation-states that were seen as the building blocks of political and symbolic authority, IS seeks to break down – and through – existing borders. As Abu Bakr al-Baghdadi, the leader of IS, puts it: 'Syria is not for the Syrians, and Iraq is not for the Iraqis. The earth is Allah's' (*Dabiq* 2014: 10). Militancy is therefore germane to IS's mission. This is best expressed in *The Management of Savagery*, a text written under the pseudonym Abu Bakr Naji, which is at the heart of IS's military strategy. For Naji, there are three stages to a military campaign: *al-Nikaya wal-tamkeen* (vexation and empowerment), in which irregular, unconventional war prompts the withdrawal of the state from a particular area; *Idarat al-tawahhush* (the management of savagery), in which chaos breeds polarization and heightened civil conflict; and finally, *Shawkat al-tamkeen* (empowerment), in which militants secure a base for the Islamic state (Burke 2015: 81: Gerges 2016: 37). As well as being a strategic imperative, IS sees violence as a cleansing force. Jihad is interpreted as an act of physical combat in which the true Muslim demonstrates their conviction by fighting for *al-hakimiyyah* – God's sovereignty (Maher 2016: 32). Apostates (*murtadeen*), heretics (*mushrikun*), oppressors (*zalimun*), tyrants (*taghut*), and rejectors (*rafida*) are excommunicated (*takfir*). The result is a sharply polarized worldview based around the concept of *al-wala' wa-l-bara'*: loyalty and disavowal (Maher 2016: 15–16). Loyalty is reserved for true believers; disavowal for unbelievers. The former offers salvation through submission and

---

[9] Many thanks to Matt Dixon for enlightening conversations on this topic.

purification. The latter legitimizes extreme acts, including murder and enslavement, as was the case for the thousands of Yazidis killed, kidnapped, or raped by IS in northern Iraq in 2014. The binary IS worldview is promoted via an extensive media department that operates over a range of platforms.

The notion of violence as a cleansing force and the wide-ranging use of propaganda represent the closest links between fascism and IS. They are not the only parallels: both share a hierarchical structure, a Manichean ideology, and a goal of seizing the state in order to enact a radical programme. Yet for all the horrors carried out by IS, there has been no systematic annihilation of a particular group and no industrial killing on anything resembling the scale of the Shoah. Nor has there been the same sense of racialized violence – for IS, the shortcoming of its enemies is not permanent points of biological difference, but wrong beliefs, which can, in theory at least, be rectified by submission and purification. The historical agent that delivers its project is the devout, a category that is earned, rather than the immemorial nation, a category that someone is born into. To put this into more formal language, where the former is achieved, the latter is ascribed.

For a time, the IS message proved to be highly successful. At its highpoint, its army boasted up to 30,000 fighters and it controlled territory as large as the UK. In 2014, al-Baghdadi announced that he was the Caliph, the supreme leader of Muslims worldwide. However, as with fascism, IS overreached, not only falling out violently with other militant Salafi groups such as al-Qaeda, but also attacking Kurds in Turkey, bombing a Russian passenger jet, and carrying out terrorist attacks in Europe. As a result, between 2015 and 2017, a concerted counteroffensive by a coalition of more than 50 states saw IS lose almost all of its territory. For two reasons, however, this has not heralded the end of the group. First, its affiliates remain active in many parts of the Middle East, North Africa, and sub-Saharan Africa, most notably in the Sahel, the vast area between Africa's northern deserts and its tropical savannah, which encompasses hotspots including northern Nigeria, Mali, and Sudan. The French state alone operates a counter-terrorism mission in the Sahel that costs $700 million each year – the region is the new frontline in the conflict between IS and its enemies. Second, the message that IS carries is one that resonates with many Muslims. It is not farfetched to think that, were other states with a significant IS presence to become as unstable as Iraq and Syria, the group would find thousands of recruits willing to take up arms.

Although united by adherence to *tawhid* (monotheism), a basic creed (*'aqida*), a common reading of history, and a shared set of intellectual influences (Wiktorowicz 2006), IS has departed from al-Qaeda on a range of issues: it attends primarily to the 'near enemy' (Muslim states in the Middle East and North Africa) rather than the 'far enemy' (the West, particularly the United States); it seizes territory in order to generate a Caliphate immediately rather than looking to build up support over the long term; and it uses violence indiscriminately rather than seeking the support of fellow Muslims for its campaigns (Burke 2015: 17–18; Gerges 2016: 4). Such adaptations are likely to continue. Joas Wagemakers (2017: 15–19; also see Wiktorowicz 2006) argues that there are three main currents within contemporary Salafism: 'quietists', who focus on education and preaching, and who see politics as diluting the purity of Islam; 'politicos', who are actively involved in politics, including on occasion extra-constitutional activities; and 'jihadis', who seek the violent overthrow of Muslim rulers considered to be illegitimate, partly through targeting their Western backers. Neither al-Qaeda nor IS therefore represent the sum total of Salafi militancy – they are nodes within a global network that includes branch offices in Europe, Asia, and Africa. Beyond this network is a wider community that shares the basic critique and worldview promoted by these groups, if not always their tactics. Given this, the ideas and practices of militant Islamism are likely to endure for some time to come (Byman 2016: 165). In this way, more than any other, the comparison between militant Islamism and fascism has something to commend it. In the long-term, both have an afterlife that endures beyond their experience as concrete revolutionary projects.

Populism

Populism has deep roots (Kaltwasser et al. 2017). The Greek historian, Thucydides, wrote about populism some 2,500 years ago. In the nineteenth century, self-avowed populist movements appeared in Russia in the 1870s and 1880s, and in the United States during the 1890s. The term was revived to describe the experience of a number of Latin American states both during the Cold War (particularly Argentina's period of Peronism) and after (most notably in discussions of the Bolivarian Revolution instituted by Hugo Chavez in Venezuela) (Molyneux and Osborne 2017: 6–8). More recently, the term has been applied to a motley cast of characters: Silvio Berlusconi, Alberto Fujimori, Recep Erdogan, Narendra Modi, Raila Odinga, Rodrigo Duterte, Beppe Grillo, Marine Le Pen, Thaksin Shinawatra, Yoweri Museveni, Geert Wilders, Evo Morales, Julius Malema, Victor Orbán, Jair Bolsonaro, Pablo Iglesias, Donald Trump, and more. The recent surge in populism is therefore nothing new. Nor is it new to see the term encompassing figures from both the left (like Morales) and right (like Trump), as well as those in-between (e.g. Grillo). Populism is nothing if not adaptable (Laclau 2005).

It is clearer what contemporary populism is against than what it is for. Primarily, populism pitches itself against liberalism (Mudde and Kaltwasser 2017), whether represented by free markets, the free movement of peoples or, on occasion, representative democracy itself. It speaks to a widespread loss of trust in mainstream politics, parties, and institutions (Brubaker 2017: 369–71), which are seen as distant, corrupt, and concerned with projects that favour some groups, particularly women and minorities, at the expense of 'real people' (Müller 2016: 19–20; Molyneux and Osborne 2017: 17). Like social-movements-come-revolutionary-movements, contemporary strains of populism are animated by the retooling of liberalism as neoliberalism, which is often referred to by its populist detractors as globalism or globalization. Populists claim to speak for those left behind by the dislocations fostered by neoliberalism/globalism.[10] As noted in the previous section, it is easy to see why their views resonate so widely: hyper-mobile markets, particularly in finance, appear to be not just uncontrolled, but uncontrollable; inequality is at unprecedented levels; and most people outside the super-rich are worse off than they were ten or 20 years ago – 80 per cent of American households, 90 per cent of Italian households, and 70 per cent of British households saw their incomes either stagnate or decline between 2009 and 2016 (Muñiz 2017: 12). Since 2008, Britain has experienced its longest period of decline in real incomes since consistent records began at the end of the Napoleonic Wars (Lanchester 2018: 5).

There is, however, a difference in emphasis between populist movements and the more overtly progressive movements discussed in previous sections. Populists stress the ways in which international competition has stripped away jobs, as well as emphasizing the role of new technologies in generating either unemployment or underemployment. The shift to post-industrial economies has seen the emergence of ever more flexible (and therefore insecure) labour markets alongside increasing automation and the loss of a range of social protections (Pettersson 2017: 5–7). This is an environment in which many people feel abandoned and even more feel powerless. Over the past generation, manufacturing jobs have retracted throughout the West, in part because

---

[10] This is not always the case. In India, for example, Narendra Modi's version of populism is one that combines a virulent strain of Hindu nationalism with *adherence* to neoliberalism/globalism. For his part, Jair Bolsonaro links a racialized view of Brazilian nationalism with a liberalizing economic agenda.

of China's hyperventilated development, in part because of offshoring and the development of global value chains, and in part because of a profound digital disruption. A slide first presented at an IBM event in 2015, and that subsequently went viral, summarizes this digital disruption crisply: The world's largest taxi company owns no taxis (Uber); Its largest accommodation provider owns no real estate (Airbnb); The world's largest global phone companies own no infrastructure (Skype, WeChat); The world's most valuable retailer has no inventory (Alibaba); The most popular media owner creates no content (Facebook); The fastest growing banks have no actual money (SocietyOne); The world's largest movie house owns no cinemas (Netflix); The largest software vendors don't write the apps (Apple and Google). Populist anger is fuelled by mega-corporations that produce little of substance, employ few people, and pay little tax.

The response of populists to these multiple instabilities is usually a combination of neo-protectionism, which is seen as a bulwark against globalization, and nativism, which is a reaction to the sense of contempt shown by both centre-left and centre-right parties to the 'cultural backwardness' of 'ordinary people' (Streeck 2017: 12; also see Hall 1979; Fraser 2017). Populists tend to reject neoliberalism/globalism on the one hand, and cultural diversity on the other, in favour of 'popular nationalism'. Both critiques combine to generate a hostility towards immigrants, a hostility that sometimes bleeds (quite literally) into virulent forms of racism. Immigrants, it is argued, do not just take 'our' jobs and drive down 'our' wages, they also pollute society. They are, in effect, impure. Populist parties combining neo-protectionism and nativism have appeared throughout the West, partly in response to increased migration and associated moral panics. Viktor Orbán is the Prime Minister of Hungary and his Fidesz party has a substantial majority in the Hungarian parliament. The Norwegian Progress Party has formed part of a governing coalition since 2013. The People's Party is currently the largest party in the Swiss Federal Assembly. Donald Trump won the American presidency in 2016. Jair Bolsonaro became president of Brazil in 2018. The linking by populists of neoliberalism with identity politics is not confined to the right – Evo Morales, the left-wing president of Bolivia, often distinguishes the 'real mestizo people', who suffer from neoliberalism, from the corrupt 'European' elites, who benefit from it (Mudde and Kaltwasser 2017: 14).

The crucial move made by populists is to align 'the people' with 'a person'. In other words, populism is the embodiment of a particular group ('the people') in the form of a ('the') leader. As Donald Trump put it at the Republican Convention in July 2016, 'I am your voice'.

The people are imbued with absolute 'moral sovereignty' – they are a 'single, homogenous bloc who can do no wrong' (Müller 2017: 20). This inviolate popular will is articulated by the leader, without mediation, hence the importance of the 'Twitter bond' between Donald Trump and his supporters (Singh 2017: 25). Unlike representative democracies, in populism, the executive and the demos are one – it is not 'we, the people', but 'I, the people'. This union of leader and people is defined by its opposition to those outside the union, who become 'un-people': the elite, which may be political, corporate, or cultural, or brought together to form a single 'establishment'; 'experts', particularly intellectuals and journalists; and even those whose only crime is to live in cities. The bifurcation between 'real people' and 'unpeople' is sharply drawn, effectively dividing society into two antagonistic blocs. It is used to legitimate a range of anything-goes policies: Bolsonaro's defence of dictatorship and torture, Erdogan's detention of hundreds of thousands of his opponents, and Duterte's extrajudicial murder of drug dealers. Populists manipulate fear of others to foster an intense, extreme politics. Often this is directed at a conspiratorial enemy within, as in Erdogan's attack on Gülenists. This amounts to zero-sum politics imagined as a state of permanent emergency: we have lost because you have won. Populism represents the politics of polarization: us/them; winner/loser; native/immigrant. Against this polarization, the unity of populism – the unmediated identity that it provides between leader and people – is a powerful, even toxic, blend.

Historically, populism has been more likely to emerge in periods of crisis – populists evoke a rhetoric of crisis in order to implore 'the people' to act decisively in the face of a threat to the body politic (Moffitt 2016: 45; also see: Hall 1979; Brubaker 2017; Kaltwasser et al. 2017). It is no surprise, therefore, that the great recession that followed the 2008 crash has helped to generate a transnational wave of populism. During crisis periods, popular anger and fear can either be contained through representative government, the separation of powers, and independent legal and media systems, or expressed through more direct channels, whether seen in the social-movements-come-revolutionary-movements discussed earlier in this chapter, or populist sentiments. Both social movements and populism give full expression to public anger. And both do so by circumventing or transgressing regularized politics. Indeed, just as Occupy and similar groups use online channels to spread their message and mobilize their supporters, populists either seek to capture media outlets (as in Berlusconi's attempt to control state television in Italy) or sidestep mainstream media altogether (as in Grillo's blog and Meetup Groups) (Moffitt 2016: ch. 5). But whereas Occupy and related groups are characterized by horizontalism, deliberation, and inclusivity, populism is hierarchical, non-deliberative, and exclusive. In this sense, they represent quite different traditions. As the last chapter showed, the former act within quintessentially contemporary revolutionary anatomies. The latter speaks to an older credo: the division of society into antagonistic blocs, the absolutism of a conviction in 'the people', a denunciation of the movement's enemies, a violent rhetoric, and the seizure of political power in order to institute a transformative agenda.

There are several reasons why the current wave of populism will, in time, recede. First, the bond between leader and people will weaken as charismatic authority becomes routinized, losing some of its intensity (Molyneux and Osborne 2017: 14). Second, populists struggle to deliver on their promises. Although populists often appear as 'plebiscitary dictators' (Weber 1978/1922): 343), standing above party politics and speaking directly to the people, political power is never total. To stay in office, populists are forced to make accommodations with bureaucracies and institutions, sometimes even former adversaries. In the United States, for example, individual states and coalitions of states have been allying with parts of the federal bureaucracy, an independent judiciary, a free press, and an active civil society to constrain President Trump's agenda (Singh 2017: 22). These accommodations water down populist policies and tame the appeal of the leader. Finally, having only ever appealed to a section of a population, populism cannot sustain itself over the long-run. Over time, the 'unpeople' fight back or co-opt the populist message, as the Conservative Party has done with the UK Independence Party in Britain. Just as revolutionary agendas are constrained by the need to trade and make alliances, so the populist agenda is constrained, if not eradicated, by existing norms, practices, and institutions.

However, even when the current populist wave recedes, it is unlikely to be too long before another appears. This is because populism speaks not just to moral panics around immigration or public alienation from distant institutions, but to a recurrent tendency within capitalism towards crisis. This is not to deny the advances that capitalism has helped to foster, from wealth generation to reductions in child mortality, and from increases in life expectancy to a decline in absolute poverty (Bregman 2017: 1–7; Muñiz 2017: 11).[11] But just as night follows day, bust follows boom. Neoliberalism contains a range of structural instabilities that, as yet, policy-makers have scarcely faced up to, let alone begun to solve.

---

[11] Some of these gains are being threatened. For example, in many parts of the West, life expectancy is beginning to fall and infant mortality is beginning to rise. This is linked to post-2008 austerity programmes and associated processes: declining household incomes, reductions in state services and spending, rising levels of drug abuse, etc.

Globalization generates instabilities that challenge both incomes and identities. Populism provides answers to these instabilities, as well as recurrent periods of capitalist crisis, which make sense to many people around the world.

Realistic Utopias

A map of the world that does not include Utopia is not worth even glancing at, for it leaves out the one country at which Humanity is always landing. And when Humanity lands there, it looks out, and, seeing a better country, sets sail. Progress is the realisation of Utopias.[12]

There are, therefore, two main revolutionary currents in the contemporary world. The first, associated with negotiated revolutions, social-movements-come-revolutionary-movements, and post-modern views of revolution shares a commitment to pluralism, participation, and deliberation. The second, associated with militant Islamism and populism, is Manichean in ideology, polarizing in practice, and hierarchical in organization. Where does this analysis leave the theory and practice of revolution?

As discussed in the Introduction to this book, revolutionaries have often claimed to be utopian in aspiration, but realistic in analysis, rooting their strategies in existing conditions and antagonisms, while imagining alternative futures (Halliday 2003a). There is a tension here. A revolution is, in one sense, unattainable – the promise of a future that exists, in some senses, only as a dream. Yet revolutionaries claim that this future *is* attainable – the future can be made the present and the dream can be made reality, made by people who will themselves be transformed through the act of revolution. In this sense, the goal of revolutionaries is to turn the probably impossible into the improbably possible. To put this another way, revolutionaries favour the formulation of 'realistic utopias' (Lawson 2008). This theme is further developed in the work of Erik Olin Wright (2010, 2013). Wright argues that 'real utopias' exist in the 'hairline fractures' of contemporary social orders. These fractures are filled by a range of schemas, from the establishment of a Universal Basic Income (UBI) to a post-work society, and from a global tax on wealth to plans for economies based entirely on clean energy. For utopian thinkers, the point is to 'think big' in order to map out an 'open ended escape from the present' (Srnicek and Williams 2015: 108).

---

[12] From Oscar Wilde's essay, 'The Soul of Man Under Socialism', published in 1891. Available at: www.marxists.org/reference/archive/wilde-oscar/soul-man/, accessed 8 October 2018.

Wright (2010: 20–5) argues that enactments of utopian thinking face three tests: whether they are *desirable*, whether they are *viable*, and whether they are *achievable*. Desirability is concerned with the construction of ideal societies, whether these are liberal, socialist, Islamist, ecological, post-capitalist, technological, or otherwise. Viability is the sense in which utopian ideals resonate with existing conditions – they are proposals for the imaginative transformation of current practices. Finally, achievability concerns the realms of agency, strategy, and context; in short: is the ideal deliverable? If revolutions in the past offered a ruptural transformation that was premised on a sharp break between existing and future conditions, Wright (2013: 20) proposes support for 'interstitial transformations' that work in the 'niches and margins' of particular societies (also see Jameson 2010). Because utopian thinking is rooted in multiple temporalities, thick contexts, and local imaginaries, it must be plural – there are many answers to the question 'what is to be done'? Wright follows Raymond Geuss (2008, 2015; also see Williams 2005: ch. 1) in embracing the tensions that arise from acting ethically within the constraints of a particular time and place. If utopianism focuses on human needs beyond existing conditions, realism recognizes that political action takes place within contexts that are historically produced. Such a combination eschews the 'colourless, odourless "value" of "pure morality"' in favour of 'making utopias real' through an attitude of contestation alongside a 'flexible strategic pluralism' (Geuss 2015: 18).

The understanding of realistic utopias fostered by Wright, Geuss, and others helps to complement and renew existing concepts of revolution. It complements existing work by seeing real utopias as a persistent feature of revolutionary praxis, actualized in the modernization programmes, technological advances, and scientific innovations of revolutionary states. It is also a reminder of the compound aspects of unruly programmes (Scott 1998: 7–9): Lenin enthused over Taylorism and other forms of capitalist production,[13] just as militant Salafists borrow from anti-colonial, Marxian, and post-modern traditions. At the same time, such an understanding renews a revolutionary tradition derived from Rosa Luxemburg (1918), which sees revolution as multiple and indeterminate. Luxemburg stressed the need for revolutionaries to 'improvise' rather than follow 'ready-made prescriptions'.[14] For James Scott (1998: 177–8),

---

[13] The title of one of Lenin's best known texts, *What Is to Be Done?* was taken from the utopian novel of the same name by the nineteenth-century writer, Nikolay Chernyshevsky. It was also the favourite book of Lenin's brother, Alexander, who was executed in 1887 for his part in a plot to assassinate the Tsar.

[14] Luxemburg's formulation was followed by Aleksandra Kollontai, head of the Women's Section of the Central Committee during the early years of the revolution. Kollontai

this revolutionary improvisation expresses itself in *metis*, from the Greek for practical knowledge, cunning, and skill. These improvisations can be found in the attempts by those in the Rojava cantons to generate radical forms of libertarian municipalism,[15] in spaces intended to foster new solidarities around ecological issues, and in cross-sectoral alliances that challenge existing hierarchies. Scott (1998: 193) argues that *metis* provides a means by which to struggle against oppression, while avoiding the 'administrative utopianism' of 'high modernity'. The work of Wright, Scott, and Luxemburg sits well in an era that has rejected the epic of modern revolutions. What Wright and others point to is a revolutionary ethos that retains a sense of contestation, commitment, solidarity, and collectivism, but which is also adaptable, pluralist, and experimental – multiple small 'r' revolutions rather than a singular big 'R' Revolution.

This ethos emerges from a range of contexts and supports a range of activities. But for all this diversity, it shares the same desire to 're-enchant modernity' that has motivated revolutionaries over the past two centuries (Toscano 2010: 203), while seeking to avoid the authoritarian statism that has often marred the outcomes of these revolutions. If big 'R' Revolution presents itself as a Messiah bringing redemption to history's injustices, small 'r' revolutions are humbler. Their promise is not earthly salvation, but the striving for the *possibility* of radical transformation, of something better, even if that something better will never be realized. In keeping with the sensibilities of this book, it is historicist in that it sees the central concern of contemporary revolutionaries as finding new ways of generating enduring solidarities in an era of individuation. It offers a relational view of revolution as process rather than outcome. And, needless to say, in a world of globalization, revolutionary movements will be international, or they will be nothing.

Anatomies of Revolution

Recent years have seen a renewed interest in revolutions, both in practice and in theory. We are, as Jack Goldstone (2016: ii) puts it, in a 'new age of revolution'. These movements are a reminder of the enduring human

---

was critical of the path taken by the revolution, particularly after the Kronstadt rebellion, arguing that there must be 'genuine collaboration' between workers and the party rather than a 'transmission belt' from the latter to the former. For more on this, see Scott (1998). On the broader issue of party form, see Dean (2016).

[15] The influence of the American eco-anarchist Murray Bookchin on Abdullah Öcalan, leader of the PKK (Partiya Karkerên Kurdistanê – Kurdistan Workers Party), is well told in Biehl (2015). Although this influence has spread to Kurdish groups in Syria, Iraqi Kurds remain tied to a centralizing nation-state model.

proclivity to confront injustice, even as the conditions from which injustice arises change across time and place. They are also a reminder that revolutionary sentiment is a vital remedy to conditions of 'butchery and starvation' (Dunn 1972: 267). It is possible to highlight a number of themes that such activities provoke for the study of revolution: first, that continuing conditions of injustice, oppression, exploitation, inequality, and debasement mean that revolutions will remain a common feature of contemporary societies; second, that such movements are vital to vibrant social orders, both in and of themselves, and because without the possibility of radical change, the possibilities for reform are also diminished; third, that revolutions will always experience tensions between the realistic and the utopian; and fourth, that revolutionary anatomies will continue to shift in form according to the contexts in which they emerge.

This book has sought to make three main contributions to the study of revolutionary anatomies. First, it has developed an inter-social account that stresses the ways in which transboundary interactions play a generative role in how revolutions begin, endure, and end. As argued in Chapters 1 and 2, most work on revolutions falls within one of two stools: first, internalist accounts that see revolutions as the result of logics that take place within a specific society; and second, comparative internalist accounts that compare these endogenous logics in discrete settings. Neither do enough to connect and theorize the space between revolutionary sites. As such, both fall victim to 'methodological nationalism' – the bracketing (and, oftentimes, the reification) of the nation/state/society as the preeminent, natural site of research (Go and Lawson 2017). This study has sought to do something different. It has adopted a *descriptive* inter-social account that recognizes the generative impact of transboundary events on revolutions. And it has outlined the parameters of an *analytical* inter-social account that theorizes the ways in which the interactions between social sites (polities, economies, cosmologies, normative frameworks, and more) enable revolutionary dynamics to take place. Such dynamics include the formative role played by inter-state competition, forms of transnational learning, the emulation of more 'advanced' social orders, the amalgamation of new technologies onto existing organizational arrangements, and more. This 'interactive multiplicity' – the way in which the connections between diversely located entities-in-motion drive social change – is a core component of historical development (Rosenberg 2010, 2016). It is also a core component of revolutionary anatomies.

Second, this book has sought to historicize revolutions. Although historical study has been a long-standing feature of revolutionary studies, this has not always equated to a historicist approach in which a concern for the constitutive impact of time and place takes centre stage. One of the most enduring features of revolution as a practice is its malleability. As this book has shown, revolutions are not a single thing, but shapeshifters that modify their form according to the context in which they take place. Being attentive to these shifting modalities starts with a concern for the singularity of revolutionary episodes. No two revolutions are ever completely alike. That said, examination of the many forms that revolution assumes demonstrates that there are regularities within revolutionary dynamics, regularities that emerge from assembling events into causal pathways, abstracting these pathways into critical configurations, and using these configurations to explain a range of cases. For example, both this chapter and the previous chapter have examined the emergence and development of negotiated revolutions, exploring the analytical purchase of this concept in diverse empirical settings and the morphing of negotiated revolutions 1.0 into negotiated revolutions 2.0. Although no two negotiated revolutions are exactly alike, it is possible to detect causal pathways within multiple cases that are sufficiently robust to sustain wider explanations. There is no single template for how such revolutions take place. What there are instead are variations on a theme, a theme that adapts to meet new circumstances.

Third, and linked, this book is premised on a relational approach that sees revolutions as emergent rather than dispositional. All revolutions are formed by the interaction of entities-in-motion – they are confluences of events that are embedded within fields of action that are, in turn, derived from historically specific conditions. All revolutions have navels – they accumulate from events and sequences that are ordered into broader configurations. This makes revolutions significant both to historical and contemporary societies. It is the requirement that revolutions contain an essential set of characteristics that led some analysts to presume that the age of revolutions was over. It is not. Rather, revolutions in the contemporary world are changing in accordance with contemporary conditions. One of the main forms that revolution takes in the contemporary world is negotiated revolutions – the previous chapter outlined their anatomies and explored their impact. The long-term significance of negotiated revolutions is unclear; their assessment represents a challenge to come. At the same time, negotiated revolutions have not exhausted the possibilities of revolution. This opens up a final challenge: the identification and assessment of future anatomies of revolution.

References

Abbott, Andrew (1988), 'Transcending General Linear Reality', *Sociological Theory* 6(2): 169–86.

(2016), *Processual Sociology* (Chicago: University of Chicago Press).

Abdelrahman, Maha (2013), 'In Praise of Organization: Egypt Between Activism and Revolution', *Development and Change* 44(3): 569–85.

Abrahamian, Ervand (1982), *Iran between Two Revolutions* (Princeton: Princeton University Press).

(1993), *Khomeinism* (Berkeley: University of California Press).

(2008), *A History of Modern Iran* (Cambridge: Cambridge University Press).

(2011), 'Mass Protests in the Iranian Revolution', in: Adam Roberts and Timothy Garton Ash, eds., *Civil Resistance and Power Politics* (Oxford: Oxford University Press): 162–78.

Acemoglu, Daren, Simon Johnson, and James Robinson (2005), 'The Rise of Europe: Atlantic Trade, Institutional Change, and Economic Growth', *American Economic Review* 95(3): 546–79.

Achar, Gilbert (2016), *Morbid Symptoms* (London: Saqi).

Ackerman, Peter and Jack DuVall (2001), *A Force More Powerful: A Century of Non-Violent Conflict* (Basingstoke: Palgrave).

Adam, Heribert and Kogila Moodley (1993), *Negotiated Revolution: Society and Politics in Post-Apartheid South Africa* (Johannesburg: Jonathan Ball).

Adams, Julia (2005), *The Familial State* (Ithaca: Cornell University Press).

Aday, Sean, Henry Farrell, Marc Lynch, John Sides, and Deen Freelon (2012), *New Media and Conflict After the Arab Spring* (Washington, DC: United States Institute for Peace): www.usip.org/files/resources/PW80.pdf, accessed 20 March 2019.

Adelman, Jeremy (2006), *Sovereignty and Revolution in the Iberian Atlantic* (Princeton: Princeton University Press).

(2008), 'An Age of Imperial Revolutions', *American Historical Review* 113(2): 319–40.

Adorno, Theodor and Max Horkheimer (1997/1944), *The Dialectic of Enlightenment* (London: Verso).

Afary, Janet and Kevin Anderson (2005), *Foucault and the Iranian Revolution* (Chicago: University of Chicago Press).

Alexander, Jeffrey (2011), *Performative Revolution in Egypt* (London: Bloomsbury).

Allinson, Jamie (2019), 'Counter-Revolution as International Phenomenon: The Case of Egypt', *Review of International Studies* 45(2): 320–44.

Amandla! A Revolution in Four Part Harmony (2002), Director: Lee Hirsch.

Aminzade, Ronald (1992), 'Historical Sociology and Time', *Sociological Methods and Research* 20(4): 456–80.

Aminzade, Ronald and Doug McAdam (2001), 'Emotions and Contentious Politics', in: Ronald Aminzade ed., *Silence and Voice in the Study of Contentious Politics* (Cambridge: Cambridge University Press): 14–50.

Aminzade, Ronald, Jack Goldstone, and Elizabeth Perry (2001), 'Leadership Dynamics and Dynamics of Contention', in: Ronald Aminzade, ed., *Silence and Voice in the Study of Contentious Politics* (Cambridge: Cambridge University Press): 126–54.

Anderson, Jon Lee (1997), *Che Guevara: A Revolutionary Life* (London: Grove).

Anderson, Perry (1974), *Lineages of the Absolutist State* (London: Verso).

(1976), 'The Notion of Bourgeois Revolution', in: Perry Anderson, ed., *English Questions* (London: Verso): 105–18.

Andrew, Christopher (2010), 'Intelligence in the Cold War', in: Melvyn Leffler and Arne Westad, eds., *The Cambridge History of the Cold War*, Volume 2 (Cambridge: Cambridge University Press): 417–37.

Angell, Alan (1995), 'Union and Workers in Chile During the 1980s', in: Paul Drake and Ivan Jakšić, eds., *The Struggle for Democracy in Chile, 1982–1990* (Lincoln: University of Nebraska Press): 188–210.

Anievas, Alex (2013), *Capital, the State and War* (Ann Arbor: University of Michigan Press).

(2015), 'Revolutions and International Relations: Rediscovering the Classical Bourgeois Revolutions', *European Journal of International Relations* 21(4): 841–66.

Ansari, Ali (2007), *Iran Under Ahmadinejad* (London: Routledge).

(2010), *Crisis of Authority: Iran's 2009 Presidential Authority* (London: Chatham House).

Ansari, Ali and Aniseh Bassiri Tabrizi (2016), 'The View From Tehran', in: Aniseh Bassiri Tabrizi and Rafaello Pantucci, eds., *Understanding Iran's Role in the Syrian Conflict* (London: RUSI): 3–10.

Arel, Dominique (2013), 'Ukraine Since the Orange Revolution', in: Vicken Cheterian, ed., *From Perestroika to Rainbow Revolution* (London: Hurst & Co): 117–42.

Arendt, Hannah (1963), *On Revolution* (London: Viking).

Arjomand, Said (2019), *Revolution: Structure and Meaning in World History* (Chicago: University of Chicago Press).

Armbruster, Chris (2010), 'One Bright Moment in an Age of War, Genocide, and Terror? On the Revolutions of 1989', in: George Lawson, Chris Armbruster, and Michael Cox, eds., *The Global 1989: Continuity and Change in World Politics* (Cambridge: Cambridge University Press): 201–18.

Armitage, David (2015), 'Every Great Revolution is Also a Civil War', in: Keith Michael Baker and Dan Edelstein, eds., *Scripting Revolution* (Palo Alto: Stanford University Press): 57–68.

Armitage, David and Sanjay Subrahmanyan, eds. (2010), *The Age of Revolution in Global Context* (Basingstoke: Palgrave).

Armstrong, David (1993), *Revolution and World Order* (Oxford: Oxford University Press).

Ash, Timothy, Janet Gunn, John Lough, Orysia Lutsevych, James Nixey, James Sherr, and Kataryna Wolczuk (2017), *The Struggle for Ukraine* (London: Chatham House).

Aslund, Anders (2006), 'The Ancien Regime: Kuchma and the Oligarchs', in: Anders Aslund and Michael McFaul, eds., *Revolution in Orange* (Washington, DC: Carnegie): 9–28.

(2015), *Ukraine: What Went Wrong and How to Fix It* (Washington, DC: Peterson Institute for International Economics).

Asmal, Kader, Louise Asmal, and Ronald Suresh Roberts (1997), *Reconciliation Through Truth: A Reckoning of Apartheid's Criminal Governance* (London: James Currey).

Axworthy, Michael (2013), *Revolutionary Iran* (London: Allen Lane).

Aya, Rod (1990), *Rethinking Revolutions and Collective Violence* (Amsterdam: Het Spinhuis).

(2001), 'The Third Man; Or, Agency in History; Or, Rationality in Revolution', *History and Theory* 40(4): 143–52.

Aylmer, Gerald (1973), *The State's Servants* (London: Routledge).

(1974), *The King's Servants* (London: Routledge).

Ayres, Jeffrey M. (1999), 'From the Streets to the Internet: The Cyber-Diffusion of Contention', *The ANNALS of the American Academy of Political and Social Science* 566(1): 132–43.

Ayubi, Nazih (1995), *Over-Stating the Arab State* (London: I. B. Tauris).

Badiou, Alain (2001), *Ethics* (London: Verso).

(2010), *The Communist Hypothesis* (London: Verso).

Bailyn, Bernard (1967), *The Ideological Origins of the American Revolution* (Cambridge, MA: Harvard University Press).

(1995), 'The American Tragedy', *New York Review of Books* 42(15): 14–16.

Baker, Keith Michael (2015), 'Revolutionising Revolution', in: Keith Michael Baker and Dan Edelstein, eds., *Scripting Revolution* (Palo Alto: Stanford University Press): 71–102.

Barany, Zoltan (2016), *How Armies Respond to Revolution and Why* (Princeton: Princeton University Press).

Barkawi, Tarak and George Lawson (2017), 'The International Origins of Social and Political Theory', *Political Power and Social Theory* 32: 1–7.

Bates, Robert, Avner Greif, Margaret Levi, Jean-Laurent Rosenthaul, and Barry Weingast (1998), *Analytical Narratives* (Princeton: Princeton University Press).

(2000), 'The Analytical Narrative Project', *American Political Science Review* 94(3): 696–702.

Bayat, Asef (2008), 'Is There a Future for Islamist Revolution?', in: John Foran, David Lane, and Andreja Zivkovic, eds., *Revolution in the Making of the Modern World* (London: Routledge): 96–111.

(2013), *Life as Politics*, 2nd edition (Palo Alto: Stanford University Press).

(2017), *Revolution without Revolutionaries* (Palo Alto: Stanford University Press).

Beck, Colin (2011), 'The World-Cultural Origins of Revolutionary Waves', *Social Science History* 35(2): 167–207.

(2014), 'Reflections on the Revolutionary Wave in 2011', *Theory and Society* 43(2): 197–223.

(2015), *Radicals, Revolutionaries, and Terrorists* (Cambridge: Polity Press).

(2018), 'The Structure of Comparison in the Study of Revolution', *Sociological Theory* 36(2): 134–61.

Beeman, William O. (2008), *The Great Satan vs. the Mad Mullahs* (Chicago: University of Chicago Press).

Beissinger, Mark (2002), *Nationalist Mobilization and the Collapse of the Soviet State* (Cambridge: Cambridge University Press).

(2006), 'Promoting Democracy: Is Exporting Revolution a Constructive Strategy?' *Dissent* (Winter): www.dissentmagazine.org/article/promoting-democracy-is-exporting-revolution-a-constructive-strategy, accessed 20 September 2017.

(2007), 'Structure and Example in Modular Political Phenomena: The Diffusion of Bulldozer/Rose/Orange/Tulip Revolutions', *Perspectives on Politics* 5(2): 259–76.

(2014), 'The Changing Face of Revolution as a Mode of Regime Change, 1900–2012', Paper presented at the Comparative Workshop on Mass Protests, LSE, 13–14 June.

Bellin, Eva (2004), 'The Robustness of Authoritarianism in the Middle East', *Comparative Politics* 36(2): 139–57.

(2012), 'Reconsidering the Robustness of Authoritarianism in the Middle East', *Comparative Politics* 44(2): 127–49.

Benjamin, Walter (1999/1921), 'Critique of Violence', in: Walter Benjamin, *Selected Writings*, Volume 1 (Cambridge, MA: Belknap): 277–300.

Bennett, Lance and Alexandra Segerberg (2013), *The Logic of Connective Action* (Cambridge: Cambridge University Press).

Bennett, Lance, Christian Breunig, and Terri E. Givens (2008), 'Communication and Political Mobilization: Digital Media and the Organization of Anti-Iraq War Demonstrations in the US', *Political Communication* 25(3): 269–89.

Bethell, Leslie (1993), *Chile Since Independence* (Cambridge: Cambridge University Press).

Beyer, Jessica (2014), *Expect Us: Online Community and Political Mobilization* (Oxford: Oxford University Press).

Bhatt, Chetan (2009), 'The "British Jihad" and the Curves of Religious Violence', *Ethnic and Racial Studies* 33(1): 1–21.

Biehl, Janet (2015), *Ecology or Catastrophe: The Life of Murray Bookchin* (Oxford: Oxford University Press).

Bisley, Nick (2004), 'Revolution, Order and International Politics', *Review of International Studies* 30(1): 49–69.

Blackburn, Robin (1963), 'Prologue to the Cuban Revolution', *New Left Review* 21: 52–91.

Bob, Clifford (2005), *The Marketing of Rebellion* (Cambridge: Cambridge University Press).

(2012), *The Global Right Wing and the Clash of World Politics* (Cambridge: Cambridge University Press).

Bossenga, Gail (2010), 'Financial Origins of the French Revolution', in: Thomas E. Kaiser and Dale K. Van Kley, eds., *From Deficit to Deluge: The Origins of the French Revolution* (Palo Alto: Stanford University Press): 37–66.

Bourke, Richard (2015), *Empire and Revolution: The Political Life of Edmund Burke* (Princeton: Princeton University Press).

Bowen, Wyn and Matthew Moran (2015), 'Living with Nuclear Hedging: The Implications of Iran's Nuclear Strategy', *International Affairs* 91(4): 687–708.

Brancati, Dawn (2016), *Democracy Protests: Origins, Significance and Consequences* (New York: Cambridge University Press).

Bregman, Rutger (2017), *Utopia for Realists* (London: Bloomsbury).

Breines, Wini (1982), *The Great Refusal: Community and Organization in the New Left: 1962–1968* (New York: Praeger).

Brenner, Robert (1993), *Merchants and Revolution* (Cambridge: Cambridge University Press).

Brewer, John (1990), *The Sinews of Power: War, Money, and the English State* (Cambridge, MA: Harvard University Press).

Brinton, Crane (1965/1938), *The Anatomy of Revolution* (New York: Vintage).

Brooke, Heather (2011), *The Revolution Will Not be Televised* (London: Heinemann).

Broué, Pierre (2005), *The German Revolution, 1917–1923* (Leiden: Brill).

Brown, Jonathan (2017), *Cuba's Revolutionary World* (Cambridge, MA: Harvard University Press).

Brownlee, Jason (2007), *Authoritarianism in an Age of Democracy* (Cambridge: Cambridge University Press).

Brownlee, Jason, Tarek Masoud, and Andrew Reynolds (2015), *The Arab Spring: Pathways of Repression and Reform* (Oxford: Oxford University Press).

Brubaker, Rogers (2017), 'Why Populism?' *Theory and Society* 46(5): 357–85.

Bruce, Susan (1996), *Three Early Modern Utopias* (Oxford: Oxford University Press).

Brunkhorst, Hauke (2014), *Critical Theory of Legal Revolutions* (London: Bloomsbury).

Bruszt, László (1990), '1989: The Negotiated Revolution in Hungary', *Social Research* 57(2): 365–87.

Brym, Robert, Melissa Godbout, Andreas Hoffbauer, Gabe Menard, and Tony Huiquan Zhang (2014), 'Social Media in the 2011 Egyptian Uprising', *The British Journal of Sociology* 65(2): 266–92.

Buchanan, Allen (2013), 'The Ethics of Revolution and Its Implications for the Ethics of Intervention', *Philosophy and Public Affairs* 41(4): 291–323.

Buck-Morss, Susan (2000), 'Hegel and Haiti', *Critical Inquiry* 26(4): 821–65.

Bukovansky, Mlada (2002), *Legitimacy and Power Politics* (Princeton: Princeton University Press).

Bull, Malcolm (2013), 'Help Yourself', *London Review of Books*, 21 February (34)4: 15–17.

Bunce, Valerie (2013), 'Rethinking Diffusion: 1989, the Color Revolutions, and the Arab Uprisings', Paper presented at the London School of Economics, 4 February.

Bunce, Valerie and Sharon Wolchik (2007), 'Transnational Networks, Diffusion Dynamics, and Electoral Revolutions in the Postcommunist World', *Physica A* 387: 92–9.

(2011), *Defeating Authoritarian Leaders in Postcommunist Countries* (Cambridge: Cambridge University Press).

Burke, Edmund (1993/1790), *Reflections on the Revolution in France* (Oxford: Oxford University Press).

(1999/1796), 'Letters on a Regicide Peace', in: *Select Works of Edmund Burke, Vol. 3* (Indianapolis: Liberty Fund).

(2005/1792), *The Works of the Right Honourable Edmund Burke, Vol. 4* (Project Gutenberg EBook: www.gutenberg.org/files/15700/15700-h/15700-h.htm, accessed 20 March 2019).

Burke, Jason (2007), *Al Qaida* (London: Penguin).

(2015), *The New Threat from Islamic Militancy* (London: Bodley Head).

Buzan, Barry and George Lawson (2013), 'The Global Transformation: The Nineteenth Century and the Making of Modern International Relations', *International Studies Quarterly* 57(3): 620–34.

(2014), 'Capitalism and the Emergent World Order', *International Affairs* 90(1): 71–91.

(2015), *The Global Transformation: The Nineteenth Century and the Making of Modern International Relations* (Cambridge: Cambridge University Press).

Byman, Daniel (2016), 'Islamic State – A Review Essay', *International Security* 40(4): 127–65.

Byrne, Jeffrey (2016), *Mecca of Revolution* (New York: Oxford University Press).

Calhoun, Craig (2012), *The Roots of Radicalism* (Chicago: University of Chicago Press).

Callinicos, Alex (1989), 'Bourgeois Revolution and Historical Materialism', *International Socialist Journal* 42: 113–71.

(2008), 'What Does Revolution Mean in the Twenty-First Century?' in: John Foran, David Lane, and Andreja Zivkovic, eds., *Revolution in the Making of the Modern World* (London: Routledge): 151–64.

Carothers, Thomas (2002), 'The End of the Transition Paradigm', *Journal of Democracy* 13(1): 5–21.

Carr, E. H. (1969), *The Twenty Years Crisis* (Basingstoke: Macmillan).

Carter, Jeff, Michael Bernhard, and Glenn Palmer (2012), 'Social Revolution, the State, and War: How Revolutions Affect War-Making Capacity and Interstate War Outcomes', *Journal of Conflict Resolution* 56(3): 439–66.

Cartwright, Nancy (2004), 'Causation: One Word, Many Things', *Philosophy of Science* 71(5): 805–19.

Castañeda, Jorge (1993), *Utopia Unarmed: The Latin American Left After the Cold War* (New York: Vintage).

Castells, Manuel (1996), *The Rise of the Networked Society* (Oxford: Blackwell).

(2012), *Networks of Outrage and Hope: Social Movements in the Internet Age* (New York: Wiley).

Chalcraft, John (2016), *Popular Politics in the Making of the Modern World* (Cambridge: Cambridge University Press).

Chandaman, C. D. (1975), *The English Public Revenue, 1660–1688* (Oxford: Clarendon).

Charap, Samuel and Timothy J. Colton (2017), *Everyone Loses: The Ukraine Crisis and the Ruinous Contest for Post-Soviet Eurasia* (London: IISS).

Chehabi, H. E. and Juan J. Linz, eds. (1998), *Sultanistic Regimes* (Baltimore: Johns Hopkins University Press).

Chenoweth, Erica and Maria J. Stephan (2008), 'Why Civil Resistance Works: The Strategic Logic of Nonviolent Conflict', *International Security* 33(1): 7–44.

—— (2011), *Why Civil Resistance Works: The Strategic Logic of Nonviolent Conflict* (New York: Columbia University Press).

Chenoweth, Erica and Christopher Wiley Shay (forthcoming), 'Updating Nonviolent Campaigns: Introducing NAVCO 2.1'.

Cheterian, Vicken (2013), 'Perestroika, Transition, Colour Revolution', in: Vicken Cheterian, ed., *From Perestroika to Rainbow Revolution* (London: Hurst & Co): 1–31.

Chorley, Katharine (1943), *Armies and the Art of Revolution* (London: Faber & Faber).

Clark, Victor Figueroa (2015), 'The Forgotten History of the Chilean Transition: Armed Resistance Against Pinochet and US Policy towards Chile in the 1980s', *Journal of Latin American Studies* 47(3): 491–520.

Clinton, Hillary (2010), 'Remarks on Internet Freedom', Speech delivered at The Newseum, Washington DC, 21 January: www.state.gov/secretary/rm/2010/01/135519.htm, accessed 20 March 2019.

Clover, Joshua (2009), *1989: Bob Dylan Didn't Have this to Sing About* (Berkeley: University of California Press).

Cobban, Alfred (1971), *Dictatorship: Its History and Theory* (New York: Haskell House).

Colburn, Forrest (1994), *The Vogue of Revolution in Poor Countries* (Princeton: Princeton University Press).

Cole, Juan (2014), *The New Arabs* (New York: Simon & Schuster).

Colgan, Jeff (2012), 'Measuring Revolution', *Conflict Management and Peace Science* 29(4): 444–67.

—— (2013), 'Domestic Revolutionary Leaders and International Conflict', *World Politics* 65(4): 656–90.

Collin, Matthew (2007), *The Time of the Rebels* (London: Serpent's Tail).

Connelly, Mathew (2003), *A Diplomatic Revolution: Algeria's Fight for Independence and the Origins of the Post-Cold War Era* (Oxford: Oxford University Press).

Constable, Pamela and Arturo Valenzuela (1991), *A Nation of Enemies* (London: Norton).

Cooper, Marc (2001), *Pinochet and Me* (London: Verso).

Cottam, Richard (1988), *Iran and the United States* (Pittsburgh: University of Pittsburgh Press).

Crépin, Annie (2013), 'The Army of the Republic: New Warfare and a New Army', in: Pierre Serna, Antonino De Francesco, and Judith A. Miller, eds., *Republics at War, 1776–1840: Revolutions, Conflicts, and Geopolitics in Europe and the Atlantic World* (New York: Palgrave): 131–48.

Cronin, Jeremy (1992), 'Dreaming of the Final Showdown: A Reply to Jordan and Nzimande', *The African Communist* 130(4): 38–44.

Crouch, Colin (2011), *The Strange Non-Death of Neoliberalism* (Cambridge: Polity).

Cull, Nicholas J. (2013), 'The Long Road to Public Diplomacy 2.0: The Internet in US Public Diplomacy', *International Studies Review* 15(1): 123–39.

Cushion, Steve (2016), *A Hidden History of the Cuban Revolution* (New York: Monthly Review Press).

Dabashi, Hamid (2010), *Iran, the Green Movement, and the USA* (London: Zed).

(2012), *The Arab Spring: The End of Postcolonialism* (London: Zed).

Dabiq (2014), 'The World Has Divided Into Two Camps', Issue 1: https://clarionproject.org/docs/isis-isil-islamic-state-magazine-Issue-1-the-return-of-khilafah.pdf, accessed 11 October 2018.

David-Fox, David (2017), 'Towards a Life Cycle Analysis of the Russian Revolution', *Kritika: Explorations in Russian and Eurasian History* 18(4): 741–83.

Davidson, Neil (2012), *How Revolutionary Were the Bourgeois Revolutions?* (London: Haymarket).

Davies, James C. (1962), 'Towards a Theory of Revolution', *American Sociological Review* 27(1): 5–19.

Davis, Mike (2011), 'Spring Confronts Winter', *New Left Review* 72 (November–December): 5–15.

De Vries, Jan (1976), *The Economy of Europe in an Age of Crisis, 1650–1750* (Cambridge: Cambridge University Press).

Dean, Jodi (2016), *Crowds and Party* (London: Verso).

Debray, Régis (1967), *Revolution in the Revolution* (London: Penguin).

Defronzo, James (2011), *Revolutions and Revolutionary Movements*, 4th edition (Boulder: Westview).

Deibert, Ronald, John Palfrey, Rafal Rohozinski, and Jonathan Zittrain (2010), *Access Controlled: The Shaping of Power, Rights, and Rule in Cyberspace* (Cambridge, MA: MIT Press).

Deleuze, Gilles and Felix Guattari (1987), *A Thousand Plateaus: Capitalism and Schizophrenia*, Volume 2, trans. Brian Massumi (Minneapolis: University of Minnesota Press).

Della Porta, Donatella (2015), *Social Movements in Times of Austerity* (Cambridge: Polity).

Della Porta, Donatella and Lorenzo Mosca (2005), 'Global-Net for Global Movements? A Network of Networks for a Movement of Movements', *Journal of Public Policy* 25(1): 165–90.

Della Porta, Donatella and Sidney Tarrow (2012), 'Interactive Diffusion: The Coevolution of Police and Protest Behavior', *Comparative Political Studies* 45(1): 119–52.

Demes, Pavol and Joerg Forbring (2006), 'Pora: It's Time for Democracy in Ukraine', in: Anders Aslund and Michael McFaul, eds., *Revolution in Orange* (Washington, DC: Carnegie): 85–101.

Desai, Manali and Dylan Riley (2007), 'The Passive Revolutionary Route to the Modern World: Italy and India in Comparative Perspective', *Comparative Studies in Society and History* 49(4): 815–47.

Deutscher, Isaac (1984), *Marxism, Wars and Revolutions* (London: Verso).

Devji, Faisal (2005), *Landscapes of the Jihad* (Oxford: Oxford University Press).

Diamond, Larry (2002), 'Thinking about Hybrid Regimes', *Journal of Democracy* 13(1): 21–35.

Diamond, M. J., ed. (1998), *Women and Revolution: Global Expressions* (Dordrecht: Kluwer).

Dix, Robert (1984), 'Why Revolutions Succeed and Fail', *Polity* 16(3): 423–46.

Dixon, Matt (forthcoming), 'Building a Global Terrorist Organization'.

Dodge, Toby (2012), 'From the Arab Awakening to the Arab Spring', LSE IDEAS Special Report: 5–11.

Domínguez, Jorge (1998), 'The Batista Regime in Cuba', in: H. E. Chehabi and Juan J. Linz, eds., *Sultanistic Regimes* (Baltimore: Johns Hopkins University Press): 113–31.

Downing, Brian (1992), *The Military Revolution and Political Change* (Princeton: Princeton University Press).

Drake, Paul and Ivan Jakšić, eds. (1995), *The Struggle for Democracy in Chile, 1982–1990* (Lincoln: University of Nebraska Press).

Dubois, Laurent (2004), *Avengers of the New World* (Cambridge, MA: Belknap).

Dunn, John (1972), *Modern Revolutions: An Introduction to the Analysis of a Political Phenomenon* (Cambridge: Cambridge University Press).

  (1979), *Western Political Theory in the Face of the Future* (Cambridge: Cambridge University Press).

  (2008), 'Understanding Revolution', in: John Foran, David Lane, and Andreja Zivkovic, eds., *Revolutions in the Modern World* (London: Routledge): 17–26.

Edelstein, Dan (2015), 'From Constitutional to Permanent Revolution', in: Keith Michael Baker and Dan Edelstein, eds., *Scripting Revolution* (Palo Alto: Stanford University Press): 118–30.

Ehteshami, Anoush (2009), 'Iran's International Relations', in: Middle East Institute, ed., *The Iranian Revolution at 30* (Washington, DC: Middle East Institute), www.mei.edu/publications/irans-international-relations-pragmatism-revolutionary-bottle, accessed 14 March 2019.

Eisenstadt, S. N. (1973), *Traditional Patrimonialism and Modern Neopatrimonialism* (Beverly Hills: Sage).

Elton, Geoffrey (1974), *Studies in Tudor and Stuart Politics and Government* (Cambridge: Cambridge University Press).

Emirbayer, Mustafa and Jeff Goodwin (1996), 'Symbols, Positions, Objects: Towards a New Theory of Revolutionary and Collective Action', *History and Theory* 35(3): 358–74.

Ermakoff, Ivan (2015), 'The Structure of Contingency', *American Journal of Sociology* 121(1): 64–125.

Errejón, Íñigo and Chantal Mouffe (2016), *Podemos: In the Name of the People* (London: Lawrence & Wishart).

Ertman, Thomas (1997), *Birth of the Leviathan* (Cambridge: Cambridge University Press).

Espín, Vilma, Asela de los Santos, and Yolanda Ferrer (2012), *Women in Cuba: The Making of a Revolution within the Revolution* (New York: Pathfinder).

Falleti, Tulia G. and Julia F. Lynch (2009), 'Context and Causal Mechanisms in Political Analysis', *Comparative Studies* 42(9): 1143–66.

Falleti, Tulia G. and James Mahoney (2015), 'The Comparative Sequential Model', in: James Mahoney and Kathleen Thelen, eds., *Advances in Comparative Historical Research* (Cambridge: Cambridge University Press): 211–39.

Fanon, Frantz (2001/1961), *The Wretched of the Earth* (London: Penguin).

Fawcett, Louise (2015), 'Iran and the Regionalisation of (In)Security', *International Politics* 52(5): 646–56.

Fedorenko, Kostyantyn, Olena Rybiy, and Andreas Umland (2016), 'The Ukrainian Party System Before and After the 2013–14 Euromaidan', *Europe-Asia Studies* 68(4): 609–30.

Ferrer, Ada (2012), 'Haiti, Free Soil, and Antislavery in the Revolutionary Atlantic', *American Historical Review* 117(1): 40–66.

   (2014), *Freedom's Mirror: Cuba and Haiti in the Age of Revolution* (Cambridge: Cambridge University Press).

Figes, Orlando (2014), *A People's Tragedy: The Russian Revolution, 1891–1924* (London: Bodley Head).

Finlay, Christopher (2015), *Terrorism and the Right to Resist* (Cambridge: Cambridge University Press).

Finley, Moses (1986), 'Revolutions in Antiquity', in: Roy Porter and Mikuláš Teich, eds., *Revolutions in History* (Cambridge: Cambridge University Press): 47–60.

Fischer, Sibylle (2004), *Modernity Disavowed: Haiti and the Cultures of Slavery in the Age of Revolution* (Durham, NC: Duke University Press).

Fisher, Mark (2009), *Capitalist Realism* (London: Zero).

Fishwick, Adam (2014), *Industrialisation and the Working Class: The Contested Trajectories of ISI in Chile and Argentina*, PhD thesis, Sussex University.

Fligstein, Neil and Doug McAdam (2012), *A Theory of Fields* (Oxford: Oxford University Press).

Flyvbjerg, Bert (2001), *Making Social Science Matter* (Cambridge: Cambridge University Press).

Foot, Rosemary (2010), 'The Cold War and Human Rights', in: Melvyn Leffler and Arne Westad, eds., *The Cambridge History of the Cold War*, Volume 3 (Cambridge: Cambridge University Press): 445–65.

Foran, John (1993a), 'Theories of Revolution Revisited? Towards a Fourth Generation', *Sociological Theory* 11(1): 1–20.

   (1993b), *Fragile Resistance: Social Transformation in Iran from 1500 to the Revolution* (Boulder: Westview).

   (2003), 'Magical Realism: How Might the Revolutions of the Future Have Better End(ing)s?' in: John Foran, ed., *The Future of Revolution* (London: Zed): 271–83.

   (2005), *Taking Power: On the Origins of Third World Revolutions* (Cambridge: Cambridge University Press).

   (2009), 'Theorizing the Cuban Revolution', *Latin American Perspectives* 36(2): 16–30.

   (2014), 'System Change, Not Climate Change: Radical Social Transformation in the Twenty-First Century' in: Berch Berberoglu, ed., *The Palgrave Handbook of Social Movements, Revolution, and Social Transformation* (Basingstoke: Palgrave): 399–425.

Foster, R. F. (1989), *Modern Ireland* (London: Penguin).

Franqui, Carlos (1968), *The Twelve* (London: Lyle Stuart).

Fraser, Nancy (2017), 'The End of Progressive Neoliberalism', *Dissent*, 2 January, www.dissentmagazine.org/online_article/progressive-neoliberalism-reactionary-populism-nancy-fraser, accessed 14 March 2019.

Frazier, Robeson Taj (2015), *The East is Black* (Durham, NC: Duke University Press).

Furet, François (1981), *Reinterpreting the French Revolution* (Cambridge: Cambridge University Press).

(1999), *The Passing of an Illusion* (Chicago: University of Chicago Press).

Gaffield, Juilia (2015), *Haitian Connections in the Atlantic World* (Chapel Hill: University of North Carolina Press).

Gamson, William (1992), *Talking Politics* (Cambridge: Cambridge University Press).

Garcés, Joan E. (1990), *Allende y la Experiencia Chilena: Las Armas de la Política* (Santiago: Ediciones BAT).

Garretón, Manuel Antonio (1980), *Procesos Políticos en un Régimen Autoritario* (Santiago: FLACSO).

Garton Ash, Timothy (1989), *The Uses of Adversity: Essays on the Fate of Central Europe* (London: Penguin).

(1990), *The Magic Lantern: The Revolution of '89 Witnessed in Warsaw, Budapest, Berlin & Prague* (London: Penguin).

Geddes, Barbara (1999), 'What do we Know About Democratization After Twenty Years', *Annual Review of Political Science* 2: 115–44.

Geddes, Barbara, Joseph Wright, and Erisa Frantz (2014), 'Autocratic Breakdown and Regime Transitions', *Perspective on Politics* 12(2): 313–31.

Geggus, David (2002), *Haitian Revolutionary Studies* (Bloomington: Indiana University Press).

(2010), 'The Caribbean in the Age of Revolution', in: David Armitage and Sanjay Subrahmanyan, eds., *The Age of Revolution in Global Context* (Basingstoke: Palgrave): 83–100.

Gellner, Ernest (1981), *Muslim Society* (Cambridge: Cambridge University Press).

(1988), *Plough, Sword and Book: The Structure of Human History* (London: Collins Harvill).

Geras, Norman (1989), 'Our Morals: The Ethics of Revolution', *Socialist Register* 25: 185–211.

Gerassi, John, ed. (1968), *Venceremos! The Speeches and Writings of Che Guevara* (New York: Macmillan).

Gerassi, John (1971), *Towards Revolution* (London: Weidenfeld & Nicolson).

Gerges, Fawaz (2007), *Journey of the Jihadist: Inside Muslim Militancy* (London: Harvest).

(2013), 'The Islamist Moment: From Islamic State to Civil Islam', *Political Science Quarterly* 128(3): 389–426.

(2016), *ISIS: A History* (Princeton: Princeton University Press).

Gerschenkron, Alexander (1962), *Economic Backwardness in Historical Perspective* (Cambridge, MA: Belknap).

Geuss, Raymond (2008), *Philosophy and Real Politics* (Princeton: Princeton University Press).

(2015), 'Realism and the Relativity of Judgement', *International Relations* 29(1): 3–22.

Ghamari-Tabrizi, Behrooz (2016), *Foucault in Iran: Islamic Revolution After the Enlightenment* (Minneapolis: University of Minnesota Press).

Giddens, Anthony (1985), *The Nation-State and Violence* (Berkeley: University of California Press).

Gil, Federico Guillermo, Ricardo Lagos Escobar, and Henry A. Landsberger (1979), *Chile at the Turning Point: Lessons of the Socialist Years 1970–1973* (Philadelphia: Institute for the Study of Human Issues).

Gladwell, Malcolm (2010), 'Small Change: Why the Revolution Will Not be Tweeted', *The New Yorker*, 4 October: 42–9.

Gleijeses, Piero (2009), *The Cuban Drumbeat* (London: Seagull).

(2011), 'Cuba and the Cold War', in: Melvyn P. Leffler and Odd Arne Wester, eds., *The Cambridge History of the Cold War* (Cambridge: Cambridge University Press): 327–48.

Go, Julian and George Lawson (2017), 'For a Global Historical Sociology', in: Julian Go and George Lawson, eds., *Global Historical Sociology* (Cambridge: Cambridge University Press): 1–34.

Goddard, Stacie (2012), 'Brokering Peace: Networks, Legitimacy, and the Northern Ireland Peace Process', *International Studies Quarterly* 56(3): 501–15.

Goffman, Erving (1974), *Frame Analysis* (New York: Harper Colophon).

Goldfrank, Walter L. (1975), 'World System, State Structure, and the Onset of the Mexican Revolution', *Politic and Society* 5(4): 417–39.

(1979), 'Theories of Revolution and Revolution Without Theory', *Theory and Society* 7(1): 135–65.

Goldstone, Jack (1980), 'Theories of Revolution: The Third Generation', *World Politics* 32(3): 425–53.

(1991), *Revolution and Rebellion in the Early Modern World* (Berkeley: University of California Press).

(1994), 'Is Revolution Individually Rational?' *Rationality and Science* 6(1): 139–66.

(2001), 'Towards a Fourth Generation of Revolutionary Theory', *Annual Review of Political Science* 4: 139–87.

(2003), 'Comparative Historical Analysis and Knowledge Accumulation in the Study of Revolutions', in: James Mahoney and Dietrich Rueschemeyer, eds., *Comparative Historical Analysis in the Social Sciences* (Cambridge: Cambridge University Press): 41–90.

(2009), 'Rethinking Revolution: Integrating Origins, Processes, and Outcomes', *Comparative Studies of South Asia, Africa, and the Middle East* 29(1): 18–32.

(2011), 'Understanding the Revolutions of 2011', *Foreign Affairs* 90(3): 8–16.

(2014a), *Revolution: A Very Short Introduction* (Oxford: Oxford University Press).

(2014b), 'Why the Arab Revolutions of 2011 Are True Revolutions: Implications and Prognosis', Paper presented at the 18th World Congress of Sociology, Yokohama, July.

(2016), *Revolution and Rebellion in the Early Modern World*, 2nd edition (London: Routledge).

Goldstone, Jack and Bert Useem (2012), 'Putting Values and Institutions Back into the Theory of Strategic Action Fields', *Sociological Theory* 30(1): 37–47.

Goodwin, Jeff (2001), *No Other Way Out* (Cambridge: Cambridge University Press).

Gordin, Michael, Helen Tilley, and Gyan Prakash, eds. (2010), *Utopia/Dystopia: Conditions of Historical Possibility* (Princeton: Princeton University Press).

Gordon, Uri (2018), 'Prefigurative Politics Between Ethical Practice and Absent Promise', *Political Studies* 66: 521–37.

Gott, Richard (2005), *Cuba: A New History* (New Haven: Yale University Press).

Gould, Deborah (2009), *Moving Politics* (Chicago: University of Chicago Press).

Gould, Roger (1995), *Insurgent Identities* (Chicago: University of Chicago Press).

Graeber, David (2011), *Revolutions in Reverse* (London: Minor Compositions).

Gramsci, Antonio (1971), *Selections from the Prison Notebooks*, ed. and trans. Quintin Hoare and Geoffrey Nowell-Smith (London: Lawrence & Wishart).

(1988/1929–33), 'Passive Revolution, Caesarism, Fascism', in: David Forgacs, ed., *The Antonio Gramsci Reader* (London: Lawrence & Wishart): 246–74.

Granovetter, Mark (1973), 'The Strength of Weak Ties', *American Journal of Sociology* 78(6): 1360–80.

Gray, John (2007), *Black Mass: Apocalyptic Religion and the Death of Utopia* (London: Allen Lane).

Gross, Michael L. (2015), *The Ethics of Insurgency* (Cambridge: Cambridge University Press).

Guelke, Adrian (2005), *Rethinking the Rise and Fall of Apartheid* (Basingstoke: Palgrave Macmillan).

Guerra, William (2018), *Heroes, Martyrs, and Political Messiahs in Revolutionary Cuba, 1946–58* (New Haven: Yale University Press).

Guevara, Che (1963), *Guerilla Warfare* (New York: Monthly Review).

(1968), *Socialism and Man in Cuba* (Havana: 5 de Mayo): 3–22.

Gunitsky, Seva (2015), 'Corrupting the Cyber-Commons: Social Media as a Tool of Autocratic Stability', *Perspectives on Politics* 13(1): 42–54.

Gunning, Jeroen and Ilan Zvi Baron (2013), *Why Occupy a Square?* (London: Hurst).

Gurr, Ted Robert (1970), *Why Men Rebel* (Princeton: Princeton University Press).

(1988), 'War, Revolution, and the Growth of the Coercive State', *Comparative Political Studies* 21(1): 45–65.

Gurr, Ted Robert and Jack Goldstone (1991), 'Comparison and Policy Implications', in: Jack Goldstone, Ted Robert Gurr, and Farrokh Moshiri, eds., *Revolutions of the Late Twentieth Century* (Boulder: Westview): 324–52.

Gustafson, Kristian (2007), *Hostile Intent: US Covert Operations in Chile, 1964–1974* (Washington, DC: Potomac).

Gustafson, Kristian and Christopher Andrew (2018), 'The Other Hidden Hand: Soviet and Cuban Intelligence in Allende's Chile', *Intelligence and National Security* 33(3): 407–21.

Habermas, Jürgen (1990), 'What Does Socialism Mean Today? The Rectifying Revolution and the Needs for New Thinking on the Left', *New Left Review* (183): 3–21.

Hale, Henry (2011), 'Formal Constitutions in Informal Politics', *World Politics* 63(4): 581–617.

Hall, Stuart (1979), 'The Great Moving Right Show', *Marxism Today* (January): 19–34.

Halliday, Fred (1982), 'The Iranian Revolution: Uneven Development and Religious Populism', *Journal of International Affairs* 36(2): 187–207.

(1999), *Revolution and World Politics* (London: Palgrave).

(2003a) *Islam and the Myth of Confrontation* (London: I. B. Tauris).

(2003b), 'Utopian Realism: The Challenges for "Revolution" in Our Times', in: John Foran, ed., *The Future of Revolution* (London: Zed): 300–9.

(2005), *The Middle East in International Relations: Power, Politics and Ideology* (Cambridge: Cambridge University Press).

(2008), 'Revolutionary Internationalism and its Perils', in: John Foran, David Lane, and Andreja Zivkovic, eds., *Revolution in the Making of the Modern World* (London: Routledge): 65–80.

(2010), 'Third World Socialism: 1989 and After', in: George Lawson, Chris Armbruster, and Michael Cox, eds., *The Global 1989: Continuity and Change in World Politics* (Cambridge: Cambridge University Press): 112–34.

Hampsher-Monk, Iain (2005), 'Edmund Burke's Changing Justification for Intervention', *Historical Journal* 48(1): 65–100.

Hanson, Stephen (2010), *Post-Imperial Democracies* (Cambridge: Cambridge University Press).

Hardt, Michael and Antonio Negri (2001), *Empire* (Cambridge, MA: Harvard University Press).

(2012), *Declaration*, http://antonionegriinenglish.files.wordpress.com/2012/05/93152857-hardt-negri-declaration-2012.pdf, accessed 20 March 2019.

(2017), *Assembly* (New York: Oxford University Press).

Harmer, Tanya (2011), *Allende's Chile and the Inter-American Cold War* (Chapel Hill: North Carolina Press).

Harris, Kevan (2012a) *The Martyr's Welfare State*, PhD thesis, Johns Hopkins University.

(2012b), 'The Brokered Exuberance of the Middle Class: An Ethnographic Analysis of Iran's 2009 Green Movement', *Mobilization* 17(4): 435–55.

(2017), *A Social Revolution: Politics and the Welfare State in Iran* (Berkeley: University of California Press).

Harris, Tim (2005), *Restoration: Charles II and His Kingdoms* (London: Penguin).

(2006), *Revolution: The Great Crisis of the British Monarchy, 1685–1720* (London: Penguin).

(2015), 'Did the English Have a Script for Revolution?' in: Keith Michael Baker and Dan Edelstein, eds., *Scripting Revolution* (Palo Alto: Stanford University Press): 25–40.

Haslam, Jonathan (2005), *The Nixon Administration and the Death of Allende's Chile: A Case of Assisted Suicide* (London: Verso).

Haynes, Mike and Jim Wolfreys (2007), *History and Revolution* (London: Verso).

Hazan, Eric (2014), *A People's History of the French Revolution* (London: Verso).

Herren, Madeleine (2017), 'Fascist Internationalism', in: Glenda Sluga and Patricia Clavin, eds., *Internationalisms: A Twentieth Century History* (Cambridge: Cambridge University Press): 191–212.

Hess, David and Brian Martin (2006), 'Repression, Backfire, and the Theory of Transformative Events', *Mobilization* 11(1): 249–67.

Heydemann, Steven (2013), 'Syria and the Future of Authoritarianism', *Journal of Democracy* 24(4): 59–73.

Hickman, John (1998), *News from the End of the Earth* (London: Hunt & Co).

Hill, Christopher (1975), *The World Turned Upside Down: Radical Ideas During the English Revolution* (London: Penguin).

——— (1980), 'A Bourgeois Revolution?', in: J. G. A. Pocock, ed., *The Three British Revolutions: 1640, 1688, 1776* (Princeton: Princeton University Press): 109–39.

——— (2002/1961), *The Century of Revolution, 1603–1714* (London: Routledge).

Hobsbawm, Eric (1959), *Primitive Rebels: Studies in Archaic Forms of Social Movement in the 19th and 20th Centuries* (New York: Norton).

——— (1962), *The Age of Revolution, 1789–1848* (London: Abacus).

——— (1986), 'Revolution', in: Roy Porter and Mikuláš Teich, eds., *Revolutions in History* (Cambridge: Cambridge University Press): 5–46.

Holloway, John (2002), *Change the World Without Taking Power* (London: Pluto).

Holmes, Amy Austin (2012), 'There are Weeks When Decades Happen: Structure and Strategy in the Egyptian Revolution', *Mobilization* 17(4): 391–410.

Holquist, Peter (2003), 'State Violence as Technique', in: Amir Weiner, ed., *Landscaping the Human Garden* (Palo Alto: Stanford University Press): 19–45.

Horowitz, Donald (1969), *Imperialism and Revolution* (New York: Random House).

Houghton, David Patrick (2001), *US Foreign Policy and the Iran Hostage Crisis* (Cambridge: Cambridge University Press).

Howard, Philip and Muzammil Hussain (2011), 'The Role of Digital Media', *Journal of Democracy* 22(3): 35–48.

——— (2013), 'What Best Explains Successful Protest Cascades? ICTs and the Fuzzy Causes of the Arab Spring', *International Studies Review* 15(1): 48–66.

Huberman, Leo and Paul Sweezy (1961), *Cuba: Anatomy of a Revolution* (New York: Monthly Review).

Hui, Victoria Tin-Bor (2005), *War and State Formation in Ancient China and Early Modern Europe* (Cambridge: Cambridge University Press).

Huneeus, Carlos (2011), 'Popular Mass Mobilization versus Authoritarian Rule: Pinochet's Chile, 1983–88', in: Adam Roberts and Timothy Garton Ash, eds., *Civil Resistance and Power Politics* (Oxford: Oxford University Press): 197–212.

Hunt, Lynn (1989), 'Masculin et Féminin Dans la Révolution Française', *Pages d'Ecritures* 3: 12–14.

——— (1992), *The Family Romance of the French Revolution* (Berkeley: University of California Press).

——— (2010), 'The French Revolution in Global Context', in: David Armitage and Sanjay Subrahmanyan, eds., *The Age of Revolution in Global Context* (Basingstoke: Palgrave): 20–36.

——— (2013), 'The Global Financial Origins of 1789', in: Suzanne Desan, Lynn Hunt, and William Max Nelson, eds., *The French Revolution in Global Perspective* (Ithaca: Cornell University Press): 32–43.

Huntington, Samuel (1968), *Political Order in Changing Societies* (New Haven: Yale University Press).

——— (1991), *The Third Wave* (Norman: University of Oklahoma Press).

Hutton, Ronald (1985), *The Restoration* (Oxford: Oxford University Press).

Ismail, Salwa (2012), 'The Egyptian Revolution Against the Police', *Social Research* 79(2): 435–62.

Israel, Jonathan, ed. (1991), *The Anglo-Dutch Moment: Essays on the Glorious Revolution and Its World Impact* (Cambridge: Cambridge University Press).

Israel, Jonathan (1998), *The Dutch Republic* (Oxford: Clarendon).

(2017), *The Expanding Blaze: How the American Revolution Ignited the World, 1775–1848* (Princeton: Princeton University Press).

Jackson, Patrick (2010), 'How to Think About Civilizations', in: Peter Katzenstein, ed., *Civilizations in World Politics* (London: Routledge): 176–200.

(2011), *The Conduct of Inquiry in International Relations* (London: Routledge).

James, C. L. R. (2001/1938), *The Black Jacobins* (London: Penguin).

Jameson, Frederick (2010), 'Utopia as Method, or the Uses of the Future', in: Michael Gordin, Helen Tilley, and Gyan Prakash, eds., *Utopia/Dystopia: Conditions of Historical Possibility* (Princeton: Princeton University Press): 21–44.

Jasanoff, Maya (2010), 'The French Revolution in Global Context', in: David Armitage and Sanjay Subrahmanyan, eds., *The Age of Revolution in Global Context* (Basingstoke: Palgrave): 37–58.

Jasper, James (1998), 'The Emotions of Protest', *Sociological Forum* 13(3): 397–424.

(2011), 'Emotions and Social Movements', *Annual Review of Sociology* 37: 283–303.

Jervis, Robert (2010), 'Identity and the Cold War', in: Melvyn Leffler and Arne Westad, eds., *The Cambridge History of the Cold War*, Volume 2 (Cambridge: Cambridge University Press): 22–43.

Johnston, Hank and John A. Noakes (2005), *Framing Protest: Social Movements and the Framing Perspective* (Oxford: Rowman & Littlefield).

Jones, Stephen F. (2006), 'The Rose Revolution: A Revolution without Revolutionaries?' *Cambridge Review of International Affairs* 19(1): 33–48.

Jordan, Pallo (1992), 'Strategic Debate in the ANC: A Response to Joe Slovo', *The African Communist* 130(4): 7–15.

Kadivar, Mohammad Ali (2018), 'Mass Mobilization and the Durability of New Democracies', *American Sociological Review* 83(2): 390–417.

Kadivar, Mohammad Ali and Neil Ketchley (2018), 'Sticks, Stones, and Molotov Cocktails: Unarmed Collective Violence and Democratization', *Socius* 4: 1–16.

Kalberg, Stephen (2012), *Max Weber's Comparative Historical Sociology Today* (London: Ashgate).

Kaltwasser, Cristóbal Rovira, Paul Taggart, Paulina Ochoa Espejo, and Pierre Ostiguy, eds. (2017), *The Oxford Handbook of Populism* (Oxford: Oxford University Press).

Kalyvas, Stathis N. (2015), 'Is ISIS a Revolutionary Group and if Yes, What Are the Implications?', *Perspectives on Terrorism* 9(4): 42–7.

Kamrava, Mehran (2014), 'Khomeini and the West', in: Arshin Adib-Moghaddam, ed., *A Critical Introduction to Khomeini* (Cambridge: Cambridge University Press): 149–69.

Kane, Anne (1997), 'Theorizing Meaning Construction in Social Movements', *Sociological Theory* 15(3): 249–76.

Karatnycky, Adrian and Peter Ackerman (2005), *How Freedom Was Won: From Civil Resistance to Durable Democracy* (Washington, DC: Freedom House).

Karl, Terry Lynn (1992), 'El Salvador's Negotiated Revolution', *Foreign Affairs* 71(2): 147–64.

(1995), 'The Hybrid Regimes of Central America', *Journal of Democracy* 6(3): 72–87.

Kasrils, Ronnie (1998), *Armed and Dangerous* (London: Heinemann).

Katz, Mark (1997), *Revolutions and Revolutionary Waves* (New York: St Martin's).

Keddie, Nikki (2003), *Modern Iran: Roots and Results of Revolution*, 2nd edition (New Haven: Yale University Press).

Kelsen, Hans (2007/1945), *General Theory of Law and State* (Cambridge, MA: Harvard University Press).

Kennedy, Paul (1976), *The Rise and Fall of British Naval Mastery* (London: Penguin).

Ketchley, Neil (2017), *Egypt in a Time of Revolution* (Cambridge: Cambridge University Press).

Khalili, Laleh (2007), *Heroes and Martyrs of Palestine* (Cambridge: Cambridge University Press).

Khomeini, Ruhollah (1970), *Islamic Government: Governance of the Jurist*, www.al-islam.org/printpdf/book/export/html/12118, accessed 14 March 2019.

(1981), *Islam and Revolution* (North Harledon: Mizan).

Kirby, Paul (2012), *Rethinking War/Rape: Feminism, Critical Explanation and the Study of Wartime Sexual Violence*, PhD thesis, London School of Economics.

Kissinger, Henry (1999), *A World Restored: Metternich, Castlereagh and the Problems of the Peace 1812–1822* (New York: Weidenfeld & Nicolson).

Klooster, Wim (2009), *Revolution in the Atlantic World* (New York: New York University Press).

Kolla, Edward James (2017), *Sovereignty, International Law, and the French Revolution* (Cambridge: Cambridge University Press).

Konrád, György (1984), *Antipolitics: An Essay* (London: Harcourt).

Kramer, Mark (2011), 'The Demise of the Soviet Bloc', *Europe-Asia Studies* 63(9): 1535–90.

Krippner, Greta (2011), *Capitalizing on Crisis: The Political Origins of the Rise of Finance* (Cambridge, MA: Harvard University Press).

Krushelnycky, Askold (2006), *An Orange Revolution* (London: Harvill Secker).

Kudelia, Serhiy (2014), 'The House that Yanukovych Built', *Journal of Democracy* 25(3): 19–34.

Kulyk, Volodymryn (2016), 'National Identity in Ukraine', *Europe-Asia Studies* 68(4): 588–608.

Kumar, Krishan (2008), 'The Future of Revolution: Imitation or Innovation?', in: John Foran, David Lane, and Andreja Zivkovic, eds., *Revolution in the Making of the Modern World* (London: Routledge): 222–35.

Kuran, Timur (1995), 'Why Revolutions and Better Understood than Predicted', in: Nikki Keddie, ed., *Debating Revolution* (New York: New York University Press): 27–35.

Kurki, Milja (2006), 'Causes of a Divided Discipline: Rethinking the Concept of Cause in International Relations Theory', *Review of International Studies* 32(2): 189–216.

Kurki, Milja and Hidemi Suganami (2012), 'Towards the Politics of Causal Explanation: A Reply to the Critics of Causal Inquiries', *International Theory* 4(3): 400–29.

Kurzman, Charles (2003), 'The Poststructuralist Consensus in Social Movement Theory', in: Jeff Goodwin and James Jasper, eds., *Rethinking Social Movements: Structure, Meaning, and Emotion* (Oxford: Rowman & Littlefield): 111–21.

(2004a), *The Unthinkable Revolution in Iran* (Cambridge, MA: Harvard University Press).

(2004b), 'Can Understanding Undermine Explanation? The Confused Experience of Revolution', *Philosophy of the Social Sciences* 34(3): 328–51.

(2008), *Democracy Denied, 1905–1915* (Cambridge, MA: Harvard University Press).

Kuzio, Taras (2005), 'From Kuchma to Yushchenko: Ukraine's 2004 Presidential Elections and the Orange Revolution', *Problems of Post-Communism* 52(2): 29–44.

(2006), 'Everyday Ukrainians and the Orange Revolution', in: Anders Aslund and Michael McFaul, eds., *Revolution in Orange: The Origins of Ukraine's Democratic Breakthrough* (Washington, DC: Carnegie Endowment for International Peace): 45–68.

Kwass, Michael (2013), 'The Global Underground: Smuggling, Rebellion, and the Origins of the French Revolution', in: Suzanne Desan, Lynn Hunt, and William Max Nelson, eds., *The French Revolution in Global Perspective* (Ithaca: Cornell University Press): 15–31.

Laclau, Ernesto (2005), *On Populist Reason* (London: Verso).

Laclau, Ernesto and Chantal Mouffe (2000), *Hegemony and Socialist Strategy*, 2nd edition (London: Verso).

Lanchester, John (2018), 'After the Fall', *London Review of Books* 40(13): 3–8.

Landers, Jane G. (2010) *Atlantic Creoles in the Age of Revolution* (Cambridge, MA: Harvard University Press).

Landsberg, Chris (2001), *The International Politics of South Africa's Democratic Transition*, PhD thesis, Department of International Politics, Oxford University.

Lane, David (2008), 'The Orange Revolution: "People's Revolution" or Revolutionary Coup?', *British Journal of Politics and International Relations* 10(4): 525–49.

Lawson, George (2004), *Negotiated Revolutions* (London: Ashgate).

(2005), 'Negotiated Revolutions: The Prospects for Radical Change in Contemporary World Politics', *Review of International Studies* 31(3): 473–93.

(2006a), 'Trends in Revolution', in: James DeFronzo, ed., *Revolutionary Movements in World History* (Santa Barbara: ABC-CLIO): 876–81.

(2006b), 'Reform, Rebellion, Civil War, Coup d'État and Revolution', in: James DeFronzo, ed., *Revolutionary Movements in World History* (Santa Barbara: ABC-CLIO): 717–22.

(2008), 'A Realistic Utopia?: Nancy Fraser, Cosmopolitanism and the Making of a Just World Order', *Political Studies* 56(4): 881–906.

(2010), 'The "What", "When" and "Where" of the Global 1989', in: George Lawson, Chris Armbruster, and Michael Cox, eds., *The Global 1989: Continuity and Change in World Politics* (Cambridge: Cambridge University Press): 1–20.

(2011), 'Halliday's Revenge: Revolutions and International Relations', *International Affairs* 87(5): 1067–85.

(2012), 'The Eternal Divide? History and International Relations', *European Journal of International Relations* 18(2): 203–26.

(2015a), 'Revolutions and the International', *Theory and Society* 44(4): 299–319.

(2015b), 'Revolution, Nonviolence, and the Arab Uprisings', *Mobilization* 20(4): 453–70.

(2016), 'Within and Beyond the "Fourth Generation" of Revolutionary Theory', *Sociological Theory* 34(2): 106–27.

(2017), 'A Global Historical Sociology of Revolution', in: Julian Go and George Lawson, eds., *Global Historical Sociology* (Cambridge: Cambridge University Press): 76–98.

Lenin, Vladimir Il'ich (1917), 'Lecture on the 1905 Revolution', www.marxists .org/archive/lenin/works/1917/jan/09.htm, accessed 20 March 2019.

(1970/1923), *On Culture and Cultural Revolution* (Moscow: Progress).

(1987/1901–2), *What is to Be Done?* (New York: Dover).

(1992/1918), *The State and Revolution* (London: Penguin).

Leshchenko, Sergii (2014), 'The Media's Role', *Journal of Democracy* 25(3): 52–7.

Lévesque, Jacques (1997), *The Enigma of 1989: The USSR and the Liberation of Eastern Europe* (Berkeley: University of California Press).

(2010), 'The East European Revolutions of 1989', in: Melvyn Leffler and Arne Westad, eds., *The Cambridge History of the Cold War*, Volume 3 (Cambridge: Cambridge University Press): 311–32.

Levitsky, Steven and Lucan Way (2010), *Competitive Authoritarianism: Hybrid Regimes After the Cold War* (Cambridge: Cambridge University Press).

(2013), 'The Durability of Revolutionary Regimes', *Journal of Democracy* 24(3): 5–17.

(2016), 'Durable Authoritarianism', in: Orfeo Fieretos, Tulia Falleti, and Adam Sheyato, eds., *Oxford Handbook of Historical Institutionalism* (Oxford: Oxford University Press): 208–22.

Lichbach, Mark (1995), *The Rebels Dilemma* (Ann Arbor: Michigan University Press).

Little, Daniel (1995), 'Causal Explanation in Social Science', *Southern Journal of Philosophy* 34: 31–56.

(2000), 'Explaining Large-Scale Historical Change', *Philosophy of the Social Sciences* 30(1): 89–112.

(2016), *New Directions in the Philosophy of Social Science* (London: Rowman & Littlefield).

Lodge, Tom (2011), 'The Interplay of Non-Violent and Violent Action in the Movement Against Apartheid', in: Adam Roberts and Timothy Garton Ash, eds., *Civil Resistance and Power Politics* (Oxford: Oxford University Press): 213–30.

Losurdo, Domenico (2015), *War and Revolution* (London: Verso).

Loveman, Brian (2001), *Chile: The Legacy of Hispanic Capitalism* (Oxford: Oxford University Press).

Luxemburg, Rosa (1918), *The Russian Revolution*, www.marxists.org/archive/luxemburg/1918/russian-revolution/index.htm, accessed 20 March 2019.

Lynch, Marc (2011), 'After Egypt: The Limits and Promise of Online Challenges to the Authoritarian Arab State', *Perspective on Politics* 9(2): 301–10.

(2012), *The Arab Uprising* (New York: Public Affairs).

(2014), 'Introduction', in: Marc Lynch, ed., *Reflections on the Arab Uprisings*, POMEPS Studies No. 10 (Washington, DC: POMEPS): 3–7.

(2016), *The New Arab Wars* (New York: Public Affairs).

McAdam, Doug and William Sewell (2001), 'It's About Time: Temporality in the Study of Social Movements', in: Ronald Aminzade, ed., *Silence and Voice in the Study of Contentious Politics* (Cambridge: Cambridge University Press): 89–125.

McAdam, Doug, Sidney Tarrow, and Charles Tilly (2001), *Dynamics of Contention* (Cambridge: Cambridge University Press).

McDaniel, Tim (1991), *Autocracy, Modernization and Development in Russia and Iran* (Princeton: Princeton University Press).

McFaul, Michael (2007), 'Ukraine Imports Democracy: External Influences on the Orange Revolution', *International Security* 32(2): 45–83.

Mack, Andrew (1975), 'Why Big Nations Win Small Wars', *World Politics* 27(2): 175–200.

McLuhan, Marshall (1962), *The Gutenberg Galaxy: The Making of Typographic Man* (Toronto: University of Toronto Press).

Macmillan, Hugh (2017), '"Past History Has Not Been Forgotten": The ANC/ZAPU Alliance – the Second Phase, 1978–1980', *Journal of Southern African Studies* 43(1): 179–93.

Maher, Shiraz (2016), *Salafi-Jihadism* (London: Hurst).

Mahoney, James and Kathleen Thelen (2015), 'Comparative Historical Analysis in Contemporary Political Science', in: James Mahoney and Kathleen Thelen, eds., *Advances in Comparative Historical Research* (Cambridge: Cambridge University Press): 4–36.

Malešević, Siniša (2017), *The Rise of Organised Brutality* (Cambridge: Cambridge University Press).

Malia, Martin (2006), *History's Locomotives: Revolutions and the Making of the Modern World* (New Haven: Yale University Press).

Manganyi, Noel C. and André Du Toit (1990), *Political Violence and the Struggle in South Africa* (London: Macmillan).

Mann, Michael (2004), *Fascists* (Cambridge: Cambridge University Press).

(2012), *The Sources of Social Power*, Volume 3 (Cambridge: Cambridge University Press).

Mao Zedong (1927), *Report on an Investigation of the Peasant Movement in Hunan*, www.marxists.org/reference/archive/mao/selected-works/volume-1/mswv1_2.htm, accessed 20 March 2019.

Maoz, Zeev (1989), 'Joining the Club of Nations: Political Development and International Conflict', *International Studies Quarterly* 33(2): 199–231.

Markoff, John (1996), *Waves of Democracy* (Thousand Oaks: Pine Forge).

Marrat, Chibli (1993), *The Renewal of Islamic Law* (Cambridge: Cambridge University Press).

Martínez, Javier and Alvaro Díaz (1996), *Chile: The Great Transformation* (Washington, DC: Brookings).

Marx, Karl and Friedrich Engels (1967/1848), *The Manifesto of the Communist Party* (London: Penguin).

(1968/1852), *The Eighteenth Brumaire of Louis Bonaparte* (Peking: Foreign Languages Press).

Matin, Kamran (2006), 'The Revolution of "Backwardness": The Iranian Constitutional Revolution, 1906–1911', in: Bill Dunn and Hugo Radice, eds., *100 Years of Permanent Revolution: Results and Prospects* (London: Pluto): 10–26.

(2013), *Recasting Iranian Modernity* (London: Routledge).

Matthiesen, Toby (2013), *Sectarian Gulf: Bahrain, Saudi Arabia, and the Arab Spring that Wasn't* (Palo Alto: Stanford University Press).

Mayer, Arno (1971), *Dynamics of Counter-Revolution in Europe, 1870–1956* (London: Harper).

(1977), 'Internal Crisis and War Since 1870', in: Charles C. Bertrand, ed., *Revolutionary Situations in Europe, 1917–22* (Montreal: University of Quebec Press): 201–33.

(2001), *The Furies: Violence and Terror in the French and Russian Revolutions* (Princeton: Princeton University Press).

Menan, Rajan and Eugene Rumer (2015), *Conflict in Ukraine* (Boston: MIT Press).

Mendelsohn, Barak (2016), *The al-Qaeda Franchise* (Oxford: Oxford University Press).

Meredith, Martin (1994), *South Africa's New Era: The 1994 Election* (London: Mandarin).

Michie, Lindsay and Vangeli Gamede (2013), '"The Toyi-toyi Was Our Weapon": The Role of Music in the Struggle against Apartheid in South Africa', in: Eunice Rojas and Lindsay Michie, eds., *Sounds of Resistance* (Santa Barbara: Praeger): 251–70.

Milani, Abbas (2015), 'Iran's Paradoxical Regime', *Journal of Democracy* 26(2): 52–60.

Milanovic, Branko (2016), *Global Inequality: A New Approach for the Age of Globalization* (Cambridge, MA: Harvard University Press).

Miller, John (1973), *Popery and Politics in England, 1660–1688* (Cambridge: Cambridge University Press).

Miller, Mary Ashburn (2011), *A Natural History of Revolution* (Ithaca: Cornell University Press).

Mitchell, Lincoln A. (2012), *The Color Revolutions* (Philadelphia: University of Pennsylvania Press).

Mkandawire, Thandika (2015), 'Neopatrimonialism and the Political Economy of Economic Performance in Africa: Critical Reflections', *World Politics* 67(3): 563–612.

Moaddel, Mansoor (1993), *Class, Politics and Ideology in the Iranian Revolution* (New York: Columbia University Press).

Moffitt, Benjamin (2016), *The Global Rise of Populism* (Palo Alto: Stanford University Press).

Moghadam, Valerie (1997), 'Gender and Revolution', in: John Foran, ed., *Theorizing Revolution* (London: Routledge): 137–67.

(2008), 'Revolution, Nationalism, and Global Justice: Towards Social Transformation with Women', in: John Foran, David Lane, and Andreja Zivkovic, eds., *Revolution in the Making of the Modern World* (London: Routledge): 112–29.

Moghaddam, Arshin-Adib (2008), *Iran in World Politics* (New York: Columbia University Press).

Molyneux, Maxine and Thomas Osborne (2017), 'Populism: A Deflationary View', *Economy and Society* 46(1): 1–19.

Moore Jr., Barrington (1966), *Social Origins of Dictatorship and Democracy* (London: Penguin).

(1978), *Injustice: The Social Bases of Obedience and Revolt* (London: Macmillan).

(2000), *Moral Purity and Persecution in History* (Princeton: Princeton University Press).

More, Thomas (2003/1516), *Utopia* (London: Penguin).

Morley, Morris H. and Chris McGillion (2015), *Reagan and Pinochet: The Struggle over US Policy toward Chile* (New York: Cambridge University Press).

Morozov, Evgeny (2011), *The Net Delusion* (London: Allen Lane).

Morton, Adam (2010), 'Reflections on Uneven Development: The Mexican Revolution, Primitive Accumulation, and Passive Revolution', *Latin American Perspectives* 37(1): 7–34.

Mosher, Michael A. (1991), 'The Skeptic's Burke', *Political Theory* 19(3): 391–418.

Moshiri, Farrokh (1991), 'Iran: Islamic Revolution Against Westernization', in: Jack Goldstone, Ted Robert Gurr, and Farrokh Moshiri, eds., *Revolutions of the Late Twentieth Century* (Boulder: Westview): 116–35.

Motyl, Alexander (1999), *Revolutions, Nations, Empires* (New York: Columbia University Press).

Mudde, Cas and Cristóbal Rovira Kaltwasser (2017), *Populism: A Very Short Introduction* (Oxford: Oxford University Press).

Mulgan, Geoff (2013), *The Locust and the Bee: Predators and Creators in Capitalism's Future* (Princeton: Princeton University Press).

Mulholland, Marc (2017), 'Revolution and the Whip of Reaction', *Journal of Historical Sociology* 30(2): 369–402.

Müller, Jan-Werner (2016), *What is Populism?* (Pittsburg: University of Pennsylvania Press).

(2017), 'A Majority of "Deplorables"?' in: Henning Meyer, ed., *Understanding the Populist Revolt* (Brussels: Social Europe): 20–1.

Mumford, Stephen and Rani Lill Anjum (2014), *Getting Causes from Powers* (Oxford: Oxford University Press).

Muñiz, Manuel (2017), 'Populism and the Need for a New Social Contract', in: Henning Meyer, ed., *Understanding the Populist Revolt* (Brussels: Social Europe): 10–13.

Nattrass, Nicoli (2013), 'A South African Variety of Capitalism?' *New Political Economy* 19(1): 56–78.

Nepstad, Sharon Erickson (2011), *Nonviolent Revolution* (New York: Oxford University Press).

(2015), *Nonviolent Struggle* (New York: Oxford University Press).

Nexon, Daniel (2009), *The Struggle for Power in Early Modern Europe* (Princeton: Princeton University Press).

Nietzsche, Fredrich (2003/1886), *Beyond Good and Evil* (London: Penguin).

North, Douglass C., John Joseph Wallis and Barry R. Weingast (2009), *Violence and Social Orders: A Conceptual Framework for Interpreting Recorded Human History* (Cambridge: Cambridge University Press).

Norton, Augustus (2009), *Hezbollah: A Short History* (Princeton: Princeton University Press).

Nzimande, Blade (1992), 'Let Us Take the People With Us: A Reply to Joe Slovo', *The African Communist* 130(4): 16–28.

Ober, Josiah (1998), *The Athenian Revolution* (Princeton: Princeton University Press).

Onuch, Olga (2014), 'Who Were the Protestors?' *Journal of Democracy* 25(3): 44–51.

Onuch, Olga and Gwendolyn Sasse (2016), 'The Maidan in Movement: Diversity and the Cycles of Protest', *Europe-Asia Studies* 68(4): 555–87.

O'Shaughnessy, Hugh (2000), *Pinochet: The Politics of Torture* (London: Latin American Bureau).

Ostovar, Afshon (2016), *Vanguard of the Imam: Religion, Politics, and Iran's Revolutionary Guards* (Oxford: Oxford University Press).

Owen, Roger (2012), *The Rise and Fall of Arab Presidents for Life* (Cambridge, MA: Harvard University Press).

Owens, Patricia (2015), *Economy of Force* (Cambridge: Cambridge University Press).

Ozouf, Mona (1991), *Festivals and the French Revolution* (Cambridge, MA: Harvard University Press).

Paige, Jeffery (2003), 'Finding the Revolutionary in the Revolution: Social Science Concepts and the Future of Revolution', in: John Foran, ed., *The Future of Revolution* (London: Zed): 19–29.

Paine, Thomas (1999/1791), *Rights of Man* (New York: Dover).

(2004/1776), *Common Sense* (London: Penguin).

Palmer, R. R. (1954), 'The World Revolution of the West', *Political Science Quarterly* 69(1): 1–14.

(1959), *The Age of Democratic Revolution 1760–1800*, Volume 1 (Princeton: Princeton University Press).

(1964), *The Age of Democratic Revolution 1760–1800*, Volume 2 (Princeton: Princeton University Press).

Panah, Maryam (2002), 'Social Revolutions: The Elusive Emergence of an Agenda in International Relations', *Review of International Studies* 28(2): 271–92.

Pariser, Eli (2011), *The Filter Bubble* (London: Viking).

Parsa, Misagh (2000), *States, Ideologies and Revolutions* (Cambridge: Cambridge University Press).

Pavone, Tommaso (2019), 'Selecting Cases for Comparative Sequential Analysis: Novel Uses for Old Methods', in: Jennifer Widner, Michael Woolcock, and Daniel Ortega Nieto, eds., *The Case for Case Studies* (New York: Cambridge University Press).

Pearlman, Wendy (2011), *Violence, Nonviolence, and the Palestinian National Movement* (Cambridge: Cambridge University Press).

Pérez-Stable, Marifeli (2012), *The Cuban Revolution: Origins, Causes, and Legacy*, 3rd edition (Oxford: Oxford University Press).

Pettee, George (1938), *The Process of Revolution* (New York: Harper and Brothers).

Pettersson, Karin (2017), 'Without Social Democracy, Capitalism Will Eat Itself', in: Henning Meyer, ed., *Understanding the Populist Revolt* (Brussels; Social Europe): 4–9.

Piketty, Thomas (2014), *Capital in the Twenty-First Century*, trans. Arthur Goldhammer (Cambridge, MA: Harvard University Press).

Pincus, Steven (2009), *1688: The First Modern Revolution* (New Haven: Yale University Press).

(2012), 'Empires and Capitalisms', Paper presented at the SSHA Conference, Vancouver, November.

Pipes, Daniel (1991), *The Russian Revolution* (London: Vintage).

Plato (1997/420BC), *Republic* (London: Wordsworth).

Polanyi, Karl (2001/1944), *The Great Transformation* (Boston: Beacon Press).

Polasky, Janet (2015), *Revolutions Without Borders: The Call to Liberty in the Atlantic World* (New Haven: Yale University Press).

Polletta, Francesca (2006), *It Was Like a Fever* (Chicago: Chicago University Press).

Popkin, Samuel (1979), *The Rational Peasant* (Berkeley: University of California Press).

Popovic, Srdja (2015), *Blueprint for Revolution* (London: Scribe).

Pouliot, Vincent (2015), 'Practice Theory', in: Andrew Bennett and Jeffrey T. Checkel, eds., *Process Tracing* (Cambridge: Cambridge University Press): 237–59.

Prestholdt, Jeremy (2012), 'Resurrecting Che: Radicalism, the Transnational Imagination, and the Politics of Heroes', *Journal of Global History* 7(3): 506–26.

Puar, Jasbir (2017), *Right to Maim: Debility, Capacity, Disability* (Durham, NC: Duke University Press).

Puebla, Tete (2003), *Marianas in Combat: Teté Puebla and the Mariana Grajales Women's Platoon in Cuba's Revolutionary War, 1956–58* (New York: Pathfinder Press).

Quandt, William (1998), *Between Ballots and Bullets* (Washington, DC: Brookings).

Rachum, Ilan (1999), *'Revolution': The Entrance of a New Word in Western Political Discourse* (Lanham: University Press of America).

Raekstad, Paul (2018), 'Revolutionary Practice and Prefigurative Politics: A Clarification and Defense', *Constellations* 25: 359–72.

Rancière, Jacques (2006), *Hatred of Democracy* (London: Verso).

Rao, Rahul (2016), 'Revolution', in: Felix Berenskoetter, ed., *Concepts in World Politics* (London: Sage): 253–70.

Razoux, Pierre (2015), *The Iran-Iraq War* (Cambridge, MA: Harvard University Press).

Reagan, Ronald (1989), 'The Goliath of Totalitarianism Will be Brought Down by the David of the Microchip', *Guardian*, 14 June.

Reed, Isaac (2011), *Interpretation and Social Knowledge* (Chicago: University of Chicago Press).

Rich, Paul (1996), *State Power and Black Politics in South Africa, 1912–51* (Basingstoke: Macmillan).

Richard, Nelly (2018), *Eruptions of Memory* (Cambridge: Polity).

Ritter, Daniel (2015), *The Iron Cage of Liberalism* (Oxford: Oxford University Press).

Roberts, Kenneth M. (1998), *Deepening Democracy?* (Palo Alto: Stanford University Press).

Robertson, Geoffrey (2007), *The Levellers* (London: Verso).

Robertson, Graeme (2010), *The Politics of Protest in Hybrid Regimes* (Cambridge: Cambridge University Press).

Robinson, Cedric (1983), *Black Marxism* (London: Zed).

Rose, Craig (1999), *England in the 1690s* (Oxford: Blackwell).

Rosenau, James (1964), 'Internal War as an International Event', in: James Rosenau, ed., *International Aspects of Civil Strife* (Princeton: Princeton University Press): 45–91.

Rosenberg, Justin (1994), *The Empire of Civil Society* (London: Verso).

(2006), 'Why is there No International Historical Sociology?' *European Journal of International Relations* 12(3): 307–40.

(2010), 'Basic Problems in the Theory of Uneven and Combined Development', *Cambridge Review of International Affairs* 23(1): 165–89.

(2016), 'Uneven and Combined Development: "The International" in Theory and History', in: Alexander Anievas and Kamran Matin, eds., *Historical Sociology and World History: Uneven and Combined Development Over the Longue Durée* (London: Rowman & Littlefield): 17–30.

Rowbotham, Sheila (2013), *Women in Movement: Feminism and Social Action* (New York: Routledge).

Rudé, George (1964), *Revolutionary Europe, 1783–1815* (London: Fontana).

Runciman, W. G. (1966), *Relative Deprivation and Social Justice* (London: Routledge).

Rupnik, Jacques (2014), 'The World After 1989 and the Exhaustion of Three Cycles', in: Jacques Rupnik, ed., *1989 as a Political World Event* (London: Routledge): 7–24.

Russell, Conrad (1990), *The Causes of the English Civil War* (Oxford: Clarendon).

Russell, D. E. H. (1974), *Rebellion, Revolution, and Armed Force* (London: Academic).

Sadjadpour, Karim (2009), *Reading Khamenei: The World View of Iran's Most Powerful Leader* (Washington, DC: Carnegie Endowment for International Peace).

Saikal, Amin (2010), 'Islamism, the Iranian Revolution, and the Soviet Invasion of Afghanistan', in: Melvyn Leffler and Arne Westad, eds., *The Cambridge History of the Cold War*, Volume 2 (Cambridge: Cambridge University Press): 112–34.

Sakwa, Richard (2015), *Frontline Ukraine* (London: I. B. Tauris).

Sanders, James (2006), *Apartheid's Friends: The Rise and Fall of South Africa's Security Service* (London: John Murray).

Sarotte, Mary-Ann (2012), 'China's Fear of Contagion: Tiananmen Square and the Power of the European Example', *International Security* 37(2): 156–82.

Sartre, Jean-Paul (1965), 'Preface', in: Frantz Fanon, ed., *The Wretched of the Earth*, trans. Constance Farrington (New York: Grove Press): 7–26.

Schneider, Cathy (1995), *Shantytown Protest in Pinochet's Chile* (Philadelphia: Temple University Press).

Schock, Kurt (2005), *Unarmed Insurrections* (Minneapolis: University of Minnesota Press).

Schroeder, Paul (1994), *The Transformation of European Politics, 1763–1848* (Oxford: Oxford University Press).

Scott, Andrew (1982), *The Revolution in Statecraft: Intervention in an Age of Interdependence* (Durham, NC: Duke University Press).

(2000), *England's Troubles: 17th Century English Political Instability in a European Context* (Cambridge: Cambridge University Press).

Scott, James C. (1998), *Seeing Like a State* (New Haven: Yale University Press).

(2012a), 'Tyranny of the Ladle', *London Review of Books*, 6 December 34(23): 21–8.

(2012b), *Two Cheers for Anarchism* (Princeton: Princeton University Press).

Seekings, Jeremy (2000), *The United Democratic Front* (Cape Town: David Philips).

Selbin, Eric (1993), *Modern Latin American Revolutions* (Boulder: Westview).

(2008), 'Stories of Revolution in the Periphery', in: John Foran, David Lane, and Andreja Zivkovic, eds., *Revolution in the Making of the Modern World* (London: Routledge): 130–47.

(2009), 'Conjugating the Cuban Revolution: It Mattered. It Matters. It Will Matter', *Latin American Perspectives* 36(1): 21–9.

(2010), *Revolution, Rebellion, Resistance: The Power of Story* (London: Zed).

Sewell, William (2001), 'Space in Contentious Politics', in: Ronald Aminzade, ed., *Silence and Voice in the Study of Contentious Politics* (Cambridge: Cambridge University Press): 51–88.

(2005), *Logics of History* (Chicago: University of Chicago Press).

Shaban, M. A. (1979), *The Abyssinian Revolution* (Cambridge: Cambridge University Press).

Shah, Alpa (2018), *Nightmarch* (London: Hurst and Co.).

Sharman, Jason (2002), 'Culture, Strategy, and State-Centered Explanations of Revolution', *Social Science History* 27(1): 1–24.

Shatz, Adam (2008), 'Laptop Jihadi', *London Review of Books*, 20 March 30(6): 14–17.

Shehata, Dina (2011), 'The Fall of the Pharaoh', *Foreign Affairs* 90(3): 26–32.

Shorten, R. (2007), 'The Status of Ideology in the Return of Political Religion Theory', *Journal of Political Ideologies* 12(2): 163–87.

Sick, Gary (1985), *All Fall Down* (New York: Random House).

Sigmund, Paul E. (1993), *The United States and Democracy in Chile* (Baltimore: Johns Hopkins University Press).

Silva, Eduardo (1995), 'The Political Economy of Chile's Regime Transition', in: Paul Drake and Ivan Jakšić, eds., *The Struggle for Democracy in Chile, 1982–1990* (Lincoln: University of Nebraska Press): 98–127.

Simmel, Georg (1978/1900), *The Philosophy of Money* (London: Routledge).

Simmons, Beth (2011), 'International Studies in the Global Information Age', *International Studies Quarterly* 55(3): 589–99.

Simms, Brendan (2011), 'A False Principle in the Law of Nations: Burke, State Sovereignty, (German) Liberty, and Intervention in the Age of Westphalia', in: Brendan Simms and David Trim, eds., *Humanitarian Intervention: A History* (Cambridge: Cambridge University Press): 89–110.

Singh, Robert (2017), 'I, The People', *Economy and Society* 46(1): 20–42.

Skocpol, Theda (1973), 'A Critical Review of Barrington Moore's "Social Origins of Dictatorship and Development"', *Politics and Sociology* 4(1): 1–34.

(1979), *States and Social Revolutions: A Comparative Analysis of France, Russia and China* (Cambridge: Cambridge University Press).

(1994), 'Rentier State and Shi'a Islam in the Iranian Revolution', in: *Social Revolutions in the Modern World* (Cambridge: Cambridge University Press): 240–58.

Slater, Dan (2010), *Ordering Power: Contentious Politics and Authoritarian Leviathans in Southeast Asia* (Cambridge: Cambridge University Press).

Slater, Dan and Nicholas Rush Smith (2016), 'The Power of Counterrevolution', *American Journal of Sociology* 121(5): 1472–516.

Slovo, Joe (1992), 'Negotiations: What Room for Compromise?' *The African Communist* 130(3): 36–40.

Snow, David and Robert D. Benford (1988), 'Ideology, Frame Resonance, and Participant Observation', in: Bert Klandermans, Hanspeter Kriesi, and Sidney Tarrow, eds., *From Structure to Action* (Greenwich, CT: JAI Press): 197–217.

(1992), 'Master Frames and Cycles of Protest', in: Aldon D. Morris and Carol McClung Mueller, eds., *Frontiers in Social Movement Theory* (New Haven: Yale University Press): 133–55.

Snyder, Timothy (2010), *Bloodlands* (New York: Basic).

Sohrabi, Nader (1995), 'Historicizing Revolutions: Constitutional Revolutions in the Ottoman Empire, Iran, and Russia, 1905–1908', *American Journal of Sociology* 100(6): 1383–447.

(2002), 'Global Waves, Local Actors: What the Young Turks Knew about Other Revolutions and Why It Mattered', *Comparative Studies in Society and History* 44(1): 45–79.

Solidarity Centre (2011), *Justice for All* (Washington, DC: The Solidarity Centre).

Sorel, Georges (1999/1908), *Reflections on Violence* (Cambridge: Cambridge University Press).

Sorokin, Pitrim (1925), *The Sociology of Revolution* (Philadelphia: Lippincott).

Sparks, Allister (1995), *Tomorrow is Another Country: The Inside Story of South Africa's Negotiated Revolution* (London: Heinemann).

Spinner, Jeff (1991), 'Constructing Communities: Edmund Burke on Revolution', *Polity* 33(3): 395–421.

Srnicek, Nick and Alex Williams (2015), *Inventing the Future* (London: Verso).

Stacher, Joshua (2012), *Adaptable Autocrats: Regime Power in Egypt and Syria* (Palo Alto: Stanford University Press).

Staniskis, Jadwiga (1984), *Poland's Self-Limiting Revolution* (Princeton: Princeton University Press).

Stein, Ewan (2012), 'Revolutionary Egypt: Promises and Perils', *LSE IDEAS Special Report*: 23–7.

Stephanson, Anders (2010), 'The Philosopher's Island', *New Left Review* 61 (January/February): 197–210.

Stern, Geoffrey (1967), *Fifty Years of Communism* (London: Ampersand).

Stinchcombe, Arthur (1999), 'Ending Revolutions and Building New Governments', *Annual Review of Political Science* 2: 49–93.

Stone, Bailey (2002), *Reinterpreting the French Revolution: A Global Historical Perspective* (Cambridge: Cambridge University Press).

Stone, Lawrence (1965), *The Crisis of the Aristocracy, 1558–1641* (Oxford: Oxford University Press).

(1966), 'Theories of Revolution', *World Politics* 18(2): 59–76.

(1988), 'The Bourgeois Revolution of 17th Century England Revisited', in: Geoff Eley and William Hunt, eds., *Reviving the English Revolution* (London: Verso): 279–88.

Stone, Lawrence and Jeanne Fawtier Stone (1986), *An Open Elite? England, 1540–1880* (Oxford: Oxford University Press).

Strayer, Robert (2015), 'Communism and Fascism', in: J. R. McNeill and Kenneth Pomeranz, eds., *The Cambridge World History, Vol. 7, Part 1: Production, Destruction and Connection, 1750–Present* (Cambridge: Cambridge University Press): 442–64.

Streeck, Wolfgang (2014), *Buying Time: The Delayed Crisis of Democratic Capitalism*, trans. Patrick Camiller (London: Verso).

(2017), 'The Return of the Repressed', *New Left Review* 104 (March–April): 5–18.

Subramanian, Arvind and Martin Kessler (2013), 'The Hyperglobalization of Trade and Its Future' Peterson Institute for International Economics, Working Paper 13-6, https://piie/com/sites/default/files/publications/wp/wp13-6.pdf, accessed 14 March 2019.

Suttner, Raymond (2008), *The ANC Underground* (Auckland Park: Jacana).

(2012), 'The ANC Centenary: A Long and Difficult Journey', *International Affairs* 88(4): 719–38.

Sweig, Julia E. (2002), *Inside the Cuban Revolution: Fidel Castro and the Urban Underground* (Cambridge, MA: Harvard University Press).

Syme, Ronald (2002), *The Roman Revolution* (Oxford: Oxford University Press).

Takeyh, Ray (2006), *Hidden Iran: Paradox and Power in the Islamic Republic* (New York: Holt).

(2009), *Guardians of the Revolution* (Oxford: Oxford University Press).

Talmadge, Caitlin (2015), *The Dictator's Army: Battlefield Effectiveness in Authoritarian Regimes* (Ithaca: Cornell University Press).

Tardelli, Luca (2013), *Fighting for Others*, PhD thesis, London School of Economics.

Tarrow, Sidney (1998), *Power in Movement: Collective Action, Social Movements, and Politics* (Cambridge: Cambridge University Press).

(2005), *The New Transnational Activism* (Cambridge: Cambridge University Press).

(2012), *Strangers at the Gates* (Cambridge: Cambridge University Press).

(2013), *The Language of Contention, 1688–2012* (Cambridge: Cambridge University Press).

(2015), *War, States, and Contention* (Ithaca: Cornell University Press).

Tawney, R. H. (1926), *Religion and the Rise of Capitalism* (London: John Murray).

Taylor, Michael, ed. (1988), *Rationality and Revolution* (Cambridge: Cambridge University Press).

Teschke, Benno (2003), *The Myth of 1648* (London: Verso).

(2005), 'Bourgeois Revolution, State Formation and the Absence of the International', *Historical Materialism* 13(2): 3–26.

Tessler, Mark (2014), 'Political System Preferences After the Arab Spring', in: Marc Lynch, ed., *Reflections on the Arab Uprisings*, POMEPS Studies No. 10 (Washington, DC: POMEPS): 30–5.

Therborn, Goran (2012), 'Class in the 21st Century', *New Left Review* 78: 5–29.

Thomas, Hugh (2001/1971), *Cuba: A History* (London: Penguin).

Thomas, Keith (1971), *Religion and the Decline of Magic* (London: Penguin).

Thomas, Peter D. (2013), 'The Communist Hypothesis and the Question of Organization', *Theory and Event* 16(4).

Thompson, E. P. (1963), *The Making of the English Working Class* (London: Victor Gollancz).

Thompson, Mark (1995), *The Anti-Marcos Struggle: Personalistic Rule and Democratic Transition in the Philippines* (New Haven: Yale University Press).

(2004), *Democratic Revolutions* (London: Routledge).

Tilly, Charles (1964), *The Vendée* (Cambridge, MA: Harvard University Press).

(1978), *From Mobilization to Revolution* (New York: McGraw-Hill).

(1985), 'War Making and State Making as Organized Crime', in: Peter Evans, Dietrich Rueschemeyer, and Theda Skocpol, eds., *Bringing the State Back In* (Cambridge: Cambridge University Press): 169–91.

(1990), *Capital, Coercion, and European States, AD 990–1992* (Oxford: Blackwell).

(1993), *European Revolutions, 1492–1992* (Oxford: Blackwell).

(1995), 'To Explain Political Processes', *American Journal of Sociology* 100(6): 1594–610.

(2002), *Stories, Identities and Political Change* (Oxford: Rowman & Littlefield).

(2003), *The Politics of Collective Violence* (Cambridge: Cambridge University Press).

(2004), *Contention and Democracy in Europe, 1650–2000* (Cambridge: Cambridge University Press).

(2005), *Identities, Boundaries and Social Ties* (New York: Routledge).

(2006), *Regimes and Repertoires* (Cambridge: Cambridge University Press).

(2008), *Contentious Performances* (Cambridge: Cambridge University Press).

Tocqueville, Alexis de (1999/1852), *The Ancien Régime and the French Revolution* (Chicago: University of Chicago Press).

Tökés, Rufolf (1996), *Hungary's Negotiated Revolution* (Cambridge: Cambridge University Press).

Tooze, Adam (2007), *The Wages of Destruction* (London: Penguin).

Toscano, Alberto (2010), *Fanaticism* (London: Verso).

Trevor-Roper, Hugh (1953), *The Gentry, 1540–1640* (Cambridge: Cambridge University Press).

Tripp, Charles (2013), *The Power and the People* (Cambridge: Cambridge University Press).

Trotsky, Leon (1972/1937), *The Revolution Betrayed* (London: Pathfinder).

(1997/1932), *The History of the Russian Revolution* (London: Pluto).

(2007/1920), *Terrorism and Communism* (London: Verso).

Tufekci, Zeynep (2017), *Twitter and Tear Gas: The Power and Fragility of Networked Protest* (New Haven: Yale University Press).

Tulchin, Joseph S. and Augusto Varas (1991), *From Dictatorship to Democracy; Rebuilding Political Consensus in Chile* (Boulder: Lynne Rienner).

Turner, Adair (2011), 'Reforming Finance', Clare Distinguished Lecture in Economic and Public Policy, Cambridge, 18 February.

Valenzuela, J. Samuel and Arturo Valenzuela (1986), *Military Rule and Chile* (Baltimore: Johns Hopkins University Press).

Van Kessel, Ineke (2000), *Beyond our Wildest Dreams* (London: University of Virginia Press).

Van Vuuren, Hennie (2017), *Apartheid, Guns, and Money* (London: Hurst).

Varol, Ozan (2012), 'The Democratic Coup d'état', *Harvard International Law Journal* 53(2): 292–356.

Vatanka, Alex (2015), 'Iran Abroad', *Journal of Democracy* 26(2): 61–70.

Vidal, Hernán (1995), *Frente Patriótico Mañuel Rodríguez: El Tabú del Conflicto Armado en Chile* (Santiago: Mosquito Editores).

Vu, Tuong (2010), 'Studying the State through State Formation', *World Politics* 62(1): 148–75.

Wagemakers, Joas (2017), 'Revisiting Wiktorowicz', in: Franceso Cavatorta and Fabio Merone, eds., *Salafism After the Arab Awakening* (London: Hurst): 7–24.

Walgrave, Stefaan and Ruud Wouters (2014), 'The Missing Link in the Diffusion of Protest: Asking Others', *American Journal of Sociology* 119(6): 1670–709.

Walgrave, Stefaan, Lance Bennett, Jeroen Van Laer, and Christian Breunig (2011), 'Multiple Engagements and Network Bridging in Contentious Politics: Digital Media Use of Protest Participants', *Mobilization* 16(3): 325–49.

Walt, Stephen (1996), *Revolutions and War* (Ithaca: Cornell University Press).

(2015), 'ISIS as Revolutionary State', *Foreign Affairs* (November/December): 42–51.

Watkins, Susan (2016), 'Oppositions', *New Left Review* 98(March–April): 5–30.

Way, Lucan (2008), 'The Real Causes of the Color Revolutions', *Journal of Democracy* 19(3): 55–69.

(2011), 'The Lessons of 1989', *Journal of Democracy* 22(4): 13–23.

(2014), 'The Maidan and Beyond', *Journal of Democracy* 25(3): 35–43.

Weber, Jeffrey (2011), *From Rebellion to Reform in Bolivia* (London: Haymarket).

Weber, Max (1978/1922), *Economy and Society* (Berkeley: University of California Press).

(1994/1910), 'The Profession and Vocation of Politics', in: Peter Lassman and Ronald Speirs, eds., *Weber: Political Writings* (Cambridge: Cambridge University Press).

(2004/1903–17), *The Methodology of the Social Sciences* (Jaipur: ABD Publishers).

Weiner, Amir (2003), 'War, Genocide, and Post-War Soviet Jewry', in: Amir Weiner, ed., *Landscaping the Human Garden* (Palo Alto: Stanford University Press): 167–88.

Welsh, Jennifer (1995), *Edmund Burke and International Relations* (London: Palgrave).

Wendt, Alexander (1998), 'On Constitution and Causation in International Relations', *Review of International Studies* 24(5): 101–18.

Westad, Arne (2007), *The Global Cold War* (Cambridge: Cambridge University Press).

(2012), *Restless Empire: China and the World since 1750* (New York: Basic Books).

Weyland, Kurt (2009), 'The Diffusion of Revolution: "1848" in Europe and Latin America', *International Organization* 63(3): 391–423.

(2010), 'Crafting Counterrevolution', *American Political Science Review* 110(2): 215–31.

(2012), 'The Arab Spring: Why the Surprising Similarities with the Revolutionary Wave of 1848?', *Perspectives on Politics* 10(4): 917–34.

(2014), *Making Waves: Democratic Contention in Europe and Latin American Since the Revolutions of 1848* (Cambridge: Cambridge University Press).

White, Micah (2016), *The End of Protest* (Toronto: Alfred A. Knopf Canada).

Wickham-Crowley, Timothy (1992), *Guerrillas and Revolution in Latin America* (Princeton: Princeton University Press).

Wight, Martin (1978/1946), *Power Politics* (Leicester: Leicester University Press).

Wiktorowicz, Quintan (2006), 'Anatomy of the Salafi Movement', *Studies in Conflict and Terrorism* 29(3): 207–39.

Wilde, Oscar (2001/1891), *The Soul of Man Under Socialism* (London: Penguin).

Willbanks, James H. (2007), *The Tet Offensive: A Concise History* (New York: Columbia University Press).

Williams, Bernard (2005), *In the Beginning was the Deed* (Princeton: Princeton University Press).

Wilson, Andrew (2006), 'Ukraine's Orange Revolution, NGOs, and the Role of the West', *Cambridge Review of International Affairs* 19(1): 21–32.

(2011), 'Ukraine's Orange Revolution of 2004: The Paradoxes of Negotiation', in: Adam Roberts and Timothy Garton Ash, eds., *Civil Resistance and Power Politics* (Oxford: Oxford University Press): 335–53.

(2014), *Ukraine Crisis* (New Haven: Yale University Press).

(2016), 'The Donbas in 2014', *Europe-Asia Studies* 68(4): 631–52.

Wilson, Charles (1968), *The Dutch Republic* (New York: McGraw-Hill).

Wolf, Eric (1969), *Peasant Wars of the Twentieth Century* (New York: Harper & Row).

Wood, Elizabeth (2003), *Insurgent Collection Action and Civil War in El Salvador* (Cambridge: Cambridge University Press).

Wood, Ellen Meiksins (2000), *The Origin of Capitalism* (London: Verso).

Wright, Erik Olin (2010), *Envisioning Real Utopias* (London: Verso).

(2013), 'Transforming Capitalism Through Real Utopias', *American Sociological Review* 78(1): 1–25.

Zeitlin, Maurice (1984), *The Civil Wars in Chile (Or the Bourgeois Revolutions that Never Were)* (Princeton: Princeton University Press).

Zimmerman, Andrew, ed. (2016), *Marx and Engels: The Civil War in the United States* (New York: International Publishers).

Žižek, Slavoj (2008), *In Defense of Lost Causes* (London: Verso).

(2012), *The Year of Living Dangerously* (London: Verso).

Zygar, Mikhail (2016), *All the Kremlin's Men* (New York: Public Affairs).

Index